OTHER SCHOOLS AND OURS

a comparative study for today

EDMUND J. KING

University of London King's College

Third Edition

HOLT, RINEHART AND WINSTON, INC.
New York   Chicago   San Francisco   Atlanta
Dallas   Montreal   Toronto   London

To my wife, Margaret,
and our four children

CONTENTS

ILLUSTRATIONS

vii

INTRODUCTION TO THE THIRD EDITION | THE APPROACH TO COMPARATIVE EDUCATION

Since the first edition of this book in 1958, comparative studies have achieved international recognition—not merely as a matter of personal interest or academic dignity but as part of the statecraft of nations. This is particularly true in the case of education. Whatever Comparative Education has been in the past, it is now very much a part of all thinking for the future—whether it concerns our own children, our own country, or the world at large.

There are now respectable and powerful departments of comparative government, comparative law, area studies, and similar kinds of academic activity in the world's major universities. Most governments either maintain research centers of their own, or rely heavily on comparative research projects in universities which they subsidize. Comparative interests are not merely liberalizing exercises; they are also part of every citizen's practical responsibilities for the future. To know what to think about our own homes we must also know about our

1

neighbors'. In the same way we can hardly know about our own country's achievements or shortcomings unless we are acquainted with the progress and problems of neighbor nations. The whole world is now our neighbor. The contraction of space and time because of technological change and modern communications has seen to that. Threats to our security by thermonuclear and other devices are part of the picture that should be before our eyes when we consider our children's security, prosperity, and education.

These aspects of life are inseparably intertwined—not in the casual way envisaged in previous exhortations by educators, but in the businesslike way required now that investment in education is often the major item of public expenditure. In other countries too, amounts spent directly or indirectly on education are assuming increasing proportions in the national budget. Therefore, the years since the first edition of this book have been a time of mounting urgency for comparative studies of education.

In the first edition I said that *Other Schools and Ours* should be read rather than studied. By this I meant that the book was intended to be interesting rather than pedantic. If a student cannot pick up a book and read it with pleasure or growing interest, something is wrong with the book as a job of teaching. On the other hand, the success of this intention and the book's readability made some professors overlook its serious purpose. The present volume is intended to encourage an interest in, and an awareness of, the cultural patterns which establish our neighbors' thoughts about education. It is also intended to provoke serious analytical thought that will enable us to ask the right questions and discern the right answers, and lead to serious research in one field or another. Among the latter we can include: comparative research in education; the sociological analysis of education in one or more countries; wider considerations of economic planning; manpower strategy; and indeed the shape of the "Great Society."

Although this third edition, therefore, maintains the essentials of the first, it is also enlarged and deepened by some new elements. One of these is a chapter on Japan. The reason for its inclusion is obvious. Of the six countries previously chosen as examples, five closely followed the European pattern, with modifications to suit their individual genius. The sixth, India, exemplified a poor and underdeveloped country seeking to strengthen its new independence with decisions for the future based largely on a choice between the traditions of Asia and the efficient but alien pattern introduced by an imperial power. Japan is distinct in many ways. It is an Asian country that has undergone many vicissitudes in the last 100 years or so. It has as deep-rooted a culture as any in the world, and an understandable pride in its art, its technical skill, and its particular internal graciousness. On the other hand, Japan was the first country in the world to be very nearly "westernized" as an alien experience, and the first to have a totally planned educational system (after 1868) linked with economic and political transformation.[1] In the post-1945 period Japan has faced several crises. It is now at a crossroads where it could affect the educational decisions of most of mankind, perhaps more than any of the countries so far conspicuous in educational activity. For most of mankind is in Asia.

All the countries first described have undergone radical reforms in structure or orientation since 1958, so the simple provision of up-to-date information necessitates a new edition. The opportunity is welcomed. We cannot make proper decisions about our own schools unless we have true information and relevant data about those of our neighbors. For this purpose the chapter on France has been almost entirely rewritten to keep up with events, and the other chapters have been radically altered. But this book, although it scrupulously tries to present accurate information, does not regard that as its main responsibility. Description is never enough. Indeed it is doubtful whether detached description in any of the social fields is possible, because when we look at other people's activity we project into that view our own patterns of perception together with our own emotionally charged scale of values. Some unspoken questions really concern us more than the neighbors we are observing. Accordingly, even what looks like straightforward examination or description is nearly always description according to the author's categories, or the enquirer's focus of interest. Rather than labor this obvious point, let us recognize why the countries to which chapters have been devoted were chosen.

Denmark deserves our interest for several reasons. It is a very small country which, with few resources and a short school life, has achieved an enviable standard of urbane civilization and international proficiency, and has indeed developed several kinds of education that have been examples to the world. It reminds us more than most countries that education is more than school, and it is representative of the admirable Scandinavian countries generally.

France is one of the great countries of the world, and its example to other nations has been even greater than her own momentous achievements. It is still the country of rationalism and intellectualism, although since 1945 there has been conspicuous attention to technological needs. This has been accompanied by radical reforms. France still highlights the problems of academic purism, of rationalist secularism con-

---

[1] The French Revolutionary and Napoleonic plans neglected many aspects either conceptualy or practically; for example, elementary education, religious reorientation, and most aspects of technological-commercial development. The Japanese did not.

tending with traditional piety, of centralization coexisting with remarkable individualism. Some current educational ideas are legacies of French thought, as are some of our most vaunted political liberties; but at the other extreme some of our educational ideas suffer their *reductio ad absurdum* in France. Even so, if we look fairly we shall see that France is in many ways the land of truly gracious living.

British society has been revolutionized during the present century, but with regrets. The sort of class struggle that Marx expected to explode with violence is conducted through the schools in accordance with the rules of the game. Antique talismans are brandished no less than genuine standards; but it is a serious and radical contest. In fact, the very existence and acceptance of so much conservatism in most aspects of life has necessitated more radical compensation in other respects than we can find anywhere outside the Soviet Union. Since the end of World War II, and even since the first edition of this book, change has affected British education in remarkable ways.

The United States is an obvious choice for any student of education —not (as some Americans might think) because the world has a high opinion of American schools and colleges generally. Despite the immense debt that other schools owe to some American innovations in the philosophy, psychology, and practice of schools, foreigners usually regard American schools as only potentially excellent, if a few conspicuous examples are omitted. The immense spate of educational literature poured over the world from American sources does little to combat this unflattering impression. Nevertheless, American technological distinction and commercial pre-eminence are the envy of the world. Clearly, their triumph indicates an exemplary educational achievement.

Some types of scholastic interest and some patterns of educational recruitment seem to belong more to Americans than to other peoples. In the immense stocktaking that has taken place since the mid-1950s, Americans have been sorting out their own standards and priorities in education; more than ever before they have been assessing the links between school and society, between schools and politics at the local and national level. These considerations alone would justify world interest in American education, quite apart from the long-standing fame of United States school patterns as the most conspicuous example of decentralization, with all its possibilities and problems.

There are still other reasons for an interest in American education as the declared mainspring of the American way of life. For many underdeveloped countries the United States represents one alternative "shape of things to come." Even if people forget that the United States is the country claimed for liberty, they see plainly that it is the land of resources and machines. If the American way of life is only the logical apex of industrialization and urbanization (as some people think), then it is hard to distinguish its material attractions from those of the alternative—the Soviet Union. Therefore it is vital for any educational observer to analyze the differences between the essential America and the essence of industrialized communism. The differences are not always those which Americans take for granted, and they are not always those most easy to maintain against two rather conflicting factors in the United States: the extremely decentralized pattern of administration, and the full logic of industrialized life with all its metropolitan concentrations of population and power.

The Soviet Union's achievements are colossal by any criterion. Many have been attributable to the schools. It is well to know what makes the second power in the world tick—and sometimes creak. Inside the Soviet Union and the Soviet bloc, the first answer given reflects communist faith—a belief in Marxist scriptures and party interpretation. But the actual practice of Soviet achievements is pivoted on its schools and colleges. There is immense enthusiasm for education in communist countries. Sometimes, indeed, satisfaction with its manifest success makes practitioners and public starry-eyed with optimism, and therefore uncritical of programs and methods. But since the death of Stalin in 1953 there have been two great changes, and a great reappraisal is going on apace. Since 1964, in particular, the whole of Eastern Europe has shown a striking readiness for serious comparative studies in education.

More than the Soviet Union itself is involved in this study. The eyes of more than half the people in the world are turned in its direction. Some gaze in admiration; some are dazzled by confusion. Too many people, even in democratic countries, cannot distinguish between what is communistic and what is merely humane or scientific. We should make that distinction very clear, not only in political theory but in educational practice. Then the hungry myriads of mankind and the vast underdeveloped regions of the earth may reach out for a better birthright without paying the price of communism. This book may help, not least by trying objectively to present a study of Soviet education.

Some of the reasons for choosing India have already been given. Like Japan, India is at a crossroads, but a crossroads a long way further back in human progress; and the multiple choice of roads is confusing. No country has more problems—economic, social, and religious, as well as those of school supply and orientation. There is another reason: it has been said that the typical member of mankind is an Indian. Statistically, he is either an Indian or a Chinese by nationality, but the

Indian's lot is perhaps more representative of the average human condition.

So the selection of these particular areas of educational interest seems justified. There are others, of course; but for a beginning there must be some limitation, and the main purpose must be to secure proper representation of the main educational types or the most conspicuous scholastic problems. The author has visited all the countries mentioned—in most cases, more than once—for careful professional study of educational characteristics. In every case, long personal contact with scholars and students has been maintained. What was said in the earlier editions has been checked and conversed about "on the ground"—even in the Soviet Union; it has also been translated into several foreign languages. These facts do not guarantee reliability, but they do clearly show the usefulness of the method here adopted to readers and researchers in many countries.

The main reason for choosing *countries* as a beginning of comparative study is that educational questions cannot really be discussed in vague or general terms. In nearly all countries, the government is charged with the responsibility for defining all (or the major part) of its formal education in accordance with laws. These are obviously limited to its own territories. They require a minimum period of attendance; they usually prescribe items of the curriculum, if not the whole curriculum; they regulate in some way the supply of teachers, of schools, and of facilities outside or after school. Above all, they largely determine the finances and economic or occupational links between schools and the nation at large. Educational problems cannot realistically be discussed without reference to these limitations, especially now that expenditure on formal education is so central a responsibility of all states.

In addition to these material considerations, there are other matters to bear in mind, more subtle and more penetrating, which in the long run equally affect educational preferences and political decision. These include such obvious elements as the language or languages spoken within a country's confines, together with all the linguistic, literary, and emotional reminders of one's national or regional "belonging." Language and its associations can envelop us like a home. The very pattern of our houses, the layout of our cities and communications, the articles or services that we use to achieve the kind of personality which seems normal to us—all these also constrain us like home influences, clothing our perceptions and ambitions like language. They add up to "the American way of life" in the United States, especially as continually enriched or checked by the infinite range of preferences daily shown by the American people. In all other countries the same kind of silent teaching or prompting or correction goes on continuously. Decisions which seem to be "objective" about schools or the theoretical aims of education are all clothed in language or institutions indigenous to us. Social words such as "school," "student," "teacher" (and indeed "natural" words like "mother") take on a different meaning from culture to culture. Furthermore, they are undergoing continuous change within each culture, as we see by comparing the assumptions made by our grandmothers with those made by our daughters. Thus all decisions tend to be made idiomatically within the evolving interpretation imposed by the cultural confines of each of our countries.

The very fact that change in the postatomic period has been so vast and swift challenges the previously accepted self-sufficiency of any cultural interpretation. Mankind needs comparative and international studies more than ever before. No norm can be taken for granted; nothing can be assumed to be changeless. It is not necessary to think only in terms of strategic interest, though this important aspect of thought about schools has come obviously to the fore since the first Sputnik in 1957. In 10 years alone all thoughts about education have been challenged on much wider grounds, and not only in the United States.

Similar, though less spectacular, changes challenge all assumptions. These changes include the emancipation of new nations, and their likely dependence in one way or another on the world's great powers; automation, and the transformation of all occupations everywhere in consequence of its development; the revolution in communications and its impact on schools, especially with increased demands already placed on a dwindling supply of up-to-the-minute teachers; the continual expansion of knowledge and change in its application; and all kinds of scientific and social discoveries.

Each one of these innovations challenges the self-sufficiency of even the most advanced country. In smaller countries change sometimes demands huge regional interdependence, as seen in the European Common Market. More often it leads to intensified specialization at particular points of research and development, combined with mutual interchange of some services. "Big Science" alone is too expensive already for most of the nations of the world. Interchange of personnel and information also necessitates some form of international "equivalance" in such things as diplomas, university studies, and indeed in workmen at every level.

In the present stage of national and educational development this generally demands a richer cultivation of each country's present resources and institutions (especially in education), combined with an awareness of outside challenges and responsibilities. Usually these events also necessitate a wider recruitment from all sections of the population for unprecedented purposes, as well as expansion for older needs which are satisfied by broadening and extending secondary and higher education. Inevitably this expansion or enrichment takes place within a national framework; but a prime requirement is that it must be internationally sensitive and realistic.

We go back to our contention, therefore, that a proper study of Comparative Education must be grounded on a sympathetic description-with-analysis of all that adds up to "education" in each human workshop—that is, in one cultural whole. National cultures are not self-justifying of course, though they usually seem so to the inhabitants. We can see how changes in the postwar period illustrate the idiomatic order of priorities which people like ourselves have evolved in other countries, so as to use existing resources and institutions to better effect. Sometimes we can learn something that could be directly copied. More often we learn something that enables us to *ask ourselves the right questions.* Nearly always we learn something more about the world in which our own children have to grow up. It is a world without precedent, with few rules unchallenged, and with hardly any signposts except those which are implied rather than seen in the present circumstances. Comparative studies, therefore, assume particular significance. The piecing together of constituent bits of information or insight makes more sense than the separate parts—if only because the total dynamic of the situation is thus perceived, together with its possible outcome and timing.

Partly to satisfy the stages by which a reader gradually finds his way into comparative study, and partly to satisfy universities' requirements for the provision of courses, the analytical insights which run through *Other Schools and Ours* are provided simply and with little elaboration. They are, however, much more strongly developed in my *World Perspectives in Education,* which illustrates and analyzes particular *problems* in education comparatively with material drawn from relevant countries. It also analyzes the decisions which have seemed necessary in different circumstances.

This second, or "problem," phase of comparative study can be a profitable one, provided that it follows a dynamic case study of the kind here presented in *Other Schools and Ours.* To do otherwise is poor pedagogy. It is also, unfortunately, poor social science. If attempted prematurely, a "problem study" in human affairs is like discussing matrimonial problems from inside a monastery, or the problems of Asian rice growers from a skyscraper office. The very "identification" of problems may be erroneous unless such identification takes place with facts and insight appropriate to each individual context. Otherwise, pseudocomparisons are made of incomparable intellectual constructs invented by the professor, or intricate decisions are misunderstood by the students. Each problem study must be constantly referred back to the needs, possibilities, and aims of its cultural context. We cannot overlook some of its irrational elements, such as its loves and fears.

At a level of greater factual or intellectual competence in coping with problem analysis by comparative study, one or more specific problems can be picked out for special enquiry. Among these are the real (not imaginary) problems urgently discussed today. These include problems of secondary school reorganization, the structure and nature of higher education, and the supply of teachers or their substitutes. Alternatively, one or more "factors" in an educational situation can be chosen for study by comparison with other contexts where an apparently identical factor occurs. Among these are language, racial diversity, and centralization versus decentralization. For research students it is profitable to prepare a dissertation or thesis on one of these topics— but only as a suitable center of interest. The topic will need constant cross-checking. If it is to be well-grounded and not just speculation, it must be referred back harmoniously to some area study or case study of the type presented here. Even though it is the nature of problem analysis to detach and "isolate" problems temporarily for examination, in that "isolated" state the problems have no more real significance than glands outside the living being in which they function, or behavior outside a social context. Problems are idiomatic. So, in the long run, are their solutions.

Is there nothing in common, then? Of course. It is a great advantage to consider our educational neighbors not as foreigners doing something outlandish but as real neighbors working in an adjoining workshop on problems that are becoming more universally similar in consequence of technological and social change. The theme of these changes is maintained throughout the present book, and is greatly elaborated in my *Education and Social Change.* For the time being we must be content to observe our neighbors scientifically, but with the sympathy of common humanity. Thus we recognize them as tackling problems which are really ours (or nearly ours) in an offbeat way, with unusual hypotheses and equipment. All these seeming oddities make us question our own assumptions about what is "natural," and perhaps make us see some things as purely accidental. Above all, we come to appreciate the force of our own cultural ecology. Our intellectual and emotional struggle to detach ourselves shows our need for complementary approaches to any "objectivity." Any alleged science without this kind of actual or informal teamwork today is useless—at any rate in the social field.

At a third stage of comparative study, where in university language we are probably thinking of the doctoral level, a new kind of synthesis in scholarship becomes possible. *Combined or coordinated studies* can be undertaken which include comparative elements from several disciplines. For example, any study of communist education should include the following: contributions from researchers into the historical, economic, and social background of countries where such education is found; insight into the previous influence of churches or other institutions of authority in those countries; literary or philosophical antecedents to more recent communist writers; and comparison between the various communist idioms developed in different countries.

As an alternative, at this same third level of interdisciplinary study, teams of researchers in sociology, economics, comparative anthropology, comparative religion, and actual "developmental" or "area" studies, could contribute to socioeconomic planning or educational reform projects for one particular region—as in South America or Africa. Indeed, in favorable circumstances a whole school or department of comparative studies can coordinate such researches as a continuous team project. Several such research units have been launched; but in only a few has the educational element been sufficiently strong or ecologically sensitive enough. In endeavors of this kind something more than practical politics is involved, though that is of vital importance in a world where most of mankind is desperately short of opportunity. There is also a truly scientific approach on a proper complementary basis, which can yield academic and humane insights of the utmost importance for education and civilization everywhere. The old cleavage between the scientific and the humane is broken down, and the old attempt to rule humane affairs by a mathematical or physical yardstick is seen as a bit of early nineteenth-century industrial archeology.

The question of *purpose* and usefulness is of increasing urgency in comparative education. Comparative studies can no longer be curricular exercises conducted in some ivory tower, or pedagogical tourism. Because of public investment and social demand, the development and reform of education are a matter of business, not conversation. If comparative studies are not permeated by a sense of questioning and purpose from the very beginning, there will be a twofold loss. The prospective teachers who follow college and university courses will gain no lasting benefit through a widening of perspectives, while the businesslike economists, sociologists, and statesmen will go ahead with their own planning and comparisons of a probably less sensitive and, therefore, less viable kind. There is an urgent need for the closest possible link between careful scholars and public men of action.

In any case, as all educational decisions are in some way social or political too, it is equally necessary that the lay public should be aware that other school systems are directly relevant to whatever is decided by the local district board or in the national ministry. Unless the kind of information presented in this book ripples outward to permeate every teacher's work and every parent's preferences, these local or national decisions will be out of touch with the world's present realities.

Other countries, already quite well-informed about foreign educational systems, are now moving from a one-sided look at their neighbors toward a full recognition that internationally-based studies of education are relevant and purposeful for their own decisions. Some recent writing in comparative education has assumed that educational decisions are "self-evident" or that the issues are simply disposed of by "juxtaposition" or "lining up." Others have attempted to produce grandiose abstract theories as though some formula of a physical kind would perpetually give a right answer. In the social field, however, no issue or problem stands by itself. All are interconnected and complex. All are housed simultaneously in many institutions, customs, and emotions. Causation is never simple, and results are seldom clean-cut, even if policies and actions are. If the truth is to be found, it is usually in subtlety and implication rather than in bold formulation.

All cultural preferences (and therefore educational decisions) are phased in time, cumulative in conviction, and the outcome of innumerable separate but complementary decisions over a wide range of people. That is what we really mean when we talk about a favorable climate of opinion. Some of the problems of educational decision are analyzed in my *Comparative Studies and Educational Decision.* Other aspects are reviewed from time to time in some of the journals dedicated to comparative studies, notably *Comparative Education,* published in England, and the *Comparative Education Review,* published in the United States.

At this level of abstraction, however, we have moved away from the carefully grounded area studies with which we began. We have passed the level of problem analysis described as the second stage of comparative study, and we have gone beyond that purposeful third stage of "thinking through" particular localized complexes for direct, contemporary usefulness. With increasing abstraction we may run the risk of irrelevance and remoteness, like that of some theologians' argument over doctrinal minutiae while the morals and pastoral needs of the flock go unobserved.

1

WE ALL KNOW BEST

When it comes to bringing up our children, we all think *we* know the best way. No one is going to teach us! But when we look at our neighbors' children, we see that some parents are not succeeding at the job, no matter how much theory they have backing them.

Is it just a case of failing to do the obvious? Or are the things we take for granted not quite so obvious after all? Get an Englishman into a corner, shake him, and ask him what education is for. With eyebrows raised he will mumble that he supposes it is for the "training of character." He may add something about "a gentleman," or something else about a "full and useful life." His choice will depend in part upon his politics.

Get your American into a corner, shake him, and ask him the same question. He will confidently reply that education is for the development of individual qualities, for making first-class citizens who will have splendid careers and will be well-adjusted members of the com-

13

munity. He will make it quite clear that he is thinking about girls as well as boys. He will go on to tell you about the usefulness of various offerings in American education for achieving these purposes. And because Americans are "sold" on education, he may go on to proclaim that it will advance the democratic and American way of life in a rather dubious world.

Get a Frenchman into a corner, and treat him likewise. With a gleam in his shrewd eye, he is ready with the answer. Education is for the sharpening of the intellect and for the transmission of *culture générale*. There is really no English translation for this phrase as the Frenchman uses it. It means being steeped in the philosophical and esthetic values of the Western tradition through an extremely thorough knowledge of the great books and of all the formal academic disciplines. But the Frenchman does not feel any need to explain this. His short, incisive sentence is supposed to be self-explanatory.

The American, the Englishman, and the Frenchman are neighbors. Like good parents everywhere, the American and the Frenchman are sure they are right. The Englishman feels fairly sure, and acts as though he could not conceive of anything else. Is the difference just one of emphasis? Will the results be much the same in the end? You would not think so if you could go into the schools of these three nations. They are as foreign to each other as can possibly be imagined. If schools are nurseries for adults-to-be, or factories for the future, it is amazing that the adult product is not more different.

Differences between nationalities are plain to see. A French girl in Piccadilly or on Fifth Avenue is French to her elegant fingertips. Her walk, her liveliness are Gallic. The keenness of her eye, the shape of her mouth, and her eloquent changes of expression are typical of France. It is hard to be precise about the difference, but few will doubt that a difference is usually there.

Similarly, it is easy to pick out most Americans in London. There is no need for distinguishing features such as clothes or hair styles. Even when Americans have lived in Britain long enough to wear English clothes and have lost other outward signs, the natives still recognize the measured, flexible swing of the typical American walk. American girls seem to the English eye to have a frank, clear gaze, a confident and somewhat boyish lift of the head, a rather large though attractive mouth, and a style of walking that might be described as "liberated." How is it that Americans, being derived from so many racial stocks that have not yet had time to amalgamate, can be so typical? Not genetically, that is clear, nor climatically, nor through occupation or class. The answer can only be that looking American, like being American and thinking American, is culturally induced.

How does this come about? We begin to guess the answer when we see how an Italian, for example, can pick out an Englishwoman abroad. He does not rely on a tailored tweed suit, or shoes, or a schoolgirl complexion, though these help. Something in the woman's bearing is usually enough to indicate her nationality. Even when seen from a distance, her mouth may announce that she is English. This is because she habitually speaks with a British accent. An Italian professor, with whom I was discussing comparative sociology, once correctly pointed out most of the Englishwomen at an international conference. He claimed that he was able to do this on the basis of mouth shape alone. He said the women looked as though they spent the whole day saying nothing but "Mew, mew." Saying "Mew, mew" can evidently become part of your physiognomy; it is probably part of your character.

Happily, no two human beings are quite alike. No matter how strong the pressure is toward standardization, there is a welcome range of personalities and appearances. No one would like his fellow countrymen to go about asking: "How typical can you get?" But no American, for example, is sorry that he looks American. In general, we can see that national habits and ways of talking or thinking become built into that outward self that is all that the world can see of me, you, or anyone else. In the long run our racial origins do not much matter. Despite our race, and even our family background in many cases, Americanization goes on all over the United States and a similar kind of nationalization goes on in England and in every other country.

But how does this happen? Are French girls taught to be chic in French schools? Hardly. Do American schools teach boys to walk as though they owned the earth? Do British schools teach boys to walk as though they didn't care who owned it? Yes and no. There are no lessons in these accomplishments, yet all day and every day they are taught by the whole community. As the school is a sort of symptom of the community and its culture, so the child's mannerisms and state of mind can only be expected to reflect the community's scale of values and etiquette.

This is particularly true in the United States, where the school is conspicuously the folk institution par excellence. The school is both the servant of today's community and the master of tomorrow's. It shoulders responsibilities that in other countries are reserved for the family or the church. It brings in the parents of its children to share its life. The social life of the school's great family often moves in an orbit round its varied assemblies and enthusiasms. The civic and vocational life of the community shows great concern for the efficiency and well-being of the school. New towns and cities plan schools before the layout of roads and houses is completed. The school is the shrine that houses the myth or prophecy of the future America. But not even in the United States does that sacred institution teach people to "walk American."

Then who or what does? Children in the United States, like children everywhere, copy the mannerisms and routines of their parents and their playmates. Without thinking about it, they value the same prestige groups and acquire the same order of priorities. Young children (though some harassed parents will doubt this) are passionate conformists. Their system of role rehearsal, therefore, and their dreams of self-identification can hardly fail to be "typical." I mean that they will exemplify the myths and imaginary self-portraits that the community dreams up for itself. In a country like the United States, where geographic and social mobility are probably more marked than anywhere else in the world, an even greater need is felt to "identify" oneself with what is "normal" and "American." There is basically little need now for the conscious Americanization of the public school system. Children are almost too ready to learn that kind of lesson. Society (that is, the organized life of people) is teaching it already for all it is worth. In the United States you *live* American—that is, you eat, buy, play, and dream American. Your father-image, mother-image, ego, and superego are American. Educators overplay the role of the school in all this. The results they achieve do not arise from the treatment they hand out—at least, not to the extent they suppose. This can be shown by the fact that American-style schools in Japan or the Philippine Islands continue to turn out Japanese and Filipinos.

It can also be indicated from evidence nearer home. I have already said that a European can often distinguish an American by his almost maritime style of walking. Americans themselves recognize a variation from the normal urban style in the swinging gait of the plainsman, cowboy, or hillbilly. Good-humored jokes are made about it. But they do not teach these things in school in the midwest. Nor do southern schools teach their young ladies to cultivate an alluring and ultra-feminine walk that somehow sets them off from their equally attractive, but nevertheless different, sisters in the north. Modes of life and superficial mannerisms are learned together, from class to class, region to region, and nation to nation. The schools play a part, but not even in the most community-conscious schools does their contribution preponderate. The same kind of schooling can be tried elsewhere with different results.

We must also notice that from country to country different ideas prevail about the role schools should play. In France, for example, it is only a few years since the public system of education was first called a system of "education." Before that it was called the public system of "teaching." Earlier, it was called "public instruction." Going back to the typical French definition of education given at the beginning of this chapter, we are not surprised to find that the school concerns itself primarily with teaching facts, or handing out great ideas, or exercising children in clear thinking. The children in these schools seem almost like young adults when contrasted with British or American youngsters. Self-determination and community life are almost unconsidered, except in a few experimental schools which are untypical. The teachers enjoying the greatest esteem are those who teach for only fifteen hours a week in straight academic subjects and do nothing else. Parents play no part in the life of the school, as a rule, except by insisting that their children complete the large amount of homework the teacher assigns. Emphasis is on work. Sports play a negligible part in the school's program, and many parents grudge the little time alloted to physical education. The French set great store by competition, and their educational system is full of it. Hence the proverb: "A Frenchman—an individualist." Teachers have one clear job to do: teach. As one of the most distinguished teachers in modern France put it, "They [teachers] are priests of the intellect." There you have it—the asceticism, the austere withdrawal, the renunciation for school purposes of the devil, the world, and the flesh.

But no one assumes that the French man or woman grows up unaware of the dangers or delights of the devil, the world, and the flesh. The French are proverbial for their *joie de vivre,* and their *bon vivant* is the prototype of the modern epicurean in any country. He does not, however, serve his apprenticeship to sensibility amid the austere exercises of the classroom—not officially, anyway.

There have been remarkable innovations in the French school system since 1945, and particularly since 1959 there has been a determined effort to realign it technologically and socially. Even so, the normal French curriculum does not yet seem to relate closely to the social and vocational needs of today, whether we consider the basic occupation of agriculture or the increasing tempo of industrialization. Many Frenchmen would like things changed in school to secure a greater realism. Emphasis is overwhelmingly on quality, and quality of mind of a particular kind; so to most teachers, and perhaps to most parents, it does not seem to matter much if vocational skill and life orientation are postponed or omitted.

For a long time there was little official concern or popular anxiety that some three quarters of the French population did not qualify for the most valued secondary education, and that effective alternatives were lacking until the 1959 reforms. Even then, anything like real equivalence in opportunities for children above the age of 11 continued to be in doubt. Proposals for "modern" alternatives to the traditionally esteemed secondary school curriculum have been treated with skepticism by ambitious parents and most teachers. This is so in nearly all countries. Nevertheless, even in those schools where the new "breakthrough" has not yet been effective, the quality of those who do succeed is astonishingly high within the broad limits of the formal curriculum. To that extent the system is successful. It has been copied in many parts of the world. This is a sobering thought for the Briton or American who feels that the successful French scholar is learned rather than educated. The French system is the basis of many nations' school programs; the American system has hardly anywhere been willingly copied, though individual aspects of it have been widely influential.

Of course, this fact tells us nothing about the real worth of the respective systems. But it does show that nations have ideas about the kind of schooling they want, and that these ideas are vastly different. No American or Briton can honestly declare that the "truths" in education are "self-evident." By seeing how other people reject our notions of how to bring up children we may come to a better appraisal of our current practice; we may alter it, or we may reinforce it. At least we may see ourselves as others see us.

Even if it were true that 50 million Frenchmen can't be wrong, as the saying goes, it is obvious that their school system is far from being the whole of their education. French life and French society are the educational matrix of the distinctive French character. Schools are an integral, but temporary part, of every Frenchman's scheme of living. They add something (it is hard to say what) to the chic turnout of the typical demoiselle. She is as ready for life as the British or American girl, although her idiom is different. She has had no formal schooling, however, in the social arts or in personality adjustment. Her mastery of the essence of being French has been instilled into her by *living* French. So it goes for every nation or cultural community.

To this extent we can see that every nation or community is totalitarian. Paradoxically, this is true even of the most liberal regime. It enfolds us at birth; we are cradled in its relationships; we acquire its language of living, its special dialogue of communication, and its idiomatic scale of values. We cannot escape from it while awake, and if we cry out in dreams we speak our mother tongue. No matter how far or in what area we wander, we have one home. Even in the secret things we take for granted, like love, there are national idioms. "What comes naturally" is often learned.

So the "self-evident truths" of child-rearing are not obvious after all. Is our chief aim to be "character," or intellectual eminence, or the production of well-adjusted and prosperous citizens? If we choose one of these, or a harmony of several, how do we set about achieving it? Those who seem to share our aims have a different family structure and different methods of teaching. Some who rely on our methods achieve different results. One might have expected "human nature" to make it all simple and obvious, but it is all very confusing.

Though we privately know best, it may be of interest to study in further detail what some of our neighbors are up to with their children. After all, their experiments can be regarded as attempted answers to our own problems, especially in the contracting world of modern travel and instantaneous intercontinental communication—to say nothing of mass production and standardization of expectation. Let us try to appreciate, indeed feel as sympathetically as we can, the intimacy of their context. That is the dynamic, ecological complex which educates them. It is frequently this conjunction of forces that solves the fundamental and, therefore, usually unspoken needs of civilized living.

Needs and expectations change; circumstances certainly change. Every new social situation produces new needs even as it copes with the old. Let us see our own homes and schools as merely passing expedients, evaluating them in the light of others' experiments and priorities.

2

DENMARK GREAT AND SMALL

The flags are almost certain to be flying today in Denmark. Soon after we see the green copper crowns of tower and steeple, and the clean warmth of brick and tile, our eyes pick out a multitude of cheerful flags. They flaunt the white cross on a scarlet background against a windy sky, which is nearly always of the palest blue or the palest gray. On every occasion possible the cheerful Danes fly their brilliant *Dannebrog* from public buildings, from houses, and from the hundreds of tiny "community gardens" that cluster together near the apartment blocks in towns. Proud of their country and fond of the land, the Danes are peaceful neighbors and hard workers, and seem to have solved many of the problems of gracious living.

Yet Denmark is geographically an inhospitable land of heath and shallow soil. It consists of a peninsula north of Germany and about 125 islands between that peninsula and Sweden. Extending altogether to 16,576 square miles, it is about half the size of Ireland and roughly one-fifth the size of Minnesota. Its population is less than 4,600,000, approximately that of the central area of London administered by the Inner London Education Authority, or half that of New York City. The climate is rather harsh, cold in winter and cool in summer. Nearly the whole of Denmark lies as far north as the northern half of Labrador.

There was a time when the Viking ancestors of the present Danes harried the seas and pillaged the coasts of northern Europe. They settled in Ireland, ruled England, and swept through the Mediterranean Sea. Until 1814, the king of Denmark was also king of Norway, Greenland, and Iceland; but after Napoleon's defeat by the British the Danes had to let Norway go. Then, though Denmark was no longer the warlike scourge of the North, its population mainly consisted of uncouth and brutalized peasants eking out a hard life in scattered communities on sodden land. Many of the landlords were foreign in their sympathies if not in blood. Yet amidst all these difficulties the Danes decided to rescue their people and country by education. Compulsory schooling for *seven* years was proclaimed in 1814—in those days an unprecedented length of time. Within about three years it had effectively begun. Today Denmark is among the best educated, cleanest, and most civilized of nations, and possibly the most democratic of all. Differences of opportunity and wealth are very small. Community life is very strong, but individual freedom is very great. Danes of all categories get along well together at home, and are sure to give a generous welcome to strangers. Though so proud of their country, and its language and cultural heritage, the Danes are great travelers and quite at ease in any community. All this they attribute to their education. Any stranger looking in on them is bound to support this testimony. It has all been accomplished in the last 150 years—the greater part in less than a century. During that time there have been foreign invasions and near-famines in this naturally poor land, yet the Danes are now materially prosperous and culturally rich. It is no wonder that they are proud of their educational system.

Only seven years of schooling are still compulsory to this day, and children do not start school until they are 7 years old. Even then they do not put in a full day, and not until they reach the age of 11 do they have a normal school timetable. Younger children are all back home by noon. This is partly to make things easier for young pupils, but also because parents usually want to share in the actual daily upbringing of their children, maintaining the country tradition. When you consider that even for older pupils the day-school program ends at two o'clock, you begin to wonder how it is all done, particularly as nearly half the children in rural areas leave school at the age of 14, and a large number in the towns as well (between 10 and 20 percent in 1966) still do so.[1]

There is even more cause for wonder when you step into a classroom where youngsters of 13 or 14 are having a lesson. They will talk to you in English—not perfect English, it is true, but perfectly adequate for the job. If you were German, some could probably talk to you in that language too. A few pupils would also be successful in French. If you were to sit in on one of the top classes of an academic high school during an English lesson, you would not only find that the whole lesson was conducted in excellent English but that the quality of the discussion would match nearly anything in an American liberal arts college or in the sixth form of an English "grammar school." It is quite uncanny. In a large town it is never necessary for the traveler to speak Danish. You are met not with the shopkeeper's or hotelkeeper's English of continental resorts, but with conversation and discussion. You will be welcomed into many homes, but you had better know what you are talking about. The Danes are perfect hosts, but will probably be a match for you in anything you discuss.

It must not be imagined that the schooling is all literary. The Danes are nothing if not practical. They live mainly by the export of dairy produce from a land that is naturally infertile except on one or two of the islands. They are great navigators and marine engineers. Danish businessmen, technicians, and scientists range the world. Visiting the home of a typical farmer (owning his own lot of little more than 50 acres), you may find it as modern and comfortable as many suburban houses in Detroit or Wimbledon. It probably lacks a few gadgets that city dwellings could well spare, but probably has some refinements (such as music and singing) from which they could benefit. The farmer himself may have a Mercedes car or a good Volkswagen at least—and we must remember that cars are less familiar in Europe. In any case, the farmer's enterprises are skillfully linked up with magnificent sales organizations. His fertilizers, foodstuffs, insurance policies, and mortgages are acquired on very favorable terms through various cooperative schemes. His eggs and pigs form part of the great flow of exports although his hens and breeding animals are few. The most up-to-date cooperative dairies process his butter and cheese. In talking to such a farmer you are certainly talking to a businessman, and you do not always need an interpreter either.

---

[1] As will be shown later in this chapter, there is a wide range of part-time provision for children to the age of 18 or beyond, which they are expected (and may soon be required) to attend if not undergoing full-time instruction. But many pupils voluntarily extend their formal education beyond the statutory minimum, and that proportion is growing rapidly.

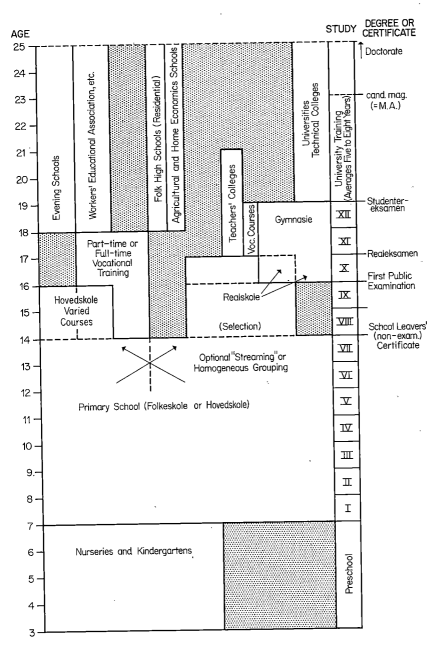

School System in Denmark

Half of all the Danes live scattered over the countryside in villages, small townships, or on small islands. A quarter of the population lives in quaint little towns; the rest in Copenhagen. It is obvious that the task of providing fair opportunities for everyone in education, communication, and urbane living is very great indeed. Denmark has no raw materials to speak of. There is no coal, no mineral wealth, no oil, no water power. With ingenuity and hard work, however, the Danes have made the effort necessary to supply the education needed. By carefully educated skill and social engineering they have managed to pay for their schools and abundant social services. Their wealth has been won by exports. In a normal year, Denmark exports more butter and produces more bacon than any other country except the United States, which has nearly forty times its population and nearly two hundred times its area. This monumental achievement would have been impossible without a happy combination of individual enterprise and close cooperation. The Danish way of education has served both endeavors and has been derived from them.

Let us look into a Danish home and see how the children grow up. Our visit will probably take us to a small apartment consisting of a living-dining room, one or two compact bedrooms, a kitchenette, and a small bathroom and toilet. The main room may contain a collapsible bed, too. The apartment, which forms part of a block maintained by the municipality, is warm and there is plenty of hot water. Other apartment houses are established on a cooperative basis, and are managed by the occupants. Some, of course, are privately managed. The rents are low.

To save space, much of the furniture is of simple but elegant design, and fitted close to the walls. An alcove or dining recess may be a feature of the room. The wallpaper is of a cheerful and modernistic pattern. Pastel shades predominate and brightly reflect the pale sunshine. Potted plants abound; some climb a trellis against the wall, others are dotted in front of the windows, and still others occupy the cool space between the double storm windows. As you have been invited for a meal, you have brought a gay bunch of flowers for your hostess. These are placed where they match the other flowers with which the room is decorated. Danes delight in floral decoration. Florists' shops are everywhere, and at all suitable seasons street peddlers sell flowers from pushcarts.

The street lies just below the window. There is no garden, but not far away the family has a "colony garden" or allotment on a communal piece of land. It has a small summerhouse where picnics are enjoyed. There are roses round the door, and a trim hedge fends off the world from one Dane's castle. All kinds of flowers are grown, as in an old-world cottage garden, and so are herbs and some vegetables. Our hostess has a pot of chervil and a pot of chives growing in her kitchen, too. When we look out the window we are struck by the number of bicycles, and by the bright colors and cheerful patterns of the children's clothing. In the cool air the children's cheeks glow healthily. No doubt their long woolen stockings, windproof jackets, and fur-trimmed caps keep them very warm. When they discard this outer clothing the house, or school's corridor-cloakroom, looks like a festive bazaar. Indoor clothing is also warm and cheerfully colored. As for color and individuality, the scene resembles that in an American school, and is in marked contrast to many schools in England.

At home the children are warmly welcomed. They treat their parents with affectionate respect, and the parents in turn treat them with courtesy. The atmosphere seems to combine the old world of childhood and the new. As children do not begin school before they are 7 (except in those urban areas where nurseries and kindergartens are provided for mothers who go out to work), a great deal of responsibility for the early stages of education falls on the family. It is not considered desirable that parents teach their children the elements of reading, however, although some do. The religious tradition among the Lutherans has always held that the home is the focus of a proper upbringing. Well over 90 percent of the Danes are officially Lutherans, and although they take their religion very lightly indeed, habits of the old faith persist. Similarly, though a decreasing number of Danes are old-style farmers and craftsmen, there is a relic still of the time-honored notion that a significant part of a child's upbringing is experienced in the family's occupation. This helps to explain why until recently there has been no widespread antagonism to a child's beginning work at 14 years of age. Schooling on a full-time basis may be temporarily discontinued then, but education goes on.

Social change continues in Denmark as everywhere else. The national union of teachers and the Social Democratic party want to raise the age of compulsory school attendance to 16. Without legislation, present trends indicate that all are likely to stay until 15 by 1970, anyway, and until 16 by 1975. Agrarian interests have resisted the extension of compulsion, and their word is powerful in Denmark. However, urbanization and urban expectations develop. Already nearly a third of all mothers go out to work, thus altering further the possibility of providing at home all the child's extracurricular needs. Therefore kindergartens and afternoon activity centers are increasingly in evidence, though as far as possible the family feeling is maintained.

When little children first go to school, they pass from one kind of parental atmosphere to another. The teacher is greatly respected. Even in kindergarten, the little girls curtsy to the teacher and the little boys bow and shake hands. In the schools of an earlier period, the teacher was also the pastor, and the dignity of that position remains to some extent. Men compose a higher proportion of teachers than we find in Britain, and a much higher proportion than in the United States.

The full school day begins at eight o'clock. There is an assembly at nine, after the first lesson. The school, especially if it has been recently built, is light and elegant. Yet economy has been carefully considered in its construction, as it has been paid for out of the town's revenues. Great attention is given to soundproofing, and to good lighting with an absence of glare. The children troop along the light-painted corridors to the assembly hall. By the usual European standards they seem very casual. Individualism prevails in hair styles as well as clothes. If the school is a *Gymnasie* (academic high school) we may notice that a few boys aged 17 or 18 are trying to grow mustaches or even beards. The head teacher enters without ceremony after the children are assembled, and greets them all. They wish him "Good morning" in return. There is a song or hymn, perhaps a short reading, an announcement or two—and that is all. There is no patriotic homage to the flag (none is on display), no declaration of allegiance, nothing solemn at all. Yet the Danes are passionately patriotic, keenly committed to education, and deeply respectful to authority. After the assembly the children troop back to their classrooms. There are no prefects, no student government. The teacher is waiting, and the somewhat austere lessons begin again.

The teacher knows fairly definitely what each week's work, or even each day's work, will entail. There is not only a division of the day into regular periods, but even a fairly minute regulation of the whole study program. The principal of the school is not, as in some countries, the chairman or leader of an almost autonomous band of teachers. He is an officer whose job it is to see that the government's regulations and other official interpretations are carried out. He is in fact called "Inspector." There may be some local adjustment of the "school plan," but the main direction comes from the Ministry. Copenhagen, where about one-fourth of all the Danes live, enjoys a great measure of local autonomy in education; but the national pattern is closely followed, except in small details, and the city's education system is centralized just like the national system.

This situation sometimes seems shocking to Britons and Americans, who cherish the idea of local autonomy. But we must bear in mind that it is possible for even an independent local authority (like the city of New York) to regulate public education minutely, and to plan the teaching program more or less as it is done in Denmark. The total number of Danes is not as great as the population thus centrally governed in

New York City. In comparing school systems we have to keep this kind of problem in perspective. It is noteworthy also that Danish teachers are more effectively able to influence the decisions of the local education authority than are their counterparts in the United States or Britain. That is because they have representatives who possess considerable powers on the local education committee. Public opinion in Denmark also accords high esteem to the teaching profession.

The Danish school year lasts from August 15 until approximately June 24, with only 26 vacation days. Children attend school 6 days a week, but classes are dismissed at noon on Saturdays. The school day is divided into six 50–minute periods, with a 10–minute break after each class and a recess about eleven o'clock. Homework takes from three to four hours a day and usually consists of a textbook assignment that must be read and thoroughly assimilated for discussion the next day. (This is a common practice on the continent of Europe.) There is little written homework. Competition among the children is keen and this is encouraged. There is now no charge for tuition, books, and medical or dental attention.

In the classroom it all adds up to a rather formal relationship between the teacher and the taught. There is much more talking by the teacher than would be considered proper in an English school, and much less activity and self-determination than is recommended by Americans. It seems incongruous, for example, to be present during a physics or chemistry lesson and find that the work is mainly done by dialogue between the teacher and the class, with a few visual illustrations and hardly any handling of anything. But the strongly verbal tendency in Danish education comes into its own in literary subjects and in anything that lends itself to discussion. Here there is very full class participation.

It is not surprising to find emphasis on the spoken word in an educational system that in times past was considered part and parcel of understanding the Word of God as set out in the Bible for interpretation among the faithful. Danish educators of the early nineteenth century were greatly concerned with rescuing the Danish language from the lowly status to which it had sunk; therefore they encouraged a sense of nationhood and self-expression by vigorous use of the mother tongue. To this day, the Danes are conspicuous for their eagerness to break into patriotic song on any excuse. It is all very happy and harmless. Far from being shut out, the visitor feels welcomed by it as he does by the gay flags that deck the streets on every possible occasion.

Yet it would be wrong to give the impression that Danish notions of education are bookish. What is done in school must be seen against the whole background of an education in society, at work, and in the home.

Even in school, close attention is given to self-expression in various manual forms of education. Many of our own notions about practical activities (and, indeed, progressive education generally) arise from the Scandinavian introduction of *slojd* (*sløyd*) woodwork in schools. Wherever possible, special teachers give instruction in metalwork, home economics, music, and so on. The public education authorities in towns of any size also conduct recreation centers where youngsters can pursue hobbies in pottery, painting, and similar crafts under the supervision of paid teachers in after-school hours. These classes are very popular.

In addition, there is an ever-present interest in physical well-being. Towns ensure that doctors, dentists, nurses, and psychologists are available directly to schools. They may employ a nurse or a psychologist permanently on the staff of a large establishment. The children usually have a Scandinavian sandwich meal (*smørrebrød*) with milk about eleven o'clock. This balanced meal in miniature has not only improved the health of the Danes in general; it has also taught generations the essentials of good nutrition. Under the name of "Oslo breakfast" it has been widely recommended by physicians in many countries to impoverished or undernourished populations. As Americans have learned from its Swedish counterpart *smörgåsbord,* a sandwich meal can be very sumptuous. This is how you will find it in the more expensive cafés in Denmark, too. It is interesting to see that what was once a social service has become a characteristic and delightful part of Danish living.

Children learn the elements of cleanliness in a practical way in many schools by having a bath at school once every two weeks. They are not, of course, allowed to suppose that this is enough! Either at school or after school they take an active part in games of all kinds. Because of the inclement climate, many games which visitors think of as outdoor games are played indoors. Gymnasiums and indoor arenas are an important part of the educational provision. Obviously in a country as thrifty as Denmark, the financial side of this accommodation may cause anxiety, but public generosity is shown everywhere. Moreover, many school swimming baths or sports arenas are available for general use in after-school hours on a paying basis. Economy is served, and at the same time home, school, and leisure activities are brought closer together. Some folk high schools (about which more will be said later) are devoted mainly to physical culture, and teachers' training colleges make a strong feature of both fitness and readiness to teach physical education. This emphasis is particularly important when we remember that many schools are small and located in rural areas.

No matter what efforts are made to consolidate schools in one locality and provide a school bus system, a farming population that is thinly scattered throughout the islands must always rely heavily on the ingenuity of the teachers in the small schools. Partly because of education's early religious associations and partly because of the undoubted devotion of teachers to their calling, the schoolmaster still enjoys great prestige. It is significant that so many teachers are men; the usual word for "teacher" is masculine. In rural areas, especially, the teacher is a power in the community as well as a factotum in the school. The schoolmaster with his violin (more mobile than a piano, and more personal) is a center of culture, an adviser, and often an organizer of adult education.

To any people seeking emancipation or social mobility, education is a ladder to greater accomplishments. The Danes are no exception. They have a fine feeling for the content of learning and for the humanities, but they are no fools when it comes to examinations. They love them—or (shall we say?) they love the certificates. Long after their formal day schooling has been completed, Danes seek professional certificates in this and that through the many opportunities available to them in further education. Their seriousness in this respect is exemplified in one fact. An apprentice between the ages of 16 and 18, undergoing a part-time course of evening instruction for a professional qualification, can actually bring a lawsuit against his teacher if he fails in his examination and can prove that his failure was due to the incompetence or incomplete teaching of his instructor.

In the light of this information, it is not surprising that until August 1959, the Danish system maintained selection by examination for the different kinds of secondary school careers. In 1937 a two-sided "middle school" (*mellemskole*) was established for children from the age of 11. One side prepared the pupils for further examinations leading to higher secondary education, and eventually to learned careers by way of college or university, while the other side was "examination-free." In most cases the two sides of the "middle school" were kept in close contact, sometimes sharing lessons. But the scheme was never completely successful. The more recent reforms were actuated by this experience, and also by some controlled experiments where moves towards unification of the school provision were observed.

A law introduced in 1958, which became effective a year later, had two main objectives: to equalize opportunity for rural children, and to unify the schooling offered those between the ages of 11 and 14, when compulsory education ends. Let us consider the latter aspect first. The gradual and permissive move towards the comprehensive principle of schooling reveals Denmark (among the Scandinavian countries) as "the most conservative in its approach to the reorganization of the structure of the school system."[2] In other words, instead of following

---

[2] Willis Dixon: *Society, Schools and Progress in Scandinavia* (1965, Pergamon), p. 86.

its Scandinavian neighbors in insisting on a "unity school" until the end of compulsory schooling—followed by differentiation afterward—Denmark preferred to achieve social solidarity, and as wide a recruitment as possible. This was done by allowing local authorities their choice between an undivided school and a "mildly divided" one for children until the age of 14.

It should not be supposed that the new dispensation merely perpetuated the old. The inadequacy of the old bifurcated "middle school" was recognized, particularly as rural children or those who most needed schooling were generally the sufferers from such a division, and talent was not effectively recruited. Hence the 1958 insistence on no more than a "mild division" into two "lines." Where this takes place, Line A leads to an expected minimum school-leaving age of 14 or, better still, to a continuation of schooling through voluntary classes 8, 9, or 10. These classes, held in the common or "main school" (*Folkeskole* or *Hovedskole*), include practical instruction in home economics, or prevocational activity of the kind that Americans call "industrial arts." The whole purpose is to provide a general, socially valuable schooling of no more than prevocational character; and pupils can transfer to the more academic line any time before or after the age of 14 if they qualify. Moreover, some local authorities have not availed themselves of even this mild differentiation, but have gained Ministerial approval for starting with the "unity school" right away.

The pupils whose records of attainment have shown them fitted to hold their own in Line B of a divided school undertake additional mathematics, separate courses in foreign languages, and other more exacting items of the curriculum. Differentiation is on the basis of the children's and their parents' preferences, supported by school records and the recommendations of the teachers. Pupils following this enriched course are neither segregated nor predestined to fame. They can transfer out of their course as their neighbors can transfer into it; in any case much of the work is common.

All children can obtain a school-leaving certificate (without a formal examination) at the age of 14, indicating their achievement so far. They are all strongly encouraged, however, to stay on beyond that age. If the brighter pupils seek an opportunity better than that offered in the ordinary classes 8, 9, and 10 already referred to, they can proceed to a *Realskole* at the age of 14. To do so, they must be recommended by teachers on the basis of their school record, and papers may be set; there is no official examination. The *Realskole* has a 3-year course.

The word *Realskole* strictly means "modern school." It was the name given to a particular kind of academic secondary school long before the recent reforms (roughly following the curricular pattern of the German *Realschule* or the *Mittelschule*). But according to the new dispensation it has a different significance in two ways. In the first place, it comes after the completion of common school at 14, and it is more accessible to all pupils. In the second place, it must now be passed through on the way to the topmost academic *Gymnasie* (for the brightest pupils, aged from 16 to 19 or 20, on their way to the university).

Though the word *skole* suggests a separate school, the *Realskole* generally forms part of the ordinary public school premises. Alternatively, it forms part of the *Gymnasie* premises, but the curriculum is the same. In either case it is a section or department of a school, not a separate school. Many a good pupil, therefore, enters school at the age of 7, and stays on at the same school until he leaves the *Realskole* at the age of 17. At the end of that three-year course he takes a *Realeksamen* (modern certificate examination), the possession of which entitles him to apply for various executive or similar posts, or for admission to certain colleges (such as a teacher-training college). It does not admit him to the universities; even for a teachers' college additional tests may be required. The *Realeksamen* is thus the first official certificate examination.

Pupils who are admitted to a *Realskole* at the age of 14, however, can present themselves for a formal public examination at the age of 16, which does not confer a certificate, but decides whether pupils can be admitted to the *Gymnasie* for a further three-year course. Not every pupil seeking this transfer is obliged to take the test at 16. Many prefer to wait until 17 to make sure of the *Realeksamen* before going on to the much tougher ordeal of the *Gymnasie* and its final examination, the *Studentereksamen*. This, as the name implies, admits a student to the university, though perhaps not to all faculties if, as for medicine, a *numerus clausus* or limited admission is enforced. The standard of the *Studentereksamen* is extremely high. Nevertheless, in keeping with the continental tradition of general education, the pupils pursue a wide range of subjects and are required to be competent in a variety of fields. More will be said about this later. Just now it is more important to complete the outline of the schools' structure. The diagram of the system given on page 23 should make things clear.

Despite the continued existence of varied options (electives) below the age of 14, and the varied levels of attainment or different paces, there is little doubt that the "unity school" is the school of the future. Already everything possible is being done to make pupils between 11 and 14 feel they are members of the same school, the same community. It should be remembered that in Denmark teachers have a great say on committees responsible for the administration of their schools.

Local authorities are not strictly allowed to introduce a "unity school" without the teachers' consent—and in any case they would be ill-advised to do so. On the other hand, teachers nearly everywhere are conservative when it comes to changing a curriculum, even when they call themselves "progressive."

The new pattern of *Realskole* is now more widely provided throughout the countryside. Any school big enough can now set up such a department, if local resources allow. If not, various arrangements are made to enable country children to have *Realskole* opportunities either by commuting for the present and transferring later, or by boarding. The Danes are great believers in flexibility and local adjustments, for all their reliance on centrally based and centrally financed minimum standards; the same flexibility is expected to enable children to take advantage of opportunities which they may belatedly show themselves fit for.

Children showing the most academic promise and the greatest persistence will thus find themselves in a *Gymnasie* after they reach 16. At this level the work is comparable to a very good English "sixth form" (though on a much broader front) or to a good American liberal arts college. Pride in these standards has created resistance to the adoption of the comprehensive principle more than any other single factor.

On the other hand, the need for expansion is shown by the fact that only about 6 percent of the total age group were successful in the *Studentereksamen* in 1960, whereas the calculated need and official expectation was that 17 percent of the age group should pass by 1980. (A not dissimilar rate of progress has been achieved in Sweden.) While teachers cast doubt on the feasibility of this plan, sociologists and psychologists have pointed out that about 80 percent of the Danes belonged to the "working class," whereas only about 20 percent—or less —of the *Gymnasie* population belonged to that category. This could mean that the working class consisted of very dull people, or that their bright children were not recruited properly. Swedish experience over 20 years of expanding secondary school opportunity has vindicated the latter view, while comprehensive schooling has been simultaneously expanded by law. Danish development has been more cautious and more sensitive to local susceptibilities.

In considering all this we must bear in mind that at the end of any briefer schooling in Denmark there is a wide range of voluntary supplements—evening classes, vocational courses or schools, and the famous folk high schools which we shall discuss later. The existence of these supplements (as in England) has unintentionally hampered radical reforms, if only because there are so many "backstairs ways" to success for the really persistent. Today, however, social conscience is less apt to leave things to chance, or to the backdoor approach. Isolation or lack of privilege may sap the hardiest initiative, and rule out even the first opportunity to compete.

Vocational certificates have economic importance in Denmark, as elsewhere; but in this country of widespread equality they have a marked social significance, too. Social etiquette (even more so than in Germany) requires full recognition not only of doctorates and higher degrees but also of diplomas, certificates, and the like. They may actually be included in a person's title when you write to him or address him (or his wife), or when you introduce him. I once wrote a "thank you" letter to a Danish pig farmer, only to discover later that the title I had correctly used on his address simply meant that he cultivated a particular size of holding.

School examinations are not used for this purpose, although some of the general pattern of academic appreciation attaches to them. Recognition of this sort does not make the Danes treat each other with snobbery, however; the impression one gets is of difference rather than inequality. The most democratic citizens value their examination certificates, and often seek opportunities to acquire qualifications of different types suited to their occupation. Indeed, the new Act requires that all schools shall provide vocational guidance from the seventh year upwards. It is realized that part of the educator's task is to acquaint pupils with the working world and its opportunities before leaving school. The Danes are reluctant to let any child miss a chance to make the most of himself. Hence, country children can travel into the towns by publicly provided bus or, in a few cases, board at some special school.

The purpose of the 1958 innovations was to minimize the risk of early segregation and to facilitate transfer from one course of study to another wherever appropriate. Also, to mitigate the accidental influence of environment, or attendance at a particular school, on the formal decision which used to depend largely on "once-and-for-all" criteria. The Danes are very careful to remove all possible barriers and handicaps to progress. In particular, they try to minimize the disadvantages of isolation on an island or remote homestead. Even before the new Act was introduced, village children living far from what was then called a "middle school with an examinations curriculum" could continue their studies in an extension of the elementary school, and could be transferred to more urban opportunities later. Similar facilities exist now in the more remote areas.

Another interest of the 1958 legislation was to encourage technical and technological expertise. At the level of classes 8–10 in the *Hoved-*

skole (main public school), some preparatory orientation towards modern employment and today's society has been incorporated in the instruction. As I have already mentioned, this is prevocational (or, as the Russians might say, "polytechnical") rather than directly vocational. The whole intention is to provide opportunity, not to cause premature stratification. Later, vocational courses of a businesslike kind are increasingly available. It can never be forgotten that for several generations Danish distinction in agriculture, marine engineering, and even domestic science and art, has been largely fostered by residential or short-term opportunities of this sort. The ordinary evening school and the nonresidential type of part-time education called "people's university" (or "folk high school") have probably catered to many more persons and needs than were ever accommodated in the much better known residential "folk high schools."

If Denmark had given nothing else to the world, it would still be famous for its development of the residential folk high school. So much has been written about this that the briefest mention will suffice. From an extremely humble beginning in the 1840s, the folk high schools expanded rapidly to provide farmers' sons with a general education in Danish literature, history, sociology, religion, and music. The courses were offered then, as now, during the long winter months when the land is difficult or impossible to work. But some folk high schools offer a supplementary course of three months during the summer, and some which offer the winter course only to men make the summer one available to women. The Danish word for "folk high school" means far more than the corresponding term in English. It carries the suggestion also of a *national* school and a *university*.

Especially as developed by Grundtvig and his admirers, folk high schools are strongly religious in atmosphere, though seldom so in formal worship nowadays. Their aim has always been to guide the moral and spiritual development of both the individual and the community, especially on the land. Yet the main emphasis in instruction in the schools is on formal lectures (here again, the influence of "the Word") followed by plenty of discussion. Continuous programs are personally tailored to suit the students' particular requirements and abilities. The principal or a tutor acts as personal guide in the preparation and elaboration of work schemes. Individual reading and inquiry are strongly encouraged.

Living conditions at a folk high school are so harsh as to be almost forbidding. Rooms and food are extremely plain. Students are expected to do manual work for the community for at least an hour a day. Traditionally, folk high school students are from the laboring class, and the continuance of rustic near-rudeness in external treatment is a salutary experience for many who nowadays are more prosperous. The surprising thing is that in a folk high school you may find a banker's daughter and a ploughman on equal terms. The banker sends his daughter because he went to the same school and appreciates it. The system works. The students soon involve you in singing or whirl you into a merry folk dance. The intellectual fare is good, the society is good, and the opportunity for a kind of spiritual retreat from the daily preoccupations of a career is excellent.

Something like one third of all Danish country and small-town dwellers passed through a folk high school in the years just before World War II, when student enrollment was highest though the actual number of schools was less than in the early days of the century. Now the enrollments are fewer and the folk high schools' influence is on the decline. That is to say, their direct influence is on the decline. As a source of democracy, self-help, and civic dignity they have indirectly led to the founding of cooperative organizations, of social service schemes, and of many other practical schools of citizenship more in keeping with the modern temper than the semievangelical message of the folk high schools themselves. Also, the direct influence of the schools may fade as the causes they fought for are recognized as having triumphed. Lastly, the appeal of the folk high school was primarily to a rural population, and Denmark is developing urban assumptions even faster than urban concentrations of population.

Those who know say that since World War II folk high schools are only shadows of their former selves. There can be no doubt, however, that these schools have contributed more to the Danish sense of democracy than any other. Sometimes the actual work accomplished in a folk high schoool has set students on the path to another profession. More often the experience of greatest significance is that of taking stock of one's life. The average age of attendance is about 23, but occasionally students are considerably older, and some of the younger ones have had the advantage of a sound academic grounding. Never does the lack of money bar any serious candidate from acceptance. For tuition, residence, and food, students are charged as little as $50.00 a month. Even this small sum may be reduced if a student earns a government grant, as the majority do. The schools themselves are private, a number being owned by their principals, but they may be helped directly or indirectly by public funds.

A number of folk high schools have a specifically vocational curriculum. A few concentrate on physical education, but a greater number cater to farmers. There is the same Grundtvigian emphasis on personal regeneration, yet the curriculum itself is mainly technical. It includes study of the Danish language and of arithmetic (because most of the students left dayschool about 14), but the main bill of fare is agricultural science from a theoretical angle. On an average, the young men have already had ten years of practical farming. The agricultural folk high school brings them up to date in farming science. Hence Danish agriculture is highly organized, with the latest strains of crops and livestock, scientific manuring, and expert marketing. But in every sense the student's stay at the school is an experience of life in a home. The principal is like a father or elder brother; his family life is identified with the school's. The Danes, with their obvious love of children, have a remarkable knack of receiving you *en famille*. This observation is perhaps even more conspicuously true of the ordinary folk high school than of the vocational type.

A few folk high schools also welcome foreigners. This is difficult, because the whole emphasis is on "Danishness," and before an overseas student can participate it is usually necessary for him to spend three months or more with a Danish family, mastering the intricate language and its difficult pronunciation. This usually means working as a farm hand. Yet the pull exercised by the folk high school is such that at Askov I have met middle-aged American women and students from the Far East. Askov, though still very Danish, is the largest folk high school. For this reason, and because of its historic associations, it is a well-known showpiece. One folk high school, however, is intentionally international. This one was established at Elsinore in 1921, in order to bring students of all origins together in mutual respect and understanding. Lectures and discussions are mainly in Danish and English, and sometimes in German. About 120 students at a time can be accommodated. Although this school is not really typical, it does give a taste of what the movement stands for, and both the founder-principal and the present principal are identified with the essence of the folk high school at its best.

On the whole, the folk high school movement has not affected the larger towns and cities directly, although a minority of students come from them. A few folk high schools, however, are associated with the Labor Party and other left-wing organizations, and are understandably more urban in their enrollment. It is interesting to visit such a college and see how, without essential loss of character, the almost religious atmosphere of personal conversion promotes a zest for political change. Grundtvig would have been aghast at some of the murals illustrating the march of the workers and at some of the blood-and-thunder songs. But he would have sympathized completely with the students' earnest self-examination. All the folk high schools impart a deep sense of personal and social commitment. No examinations are set;

no certificates are issued. What people get out of it all is something they understand very well, but is very personal.

The *mystique* or semievangelical enthusiasm associated with the Danish folk high school has inflamed its admirers in many lands— even where actual contact with Danes is almost nonexistent. In Britain and the United States, to say the least, attempts to foster the cult in its specially Danish form are usually incongruous. Although we all need more person-to-person communication, and more time and opportunity to think over the questions that occur to us in the sort of atmosphere achieved in the folk high schools in Denmark, our context is quite different. The Danish movement triumphed because it was topical, intimate, and a real answer to the needs of a particular people in special circumstances. Anything that merits the same description for any other people is bound to be different.

Indirectly, the folk high school movement may have prepared Danish farmers for the establishment of many cooperative organizations during the terrible depression years of the late nineteenth century. Danish agriculture, until then, had relied mainly on the export of grain on a family or individual basis. It was soon faced with the need for radical reorganization of buying, producing, and selling on a cooperative basis as the only alternative to starvation. Now, life in Denmark without cooperatives is almost unimaginable. The system, considered generally, combines the best of private initiative with social safeguards for those needing help through no fault of their own. Although the cooperative ramifications of Danish life are in no literal sense a school system, there is no denying that the educational emphasis of Denmark's life would be totally altered without them. To think of it is like imagining the United States without a credit system or England without committees and "team spirit."

To pass from the folk high schools (the name in Danish means nearly the same as "people's universities") and come to the universities proper is to make a great jump. The Scandinavian universities for centuries have maintained a high standard of scholarship, and far from altering that now, they seem to be making their courses tougher. After all his careful preparation in the *Gymnasie,* the student faces an arduous curriculum before attaining his first university degree. Admissions are severely restricted, yet even so a large number of admitted students fall by the wayside in their first or second years.

Partly for this reason, and partly because of the pressure of numbers, the *Studentereksamen* alone does not entitle its possessors to enter higher education, as it did traditionally. A higher grade in certain subjects is usually required. Furthermore, the course for a degree is divided into two cycles, the first of which may be completed in about three and a half years. After succeeding in this first part, the student may proceed with greater specialization towards the final degree, which is at least comparable with a master's degree in Britain and most doctorates in the United States. Even after cutting down the length of courses (to insist on more rapid progress and to eliminate weaklings), to obtain this first degree in Denmark requires a minimum of five and a half years from first admission as a very well qualified student at the age of 19 or 20. Far more often, the course takes seven years. Many students, for economic reasons, must work part-time. In recent years, as many as 60 percent have failed to complete the program. Nevertheless, a university degree is necessary for those who wish to teach in a *Gymnasie.*

Difficulties and wastage on this scale seem unthinkable to many outside observers, but the Danes point out that their small country cannot absorb all the skilled workers and scholars they already have available. Learned and skillful Danes are exported all over the world. One remedy might be to diversify the kinds of provision made. Originally there was only one university, in Copenhagen. More recently, another (with most interesting architecture) was founded in Århus. The Danish Institute of Technology in Copenhagen enjoys university status. It mainly recruits its students from those who have completed the mathematical-scientific side of the *Gymnasie,* but also accepts some who have attended a technical college after passing the *Realeksamen.*

Teachers' colleges, and institutes for pharmacy, agriculture, commerce, and the like, do not have university status. At this level, lower than genuine "higher education," there is a wide range of technical institutions that have been strengthened since 1960, when a Vocational Training Act was passed. Most of the provision in such colleges is for technicians, and a large part of it is based on a "sandwich" arrangement alternating theory with practical training. The technical colleges run for three years following the *Realskole.* The students who start after-school life as apprentices (a four-year stint) can proceed to three years in the *Realskole* and then go on to a technical college (*Technikum*). Not only is there a variety of provision, but bridges at all stages between the various sections and levels.

Nevertheless, despite the abundance of opportunities and their growing accessibility, the work is arduous and the ultimate objectives lofty. To obtain a doctorate in Norway, Sweden, or Denmark is a far more grueling ordeal than in Germany, or even in England. The American colleges requiring comparable excellence before conferring their highest awards could probably be counted on the fingers of one hand.

University lectures in Denmark may be freely attended by anyone, though no one lacking the requisite examination qualifications will be admitted to the university examinations. There is no tuition fee. The public can be present when a doctoral candidate defends his thesis. In essence there is no divorce between learning and living in Denmark. Though there are, of course, many things which progressive Danes would like to see altered (as happens in every country's stocktaking), Danish achievements can only be described as magnificent.

Our recognition of Danish success does not blind us, however, to some problems still unsolved or to newer reasons for disquiet. The crusading zest that was typical of the folk high schools during the past century, for example, seems to be fading in both Denmark and Sweden. Neither of these countries suffered greatly in World War II, in comparison with most European nations. Life is relatively easy, but the very absence of crying evils needing educational, social, or political remedies seems to have aggravated a kind of fatigue or malaise. Most of the ordinary exigencies of life are prepared for by an adequate educational and political system, and most of the accidental perils of life are taken care of by social insurance and the welfare state. These safeguards are specially necessary in the precarious economy of tiny European nations so easily tossed about in the storms of international economics.

Yet welfare states must be re-earned every day, as the Danes maintain their economy by daily cooperation. Partnership in industrial, professional, and political roles must be continuously reenacted with responsible understanding by every citizen. Many Scandinavians wonder if this is being done. Military conscription usurps the time and kills the enthusiasm once devoted to a period in the folk high school. Jobs—good jobs—are more easily won. People prefer to be at home rather than involved in community action; books, radio, and movies appeal to them separately. People want to "live their own lives." This could be healthy, but alcohol is an increasing problem and Denmark has an even higher divorce rate than the United States. In 1964, the Danish Doctors' Association declared that over 92 percent of Copenhagen's teenage brides were pregnant when they married, and that the hospitals treated some 15,000 abortion cases every year. (In all countries of the world, such figures are generally higher than the public realizes, but in Denmark the figure is especially high.) New problems clearly need new solutions, and the Danes are anxiously seeking them.

In some ways Denmark, like Athens of old, has itself been a school for many of its contemporaries. The attention it has rightly earned has certainly not been for its scholastic system in any narrow sense, though many of its excellent experiments challenge the professional observer. The Danish educational system is inseparable from the whole pattern of Danish living; it is identified with it.

This is a lesson we must learn when we look at any of our neighbors' ways of bringing up children. The absurd notion (presented in some American writing on Comparative Education) that one can compare the length of school life and the numbers of children involved, and thus reach a fair relative assessment of two educational systems, is manifestly based upon a complete misunderstanding of what education is. It ignores the fostering influence of individual families, the whole social matrix that develops the maturing personality, and the vast range of institutions or educational contacts that may be alternatives to the influences at work in our own culture. In Denmark, "Danishness" is not the monopoly of the public school system, or of the folk high school, or of any other sector of public or private activity. It permeates life; it is practiced in the cooperative societies and welfare organizations so conspicuous to the traveler, but taken for granted by the Danes as an inevitable part of their lives. The songs and flower-decked tables are as symbolic as the flags. A daily attestation of loyalty would be as embarrassing as it is unnecessary—in Denmark. For Danish schools—even in the gloomy years following 1814 or the hungry gap when Danish grain exports were swamped by the golden flow from the prairies—there has never really been any need to process Danes in the all-inclusive way of the public school in the United States. The schools of any country do as much or as little of the work of educating as its inhabitants find necessary or useful. There is a good object lesson on that in Denmark.

Of course, times change. The increasing complication and costliness of all educational completeness tends to take responsibility for it away from the homes, farms, and voluntary endeavors of those who have contributed to it for so long. Less and less education is fulfilled in the village or homestead; but by the same token less and less is completely possible in the little red schoolhouse or the little school district. Furthermore, though the Danes so far do not experience quite the same teacher shortage as many other countries, and though they have managed to retain more respect for teachers and for learning than do most of us, the general *embourgeoisement* or middle-class-making of our modern world affects prospects in Denmark too. There are also mobility, communications, and different occupational patterns to consider. These preoccupy the Danes as they do us. But in Denmark's cautious changes empirical solutions are sought in a quieter corner than we can ever enjoy. The complications can be unraveled more slowly.

Certainly, no solution can be imported as though it were a ready-made machine—not even from neighboring Norway and Sweden, where strong Scandinavian affinity is felt. Within all its diversity and occasional unevenness, the Danish system clearly enshrines democracy and educational commitment of a genuineness that few others can match.

It is no help to any serious parent or student if a book or adviser uses clichés such as "a one-track system" to recommend the American school provision because that is supposed to be more "democratic" than any system which is not "one-track." It is no help to use words that do not mean anything, and it is downright misleading to ignore the facts. Danish schools are certainly not one-track systems of education. Even after recent reforms they retain differences and perhaps make them. They may even still be said to risk causing inequality. But whatever we think about this, the results are far less painful when society at large is full of lessons in equality and democracy.

Do we agree that in order to be democratic (and we have not settled what that means!) we want all children to have exactly the same type of schooling? If we do, then we must abolish elective subjects. We must enforce attendance in exactly the same classes of all children, boys and girls, slow and quick, "bookish" and "practical," of all income groups and of all professional futures, in every single school in the country. We must rule out local and parental preferences. We must prevent persons or communities from providing anything better than what is offered to the least privileged members of our society. We must certainly eliminate favored school districts, and their autonomy.

No one in a Western democratic society really wants this state of affairs. In other words, no one, simply because he is a democrat, truly wants a genuine "one-track" system. A democrat, or indeed any farsighted citizen of any free community, wants to provide children with the best opportunities for self-development, social adjustment, and community service. None of these can be provided by turning mass-produced articles out of the same mold. We all want to see individual qualities encouraged—even by different methods of schooling. One of the most important problems in social philosophy reveals itself in our schools: how to provide true equality while recognizing complementary differences. We recognize these between men and women, while admitting an essential equality. Though we long for equality we want our community to be enriched socially and professionally by different contributions. At the same time we seek to encourage sympathy and harmony, not just in the public school system but in all the formative contacts of public life.

Teachers and parents must therefore be on their guard against misleading appeals on behalf of the "one-track" or any other system on the automatic assumption that "we know best." We might ask ourselves if our own particular system is what it is alleged to be—either "one track" or "fair shares" or "democratic" or anything else. When we put any system to the test we see that it is riddled with inequalities, inconsistencies, and educational superstitions. We also see that, if it works pretty well on the whole, its success depends not just on what is done formally by parents and teachers but on the whole complementary pattern of public life. In other words, for an educational system to be sound it is necessary to have home and school and work and public life helping one another in a realistic way. To be "real," the system must be true to its context; its idiom must suit the circumstances.

That is why it is wrong to expect other parents and teachers to see eye to eye with us, even though we are all asking the same fundamental questions about bringing up children. We live in different worlds of activity; we have different problems and opportunities; our value systems are as different as our idioms of language and dress and food.

From what do these differences arise? From history, geography, state of economic or social development? Do they arise from the language we speak, the religion or philosophy we profess? Are they closely linked with our patterns of schooling, or does the form of school structure and relationships not seem to matter as much as we thought? Can different ways of learning and teaching achieve similar objects? Can similar ways of learning and teaching produce different results in different external circumstances? These are the sort of questions we inevitably ask ourselves in any comparative study. When we see a whole educational or cultural system working as a microcosm (with the school system as its core), we have a living laboratory before our eyes—a *living* laboratory that shows up the tricky interplay of ecological factors and of topicality as no sterile theory could.

Although there is so much self-sufficient "adding up to sense" in any country's way of life, it still remains a local and temporary idiom. If it were an exclusively *foreign* expression, however, there could be no communication between our neighbors and ourselves. There could be no general analysis, no comparison. It is the possibility of comparison that makes us try to pick out the essential from the peripheral, the merely foreign aspects from the broadly human. Our analysis is reaching out for an understanding of what is widely relevant.

Just as communication and clothing and nutrition are everywhere essential human needs, and just as we can better appreciate the main theme by studying its variations, so can we greatly profit our own families by looking at what happens to other people's children. Some small things we may copy outright for our own program. More often we may find our idioms challenged and needing greater clarification. We may need to rephrase our most pious proclamations, having learned to see the truth of our situation as never before. At least we may acknowledge that there is more than one way of doing something effectively.

Even if we think that our review of other people's educational practices and notions has done no more than show up our own family portrait in a sort of distorting mirror, or echoed our pedagogic principles in some monstrous "double talk," we shall have begun to see ourselves as others see us. That is sometimes amusing. It is sometimes the beginning of wisdom.

For many readers of this book it will be sufficiently instructive to do no more than read of other people's educational preferences or experiments. Those who wish to pursue the study further should begin by asking themselves a few basic questions as they read on. They may ask the seemingly obvious (for example: what is education, and who is educated, and to what end?) in circumstances where the answer does not seem obvious after all. They may go on to wonder if their own or their neighbors' practices have anything more to justify them than longstanding habit. A further stage might be the more professional type of enquiry (for example: how the secondary schools lead on from the primary stage; how selection or differentiation takes place if there are alternative kinds of schooling or elective subjects; how teacher and administrator allocate their responsibilities). Some questions are philosophical, or sociological. But instead of being abstract, they look real; flesh-and-blood answers are forthcoming when the problems are seen in context.

Of course, for the really serious student of comparative education it will be necessary to proceed with deeper enquiries afterwards. Some indication of these was given in the Introduction. A more intensive analysis will be outlined in the last chapter. But at this stage the best plan is to think through our neighbors' problems *with them,* recognizing intimately their relevance to ourselves. That is not only the basis of any research (no matter how "scientific") in any of the social sciences; it is also the very essence of any humane awareness. In a comparative study of education, that most characteristic and universal of human attributes, we are cultivating the sciences and the humanities at the same time.

We are also embarked upon the very business that may make more sense of our own children's education, if only because their world is a wider and more purposeful world than most of us grew up in.

3

FRANCE THE CENTRAL LIGHT OF REASON

La belle France! There we have it; some countries are territories, some are nations, but France is a person—fair and feminine, inconstant and sometimes tempestuous, yet essentially true to character in all her moods. A French proverb puts it well: "The more we change, the more we stay the same."

Frenchmen of all factions think of their land as their love, their inspiration, and their joy. They are more radically divided than most other nations in politics, religion, and sympathies, but they are fanatically loyal to the France of their dreams. Before foreigners they close their ranks, and their quarrels are nearly all among themselves. Strangely enough, French discrepancies are all truly French in essence and expression. It would be hard to find any other country where national characteristics are so indelibly stamped on nationals' behavior. That was true centuries ago. History shows the essential France of to-day evolving recognizably through the past two thousand years or more, despite all the stormy changes that have taken place. What is more, this evolution has produced not only modern France; it has given the free world a wealth of inspiring ideals.

In Britain and some other nations men have worked out empirical solutions to local problems, and their practice and institutions have sometimes been a great example to the world. But it is from France that we have received the great declarations of human rights in their most universal and radical form. Our liberal society and our enlightenment draw their inspiration from the almost intoxicating "universal principles" which French *philosophes* and their international friends distilled from contemporary Europe (especially Britain) and from the ancient world of Greece and Rome. The United States is probably more indebted to France for its democratic daydreams than to any other nation or culture. The American Declaration of Independence and the Bill of Rights echo the very phrases (let alone the ideas) of the *philosophes*. The French Revolution's declaration of human rights owed much to the part played in its drafting by Benjamin Franklin and Thomas Paine; but those notions of natural law, natural rights, and self-evident truths were molded in their revolutionary form by French political theorists. "Freedom, equality, and brotherhood" has been a clarion call round the world for two centuries, and the note was first sounded in France.

How does it come about then that British and American achievements in democracy, industrialization, and learning are now so different from those of France? France is less than thirty miles from England; their capital cities are now less than an hour apart by air. Yet the daily idioms of the two countries could hardly be more different. Probably only the United States is more different from France than is Britain. If we had not been trained to notice the overwhelming influence of institutions and social background on our educational and political programs, we would have expected close similarity. Jefferson, for example, was much attracted to some of the French ideas on education. But both the United Kingdom and the United States have experienced the stimulation of French radical ideas without becoming French. Why? Because the familiar institutions and practices of both Anglo-Saxon countries are fundamentally different. It is these, rather than the rational ideas, that have so profoundly shaped their national character and aspirations.

It is of cardinal importance in any educational study to appreciate the force of institutions as teachers or habituators. People go to church, sit on juries, or are themselves apprehended by the police. Each of these experiences at first hand enunciates certain social principles of behavior, recommends them as "normal," and sets particular practices

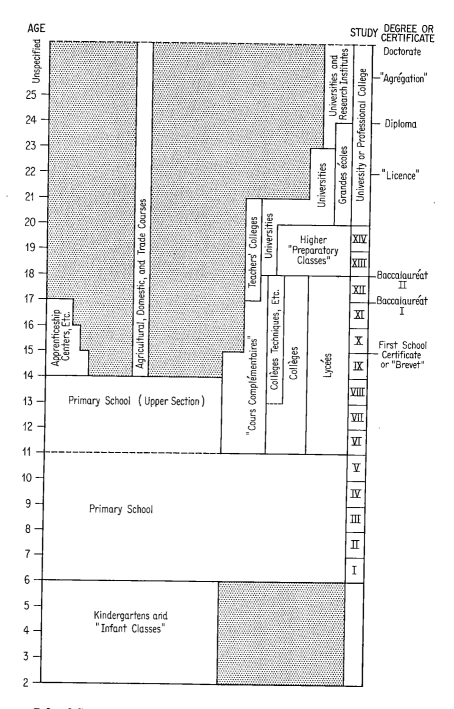

School System in France: Before Implementation of 1959 Reforms

46

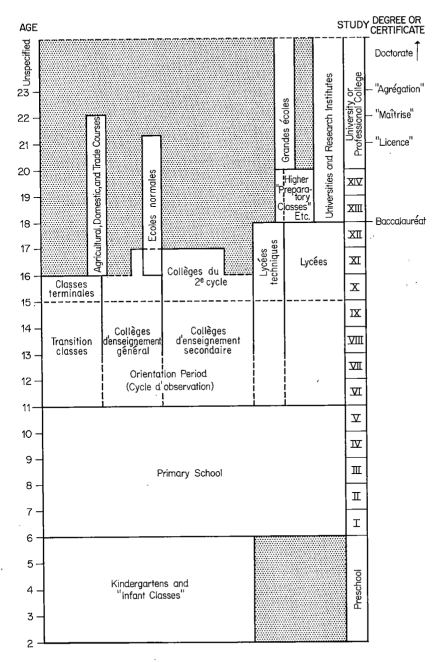

School System in France: In Transition 1959–1972

47

or aspirations into some sort of order. When we speak of institutions, too, we need not always think of something very grand. An alarm clock and a timetable may differentiate the country from the town, the East from the West. One by one, perhaps, institutions may not seem so potent; but, taken all together and added up in a kind of cultural persuasion, they are like the phrases of a language, or the rhythms of a constant social intercourse, which we automatically internalize as "values" throughout all our perceptions.

Thus the comparative study of education can never divest itself of the study of institutions—of *social* institutions—before any scholastic building, pattern, or pronouncement is taken under scrutiny. Every individual is part of some social group innumerable times over: of his family and home, of his playfellows and workmates, of his neighborhood and occupational routines, and so on endlessly. Thus identification of self is very often the result of experiencing "others" in circumstances which show them to be different or complementary. The institutions therefore that surround us all the time are, as it were, a matrix of our personality. Institutions that lie further afield (such as church or school) still identify us with groups; and the groups themselves are grouped into patterns. These add up to cultures, reinforced even more penetratingly by roles and rituals than by any formal pronouncements, because there is nothing so obvious to contradict.

These generalities may seem obvious, and would not be stressed here if France did not provide so telling a lesson of apparent identification with ourselves in rational, international principles—contrasting with such a distinctive idiom in actual practices and institutions. What is more, France is not somehow diminished by this human attribute; she is enriched and made more personal. The great fluctuations of aim and achievement to be described in this chapter are as human as the French language, just as logical and illogical, just as full of reason and of passion. In our own idioms, we too are in a similar plight. All this involvement schools us before we see any school, argues with the school during our school days, and sets limits to the "meaning" of school afterward. In the country dedicated to reason *par excellence* we need to be doubly reminded of the lower-than-rational.

What of France itself? France is a country of ideas, over which men fight as elsewhere they compete for money. This is especially true of her school system, but it is also true of her political structure and public life. What divides France is not differences of race or climate, occupation or class (though these are considerable); the sources of disagreement are nearly all of intellectual origin. In other respects, France is remarkably united—from the vineyards above the Rhone to the rocky fisheries of Brittany, and from the dairies of Normandy to the parched coast of the Mediterranean. Thriftily and industriously, the Frenchman and his family enjoy their vivacious lives in characteristic fashion, remaining essentially Gallic no matter where they live or what their livelihood. French life is a rich and public thing, and the French pursue it with passionate individuality. In France more than in most countries, the schools themselves play a great part in fomenting both unity and disunity. This is especially strange, because French schools are devoted to reason beyond all else. This paradox is itself a direct outcome of French religion, French politics, and French philosophical contributions to the world. Let us see how it works out.

As in every other country, the public school system forms part—and only part—of the formal apparatus of state. This apparatus is intended to formalize, safeguard, and control some of the more central activities of society at large. The French school system in particular reflects what society has generally believed to be "more central," leaving much of the periphery to private enterprise and uncertainty, to variety and enjoyment, to culture and values. In the old days the stress in school was exclusively on rationality, on a modicum of sound knowledge (according to one's station), and on a preparation for the competitive contests of public life. For various reasons the French system of schooling has been typical of continental systems generally, and has helped to form many of them directly or indirectly. Thus, many basic descriptions and explanations appropriate to France apply to others in large measure.

It was characteristic of nearly all school systems before recent reforms to provide only a few people with better opportunities, and these mainly in "secondary education;" most people had to be content with elementary school. Elementary school did not mean that which preceded secondary school and ran right on into it, but parallel schooling on an inferior plane. Those in elementary schools were likely to stay until the end of their pupilship on a lower level than the "secondary" people above. They were also likely to leave school much earlier—sometimes before 14, the official leaving age in France until 1972. If a bridge were available for crossing from elementary to secondary education, it was by selective examination, sometimes of a rigorous kind. Upper-class pupils might begin their school days (as still happens in most countries, perhaps) in a fee-charging preparatory department serving the secondary school and more or less guaranteeing access to it. In some countries (France included) a few public secondary schools once had attached fee-paying departments.

The representative school system during the transitional stage of the immediate postwar period could thus usually be represented either as two upright columns (one much shorter than the other), linked by a precarious bridge, or by a diagram showing most children in the strong trunk of a primary school topped by a short limb of upper primary school for the majority and a slender, long branch of secondary school for those most favored socially or academically. It will help us to understand recent changes in France if such a rough and ready diagram is borne in mind as the school pattern into which the reforms of recent years have brought alterations.

Every child's first day at school is an impressive occasion, but if a French 6-year-old could stop to think about it he would find his first contact with school overwhelming. At eight o'clock on September 16 every primary school child in northern and eastern France, duly enrolled by the mayor of his town, begins the morning shift of three hours. (In the south and west of France, school opens 10 days later.) In the afternoon there is another three-hour shift beginning at one o'clock. The term lasts until the evening of December 23. The five-day school week is arranged so as to leave Thursdays (not Saturdays) and Sundays free, so that parents who so desire may have their children instructed in religious matters. All publicly-provided schools are secular. Holidays are fixed by the Order of February 11, 1939, and subsequent modifications. The choice of subjects and the distribution of lessons are equally fixed by Article 19 of the Order of January 18, 1887, the Order of 1939 just referred to, and several others—all of which secure uniformity throughout the country.

Boys and girls are usually separated (except in experimental schools), but the programs are almost identical. Only minute variations are allowed, and special permission must be secured for these. Everything is ordered. The teachers are all civil servants, selected on the basis of state qualifications that are the same for the whole of France. They are paid by the state according to a national scale, centrally directed and supervised, and charged with the execution of the educational laws. Though it is not quite true that every child in a given class is taught the same thing at the same time, any one examining the minutely regulated school programs might very well think so.

A growing number of nursery schools and classes (attended by more than half the children of France) are progressive and humane, but the compulsory primary schools for children over 6 are places for hard work. As the Circular of July 27, 1882, puts it: "The primary school's ideal is not to teach a great deal, but to teach it well. Children leave schools with a limited knowledge, but what they have been taught they know thoroughly; their learning is restricted, but not superficial. They do not possess half-knowledge . . . for what makes any education complete . . . is not the amount of information imparted, but the manner in which it is imparted." This order seems to most foreign observers to err only on the side of understatement, for French children's "limited knowledge" would seem considerable to most British teachers and to all Americans. It is duly examined and recorded on a formal certificate at the completion of school.

Yet French educators, for all their insistence on knowledge, are not primarily interested in factual learning; they insist that "the intellectual faculties shall be developed," and that children's minds shall be "trained, enriched, and broadened." This is what the law for elementary schools prescribes. The higher schools do the job much more thoroughly. The quick, alert eye of the French man or woman (or even the French child) pays testimony to the unsparing exercises of the French school.

French meals are a delight to any connoisseur of food; but to the Frenchman they are leisurely occasions (nearly always lasting one hour, and very often two) where sparkling conversation is no less important than savory dishes and good wine. A visit to a village shop or café is often an intellectual exercise, an enjoyable one if your French is equal to it. You must also know what you are talking about, for the French do not tolerate fools gladly. Almost everyone you meet in such circumstances left school at the age of 14, when compulsory attendance ended (until the 1959 decrees provided for the gradual extension of compulsory attendance until 16 during the next decade or soon after). Exact figures are hard to come by, as there is so much uncertainty about what should be classified as "secondary" education. As late as 1962, however, despite much voluntary extension of school life, only some 20–25 percent received secondary education. Now the great majority receive some form of secondary schooling, although French wits have been well sharpened without it for a long time.

But is this what education is for? The average Frenchman is inclined to say yes. School is for intellectual matters. Parents support the school's aims with real conviction, and watch over their children's progress accordingly. They do not do so through American-style parents' associations (which, though encouraged, are negligible except in a few areas), but through insistence on hard work at school and in homework. In 1957 an order was issued that made homework illegal for children under 11; but it will be some time before it can be effectively enforced. Until 1957 admission to secondary education in a *lycée* or *collège* (academic high school) was only through examination; homework was assigned to prepare children to take the examination about the age of 11. Between 1957 and 1959 children were selected for academic secondary education mainly on their previous teachers' recommendations. Only those who were "uncertain" were required to take a written examination. (The children whose primary education had been in private—usually Catholic—schools were all officially "uncertain.")

Since September 1959, a new law has reconstructed French secondary education, envisaging some changes to take place gradually until 1969 and entailing many others thereafter. It incorporates many ideas from the Langevin-Wallon and similar proposals of 1946–1947, which had stormy passage and have since caused much legislation (even of a noneducational kind) to founder. Governments have been overthrown in consequence. It therefore remains to be seen how fully and permanently some of the new proposals will be implemented. The first few years of the process certainly induce caution in the observer, particularly as this has been the characteristic reaction of Frenchmen themselves.

We have not yet reached the place for a detailed study of these unprecedented and important reforms, but we can glimpse them generically because they promise to transform the whole prospect and recruitment pattern of French education. The law of 1959 (often called the "Berthoin law" after the Minister in office) was in itself far-reaching and radical. Administrative interpretations and edicts have subsequently brought about changes on an even more sweeping scale, notably because administration since 1962 has been more closely coordinated than ever before.

In a centralized country, such innovations can theoretically be introduced by a stroke of the pen. It should be remembered, however, that more or less identical proposals were advanced soon after the first world war, revived in the Langevin-Wallon proposals, and have certainly been in the air ever since. They were rejected by most French experts and clerics on the grounds of "intellectual betrayal," "materialism," "atheistic communism," and the like—besides being suspected by many ambitious parents and, more notably, by teachers. But at the right time—a political crisis in which General de Gaulle's "tough line" was thought to be indispensable—the "atheist" and "anti-intellectual" innovations were enforced by that devout, conservative Catholic who was determined to save and enlarge France's intellectual attainment through a modernized system.

The official educational newspapers, and a great many teachers, have maintained a steadily enthusiastic welcome for the post-1959 reforms, especially now that they seem feasible and have been supported by so much follow-through action both in the Ministry of Education itself and in other official quarters connected with national planning. At the same time, when going round the schools (particularly those outside "progressive" centers) an observer is struck by the persistence of previous assumptions and practices. Cartoons, even in official newspapers, reflect characteristic attitudes in favor of academic selectivity and competition. Such caution is not surprising in view of the recency of reform.

The most important features of the new legislation were the proposed raising of the minimum school-leaving age to 16 by 1967 (but later fixed for 1972), and the institution of a period of "observation" or orientation beginning at the age of 11. At first, official pronouncements gave the impression that all children would benefit by this "observation cycle"; but later it became clear that some children would not experience it for several years to come, if at all. Obviously, in rural districts with small and scattered schools and a meager supply of teachers, a reform so manifestly requiring a consolidated or combined type of provision might have to wait. Moreover, although an observation cycle was (and is) conceived to be ideally universal, its first cautious provision was limited to those most likely to benefit. Thus, much reliance was placed on a combination of parental demand, teachers' recommendations, and local opportunity to decide which children could benefit. By 1962–1963, half the children in France were already passing through an observation cycle. It also became clear that by about 1970 at least 75 percent of all children would demand and be available for the observation cycle. The development of new types of school and the supply of suitably trained teachers facilitate the provision of this remarkable opportunity. Children are sorted out with less differentiation (or with less finality) than ever before in the history of French schools. Examinations at the age of 11 have disappeared, except for "marginal" children whose parents dispute the school record.

Administrative decisions and public acceptance do not produce schools automatically or convert teachers to a state of readiness. Old buildings had to be used. The old-established and often venerable institutions housed in some of these buildings retained the direction and impetus which had maintained them for generations, and parents fortunate enough to secure their children's admission to privileged instruction and prospects were unlikely to throw away their chances. Apart from all these considerations, a given way of life is not easily subverted. Therefore differences in child population, in teachers' competence, in teacher-child ratio, and in subject-complexion were bound to continue for a while—given the best will in the world. Many otherwise well-informed people could not see that *entrée en sixième* (admission to the first "real secondary" year) was really intended for all or even the majority of children.

Consequently, although the first term's work for all children after the age of 11 is officially the same (insofar as it can be in such different circumstances), radical and prognostic differences begin in January of that school year. Notable among these differences is the beginning of Latin by the brighter children. Nonetheless, a sincere attempt is made to minimize such differences from this point on. Some special combined "secondary schools"—*collèges d'enseignement secondaire*—have been established either as new institutions or as modifications of older schools. They group together some 600 children, including a *lycée* section. By the end of 1965, some 400 CES had been set up, with an enrollment of 193,000 pupils; the number has since rapidly increased. The CES, representing a kind of multilateral or comprehensive school for the period of at least 11 to 15 years, is a significant example of that growing European development: the combined "middle school" for lower secondary education. This is usually followed by differentiated opportunities in upper secondary education.

The establishment of a CES is not everywhere practicable, and it is doubtful whether such a plan could prosper in the presence of a well-established *lycée*—at any rate without prospect of academic segregation. The more usual practice is to retain existing institutions, and to establish the *cycle d'observation* right across the base line of those still distinct scholastic enterprises which remain separate units even when under one roof.

Consequently, a *cycle d'observation* may be experienced in a *lycée,* in a CES, or in a *collège d'enseignement général.* (The latter is the newer name of the old supplementary courses or *cours complémentaires,* and means "general education school"). In anything other than a *lycée,* the instructors assigned to the observation cycle are almost certain to be primary school teachers, with qualifications and scholastic experience much inferior to those possessed by *lycée* teachers. Nonetheless, this drawback is remedied as far as practicable by new regulations for the training and supply of teachers, which will to some extent even out attainment and distribution in due course. In 1966 there were 948,000 pupils in *collèges d'enseignement général.*

A clearer picture of these schools will be drawn later in this chapter. Without envisaging the broad outlines of the new structure, however, it is not easy to appreciate the significance of the recent changes, or the challenge they offer to education as nearly all Frenchmen think of it.

After the "common trunk" (as it is sometimes optimistically called) of the new-style observation cycle, there are four or five distinct branches after the age of 15. One of these is the "long general education" in a *lycée,* further ramifying into a range of elective courses or options, before proceeding to the *baccalauréat* examination about the age of 18. A second branch is that of "long technical education" until a similar age, leading either to the *baccalauréat* in some tech-nical or commercial subjects, or to qualifications of a more vocational kind. A third branch is "short general education" to the age of 16 or so; a fourth is "short technical education", which might begin an apprenticeship or lead to practical or technical training. For some chil-dren, at any rate, the last year may have to include some corrective work, or simply prepare them for life on the farm or in the kitchen.

Manifestly, these four or five upper-secondary branches do not sud-denly appear at the age of 15. Quite apart from the reality of the sepa-rate schools, and separate curricula served by separately qualified teachers, it is clear that a general sorting out of pupils takes place long before the age of 15. In fact, only the highly experimental and favor-ably placed *lycée* at Montgeron (one of six officially designated "pilot *lycées*") makes no distinction between the children during the *first* sec-ondary school year. Even there, as in most big schools, there may be four distinct categories of teacher with different work loads, different pay scales, different backgrounds, and different prospects.[1]

This early provisional outline of secondary school reorganization through one single act of parliament places before the observer a great tangle of interests and problems. Some of these are plainly educational; the majority are institutional and social. This the administrator recog-nizes; but from the child's point of view it is perhaps more important to recognize that years must pass before equality of access to life can be fully guaranteed. In this respect, France is representative of most European countries—indeed, of most countries. At least, the intense commitment to change and flexibility that we recognize in leading French educators is a creditable reflection of the revolutionary zeal and egalitarianism which once made France the admiration of radicals everywhere.

In our own day, France is not unique, for changes like those described above are becoming widespread. What is astonishing today is the conversion of so intellectually proud and so systematized a country in the direction of flexibility and comprehensiveness. None of these changes is intended to "soften up" the country. On the contrary, France's own self-criticism on the grounds of effeteness in 1940 and stagnation in the postwar period has eventually led to the determina-tion to use all resources well in modern as well as traditional ways.

Though we began this survey of reform at the break-off point be-tween primary and secondary education, there have been changes in

---

[1] These are the *agrégés* or top specialists in subjects; the *certifiés* with a secondary schoolteacher's certificate, also specialists; the craftsman-teacher for workshops; and the former primary schoolteacher (*ancien instituteur.*)

primary schooling itself. The previous outstanding move toward "democratization" was in 1937, when Jean Zay, the Minister of Education, ensured that all public primary schools would follow an identical curriculum and be free of charge. Before that time, the great *lycées* had run their own preparatory departments or "little classes," for which fees were charged. Children from these favored schools almost inevitably went on to the *lycée,* even in the days of selective entrance examinations. Such schools attracted the best teachers, who often preferred to teach there rather than in the less highly esteemed secondary or near-secondary schools. Even children in a primary school were thus almost guaranteed a good secondary school future, with fair prospects of still higher education and a successful career. At the time of writing, though the primary classes still associated with *lycées* are technically on the same footing as other primary classes, most of the children proceed to an observation cycle in the *lycée* of their choice. Sometimes, in prosperous suburbs, a situation can arise rather like that in certain "country club" suburbs of the United States or upper-class wards of Tokyo. This is a "straight through" prospect of social and educational privilege in publicly provided schools! Once more we see that the structure as outlined on paper is not the best clue to educational dynamics.

It would be unjust to some of France's privileged schools if we failed to acknowledge that many of them have been centers of experiment and innovation—social as well as instructional. This has redounded substantially and directly to the advantage of other publicly provided schools. The privileged schools have not basked in isolated advantage, but have been at the forefront of most of the reforms since 1946. In particular, they have been the disseminators of "new methods" imported from America or Britain and sometimes indigenously developed in France.

Blueprints for educational reform in postwar France have been part and parcel of long-term economic, social, and demographic study conducted by scholars and permanent officials. They have been embodied in a series of national plans, the first of which ran from 1946–1953 and the second from 1954–1957. Neither of these made strong reference to education as such. The third plan (1958–1961) and the fourth (1962–1965), however, were concerned respectively with problems of secondary and higher education. The fifth plan (1966–1970) again relates the educational provision to social reform and communications, and is concerned with making good some continuing omissions. It also invests heavily in research development. Planning alone would be of little constructive help; but in the detail with which Frenchmen pursue it, it is valuable as a study in feasibility. It has frequently also produced evidence which has had a cumulative effect on public opinion.

On the other hand, French theorists and planners in the past have often run ahead of possibilities, and realism based upon actual achievements so far suggests that the 1959 reforms are unlikely to meet the proposed datelines. This should not prevent us from giving them credit, or recognizing their achievements.

No doubt the ladder of opportunity will be strengthened and broadened, especially with the growth of the European Common Market and the rapid expansion of industry and commerce. These developments necessarily entail a cultivation of youthful talent from a wider social background than before, and call into question the "steeplechase" of academic elimination processes. They also demand a more careful fostering of technical and scientific skill, and the recognition of social and applied studies as distinct from purely intellectual knowledge and agility. So much is true of changes at the secondary and immediate postsecondary stages where we paused to size up the importance of France's recent reorientation. But changes in higher education are of equal or greater significance because this was the area of ultimate justification for so many educational decisions. Since Napoleon, France has seen herself as the land of *la carrière ouverte aux talents,* or "meritocracy," though the number of field marshals' batons available for competition has hitherto been closely restricted. Technological and social changes, combined with France's altered setting in the European community and the world at large, have necessitated reforms which no amount of intellectual persuasion has hitherto made acceptable.

Although her direction appears to have been altered in principle, France remains a land of people intimately aware of the aspirations and envies of the past. Despite the great opening up of new fields and careers, and the spreading scholastic net that is bringing in children whose parents never thought of a secondary education, it is usually only a "long secondary education" that leads to the university and the liberal professions. We must suppose therefore that, for a generation at least, this is what typical European opinion will prefer. Anxiety, and unofficial coaching of children below the age of "observation," are likely to prevail.

When we set aside our description of French schools for this important analysis, we left the 11-year-old French child at the point where a decision had to be made about his secondary school career. Note—the decision *is* made for him, *he* does not make it. If his parents dispute the school's recommendation, there is a test. Copies of such tests, relating to selection in 1966, are in my possession. They show the old rigor unabated. Popular parlance and official journals alike refer to only part of the after-11 provision as *sixième* or "sixth class"—the *first* year of real secondary education. (French secondary schools number

classes backward.) That is to say, it is currently used of the lowest
classes of *lycées* and the *CES* (the new secondary schools of comprehensive character). It is not normally used for the *collège d'enseignement général* (old "supplementary course" or *cours complémentaire*).
Therefore, even with an observation cycle in prospect, the child and
his parents are aware of critical decisions to be faced.

Once admitted to the orientation cycle (especially if it is in a *lycée*),
the French child does a great deal of homework. Much concern about
the effects of this on a child's physique, and even on his mental alert-
ness, has been expressed by doctors and parents since the war. So educational reformers have taken steps to reduce the amount of homework, especially for the lower classes of secondary schools. Homework
often lasted until very late in the evening, and in the crowded circumstances of many French homes the mere mechanics of its preparation
was a real problem. It has become usual in many cases now to do the
devoir at school, after the end of formal lessons. Parents still take a
keen interest. The direction of that interest is illustrated by the
following anecdote.

An American mother who went to live in Paris was very proud of
her two robust sons. A French neighbor was helpful and friendly, but
one day she confided to the American mother that it was a pity her
two sons looked so much like peasants. After a term in French schools,
however, the American boys were so pale and tired from nightly homework that their mother was anxious. Just at this time the French-
woman congratulated her neighbor on the boys' development and
stated that they now looked more like scholars. One medical survey
after another shows that French children suffer from overwork at
school. Educators often agree, and so do parents when they are off their
guard. Every now and then you hear complaints of *bourrage* (stuffing),
and proposals to abolish the public examination system in its present
form. Yet very little is done. Why? Because French public life, including most of the better jobs, is arranged on the basis of selection examinations. You either qualify or you don't.

The examinations are the same everywhere—in Paris, in Brittany,
on the Riviera, and in distant tropical territories of the French Community. That is to say, the examinations are officially set and regulated under centralized control. But an already noticeable variation
in marking standards (between different types of school) seems likely
to be accentuated by the 1962–1963 changes. These make the *baccalauréat* more of an "internal" examination like the German *Abitur* or a
"partly internal" examination like the Italian *maturità*. The fact that
so many new kinds of secondary school are approaching full academic
respectability makes conscientious markers more considerate than

strictest equity would demand. This does not imply that there is soft-
ness or corruption; only that there is a little flexibility in special circumstances.

In recent years there has been some criticism, even though the examinations and standards are the same for all children, because the
candidates are in different states of readiness. Coming from a small
school in a backward province or in an overseas territory, or from a
socially handicapped home in the metropolis, a pupil is bound to be
at some disadvantage. In the rational pursuit of absolute equality, the
French have tended to overlook contextual irrationalities. Undoubtedly, dedication to equality has been preferable to privileged intro-
ductions or family advantage. On the whole, the examination system
has been a great equalizer, and the broad avenue to success for many
thousands. The recruitment basis for access to secondary and higher
education has almost certainly been wider in a social sense than elsewhere. Many other countries have hailed the French system of competitive examination (originally derived from the Chinese at the time
of the French Revolution) as both democratic and efficient. Once
fairly launched into the competition, the bright and diligent child can
reach the very top. Equality and excellence are both apparently served.

France herself benefits by a remarkable development of her brightest children's intellectual powers. The brilliant, once spotted, are given
every chance and encouragement. Of course, there is a tendency to regard a good instrument as perfect. Selective tests were originally intended to recruit boys with linguistic and mathematical abilities, and
lead them on in either the same fields or else toward philosophy and
other abstractions. How about the new categories of knowledge? Or
the need for personal attributes different from those of speed and
nimbleness? How is it that, although girls generally are more diligent
than boys, they do not do quite so well at the *baccalauréat*? Are the
wrong questions being asked? Or the wrong aspects emphasized? Or
is there something unintentionally exclusive about the examinations'
methods or concepts? Or is the problem still a social one? In any case,
can France's modernization and expansion pay the heavy price of so
much wastage of unrecruited or half-successful talent, or such one-
sidedness? The very instrument of equality and excellence is thus
questioned for failing to guarantee either in any full, modern sense.
This criticism still does not take into account the need for great numerical expansion, such as has already been taking place before the
school and examination apparatus is ready for it.

Before the 1959 reforms, official surveys conducted by Roger Gal
and others showed that, although no favor was shown to money or
family connections, an impressive majority of the children in academic

secondary classes were from "white collar" homes. A disproportion-
ately small number of *lycée* and especially university students came
from the working class or farming community that make up the majority of the population.[2] Once again, this raises questions of equal
access, equal starting conditions, and handicaps in the great academic
steeplechase. Although in more settled agricultural days it might have
been possible to predict with some assurance what kinds of quality
might be needed for recognizable forms of preferment and office, there
can be no such assurance in times of rapid technological and occupational change. We do not even know what kinds of knowledge young
brains will have to cope with in 10 or 20 years time—let alone what use
they must make of it, or in what circumstances of human interchange
such exercise must take place. Intellectualism is a French tradition.
Fairly competitive recruitment of "talents" is a Napoleonic legacy.
Equality is in a republican's bones. The drive for modernization is on.
The older school system no longer seemed to provide equal opportunity for all these things; hence the reforms.

Before we look into the question of equal opportunities in the strictest sense, we should ponder the outstanding feature of French education and government, namely, centralization. Paris is the hub round
which France rotates. Just as in the ancient world all roads led to
Rome, so in France today all roads lead to Paris, literally and figura-
tively. France has a unitary system of government. The 94 *départe-
ments* (like counties in some ways) have local administrations, and so
do the cities and townships. But each nucleus of French life is directly
manipulated by the central government, and subjected to meticulous
regulation. In education the same is even more specifically true. There
are major educational regions called *académies* (23 in 1966), each with
its university and its *recteur* who is in charge of all education from the
university down to the level at which the "prefect" of the *département*
takes over responsibility for elementary education. Even here the
prefect is responsible through the *recteur* to the Minister of Education
in Paris. The system can be likened to a wheel whose spokes are based
on Paris—each spoke at its outer end terminating in another little
wheel, again with a central hub and radiating spokes. So it goes on
down to the level of the individual school, the individual teacher, and
the individual child. If you look for a particular item in any part of
the system, you may find identical items in the corresponding position

---

[2] We saw the same thing in Denmark; it is a worldwide phenomenon, worse in some
places than others. For figures relevant to France, and for the whole question of "social
exclusion" or even self-exclusion from educational opportunity, see my *World Perspectives
in Education,* 1965 edition, Chapters 3 and 7, and especially pp. 127–128.

in the whole of France. Only technical education (a small proportion) shows any noticeable local variation, if we except Alsace and Lorraine, to whose German-speaking populations some concessions have been made since the war.

On the other hand, though structural identity prevails in a remarkably uniform way, there may be many hidden differences in quality. There is certainly a variation in degrees of initiative. It has long been felt that a progressive denudation of provincial resources—in manpower, investment, and opportunity—is a serious social disease. During recent years administrative decisions have been made to correct this cityward gravitation, some of which affect education. Among these have been an increase in the number of *académies* (and therefore universities) from 16 at the end of World War II to 23 at the present date.

Moreover, there has been progressive devolution of some responsibilities (for example, for providing the first year or so of university studies) to a lower level of *collèges universitaires* in several large cities. (These roughly correspond in function, but not in character, to the more academic junior college in the United States in so far as they provide one or two years of university work. They are certainly not "community colleges," however, or adult education centers in the American sense. Nor must they be marked down academically with the downgrading implicit in the California Master Plan, for instance.) A further significant development, for both technology and decentralization, has been the local growth since 1965 of *instituts universitaires de technologie,* or technical colleges at a quasi-university level. But it must never be forgotten that these are not spontaneous local growths; in every case they represent centralized devolution according to an official plan. Five were established in the academic year 1965–1966 (at Rouen, Nancy, Toulouse, and two near Paris) and nine in 1967; but they were already described as "pivotal" to the modernization and amplification of tertiary education (that is, after the *baccalauréat*), especially in view of huge expansion, with over 150,000 in the IUT alone.[3]

Preoccupation with long-term planning is characteristic of French centralization in all major aspects of public life. Centralization took place in the name of equality, at least in modern France. In the past, the centralizing tendency was already manifest in the Roman Empire before Christ, and in the Roman Catholic Church which has shaped so much of Christendom. France has many living legacies from both. French cardinals and French kings were extremely powerful before the Revolution (1789), and gathered political and ecclesiastical control

---

[3]*Education Nationale,* 11 November, 1965, and 15 September and 1 December, 1966.

tightly into their hands. Both Church and State were authoritarian. The gravest social and economic inequalities were prevalent in all aspects of life. Outlying provincial areas were neglected, despised, and exploited. But before the Revolution was anything more than a distant cloud, the *philosophes* of the eighteenth century had expanded British claims for individual independence into political manifestoes for the world. Among these were claims for education that should be available to all men. All men were equal in essence; they should be made so in opportunity. If this were done, mankind could be infinitely perfectible. Men could go from strength to strength through the pursuit of reason, strengthened by useful knowledge. The privilege of ruling, of acting as champions for the less luckily endowed, would be entrusted to those who showed themselves the fittest. Fitness should of course be judged by reason—for reason, not faith or tradition or family power, gave the key to human progress.

During and after the Revolution every attempt was made to bring these fine notions (though they reveal manifest pitfalls to us) into reality. Eventually, under Napoleon in 1808, French education took on the essentials of its present form. Napoleon was no democrat, no liberal humanitarian, but he was a man of the people who had had to struggle upward to eminence. As emperor, his main concern was to strengthen France as a military power by drawing out the finest qualities of leadership. He wanted officers in military and civil life. He therefore reorganized the university and secondary school system. Though he paid no attention to elementary education, being willing to leave that for the time being to what he called the "Ignorantine Friars" (namely, the teaching orders of the Church), he gave the State a monopoly of university and secondary school teaching, and also a monopoly of examinations. Recruitment for military or civil service, and professional eminence was to be by way of these examinations. All Frenchmen, whatever their social or geographic origin, were to be given an equal chance to serve France by uniform methods of selection and disciplined training in hard work. The first modern *lycées* were founded for this purpose. Their strict regime can be fairly compared to that of the old-time barracks.

Napoleon's egalitarian approach led to the development of plans for universal elementary education. A society was founded for this purpose in 1810. Despite the many political upheavals that have taken place since Napoleon's downfall (two kingships, one emperor, five separate republics, three near-dictatorships, and so on), the Napoleonic system is in full force today in the schools of the fifth republic. It is highly centralized; it is secular (that is, it allows religion no place in the public system of schools); it is uniform throughout France; it is compulsory in the sense that all children between the ages of 6 and 14 (16 after 1972) must go to public or private school; and both public primary and secondary education is free. The state still maintains a monopoly of approved examinations, which are centrally supervised. Even children who go to private schools (mainly Catholic) are compelled to prepare for public examinations which effectively determine the choice of curriculum and also indirectly affect the teaching methods.

In actual practice, however, even here we have already noted some tempering of uniformity. The examinations are the same, but the criteria are not always the same. The final decision about who passes and who does not rests with a local *jury* selected by the authorities of the *académie*. A loophole for human frailty can be discerned here. Sometimes it is utilized for humane purposes. For example, a *jury* will frequently permit itself a slight lowering of standards when deciding whether or not to pass *baccalauréat* candidates from *lycées* known to be of lower caliber. Frenchmen are aware of this problem and not infrequently stretch the law to cope with it. This adaptive device seems likely to be used more and more during the difficult period of equalizing secondary education that began in 1959.

The vital principle of *laïcité,* or secularism, in the public schools is one which once allowed no modifications whatsoever, and kept all religious schools (mainly Catholic) from receiving any tax help. In fact, government after government has been wrecked on this principle, not to speak of private careers. The very words *la question scolaire* ("the schools question") simply mean whether church-associated schools should benefit by tax aid. In the past, conservative and royalist governments tended to favor Catholic schools, extending them financial aid and other privileges. At the same time, they taunted their opponents by curbing secularism and cutting down the amount of science in the school curriculum. The most loathed of such governments was that under Pétain's administration during World War II, which went even further by abolishing teacher training colleges (*écoles normales*). In 1946, the principle of secularism was re-established. Though this seesaw of antagonism, common to many Catholic countries, explains much bitterness on both sides, there has been a growth of tolerance since the war, with coexistence and, indeed, growing financial cooperation.

For a long time, priests, rabbis, and ministers of other faiths had been permitted access to public boarding schools to give unpaid religious instruction to children whose parents specially asked for it. (Many *lycées* have a residential section to accommodate children whose homes are at a distance.) But a great innovation took place in 1951, partly in recognition of the State's need for the supplementary secondary school provision made by the Catholics. It now became possible for the religious schools to receive *indirect* subsidies. Every parent of a primary school child became entitled to 10 new francs each term (later raised to NF 13 or three dollars). This sum was turned over either to the public committees or to parents' associations for private schools, for general scholastic purposes. In the case of private schools, the sum was expressly intended to raise Catholic teachers' salaries, which are unsatisfactory. A total of 10 percent of the local educational budget might also be allotted to school needs designated by either public school parents (through public committees) or by private school parents (through parents' associations).

In a bill introduced in 1959 (as a result of the Lapie Commission), three new relationships between private schools and the State were envisaged. On request, such schools could be entirely adopted by the State; alternatively, certain teachers or activities could be entirely financed by the State; or thirdly, varying degrees of cooperation be- tween private schools and State authorities could be negotiated, with proportional aid in return. Under previous arrangements Catholic schools, and other nonpublic schools, could receive a maximum of 10 percent of their running costs in money or kind from the State, the *département,* or the local community. But the express permission of the Minister's Central Advisory Council was necessary in each individual case. This reluctant support probably recognized two factual situations that go against the general principles of French education. First, such help was given more freely under the Pétain regime, and still survived in part; second, financial difficulties prevented the public authorities from establishing the desired number of (secular) secondary schools, so it seemed preferable to make use of the existing Catholic institutions. In any case, the presence of tax-supported scholarship-holders in Catholic schools was a source of revenue from public funds. Nonetheless, the 1959 formalization of financial opportunity for Catholic schools, in return for varying degrees of cooperation (at the Catholics' request), marks a radical change in Church-State relationships. English readers will recognize similarities to their own "dual system." It took the near-dictatorship of General de Gaulle to achieve this solution, and it still remains to be seen how far these recommendations can be implemented. By 1960, however, about 12,000 of the 14,000 private schools had applied for the "simple agreement" which would pay teachers' salaries.[4]

It will be noted that under the pre-1959 arrangements, and after the

---

[4] For details, and a discussion of the whole background, see W. D. Halls: *Society, Schools and Progress in France* (1965), pp. 75–81.

Lapie proposals, aid to private schools is permissive and not obligatory. It will also be seen that parents with children in private schools do not receive anything that parents of public school children do not also receive. In addition, of course, public schools are built by the local community (with varying amounts of aid from the central government), and public school teachers are civil servants with satisfactory wages. Private school parents must somehow find the necessary money themselves, unless they contract with the State under the new law.

Teachers in the publicly maintained schools have to be well educated and efficient by strict official standards. Many in private schools are also efficient, of course, but not all. Salaries for private school teachers are unattractive, except in the very few prestige secondary schools which correspond to English "public" and American "ivy league" schools. Prospects of promotion for private school teachers are also rather dim. For these reasons ambitious teachers and parents tend to look elsewhere, even though exceptions to this rule (as we shall soon discover) continued to grow and caused the secular government some embarrassment.

The importance of private schools is shown by a few figures. In 1966 the approximate number of children in state schools was 8,900,000; in Catholic schools about 1,910,000. These figures may be broken down as follows: in public primary schools there were 4,836,000; in Catholic primary schools about 825,000; in public secondary schools of all types 2,264,000; and in Catholic secondary schools 596,000. Public universities and technical or professional institutions catered to some 413,000 students on the basis of strict competition. There are about 24,000 students (who will sit for state examinations) in denominational private "faculties," and about 5500 in theological colleges.

It will be seen that although fewer than 18 percent of French children go to private elementary school, the secondary school population shows above 26 percent of its total in private schools, mainly Catholic.[5] Many of the private pupils are, of course, girls whose mothers want them to have a convent education, but many others probably go to Catholic secondary schools because admission is easier. Those who fail to be selected for public *lycées* may nevertheless be allowed to attend Catholic schools, especially if they can pay the fees. Moreover, the academic regime in the public secondary schools is stricter; if children cannot keep up with the pace of work and fail the various examinations

---

[5] If attention is paid only to schools of *lycée* type (that is, excluding *collèges d'enseignement général* and *collèges d'enseignement secondaire*) the Catholic secondary proportion rises to nearly 40 percent. There were *no* Catholic CES in 1965–1966, and private CEG's accommodate less than 20 percent of CEG enrollments.

they may have to leave, whereas in Catholic schools they are more often allowed to repeat the grade and have a second chance. This seems more humane to outsiders, but it causes many French parents and students to criticize the Catholic schools for unfairness and too much regard for money.

This is not, however, the main reason for criticism, which is bitter and almost obsessive with the anticlericals. (Many of these are Catholic in faith, or even in practice; a few are Protestant; the majority agnostic.) They passionately resent clerical control of any schools and fear its spread. The dread of many republicans is that there will be a reversion to the *ancien régime* of king or emperor or aristocratic privilege, with Church dignitaries in powerful alliance. During the past century's ups and downs each antirepublican government has allowed the clergy more control of education and more financial and political strength. This does not say anything about Catholicism in general, of course, but it explains why so many Frenchmen fear, despise, or even loathe the clergy in France.

La question scolaire has been temporarily shelved, but the words still cause a shudder in many quarters. A similar controversy long split Belgium, affecting policies and politics over a wide area. In another form it arouses bitter animosity in Holland and other European countries. Anticlerical fears can cause people who in other countries might be just republicans or Protestants or freethinkers to look with a friendlier eye on Moscow. The two factions drift further from under-standing—anticlericalism is countered by an obsessive fear of com-munism. In Italy, this impasse kept Florence without a mayor for three years. It is peculiarly difficult for the Frenchman to keep a cool head in this matter and concentrate solely on the extension of educa-tion and its modernization. It is surprising that so much had been achieved even before 1959. The paradox of that year was that President de Gaulle, having made himself indispensable, was able as a conserva-tive Catholic to introduce the educational reforms advocated by secularist, radical, left wingers for two generations past, and also to secure State aid to Catholic schools (or other denominational schools, which are few). Once again, a centralized decision settled the affair.

France is one of the larger countries of Europe. It covers two and a half times the area of the United Kingdom, or four-fifths the area of Texas. Its population is over 49 million. There are distinct regional variations of terrain, of occupation, and sometimes of racial admixture. Though there are important heavy industries in densely populated towns and cities, and also rich mineral industries, almost one third of the whole population is directly employed on small mixed farms. These are cultivated with the greatest care (one might almost say affection).

A vivid memory of any part of France recalls weed-free fields of vegetable crops, as well as bountiful grain. Wine production and fruit-growing are very important, and there are extensive fishing enterprises. The secondary industries supported by agriculture, and the many service occupations, keep a large part of the nonagrarian workers in small towns and villages. These people generally have strong individuality and deeply rooted traditions. In the intellectual professions success may be literally measured by nearness to Paris, but most Frenchmen love Paris better from a distance. Though centralization is strong—not just in governmental affairs but in all the nationalized industries and their subsidiaries, such as railways and banks—France is made up of localized industries, shops, and other independent enterprises. "A Frenchman—an individual!" they say, and mean it.

In these circumstances, to say nothing of its turbulent politics, it cannot have been easy to secure equality of educational opportunity. Perhaps that is one reason why the revolutionaries were so eager to maintain the traditional centralization. Otherwise, there might have been educational backwaters, and there would certainly have been local fortresses of reaction. It seemed advisable, therefore, to insist that education belong to the State, and that teachers be free from the contemporary equivalent of un-French activities.

Republicans have always pushed ahead with educational expansion. As an opposition senator said in 1880: "A demand for compulsory schooling is to be expected from a secularist, just as tyranny is to be expected from a usurper." This point of view illustrates the bitterness of opposition. The champions of education had their way, but Jules Ferry, in 1881, estimated that one sixth of the State's entire revenues would have to be allotted to the public education of children. Local resources in cities and towns are expected to provide the cost of buildings, but these can be helped out by central funds. No industrialized country spends anything like one sixth of its income on education today. This is a measure of French eagerness. Now every village has its own school. Every child's standardized schooling is made uniform in the interests of equality of opportunity in all parts of the land.

There are some real drawbacks. Judged by modern standards in more experimental countries like the United States and Britain, the French system is excessively formal and bookish. In actual practice, in the average school, it still bears little relation to the everyday life of the average French community. Even after reform it still takes fatally small account of France's urgent need for greater industrialization and modern workaday know-how. This the outsider can see. The French peasant, still wearing the traditional blue garb of his calling, sees even more to complain about. At home he may speak a local patois, sing local songs, dance traditional dances; the whole of his life rotates around the farm, the store, and the café. For all it means to him, the school's strictly correct French and standardized offerings might be far away in Paris. It is true that the local school is still every child's avenue to professional success; through it opportunity lingers in every village. But the teacher in the small village school is seldom as good or as experienced as the one who has found promotion in a larger town. Not every parent wants his boy to have a "remote" education anyway. Absenteeism is therefore a problem, and is only combated by the discontinuance of state family allowances if it happens too often.

Not surprisingly, the proportion of country children who succeed in competitive examinations is lower than that of town children. Parents with modest incomes, especially those who live at a distance from large towns, may not seriously consider a *lycée* for their children. If a youngster is selected for a *lycée* by the age of 15, he may have to live away from home. Costs at boarding establishments are low, and financial assistance is available where necessary from public funds, but rural parents must reckon with upheaval and sacrifice. Many parents do not want their daughters, especially, to be away from home.

It should be realized how thinly the French population is spread over the land. Transportation is much more limited than it is in Britain, to say nothing of America. On the other hand, school resources do come evenly into the countryside; local disparity of opportunity on the American scale would be entirely unacceptable in France. It certainly helps to improve rural schooling when all teachers are paid equally, according to their qualifications and experience, and when even able primary schoolteachers fresh from college are directed to wherever their services are most needed. But no one can pretend that identical competitions are quite fair for rural children.

A greater criticism of the system to anyone brought up on Anglo-Saxon methods is that the vast majority of French children, undergoing a "general education" of standardized type, encounter so little of topical interest to bring their schooling to life. Reform movements have not impinged markedly on the system in the remoter areas. Such criticism does not worry the French parent or teacher as much as we might expect. Old-style rationalist notions are as strong among Catholics as among their opponents. "General education" (*culture générale*) is believed to result from formal intellectual exercises, and from acquaintance with great ideas, great books, and supporting facts. Vocational and prevocational orientation have traditionally come after school life, and still substantially do despite all the postwar proposals and reforms. In the most technical or professional training, thoroughly practical though it may be, the sense of training the intellect is still paramount; this emphasis continues throughout all schooling. Reason is used as a searchlight on life, illuminating whatever it brings into focus. There is little of the British or American feeling that by grappling with practical problems, or by organizing experiences, the child can build up a pattern of understanding that is none the worse for being tentative or only partially completed. The Frenchman wants a short cut to the "principles."

There is another factor that supports this interpretation. Catholicism has always been conscious of "original sin." Natural curiosity and natural inclinations are said to be "prone to evil," and to "need correcting by discipline and self-denial." Play-ways and the experimental approach are not, therefore, supposed to have the magical potency attributed to them by many of our own countrymen. These activities are known to be pleasant, but they are not thought to be automatically enlightening. "The world" and "the flesh" are well understood in France; but there they are so often distinguished from the mind and the soul (which are supposed to triumph) that a little mistrust of them (or at least impatience) is carried over into educational attitudes.

That is not all. Even the anti-Catholic faction (that shares many of the above-mentioned suspicions) has its own reason for supporting the mind as distinct from physical involvement in one's daily context. The influence of Plato and of Descartes is very strong. In fact, Frenchmen are proud to boast that their educational system is "Cartesian." Descartes stressed that the intellect is paramount; for him it was the rational process, not the near-animal propensities of the body, that give man his essence. Instead of encouraging educators to think of personality as a harmony of complementary activities, the French view emphasizes the ascetic cultivation of "the mind." "We are priests of the intellect," says the representative teacher.

So the French 6-year-old on his first day at school sets his foot on a sternly intellectual road. Battles continue to rage around him, and new notions of how to bring up children rather timidly seek admission. Parents and teachers, priests and politicians almost all agree that school is for "the mind," and the child had better pay attention to it. Human reason gave the "open sesame" to the philosophers and revolutionaries. The power of the mind will prevail over all imperfections according to both the priestly and the secular dispensation, provided that the mind is well disciplined and enlightened by the great traditions. As Plato would have approved, the program is strictly coordinated to this end. "The good" that the child pursues is unchangeable. It is a marvel that there have been so many concessions to the times.

All the boys and girls in elementary schools wear a standard pinafore or overall. Sometimes it is blue, but usually it is·dark steel gray. Some new schools are of exemplary cheerfulness; most are gloomy and oppressive. The books nowadays include some attractive publications, but the majority are cautious and dull. They are all official. Americans will not find the head teacher's role as a sort of regulation-observing official quite so astonishing as would British observers. In small towns and villages there may be only one or two teachers. The senior teacher will also be official secretary to the mayor, and will help to issue such documents as fishing and shooting licenses. The elementary school teacher (even if he takes extended classes up to the age of 16 or 17) is called an "instructor" (*instituteur*), a name that sets him in an inferior category to that of the secondary school teacher (*professeur*).

It is worthwhile to pause at this point, and once more emphasize that the word "teacher" in English covers categories that in other languages are markedly distinguished. These other languages may have no generic word for "teacher"—certainly not one which can extend (as in England) from university teacher to nursery-school teacher. Leaving to one side any fictitious hierarchical distinction that may arise from the social aura of words like "secondary", care is often taken linguistically to distinguish between genuine differences in function— for example, as between a child-minder, a technical trainer, and a purveyor of abstruse knowledge. Speakers, therefore, may be left without a word to indicate the modern function which many of these people have in common, namely, the educative evocation and encouragement of youth. In several European languages such a word has had to be invented since about 1950, if only to apply to associations catering to the interests of various kinds of teacher. Such a word is particularly necessary since school reorganization has blurred some previous distinctions and brought different functionaries together, especially in the lower secondary school range. All this has been helped by the 1962 coordination of once insulated "administrations" for primary, secondary, and technical education under a single secretariat-general.

Teachers of all types are now recognized as needing more extended education and more training; but old distinctions remain. They are particularly noticeable in a country like France, where differences in scholastic attainment have been deeply marked. The *instituteur* has not had the same education and training as the secondary school teacher. The older members of this group passed from a special course in the top level of an elementary school to a teachers' college (*école normale*) when 16 or 17, after successfully competing in a difficult examination. Each *département* has two *écoles normales,* one for boys and one for girls (apart from a very few mixed institutions). These are maintained by the primary education administration. The typical *instituteur* of prewar days (and the majority still in practice) had probably never had any experience outside of the primary or elementary system of schooling. It is true that his studies included a four-year teachers' college course, and this in more recent years took him up to and beyond the *baccalauréat*, the highest secondary school examination. It could be that this latter experience exercises a student academically as much as most American teachers' colleges, or as some British colleges of education. The fact remains that the older elementary schoolteacher in France is still, in most cases, a lifelong product of the elementary school system itself. In former times especially he had no experience of *lycée* or *collège*, and was even further from the university.

As late as the end of 1957, a small majority of students in the *écoles normales* turning out France's primary school teachers had not been to a proper secondary school but to the *cours complémentaires*, or supplementary courses. There all the courses of study and all the teachers, though undoubtedly of good quality, had been under exclusive control of the primary administration of the Ministry of National Education. Such a future teacher was never called "student"; the word for him was *élève* (pupil), the same as for a 6-year-old beginner.

The traditional European divorce between elementary education for the masses and a superior opportunity for the elite is gradually breaking down; but in France change is slow. Both by choice of words and by carefully nourished attitudes, public opinion hangs on to the old estimation. At the same time, it should not escape our notice that these "inferior" teachers now get the *baccalauréat* that entitles them to begin a university course when they so choose. More than that, a few of the best students every year in an *école normale* can now win their way by difficult scholarship examinations to an *école normale supérieure* (higher teachers' college), and thus become very much members of the elite among university students. The *école normale supérieure* is one of the *grandes écoles* or higher professional colleges to be described later. Like them, it is open only to those who pass a harshly competitive examination, usually at the end of a brilliant career in a *lycée* and intensive preparation for two years in special classes. It is primarily intended to provide the specialist subject teachers for the most advanced and academically formidable secondary schools; but a measure of its distinction is the fact that a majority of university teachers in the faculties of Arts and Science are among its alumni, as are many statesmen and high administrators. So the great gulf between the primary school and the most elevated plane of the university can be bridged, though the bridge is flimsy and precarious, while the chasm is deep.

It should be noted that in actual practice the possessor of the *baccalauréat* may not only succeed in obtaining a post in a primary school in the many places where there is a shortage, but may be registered as a qualified teacher (*titularisé*) after five years if he attends summer courses in "pedagogy." This fact indicates the gulf between the most esteemed secondary school teachers and their colleagues under the primary school administration.

French austerity in these differentiations should not be judged too severely. Though we must emphasize that education for all children under the age of 11, and later for those in C.E.G. courses, is always considered inferior to the more academic kind, foreigners should not feel too smug. Popular education is usually treated rather shabbily in the most sympathetic of communities. If we make due allowance for the French preoccupation with intellectual eminence rather than breadth of experience, French teachers' colleges do as complete a job as their British or American equivalents. The future teachers have competed strenuously to get into the colleges and later to meet the qualifying standards at the end of the course. These may be academically advanced by our standards. The proper comparison, however, is that by French standards they are inferior in quality and training to the teachers in secondary schools. Their pay is lower; and their prospects of promotion, of geographic and social mobility, and of social acceptability are much less.

All this discrimination has its effect on the children in those schools. Despite all the changes, it perpetuates in France a class distinction whereby some children are given a socially superior education after age 11 or 15, and others carry on with what our grandfathers were honest enough to regard as an education for the lower orders. At least, selection for higher prospects in France is ensured by the same intellectual criteria for all. In Britain the method is partly similar, partly very different; it depends to some extent on parental status or on where you live. In the United States disparity is prevalent, though the mechanism of discrimination is dissimilar, and the ages are different. (This is a warning of storms to come.) The French are supremely logical, and will not stand for humbug. Though they would very much like to offer equality of educational opportunity, with widespread differentiation of equally acceptable types to suit different children and different careers, they have not progressed so far just yet. Therefore they do not pretend that progress is achieved by altering a name or two.

Until 1959, French schools were in a not very different position from those in England and Wales before the 1944 Education Act, or from those in Germany before World War II. It is a shorter time than most Americans realize since a similar situation prevailed in the United States, especially in the rural areas. No country has yet rid itself of the "lower orders" pattern of thought about children and schools. If we pretend otherwise, we are only delaying the cure. As we have recognized, the French elite is an intellectual one, which is recruited as fairly as centralization and uniformity can make it. The system's inequalities derive from regional or rural difficulties, from the unequal status of teachers, and from the assumption that the "mind" and old-style intellectual callings must be given unchallenged pre-eminence. It must be admitted that this last assumption is particularly associated still with distinct types of schools.

It therefore seems likely that the pre-1959 pattern and the new must coexist for some time, if only because buildings, teachers, and assumptions last so long. Officially, the extension of compulsory school attendance to 16 was to reach its completion in 1967, when children who entered school in 1959 (and thus became subject to the reform law) reached the age of 14. Enforcement is not quite the same as a statement of principle, however, especially in France. The fifth plan, in 1966, acknowledged that the school-leaving age would not effectively advance until 1972. Teacher supply and other considerations are bound to delay complete transformation when so many reforms, proceeding simultaneously in many sectors (technical and higher education as well), draw on the scarce resources of highly educated personnel.

It is appropriate now to review the distinctive characteristics of pre-1959 secondary institutions, for these are either still recognizable as separate schools or detectable as constituent parts of reformed establishments.

Before 1959, three types of secondary school had already grown up in addition to the continuation of elementary school beyond the age of 11. The secondary schools included the *lycées,* the *collèges,* and the *cours complémentaires.* The *lycée* was undoubtedly the prestige school, as it still is. Then, in particular, the term applied only to the definitely preuniversity school concentrating on the classics or on a particular group of bookish subjects. More recently the term *lycée* has come to be applied to all the varied kinds of school which before 1959 were called *collège.*

Since World War II there has been a steady process of promoting formerly inferior kinds of secondary education to a more highly esteemed plane. *Collèges modernes,* for example, used to be called "higher elementary schools." They gradually included more academic subjects and extended their provision beyond the age of 15 or 16. Many were indistinguishable from the traditional *lycées,* though their standards of attainment and their teachers were usually inferior. (A well-informed French spokesman described them as "a sort of *Mittelschule.*") Though the past tense is used here, the present must continue to be understood, too, in some cases.

Since 1959, all former *collèges* have been called *lycées,* while the term *collèges* is now applied to such institutions as the former *cours complémentaires.* The latter were senior classes parallel to the upper grades of elementary school, offering a more "secondary" curriculum, but taught by elementary school teachers. Children went on from the *cours complémentaires* at the age of 15 or 16 to employment, or sometimes to other forms of training. Thus we observe that, as the old higher elementary schools became *collèges modernes* (spreading a proletarian wave into secondary education), so the *cours complémentaires* are now sweeping on into the "first" or "observation" cycle of secondary education as *collèges d'enseignement général,* or as parts of the more comprehensive *collèges d'enseignement secondaire.*

A similar phenomenon has been detectable over the generations in a number of countries. In France, some of the former *cours complémentaires* in outlying towns were not schools of great distinction. In fact, they differed from elementary schools only by offering some commercially or industrially useful supplement to the elementary fare. On the other hand, some of them had devoted *instituteurs* filled with ambition for their pupils, and some continued to provide high quality training-with-general-education beyond the normal age of 15.

Paris in particular provided some very advanced *cours complémentaires industriels* with a commercial or industrial emphasis. These recruited children of promise through a competitive examination after the completion of the ordinary *cours complémentaires.* They offered advanced courses in technical theory and practice combined with an all-round education. Identical courses continue, but are recognized as integral parts of a more extended technical education. Courses in such establishments are arduous, demanding forty or more hours a week of attendance—half practical, half theoretical-and-general. There is also homework.

The same organizational pattern is now basic to the regime of the *collèges du second cycle* and of those *collèges d'enseignement général* which run a vocational or prevocational emphasis as part of their programs. (*Collèges du second cycle*—literally "second-cycle secondary schools"—is the term now applied to institutions which since World War II have been called *centres d'apprentissage*—"apprenticeship centers"—and *collèges d'enseignement technique* or "secondary-technical schools.") When youngsters graduate from such schools at the age of 17, they are skilled craftsmen with a preliminary trade certificate (*certificat d'aptitude professionnelle*), which they can exchange for the full-fledged status of craftsman after satisfactory practical experience and a further test. The standard, educationally and technically, is high. Alternatively, at about the same level and age, boys and girls can obtain similar *brevets* (certificates) of general education, of agricultural or domestic training, or as a technical assistant (*agent technique*).

The upgrading of *cours complémentaires* by enrichment of programs as well as by the title of *collège* combines the government's interest in ambitious pupils with a noteworthy tendency to continue in school anyway. In 1958, roughly 15 percent of the boys and girls stayed on at school until the age of 18, and about 25 percent until 17. Careful forecasts based upon extrapolation of present tendencies indicate that by 1975 about 35 percent are likely to remain until 18, and nearly 50 percent of all the children until 17. It is in this generalized middle area of schooling that growth is expected to be most rapid. An analysis of the occupational distribution of French workers in 1960 showed that 5 percent were in the top cadres, 35 percent in clerical and minor service occupations, and 60 percent were manual workers. It is envisaged that in the lifetime of children now at school the proportions will be 25, 55 and 20 percent. For these reasons alone, a follow-on from *collège* to higher vocational or more academically "higher" education is likely to be demanded in due course.

There has, in fact, been a long tradition of vocational training after school—a tradition still more marked in Germany. In France, the great move forward was with the Astier Law of 1919, which set up vocational training centers and financed them with a national tax on industries that did not provide in-service training. In 1920, vocational education was attached to the Ministry of Education, and in 1933 fees were abolished. In 1944, new-style apprenticeship centers were set up, and boys and girls not undergoing full-time education were required (in theory) to be trained as apprentices at least part time. In some cities the provision was good, but not everywhere, and attendance was patchy. The present incorporation of this provision in the second cycle of secondary education should consolidate it, and also help to make it "polyvalent"—that is, widely educative in a technical sense rather than prematurely or narrowly vocational.

Alongside this intermediate kind of provision a more scientifically based preparation toward technological careers is given in *lycées techniques* (formerly *collèges techniques*) which may lead to the *baccalauréat* or more often to a technician's or pretechnological certificate (*brevet de technicien*). This, in turn, can lead in certain circumstances to higher education or to training as a technologist (*technicien supérieur*). There are also several systems of admission into higher apprenticeship in private or state enterprises. It goes without saying in Cartesian France that the intellectual and theoretical content of any such provision in the technical field is exacting, although the practical side is indeed businesslike.

All this upgrading and diversification of educational opportunity for intermediate workers is of great importance—socially, as well as vocationally and academically. But the overwhelming prestige given to intellectual attainments and the liberal vocations acts as a serious brake on any alternative system of schooling. The hierarchic structure of all public life perpetuates a vested interest in the older interpretation. Parents know what's what. Teachers, especially those in higher ranks, are often unwilling or even unable to change their notions. For example, a *professeur* (note the word) in a *lycée* or *collège* has a high social status, is well paid (comparatively speaking), and teaches as little as fifteen or eighteen hours a week, with no extracurricular duties whatsoever, and no marking to do. As is usually the case with teachers of this rank in continental countries—such as Germany, Austria, and Italy—the *professeur* may give a few courses at a university, or undertake seminars with teachers doing in-service training. For this he is handsomely paid, and the prestige value is great. Continental university teachers are frequently recruited in this way. The *professeur,* therefore, tends to be constantly looking over his shoulder at the university where he would much prefer to be. In these circumstances, the solidarity of the teaching profession is a remote chimera.

To be rather cynical, one may wonder if the teaching profession in any country will ever be more united than it is now. With increasing demands being made upon scarce manpower—in industry and commerce, in administration, and in higher education itself—some hierarchy-building in schools at the secondary level seems inevitable, whether we like it or not.

The French have done their best to improve the supply of good teachers, and have certainly improved the qualifications of the lowest. At the same time, moreover, they have always had the power to post teachers wherever they are most needed, and this power has been particularly applied in the more distinguished *lycées*. These *lycées* are staffed on a national basis, albeit with some concession to the teacher's preference. Here we are likely to find more *professeurs agrégés,* or subject-specialists, with qualifications entitling them to teach in universities.

In the post-1959 rearrangements, some good teachers (or learned teachers, it would be truer to say) have been redistributed to strengthen the newer kinds of secondary schools. This redistribution policy has been applied chiefly to the younger teachers; the older ones stay where they were. Beginning in 1965, however, new *professeurs agrégés* are assigned only to upper secondary schools, or to the universities, not to the teaching of younger children. But for some time to come, the academically oriented courses or schools at any age level will continue to be more strongly staffed.

So the child securing admission to an academic type of *lycée* is very much a chosen child. He may be only 11; nevertheless, he and his parents are conscious of a real distinction. Financial and other difficulties will not be allowed to stand in his way. His tuition is free and, if he has to reside away from home, he can get a scholarship. If he is successful, not only in the yearly examinations but in the impressive vista of competitive examinations looming ahead of him, he can win his way to the highest positions—beyond school, beyond the university, beyond the research studies of a graduate school. There glows in front of him the vision of a modern French equivalent of Napoleon's baton. But the cost is heavy, nonetheless. A large number of children are unable to keep up the strenuous ordeal, and are weeded out either in the annual examination or at the end of the school's first cycle (we might almost say "first round") when they are 15. In fact, many secondary schools do not take children beyond this phase. If the pupil holds his own, he can undertake the more arduous training for the *baccalauréat*.

The *baccalauréat* has varied in external details during its history, but it has always been pivotal in French education. It was traditionally the criterion to determine whether or not a pupil might become a university student. That is, it decided if one might qualify for the top socioeconomic class. Originally, the *baccalauréat* was mainly an oral examination of searching intensity. The oral part subsequently lost in importance to the written, and, in 1960, was abandoned temporarily —except for languages and to decide the fate of marginal candidates. It was restored again in 1966.

At one time, too, the *baccalauréat* was centered on the classical and other literary or humanistic studies, but mathematics and philosophy were also always important. Since 1945, however, the number of elective subjects has grown, and in 1966 there were five main subject-groupings. These, with their subsections, offer candidates seven "sections" of *baccalauréat*. Four of the "sections" are science-centered or modern, but so far these have not attracted as many candidates as the more traditional studies. For each type of *baccalauréat,* however, every candidate will have pursued nine or ten subjects continuously throughout his school life, concentrating on a certain few from the age of about sixteen. Even so, all candidates take a language and mathematics and philosophy in the examination, whatever else they do. Four subjects are closely examined by written papers, the other five orally. A general education (*culture generale*) must never be lost sight of. Indeed, to make sure of that, all candidates must also undergo a test in physical education too, including swimming 50 yards, climbing a rope, and running!

The *baccalauréat* examination used to be taken in two parts separated by a year. Each part was a formidable obstacle. In 1959, 45 percent of the candidates failed Part I, and of those who passed 37 percent failed Part II, many trying several times. Until 1962, no candidate was admitted to Part II without having passed Part I, but in that year a provisional examination (*examen probatoire*) took the place of Part I. Almost 60 percent of the candidates for the final *baccalauréat* passed in 1963, and 63.4 percent passed the final in 1964. In 1965 the figure was 62.7 percent. (A vast improvement over 1957—a representative year of the old dispensation—when only 39 percent passed the final examination, and 61 percent failed!) In 1966 the pass rate was 50 percent.

For a number of years, in order to make sure a student was fit to pursue university studies (not even the tough and broadly based *baccalauréat* could assure this) a preparatory year (*année propédeutique*) was added to the university program. This year was crowned by an examination so formidable that, in 1964, 44 percent of the first year candidates in mathematics and physics just could not face it. Undergraduates who had switched from their major school subjects to other specialized fields were even worse off. In 1963, only 21 percent of the undergraduates who had passed the *baccalauréat* in philosophy passed the *propédeutique* in their newly chosen field of physics, biology, and chemistry entitling them to move on to medical studies. Success in the same examination for "experimental science" *bacheliers* was only 43 percent, and 47 percent for those with a *baccalauréat* in mathematics. A higher proportion of candidates passing the *baccalauréat* did not mean, therefore, a smooth road through the university. It was said that the *propédeutique* examination was being used to "restore the standards" as the *baccalauréat* became "easier."

Recently, many alterations have been achieved, set in motion, or proposed. In the concluding year at school (*classe terminale*), there is now one main examination for the *baccalauréat*. What used to take place in Part I of the *baccalauréat* (and later by the *examen probatoire*) is now achieved by a class-council or unofficial examination in school, which decides the pupil's admissibility to the top class. In 1965, 76 percent were so admitted. A second chance is given to those who repeat the year. Similarly, those who get as far as taking the *baccalauréat* examination, but fail it, can have a second shot in September—an old practice that was discontinued for a few years, but restored in 1966. Not everyone is pleased with this restoration, but until 1968 some maneuverability is permitted to those reforming the *baccalauréat,* because only then will the final shape be established.

Another alteration of consequence is that in the future the *baccalauréat* will not automatically admit its possessors to the university faculty of their choice; they must have a good mark in an appropriate group of subjects before they can be sure of admission. When the new form of *baccalauréat* is in force, the "three cycle" university structure will already have been firmly established, as it began in the autumn of 1966. In preparation for it, the university's *année propédeutique* (and the examination) were abandoned in the same year. These changes sound complicated if we pursue the details. The main outlines of reform become clearer if we remember that their purpose is to open up more avenues to more people and more studies, and at the same time to encourage interchange of interests—particularly toward the scientific, technological, and modern fields. That aspiration is, however, slow to be realized.

The *baccalauréat* is, as the French say, the "sanction" of the secondary school career. But it is not really a high school leaving-certificate or school graduation; it is technically the first examination of the university. Elaborate moves are afoot to make it more of a school examination, particularly in view of the estimate that by 1975 over 30 percent of the population are likely to stay on until age 18. Careful studies have been undertaken of those who "just miss" or fail outright in the *baccalauréat,* and, as a result, new qualifications (such as the *brevet de technicien*) and new careers have been introduced.[6] This concern is not surprising, with 25 percent of the pupils "repeating" the last two years of the *lycée,* and something like 12 percent dropping out of the competition altogether in the penultimate year—so near to their goal![7] The provision of near-university *instituts universitaires de technologie,* with two–year courses for well-qualified students over 18, must also be considered in this connection. Until all these modifications become effective, it still looks as though the chief justification for the *lycée* is to prepare for the *baccalauréat.*

Until recently only the small proportion of children who gained their *baccalauréat* were entitled to enroll in universities. Since the end of 1957, alternative means of entry to higher education have been provided, in the shape of special examinations. Undoubtedly this helps

---

[6] See, for example, *Avenirs,* April 1966.

[7] *Avenirs* (April 1966), pp. 10–11.

those who are suited to advanced study in one particular area, but who do not possess the wide knowledge or verbal skills appropriate to the *baccalauréat.* But we must not forget that, like the *baccalauréat,* these new entrance examinations are intended to encourage quality quite as much as to entitle boys and girls to higher education. Since 1959, particularly, admission has been easier for able pupils who are short of some requisite qualification, and "university colleges" are more widely available for first year work.

Higher education fees are nominal. Thus few people of the right quality can ever be debarred on financial grounds. Moreover, there are scholarships to enable students to bear the additional costs of living away from home. Inexpensive meals and lodgings are available, especially at a "university city," and students can benefit by reduced admission charges to establishments of an educational kind. Admission to a *faculté* in a university, however, gives no firm assurance of a royal road to success. Lectures are given to disconsolate and lost-looking students who sit in huge numbers while the professor drones on in the most impersonal way. Loudspeakers are widely used at overflow meetings; counseling and tutorial advice are unknown. Every student must fend for himself. It is not uncommon for even the children of professors to feel disoriented in their strange surroundings. Buildings and libraries are such as to deter all but the most resolute student.

In increasingly crowded cities, the mounting tide of university students (460,000 in public higher education alone in 1966–1967, without counting the private institutions or nonuniversity establishments) find it difficult to secure proper accommodation. In the Paris region, where a disproportionate number of students congregate, the problem is specially severe—not only in terms of accommodation, but educationally. A café is no long-term substitute for a common room. The wastage in most continental universities is very high, particularly by British standards. One of the problems internationally is that students take jobs to maintain themselves during the term, though some of the best ones can now get a state *présalaire,* at least for enrollment in the highly competitive courses. Another problem is the "phantom student" who never (or hardly ever) sets foot in the university except at registration time. Therefore the rate of failure is high. The time it takes to get a degree is about 25 percent longer than it should be. Only about 60 percent of the students actually take the examination at the appropriate time in several faculties, and half of these may fail.

Though the reference here is to France, it is probably a paler portrait of the severe problems of universities in other continental countries. Questions of purpose and continuity in study; of proper service to the students and proper course requirements from the students; of face-to-face acquaintance with student or professor; of actual *training* for a profession; of efficient methods for learning, teaching, and research; of using valuable human material and satisfying social demand; of transforming society and economy—these are just a few of the problems anxiously discussed in many languages throughout Europe.

Some of these problems seem to be philosophical matters of principle, like that of academic freedom. Some seem to be economic, like that of investment in the student or supporting the poor but ambitious student. Others seem to turn on decisions about society and politics: whether the university is to be the privileged and dilatory upper class club of tradition or the well-équipped laboratory of the future.

Whatever the decisions, they are bound to transform society—even as they respond to social change. Therefore it is certain that deliberate and carefully phased changes must come in the university population, in programs, purpose, structure, and control. It seems inevitable that higher education's new responsibilities will be linked with long-term planning, whether this takes the form of the French Fifth Plan, or the commissions familiar in Britain and the United States. Immediate decisions are to rid the universities of the "phantom students" and "graybeard students" who make no real contribution or progress. This process has begun by tightening up regulations for admission, and for checking student progress through the university's stages.

Before any of these changes were under way, France already had businesslike institutions in higher education which many other continental universities lack. These are the simply named *grandes écoles* (great schools), which are among the most distinguished institutions in the world. Several owe their foundation to the Revolutionary period. These include the *Ecole Polytechnique* and the *Ecole Normal Supérieure*, which between them have tended until fairly recently to monopolize the processing of talent for huge sectors of public life, industry, and scholarship. Admission to these two institutions (and most of the later *grandes écoles*) is almost impossible without two or three years of intensive work in special "preparatory classes" after passing the *baccalauréat*. Nearly all these brilliant students pass their difficult final examinations.

This sector of higher education thus preselects students for academic and professional distinction before the strict level of higher education ostensibly begins. On admission to a *grande école* the student is manifestly at a level equivalent to that attained by ordinary students after two years' work in an ordinary faculty. Students of a *grande école* sign an "engagement" for a specified period, and are acknowledged as probationary civil servants (since each *grande école* predestines for public service generally, or else for a particular range in a specialized profession). They are paid a modest salary besides benefitting from good accommodations and contact with superb brains and facilities. The students are often provided with special courses on their own, in addition to those in the university faculties which they attend with other undergraduates.

The ordinary students in the regular faculties of a university, therefore, may be described as having been "creamed off" before embarking upon their courses, or before there is any threat of elimination. (We must not forget, however, how distinguished they are already, by international criteria, in having obtained their *baccalauréat.*) Because the *grandes écoles* have traditionally limited their admissions by ruthless competition (and are likely to go on doing so), is there to be the same restriction in a university generally? Many continental universities impose a quota, a *numerus clausus,* at least for certain faculties where accommodation or practical facilities are scarce. We can understand that French educators are intent on obtaining excellent students, but we might not believe that the selfsame process can deliberately keep down student numbers. Yet this has long been true, and intentionally so.

Here we face one of the dilemmas of Europe—one which will appear again and again. In the old days, social privilege and access to governmental positions were regulated exclusively by family position and wealth. A reinforcing instrument in the process of exclusion was the criterion of education; it was necessary to have schooling of a particular kind. At one time this schooling was recognizably vocational (including the necessary Latin, and so forth). More recently, as in France, access to education has slowly become more nearly universal, with the result that there is enhanced competition for positions of wealth and privilege. It may perhaps become fiercer because of an overproduction of certain kinds of trained or learned personnel. In some countries (notably Italy and Austria) there is more unemployment and frustration among well-schooled people than there is in France. In France, administrative and top-level executive posts cannot absorb all the available people. Manual occupations of every kind generally lack prestige, and therefore are no more likely to be sought by Frenchmen than jobs with poor pay are likely to be sought by Americans.

Without industrial expansion (which in itself will bring unforeseen social changes, especially with automation), France's economic position is such that the country just cannot afford to employ all her well-trained personnel in suitable positions. Intentionally or not, the present selection procedure does serve to prevent one serious social embarrassment while it aggravates another. The disappointment and frustration in French education cannot be considered apart from the basic problems of economic change and a possible revision of the hierarchy of social esteem. When we examine the French school system in non-French terms, which make us fasten on to its ruthless efficiency as an instrument of selection to such an extent that we think of much secondary schooling as "unrealistic" or "purposeless," we are failing to apply fairly the criteria used by the French themselves.

The position in France, though disturbing, does not seem quite so objectionable to the French themselves. Even if the bookish and academic studies of the majority do not reach a successful conclusion in the university, it is believed that the "general education" of the mind will equip them well enough for any job they undertake. The searchlight, so to speak, is as high-powered and as carefully beamed as could be expected in their case.

In truth, the sheer amount of knowledge which a French child has amassed when ready to leave the *lycée* is enormous by any standard. Specialization has been rather limited; about nine subjects, selected from a wide range, have been thoroughly tackled by every child. The list comprises philosophy, French, Latin, Greek, two modern languages, history, geography, mathematics (including very advanced work indeed), chemistry, physics, biology, and physical education. Though subjects are grouped according to five different types of *baccalauréat,* with seven possible combinations of subjects finally selected, all of them (including the "technical" and "commercial" *baccalauréat*) require candidates to be examined in a wide academic field. At the same time, each subject is intensively studied. By way of comparison, the French candidate offering English (as a foreign language, of course) has to cover as many authors and answer questions just as difficult as an English child must when presenting himself for the advanced level of the General Certificate of Education at 18 or 19 in *his own* language. In fact, the French *baccalauréat* looks slightly more difficult.

It is impossible to make a comparison with the United States' system, because there is nothing comparable. Robert M. Hutchins, former president of the University of Chicago, has said that the pupil who passed the *baccalauréat,* or the corresponding examinations in Italy or Germany at the beginning of the century, knew as much as three American college graduates put together, and in addition had a mastery of his mother tongue. The European would be 18, and the American 22 years of age.

This is an example of a comparison which is no comparison, really, because the European systems and the American are not intended to accomplish the same thing. It should cause some misgiving, however, when Americans ask themselves questions about the standards of technical knowledge and academic equipment they used to maintain.

The proportion of American college graduates is much higher than the proportion of French youth passing the *baccalauréat*—but the proportion of French children could be greatly increased by broadening the basis of the subjects examined, and still more by lowering the standard slightly. This brings us to considerations of resources and volume, and not of quality. The criterion Dr. Hutchins uses is that of quality or thoroughness. It might be possible to modernize and democratize the system in France without sacrificing integrity of learning or a liberal understanding of mankind's recurring problems in their modern context, and that is just what many alert French educators would very much like to do. American and British examples influence them strongly, but progress until recently was very slow. It is difficult for Frenchmen to throw off their shackles of excessive intellectualism.

The approach of reform could best be foreseen in the field of technical education. Some of this (especially in the *lycées techniques*) is still not very different from the ordinary programs of the academic *lycée,* though with a scientific bias, rather than a technical one. Nevertheless, as many French children are now in technical or professional education above the age of 15 as we can find in old-style academic schools, and the number is growing. For many reasons, technical education in France is more free to develop in size and scope than formal secondary education, even where it suffers from handicaps of money, inferior status, and prejudice among parents and teachers. However strongly conservative attitudes may prevail in some quarters, the metropolitan area of Paris has some remarkable enterprises to show in technical education at *lycée* level.

Notable among these is the experimental *lycée* at Enghien, an expensive spa suburb. At this school there are all the normally expected excellences of a first-class *lycée*—but, for a large number of the pupils, the excellences are mainly oriented toward technical and scientific studies, or toward comparable studies in commerce. Alongside these, there are the usual sections in classics and modern studies. So it would be wrong to suggest that the *lycée* is a technical one, although a visit to the magnificent plant ranging from heavy engineering to the latest electronics might make one think so. The presence of the traditional and the ultramodern on the same site, both admirably exercising intellectual qualities, must be very persuasive to the many visitors from other French centers. On the same campus, too, there are an ordinary apprenticeship center (*collège d'enseignement technique*) and preparatory classes for the *grandes écoles*—the intellectual elite. The very coexistence of such diverse elements must come as a surprise to many French people—especially as so much harmony seems to be assured on one campus. Furthermore, the continual personal encounters, and academic interchange in some cases, encourage greater staying power on the technical education side and earn respect for it. Though in many ways Enghien is unique, its example can be paralleled in several other quarters, especially around Paris and in such provincial centers of new industries as Grenoble and Toulouse, famous for nuclear research and aeronautics.

Most Frenchmen believe that France already excels in technical education, because those who successfully complete academic school and triumphantly graduate from the *grandes écoles* compare favorably with the products of higher technical education anywhere. But the proportion of French children with any chance of such ultimate excellence is minute. Engineers and technologists generally (as these categories are understood in the United States or Britain) are not produced in anything like the required numbers. Still worse is the shortage of trained technicians, maintenance staff for elaborate plant, production and distribution personnel, and so on. The present growth of technical education in the face of discouraging difficulties is to be welcomed, therefore, by anyone who considers French progress as a whole. It might even be said that only development of this bread-and-butter side of French enterprise is likely to pay for the comparative luxuries of literary and philosophical brilliance. This is an inescapable consideration, no matter how much defenders of general culture shut their eyes to it. But to bring matters down to the level of the child's personal education, or of those social and political arguments that tear French cohesion to shreds, technical or vocational education may offer France a possibility of evolution blocked elsewhere.

For one thing, it can absorb many persons who would be declared (or who would feel themselves to be) failures in a strictly academic system. These people can make good, and contribute to the good of France. They can matter. Secondly, working-class solidarity in France needs to be experienced to be believed. Many town and country workers would not think of sending their children to academic schools even if they could; they are suspicious of the local *bourgeoisie,* and they despise central administrators selected by the *lycée* system. An education that seems real rather than "otherworldly" is more welcome, especially when the children bring home evidences of manual and creative skill.

In this connection we should also heed the French tendency for a child to follow his father's occupation—a tendency hard to break unless children get a chance in school or in after-school training to manifest unsuspected skills that will bring in hard cash, or at least be practically helpful. Children can thus get on in the world without being suspected of a rather unnatural betrayal of their home circle.

Thirdly, the Church does not take much practical part in the development of technical education in France (though it does in Belgium); therefore, this is one sector of education in which all French boys and girls can get together educationally without being proverbial sheep and goats. Education can get on with its job without unhelpful distractions from outside.

Fourthly, it is only in technical education that private enterprise (being secular) is both recognized and aided by the state. Some private diplomas have public recognition, firms with private apprenticeship training are exempt from the apprenticeship tax, and there is mutual support in other ways. Good relations are enjoyed not just with employers but with the trade unions as well. Technical trainees in public schools or centers have opportunities to work according to trade standards under trade conditions; technical teachers of practical subjects are recognized journeymen. Finally, it is only in vocational education that the prevailing centralization of French education is really modified for varied development. This may seem a small matter to those who normally experience decentralized responsibility; but a change in this direction might be a great chance for France.

As has been shown already, the former apprenticeship centers which used to follow elementary school, or come after *cours complémentaires,* have now been integrated into the second cycle of secondary schooling. These centers are now called *collèges d'enseignement technique* (technical-secondary schools) by most of the people employed in or administering them, although a newer term—*collèges du second cycle* (second-cycle secondary schools)—has recently come into use. At the same time, the rather more academic but not ultra-selective *collèges techniques* (secondary-technical schools), which used to run alongside the *lycées* on a separate but not-quite-equal level, have tended to lose their junior classes by incorporating them with other elements to make a combined "observation cycle." So it looks as though the very thorough programs of combined academic and vocational work will in future serve a more widely recruited population after the end of the first cycle. Thus a fusion is taking place, aided by another fusion at the university and near-university levels, and by still another between hitherto isolated types of teacher.

We have observed that the elementary school teacher (*instituteur*), once highly esteemed in the country, is now considered socially inferior even in his own profession. Those who teach in academic schools are similarly stratified. In the lowest strata are those who have only their university degree. They are seldom regarded as real teachers, even though they teach. Their main responsibility is to help out the *professeurs* by supplementary teaching, or to supervise homework periods and mark the work done, or to supervise such extracurricular activities as boarding arrangements and meals. Established *professeurs* do none of this. Either they have completed their professional training in an *école normale supérieure* (of which there are now four), emerging from the competitions as young *professeurs agrégés* (registered specialist teachers), or they have subsequently attained this dignity by intensive scholarship in their own academic subject (classics, or chemistry, or philosophy, *not* "education"). In either case, to be admitted as *agrégés* they have to crown all their studies with what may be the most exacting academic competition in the world. Very few indeed get as far as even competing for it, and out of these seasoned and intrepid competitors only a small percentage pass. The number varies from 6 percent in philosophy to 30 percent in some of the science subjects.

Those who fail to be accepted as *agrégés* can compete for the next best thing—the Certificate of Aptitude for Secondary Teaching, usually known by its French initials CAPES. This certificate was instituted in 1950 to follow a year's course in the theory and practice of education. Practice-teaching facilities are provided at an educational center in each university town under the tutelage of teachers called "educational advisers." There may be as many as six, or even ten or twelve, of these advisers on the staff of a chosen *lycée* where the brief practical part of the course is spent. The very idea that secondary school teachers should actually be *trained,* as distinct from being educated, was novel at the time. It has still not been accepted in most of Europe, though the French have come to terms with it.

The centers where secondary teachers receive their combined training-and-education at the postgraduate level were first called regional educational centers. Since 1957, mainly because of the shortage of well-qualified applicants, a new strategy has been employed. In that year, a special competitive examination was offered students at the end of their first university year—or during their preparatory classes for the *grandes écoles*—to recruit them for the teaching profession. Accepted students go on to study for their degree in the usual way, and at the same time study for the theoretical papers of the CAPES. This they do at an *Institut de Preparation aux Enseignements du Second Degré,* or IPES (Institute for Training Secondary School Teachers). If they are successful, they move on to a regional educational center for a further year of practice and theory. (The regional educational centers still exist, and serve other teachers who have not been to the IPES but want to prepare for the CAPES final examination). A few highly promising students stay on in the IPES, and prepare for the exceedingly competitive examination of the *agrégation.*

Students admitted to an IPES, like all other students admitted to teacher-training institutions or to the *grandes écoles,* sign a contract to

serve for ten years. In this case, they promise to serve as teachers or
as researchers. The 10-year period of service may include their training.
In return, the students receive a small salary as probationary civil
servants, and assured jobs await them on successful conclusion of their
courses. With the CAPES they are known as *professeurs certifiés* (certificated secondary school teacher), as distinct from the *professeurs
agrégés* and the *instituteurs.*

The CAPET, a separate and less highly esteemed certificate for
technical subject teachers, used to be similarly obtainable in appropriate institutions. This is now also called CAPES because, in consequence of recent reforms, "there is no longer any reason for maintaining
any discrimination between the CAPES and the CAPET."[8]

One or other of these certificates is now nominally required of new
teachers in all kinds of *lycées,* professional schools, and teachers' colleges. A strong move is afoot to supply enough of these *professeurs
certifiés* to serve the new observation classes, too—in *collèges d'enseignement secondaire* and *collèges d'enseignement général* (CES and
CEG). So far, these lower secondary, or middle, schools have been
staffed by *instituteurs.* Here again the trend is not merely to rename
such *instituteurs* as *professeurs* if they teach in an observation cycle,
but to encourage the best of such teachers to have at least some
university courses behind them before taking up their posts. It is
envisaged that, eventually, all teachers in the CEG and the CES for
the observation cycle of secondary schools will have completed three
years at the university, and possess a new style—and some say, cheaper
—*licence* (degree) for this purpose. Even the *instituteur* in a primary
school will pursue at least some university-level courses on a more
limited front. The future is obscure, but the purpose is clear: to merge
the various strata of the teaching profession by encouraging the lower
ones to improve themselves.

The implementation of these important changes depends upon the
fulfillment of the reforms which began to take effect in the autumn
of 1966. To simplify matters, we shall round off with a brief outline.
The *baccalauréat,* which used to give automatic right of enrollment
in any faculty, no longer does so without question. Students must have
good marks in the right subjects for a particular faculty. There is
now no preliminary first year (*propédeutique*) at the university, followed by the four certificates which used to confer a *licence.* Instead,
the university curricula have been reorganized, according to plans

<hr />

[8] Quoted from the official report "The Educational Movement in France in 1964,"
published in 1965 by the *Institut Pédagogique National,* Paris.

which had been hinted at for some years. Now there are three distinct two-year cycles in higher education. Each year of the first cycle is concluded by an examination. Only one attempt may be made at each one.

The first university cycle in science consists of four elective sections. After passing the examination in his chosen section, the student is awarded a diploma (DUES). He is also advised as to whether he should work toward a degree of high or low caliber, or switch to another institution, or turn his qualifications into a job. The written papers for the DUES are, in fact, said to be "eliminatory." Similarly, in the arts there is a two–year cycle, with five sections to choose from for those who aspire to teaching. Non-school subjects are also available in four other sections for non-teachers. As in the sciences, a diploma (DUEL) is awarded to those who pass the second–year examination, also with "eliminatory" papers before an oral examination in depth.

The second cycle contains something novel and something more controversial. It offers to the more distinguished students a two–year course leading to a *maître* or master's degree—something which has not existed since the Revolution. (Interestingly enough, a similar revival has been mooted in some German universities, at about the same level.) The *maître* is intended mainly for future researchers. In the sciences there are twelve fundamental branches of study. Candidates must obtain four certificates (two each year, as in the old pattern for the now superseded type of *licence*). In the arts, candidates must earn two preliminary certificates and then write a thesis for the *maître*. Though this seems novel, it is not the really controversial element just mentioned. That is the proposal to award a *licence* or teaching degree at the end of the first year of the second cycle, for which candidates must have specialized in one or two schoolteaching subjects.

Anyone thus obtaining a *licence* at the end of his third year could go on to further study. But it is expected that those seeking a *maître* will make up their minds to do so at the very beginning of the second cycle. Otherwise they will have to familiarize themselves with knowledge and skills differently slanted from those leading directly to a *licence*. Thus a two-level system of recruitment even for graduate teachers seems built into the new pattern.

The arrangements hitherto described for teacher recruitment and training through an IPES continue to operate. Candidates are still recruited at the end of the first university year, or its equivalent, and are then fostered by the IPES. They are not considered to be officially engaged as future teachers, however, until they have their *licence* or their *agrégation*. The *agrégation* in future will be competed for in the year after the *maîtrise;* that is, at the end of the fifth university year.

Since 1965–1966, *agrégés* are not assigned to the first cycle of secondary schools, but to the upper half, or the preparatory classes of the *grandes écoles,* or to university teaching or research.

Concluding the third university cycle, a new research doctorate is available to highly competent researchers. It is too soon to say much about this, though it is a development which has been under discussion for a long time. It is complicated by two facts: (a) the most distinguished academics are not in the ordinary faculties, but in the *grandes écoles* whose status is already so Olympian that there is no need to add lustre with doctorates; and (b) most research is done in special institutes outside the universities. The fusion of teaching and research so strongly cherished in British universities and American graduate schools is not a formal part of the French tradition.

Alongside all these changes, the two–year technological subuniversities (*instituts universitaires de technologie*) are worth close observation, both for themselves and for what they may portend. At the moment it is clear that they are intended to house and husband the kind of intellect or skill which does not quite make the theoretical grade of university study. By 1967, thirteen *IUTs* had been established. Both their number and their function can be expected to expand.

Though the cataclysmic changes described above can readily be formalized by the edicts of a centralized Ministry, the spontaneous self-reorientation of higher education familiar in Anglo-Saxon countries is by the same token excluded. So is that cross-disciplinary "bursting at the seams" which has created such response in English-speaking universities to the explosions of knowledge, of student population, and of social demand. On the other hand, a firm sense of destination can be imparted, money can be provided, and personnel can be reassigned to areas of academic and technological productivity. These are some of the points we need to ponder in reviewing the phenomenal reformation of French education since 1959.[9]

In all these developments we discern France's carefully integrated coordination of school, university, teaching profession and socio-economic evolution. Though revolution rather than evolution seems to have overtaken French education, we may be sure that further evolution or expansion of a most impressive kind will continue for

---

[9] For a penetrating, authoritative, and interesting survey of all these problems by a Frenchman who has been at the center of it all, see J. Capelle: *L'Ecole de Demain Reste à Faire* (Presses Universitaires Françaises), 1966, or its English translation published by Pergamon Press, in 1967, under the title *Tomorrow's Education—the French Experience.* See also W. D. Halls: *Society, Schools and Progress in France* (Pergamon Press) 1965.

decades from the changes described—even though some will be abortive **o**r diverted, as so often happens in France. There can be no restoration **o**f the old regime. Too many people, from the industrialists down to the poor, and from the *recteurs* of universities down to the *instituteurs,* **h**ave seen where the advantage lies.

On the other hand, most critics are still just stunned, and most **a**dvocates still intoxicated. Just before this book went to press, some **e**minent Frenchmen made such statements as: "There is a perpetual **s**truggle of parents and *professeurs* never to set foot inside a *collège l'enseignement secondaire;*" "The Minister did not dare to suppress **t**he first cycle of *lycées,* but had to let them continue alongside." The **o**rdinary man in the street, and many of the parents and teachers involved, do not yet even know the meaning of the names used for various institutions and projects under the new dispensation, let alone their **s**ignificance. The whole thing must simmer down for some years, while some of the prestige institutions (such as the *grandes écoles*) will go on as before, benefitting by university instruction and facilities but in many ways being independent and enjoying unique privileges.

It should be remembered that these are all state institutions, and that the state has a monopoly of examinations. There is no alternative way of attaining the distinctions thus held out. Wealth or favor has as little influence as human ingenuity can contrive. Students are specialists but have previously triumphed in "general education." The importance of these arrangements generally is shown by the field covered. Rigorous professional preparation is offered by the *grandes écoles* in each of the following interests: public administration, teaching, cartography, engineering, manufacturing and various technologies, fine arts, drama, physical education, agriculture, forestry, veterinary science, economics, statistics, war, aeronautics, naval studies, communications, roads, railways, physics, chemistry and so on. Many of the *grandes écoles* are supervised by ministries other than the Ministry of National Education.

Still, even with this impressive array, the nonscientific and nontechnological interests have predominated. Of all those who held French university degrees in 1950, nearly 30 percent had degrees in law (for administration), about 25 percent had degrees in literary subjects, 26 percent were graduates in medicine or pharmacy. Only 19 percent had degrees in science, either pure or applied. However, changes are afoot. In 1965–1966, the number of undergraduate students in law or administration were about 21 percent of the total; those in the literary or social field numbered 34 percent; in science and technology, 32 percent; in medicine and pharmacy, 15 percent. It is anticipated that in 1972 the proportion for science and technology will be

43 percent, and that will be out of a greatly increased university stu
dent body. The total 1972 enrollments are expected to exceed 750,00(
—more than twice as many as in 1963—not counting fifty thousan(
foreigners.

Many of the pursuits and callings prepared for by public educatio:
in other countries are in France considered to be either the concer:
of noneducational ministries, or are allowed to fall down the clefts i:
the school system. Also, attempts to secure fairness by centralizatio:
results in the neglect of local needs and possible local "growing points.'
Religious and political quarrels breed intolerance; cooperation an(
compromise are little known in France. The pursuit of rationalism
makes everyone certain he knows best; those who do not preacr
rationalism tend to preach authoritarianism with divine or politica:
sanction. Recruitment by competition causes frustration and disaffec·
tion. France is divided by intellects—brilliant and lively, but often
implacable.

Let us summarize our observations. The school system until recently
has been a source of disappointment and frustration to the majority.
For instance, half the adult population is self-employed in small-scale
private enterprises, many as peasant farmers. What realistic offering
does the school set before them? In the larger towns and cities a high
proportion of industrial workers look to the gospel of Marx and his
disciples. In recent general elections Communists totaled a quarter
or more of the votes. They were sometimes the largest single political
group. In a political and educational system where the devolution of
responsibility on a decentralized basis is unfamiliar, such figures are
understandable. People have no feeling of partnership.

Moreover, in 1943 it was estimated that in France there were eight
million "pagans" (or near-atheists) to whom the Church meant nothing
but an abomination. So the Church could not supplement for them
the educational work of other institutions. Hence the attempt to train
worker-priests who would conduct missionary work while employed
in ordinary labor. At one time there were 350 of these worker-priests
in the large cities, but in 1954 their ecclesiastic superiors closed down
their activities. They were considered too outspoken and fractious, and
their championship of the inferior and despised sounded patently left
wing to the luckier ones. Fortunately, the worker-priest system was
authorized again in 1965 with Vatican approval, but with safeguards.
Though some connections—such as family ties—are stronger in France
than in other countries, and though local patriotism is also strong,
there is a general absence of personal contact in schools and a corresponding absence in public life. Once again, "a Frenchman is an
individual." But in the complicated modern world a frustrated indi-

vidual is not simply uprooted; he is ripe for violence or at least cynicism.

To do them justice, the French themselves are fully conscious of these problems. They try to make schools less formal. "New methods" are officially encouraged and demonstrated by the Ministry of National Education; "pilot classes" are found in all regional centers, and "experimental *lycées*" are maintained at six points. In Paris, the Ministry maintains an International Center for Educational Study, where educators from all over the world meet in delightful surroundings to exchange ideas with their French counterparts. There are contrasts of opinion, of course, but progressive ideas are usually acceptable to the French. The problem is that of embodying the ideas in practical programs.

Therein lies the importance of the demonstration centers distributed throughout France. The regional educational centers (*centres pédagogiques régionaux*) help as a focus of in-service training, but they are criticized for having young teacher-trainees copy the practice of the senior teachers in observation schools, and follow closely. The International Center for Educational Study (in the Paris suburb of Sèvres) has been far more significant in promoting "active" education, with the teacher as a guide and counselor, instead of the traditional lecturer "who never sees the pupils' faces—only their heads" (as they write). Especially under the guidance of Madame Hatinguais, who retired from the directorship of the center in 1966, a strong point has also been made of getting the schools to run "in parallel" with life outside, and to promote initiative, together with a sense of social responsibility and personal taste.

All this is castigated by many older French teachers. They speak of the "destruction" of the educational system, and complain of "revolutionaries." But from 1945 on, when the first "new classes" were formed, the effects rippled outward. Within seven years there were many thousands of such classes in France. Their title was changed then to "pilot classes," indicating their role as guides for the future. The principles illustrated were encouraged, where possible, in all the initial two–year programs of *lycées* throughout France. Each regional center maintains two series of pilot classes as demonstration units or laboratories. The six *pilot lycées* already mentioned were chosen to contain only pilot classes—four in the Paris region, two in the provinces. In 1960, when the observation cycle was first instituted (then for only two years, later extended to four), it provided the opportunity to generalize the modern idea across the whole lower secondary system. Along with the change in spirit or orientation there has been a corresponding development of guidance, teamwork among teachers and pupils, class conferences, and pupil self-organization. Not all of this seems very startling to Britons—much less to Americans; but for France it represents a radical break. And the example of France is once more likely to tell in Europe.

The concept of an education that is self-experienced or self-organized, in keeping with the experimental adjustment one daily makes to life and its new perceptions, has not so far really taken root in France. That is why educational self-determination has been fostered from the center—a paradox when so much of political argument, economic practice, and personal preference is extremely localized and individualistic. At the same time, the change is noticeable, being reinforced by the manifest gains from once excluded elements such as physical education, holiday camps, and any real care for the well-being of children. All this is altered, and many parents are convinced that more must be expected from education than was once supposed. Certainly, the religious faction has often enough called active education "godless," while the prosperous call it "communistic." In all countries similar charges are leveled at educational change.

Especially in a country like France it is likely that educational and social reformers lay themselves open to such charges. The formal and informal power of centralized State and Church is so deeply entrenched that only radical measures seem sufficiently potent. Many reformers are occasionally too outspoken. It is notable that some of the prime movers behind the recommendations of the Algiers Commission of 1944 and of the Langevin-Wallon reforms of 1946 were well to the left of center in their politics. As we often have occasion to note, people who in open or fluid democratic societies would merely be mild protestants may be driven by frustration to become iconoclasts in rigid societies. Moreover, quite apart from historical and personal backgrounds, phrases such as "democratizing" education are highly suspect in a country which habitually prides itself on the excellence of its elite, on quality rather than quantity. Therefore sound proposals have come up before parliament again and again, only to be rejected or to become dead letters if they are passed as law. The 1959 reforms were passed by decree under the direction of General de Gaulle.

But every day's delay complicates the dangers in France, which is temperamentally (if not practically) a most progressive country. The legend of past glories and revolutionary principles lives on; yet the millennium does not come. Jaded with overwork and disappointment, but irrepressibly vivacious, French youth plays hard. The worldwide youth problem is especially acute in France. Alcoholism is a national problem affecting even children. Sexual promiscuity is common among students. It looks as though the consequences of demanding too much of youth in school equal those of demanding too little. On the other hand, youth seems to care more than the parents about some things. Among these are European unity (on which young Frenchmen are generally "sold"), social justice, the fusion of classes, and technological advance.

It is obvious by now why it is important for anyone concerned with education in any country to pay close attention to the problems of France. We are not simply looking at a perplexed neighbor. We are looking at some of our own problems in an intensified form. Moreover, those who live in the United States and in Britain should note that when a hitherto underdeveloped country wants an educational model, it does not go to them, but to France. The French system is not only like those of Mediterranean Europe and Latin America; it has been copied extensively even in those Moslem countries which charge France with colonial oppression. This is not because of historical imperialism; it is because the French system is radical, intended eventually to be a universal provider of freedom, equality, and brotherhood, and also suitable for the quick preparation of a professional elite under close government control. Countries such as Afghanistan and Iran, which have no historical connection with French imperialism, need to modernize quickly and perhaps ruthlessly; they have none of the deeply rooted institutions that are a prerequisite of Anglo-Saxon systems. Therefore it is to the "universal mission" of France that they look for their interpretations of education. Desperately depressed countries cannot afford the luxury of waiting for experiments; even if they felt so inclined, they do not have enough financial and material resources. They look for something streamlined and efficient for their purpose. They see it in France. The centralization of the Soviet Union owes much to France.

Countries with a highly centrifugal and locally empirical tradition derived from Britain or copied from the United States (such as Canada, Australia, and New Zealand) often tend towards centralization on the French pattern when faced with geographical difficulties or social and financial inequalities. This tendency is growing on a world-wide scale. It is often an unconscious or unrecognized consequence of industrialization, or a concomitant of great commercial organizations. The centralizing or standardizing assumptions of these can have immense cultural power even where the governmental or scholastic tradition is decentralized, as it is in the United States.

People in countries like ours, therefore, who are concerned about the maintenance of what they believe to be the most democratic standards—equality of consideration that develops the *complementary* partnerships of differing and responsible individuals—may look with anxiety on the world-wide spread of competing alternative ideas. Three quarters of the world's population (probably more) have no idea of democracy. If they have heard of it, they think it incompetent. They may even think it is wicked, for they know that competition is not absent from Western democracies, and they often think that our competition is conducted on the least satisfactory basis. The French system, by contrast, seems to such observers to be both efficient and egalitarian. Still more, it is believed to pick the winners in the international race. The countries longest industrialized can afford (especially if they are rich in the supply of raw materials) to play their way through education. They can perhaps delude the masses with a semblance of universal education, while secretly "creaming off" the elite either by a lengthier schooling or by a more expensive education outside the regular public system. The result, the antidemocratic observer thinks, is the same: the brainy and the skillful are put in charge of development. It may be alleged that the retention of wealth by successful families blocks the adoption of a more efficient system like the French. Underdeveloped countries want food, not frills.

Without accepting these ideas, we can see that others welcome them. They challenge us on our own assumptions about technological superiority and its maintenance; they should make us ask if our own systems are as fair as we suppose. They certainly remind us that if we want our cherished notions to survive we must do some rethinking about the new neighbors we have to understand, and that we can only justify ourselves after radical examination of our consciences.

For these reasons the turbulent story of France seems particularly helpful. Centralization, uniformity, and intellectualism are her disadvantages. They were intended to promote a rational and equal approach to the perfect state that would solve all problems. Now many of her inherited assumptions and methods are outmoded. We too should beware lest our assumptions and confidence outlive the world changes which inevitably envelop us. Even on the home front we should beware of being sure we know the right answer.

What does it really mean if we claim to know the "right" answer? The French for "to be right" is literally "to have *reason*." The same turn of phrase is used in many Latin countries. We of the Anglo-Saxon tradition believe that a thing is all right if it works, but when we come to the deep moral and philosophical problems we are seldom able to rely on pragmatism or expediency. We are not too happy, however, about relying on reason alone, especially in education and public life. Some men claim to "have reason" as others claim to "have religion."

Their neighbors are not so sure. If they are poetic, or perhaps just muddled, they counterclaim that "the heart has its reasons" too.

When we assess anyone else's way of bringing up children we need to use every criterion available—reason, pragmatic or instrumental considerations, together with thought about the separate human beings involved and about their relationship with their neighbors. We cannot just plump for one criterion and stick to that. So it is when we turn around and look at our own system. Fundamentally that is the main purpose of our exercise in looking elsewhere.

In France, the land of theories and principles, and exercise of the intellect, we see how important it is for any social study to pay careful heed to untheoretical entanglements of the context. This context is not simply the web of present connections with the environment, dynamic though these may be in total effect. The context in time matters equally. It is the *contemporary climax* of so many concurrent influences on educational or political decision that will turn the destiny of schools and children for generations to come. Whatever decisions are taken will have to be voiced in some sort of language—the mother tongue of the people; the language of their institutions; the language of children's own awareness and teenage aspirations; the language of the international setting of commerce and communications. How many of these aspects can be confined in the formal school structure, or in the official program?

This manifest need for proper attention to ecology and social dynamics makes nonsense of the abstract formulae of some would-be sages of Comparative Education who wish to tabulate, "juxtapose," or "isolate the variables" for paper predictions to their students or readers. The business of educational planning is not run that way. The daily business of feeling for education on the ground, and helping it to reach its own decisions in a living context, can even less be run that way. Of course there must be meticulous, scientific attention to data like those of population, finance, occupational structure, and the like—each relying on methods appropriate to its constituent social science. But there is no overall method for social study. And when all is said and done, the anatomized elements of our information are still *disiecta membra;* they do not add up to the living body with all its subtle perceptions, or the tricky interplay of its ecological responses. To argue otherwise is to argue one's own irrelevance to the educator and the person being educated; for culture and cultural participation are a series of occasions, each one of which is charged with special significance, but all of which somehow cohere in a kind of total "understanding."

So we leave France, where life still goes on for many at the pace of the ox, where the prizes of the school system are still only a mockery or disappointment to a large section of the population, and where many of those who most passionately love their country quarrel over her as over a mistress. It is paradoxical that France, the land of historical stalemate, is also the source of many of our most progressive ideas. In the eighteenth century these helped to transform the world's political expectations. In the twentieth, new movements of scholastic reform may help to transform access to the traditional treasures of learning in Europe, and unlock them for new applications.

4

GREAT BRITAIN | REVOLUTION WITH RELUCTANCE

About twenty miles of sea separate England and the continent at the nearest point. That narrow but often turbulent sea is part of British minds. In their island fastness the British peoples—the English, the Welsh, the Scots, and the Irish—know that whatever family disagreements they may have at home, together they share something that makes them different from continental communities. It is not easy for a Briton to think of himself as a European, although most British ideas and institutions are part of the European tradition, and although British social philosophy and political experiment were rationalized by the French revolutionaries in European terms that influenced the rest of the world.

This exemplifies the paradox of British life. Throughout history the English Channel and the North Sea have brought invasion after invasion, as well as many cultural influences. In more recent centuries, as increasing national unity brought strength, the English and their

sturdy sister nations have relied on the Channel as a bastion on which
they could mount their resolute defenses, while they have swept the
world in one bold enterprise after another. It is not from insularity that
the English-speaking peoples ring the globe in a Commonwealth such
as history has never known, and that the main world language of today
is that spoken in Elizabethan times by a rather isolated nation of about
four million people.

In the very act of turning their backs on the continent (until the
twentieth-century Common Market), the British looked out upon the
strange but not unfriendly world across the seas. The English words
"overseas" and "abroad" have an inviting sound, unlike the corresponding words in the languages of landlocked peoples. The British, proud
of their bold ventures, are not afraid of experimental uncertainty. They
feel sure they can "go one better" than anyone else. To this extent
their emphasis is on advance, even when lines of advance are tenuously
stretched. Yet they are reluctant revolutionaries and will not be
hustled, although their evolution has, in fact, brought about more
changes than most revolutions.

British self-assurance made victorious Napoleon balk at the Channel.
The same incapacity for acknowledging defeat made Britons stand
quietly firm under incessant aerial bombardment while Hitler's overwhelming might massed invasion forces everywhere. Stubborn habit
rather than logic still makes Britons confident that their way is right
even when others lay down the law. They will work things out their
own way, and change only when a better method has been roughed
out. The British themselves call this "muddling through," and laugh
about it. Philosophers call it "empiricism," a school of thought characteristic of Britain for centuries. Educators call it "pragmatism."

This peculiarity of the British (shared in some measure by other
nations who have copied their habits) claims special study by anyone
interested in education, because it shows the virtues of an evolutionary
approach and at the same time reveals the weaknesses of a patchwork
policy in an increasingly streamlined world. After all, nobody believes
that the medieval strip pattern of agriculture is a serious possibility
today; nor does anyone care to tinker with an old car beyond a certain
limit. Changed technology requires new methods, new models; it also
brings other objectives in view, and provides the means to reach them.
We recognize these truths in our daily life, but we forget sometimes
that they apply equally not only to educational systems as a whole but
also to our ideas about valuable or desirable types of man, about school
subjects of lasting value, and about our own educational activities in
relation to the human problems beyond our frontiers. Britain's external
circumstances have undergone immense alteration in recent history.

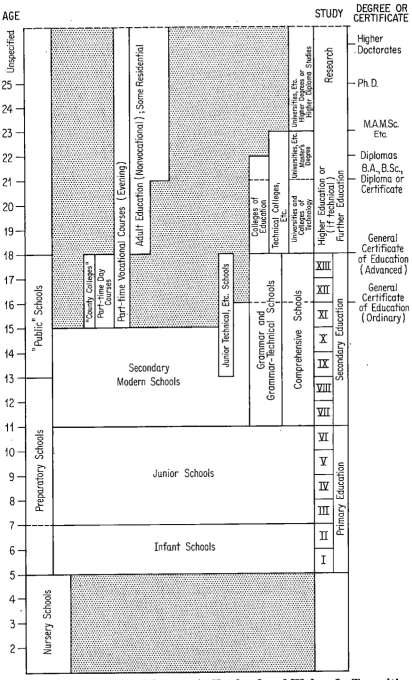

School System in England and Wales: In Transition

Every historic change alters the structure of civilization. However slightly, it modifies the formative pattern of human relationships; that is to say, it teaches people to behave differently toward one another. If people go on learning the old tricks while the world changes around them, they will soon be like educational dinosaurs armed cap-à-pie for the contingencies of yesteryear and just about as useful as dreadnoughts on dry land.

Historically speaking, the empiricism of the British has been a progressive movement. It has emphasized a changing response to changing challenges. It has encouraged a willingness to experiment, and a readiness to tolerate other people's experiments. So British political and educational ideas have not been proclaimed as manifestoes to be forcefully established by this revolution and to be forcefully torn down by counterrevolution. They have tended to be short-term, practical experiments awaiting a pragmatic justification or doomed to rejection if they do not work out. On the other hand, the near-agnostic British feel a deep reverence for anything that has worked for a long time, whether materially or spiritually. Thus they have a monarchy, archaic trappings in government and law, and so on. But these do no harm because their emotional claims do not hinder republican assumptions or modern citizenship.

Yet it can happen that a particular experiment (like the concept of the liberally-educated "gentleman"—not at home in France or really native in America) survives its technological justification, at any rate in its ancient form. We tend to forget that a "gentleman" is an item of technology, a device for a certain social and economic purpose, whose usefulness is conditional upon its being present effectively and in the right number in appropriate circumstances. British domestic and imperial history has made the "gentleman" an effective instrument of government, public relations, and even of research; but the question is now being urgently asked if there has been overproduction of this commodity, at least on the mid-nineteenth-century model. Almost every Briton is fully in favor of having as many "ladies" and "gentlemen" as possible; but the whole context of "gentility" (though not necessarily its essence) has been changed by the specialist demands of the scientific and industrial revolution, and also by the fact that most children sooner or later realize they too can lay claim to it.

The success of the National Health Service and other aspects of the "welfare state," combined with higher standards of living and the widespread availability of good, cheap clothing, makes it impossible now to distinguish "women" from "ladies" or "men" from "gentlemen" by those external marks which used to be so obvious. Furthermore, expanding fields of knowledge and enterprise call for other attributes than the generalized polish on the character which was once so dazzling in social encounter. Knowledge, efficiency, and a wider sensitivity are now called for. It is recognized that these things are not inherent in anyone, nor simply acquired by appropriate routines during childhood, but are part of a continuous contact with life as an adult working citizen. The realization of these facts is particularly critical for Britain. This social and technological reorientation is pivotal to the educational changes now going on. Therefore, the "gentleman"-producing schools, methods, and subjects are now being re-examined, and in time they may reach a pragmatically justified relationship with the actual conditions of modern Britain.[1]

This sort of process goes on in all countries, of course, but there are not really many places where there is so little bitterness, or where such colossal changes have peacefully and permanently taken place. Parents and teachers everywhere want to combine the "best of the old" with the harsh realities of the new. In Britain they can see this tug of war going on under the rules of fair play. The solution is not yet clearly in sight, but the play is. Furthermore, in Britain it may be possible to foresee some compromise between claims of centralization and those of decentralization. France's system was centralized and planned by history and by revolutionary renovation; Britain's long standing reliance on growth and local empiricism, her mistrust of planning and centralization, have perforce given way to national arrangements of a comprehensive kind. The chop and change of British educational development has left many serious anomalies still far from being resolved; but it has also brought in some straightforward and exemplary solutions, and it shows some praiseworthy (perhaps temporary) compromises that others may envy. British religious and political history encourage tolerant experiment.

Though the British are habitually protestant, they have evolved hybrid forms of Protestantism very different from those of Europe. British socialism, too, is unlike the continental varieties; it mistrusts theories and insists on evolutionary change. Radicalism is fairly polite, therefore, and cautious. The official Conservative and Liberal parties, instead of being more intransigent in their particular beliefs than their European counterparts, are less so; they are more socialistic, and are wholly committed (for example) to the social services program.

To an outside observer, Great Britain is a land of paradox. There is an easy assumption that radical self-government is everyone's right; yet there is a monarchy and an hereditary peerage. The average work-

---

[1] See the appendix on "The Gentleman: The Evolution of an English Ideal" in my *World Perspectives in Education,* London: Methuen; and Indianapolis: Bobbs-Merrill, 1962.

ing man, until recently, had an earning power not much higher than the average American Negro's; but he and his family have complete social security in health, pension, and unemployment services, and a university or professional education need not cost him anything. There is also strict public control over the rich, their incomes and their legacies. Class distinctions are strong, and subtly graded from the highest to the lowest; but external politeness should not hide from an overseas observer the fact that money and family prestige alone buy other people's respect and compliance less in Britain than, for example, in the United States.

Local self-determination is strong, not just in municipal and county government but in the thousands of voluntary organizations that make British life such a nucleated system of attachments. These even impinge directly on national activities such as politics and education. Yet British central government is also strong. Technological efficiency, and the requirements of external trade in a world devoid of imperial advantages, impose some centralization on what was a deeply decentralized way of life. They thus necessitate rationalized budgeting and careful planning for society as a whole. Though there are still many social and economic inequalities, more social changes took place during the first fifty years of this century than most bloody revolutions elsewhere were able to achieve; and since about 1944 an even more remarkable social revolution has been quietly engineered and consolidated through the schools.

Later in this chapter we shall see that recent changes in university and technological education seem likely to produce an unprecedented challenge to prevailing assumptions about the social order and to traditional prerogatives in the school system. Just here we should notice that such changes have involved urgent national planning, as distinct from locally based and empirical evolution. They have been particularly associated with postwar economic development; thus they have tended to escape notice as social and educational reforms also. It seems likely, or possible, that measures of this sort may bypass many traditional stumbling blocks, or make them gradually irrelevant. However that may be, planning is a growing and accepted feature of all public administration. Of socialistic origin, planning has been equally marked during the 1950s and 1960s under Conservative governments. It was under Conservative auspices, for example, that the National Economic Development Corporation was established, preparing the way for a labor government's National Plan in 1965, with its important repercussions on schools as well as economics. Conservatives, too, saw that higher technological education was put on a new footing, and that university expansion was accelerated. But because these or comparable schemes have long formed part of their political opponents' plans, the logic of their implementation is often resisted by Conservatives when we come down to the practicalities of local government, or to the question of which pattern of schooling is likely to be fairest and most successful in developing and discovering talent. Hence the resistance to the comprehensive school, and to any substantial change in the prerogatives of private schools. Yet many influential Conservatives—including a former Minister of Education—have declared their acceptance of comprehensive schools established voluntarily or "eventually." The big quarrel has been about pushing slowly moving local authorities to move against their inclination.

These apparent inconsistencies can be understood in the light of what has been said before, that a fundamental assumption of British life is that every person or group is entitled to attempt a satisfactory way of living or doing things. Britons do not always live up to their principles, of course; but the "hands off" tradition is very powerful. Respect for disagreement has positive results in the response of minorities, which are very orderly because they do get a reasonable chance to develop. At a more trivial level the survival of ancient buildings, archaic roads, effete machinery, and so on, is due to unwillingness to destroy a thing that somehow works. Though British public administration is in some respects much more socialistic than that of the United States, for example, there is far greater reluctance to commandeer land for roads, or to undertake big reconstruction schemes in the public interest. So many legal and customary safeguards protect the "small man." "An Englishman's home is his castle" is still a favorite saying.

It is difficult to find room for all the castles and prerogatives that this belief should justify. The United Kingdom (that is, all the British Isles excluding the autonomous Republic of Eire) has 53 million people in an area smaller than the state of Oregon. Of these, 45 million live in England, which is only slightly larger than the state of North Carolina. England's population density is over 823 to the square mile—a figure which is more astonishing when we take into account the moorland areas and regions that are predominantly agricultural. In spite of the English moors, to any Englishman traveling abroad the predominant impression is that of space. The United States looks particularly empty, even in the industrial East.

The mention of travel reminds us that people nowadays do not "stay put," not even in castles. There are still villages in Britain where not even modernization of some externals prevents us from imagining what life was like before the Industrial Revolution. In them, and in many small towns, it is easier still to overlook some of the implications for social mobility of all those more recent British inventions: the railroad, radio, television, radar, and jet aircraft—to say nothing of devices learned from other countries, such as the automobile, which has given Britain by far the most congested roads in the world. There were huge internal migrations at the time of the Industrial Revolution. The world's modern urbanization problem began in England. But when the population settled down again after the eighteenth- and nineteenth-century upheavals, patterns of residence, employment, local government, and emotional attachment developed that in some ways have kept Britain more locally entrenched than any other industrialized country in the world. The tension between organized local interest and wider national need—not least in questions of job-seeking and education —is one of the serious complications of government today.

Since 1945, however, new industries have grown up faster and others have been redistributed spontaneously without official intervention. Thus some regions that were industrial beehives a century ago are relatively depressed and fading. Moreover, the migration of the young or talented toward the Southeast (already noticeable in the 1920s and 1930s), became more marked after World War II. The result was not merely metropolitan conurbations which are any planner's nightmare, but deliberately planned new towns. Coupled with this process, we must reckon in a growing readiness of private industry and public government to agree on the need to replan industrial siting, communications, and housing on large regional bases. All these developments have a direct bearing on the distribution and control of schools, colleges, and other aids to education. It is, therefore, convenient at this point to review the administrative structure.[2]

Northern Ireland has its own parliament, but the rest of the United Kingdom is governed by Parliament in London, although certain powers (such as Scots law and the control of Scottish education) are entrusted to the separate jurisdiction of the Scots. Education in England and Wales is subject to the supervision of Parliament insofar as it receives full or partial financial support from taxes. The very important private sector was not supervised before October 1, 1957. Although the 1944 Education Act, which reorganized the system in England and Wales, enabled the Minister of Education to inspect private schools, this inspection is only now beginning. The Ministry of Education (now called the Department of Education and Science) does not own or operate any schools, employ any teachers, or draw up any

---

[2] Further information about the background of occupational change and administrative control in relation to the need for flexibility is given in G. Baron: *Society, Schools and Progress in England,* 1966, especially chaps. 2 and 3.

yllabus. It is the Minister's responsibility to make sure that each
ducational district in England and Wales (called a Local Education
Authority, or LEA) has a satisfactory provision for education at all
tages within the framework of the law.

With the unique exception of the Inner London Education Authority
which in 1965 took over the educational responsibilities of the former
London County Council), the LEAs do not exist independently as
single-purpose educational enterprises; they serve as the education department or committee of multipurpose local government units, which
are usually counties or county boroughs—that is, large towns with
county powers. The Inner London Education Authority, however,
plans and administers the school and college systems (and other educational enterprises, such as an educational television service) for the
central metropolitan area once administered by the London County
Council. Strictly speaking, the Inner London Education Authority is
a special committee of the Greater London Council which, in 1965,
was set up to take charge of and coordinate all administrative services
both for the inner London area and for the newly formed outer ring of
"London boroughs." Each of the latter is an education authority (LEA)
in its own right. The Inner London Education Authority conducts a
larger educational enterprise than the ministries of some European
countries, such as Denmark.

Some of the other LEAs administer education for populations exceeding one million; others for fewer than 100,000. Within an LEA,
some districts with more than 60,000 inhabitants are allowed considerable independence in school matters; these are called "excepted
districts." The total number of Local Education Authorities in England
and Wales in 1966 was 162 (comprising 59 counties, 102 large boroughs,
and the Inner London Education Authority). Education now absorbs
two thirds of any local administration's budget. Although centralized
reimbursement generally pays back about 60 percent of local costs,
anxiety is caused financially and also sometimes because of fears of
local incompetence in other respects.

Until the 1950s, reimbursement of local educational expenditures
(from central taxation resources administered nationally) was undertaken on a proportional basis directly related to school expenses, with
further aid according to special need. Some elements are still so treated,
as an exception, like teacher preparation (which is totally reimbursed),
and technical education (which is specially encouraged). But on the
whole, education costs are now lumped together with all other local
administration costs in calculating the proportion of expenditure which
local government can claim from central government resources. (Some
of the costs they themselves must always bear, of course; reimburse-

ment is only for generalized public services.) One result of these changes is that progressive local education authorities are inclined to be more generous than some others. If it were not for the strict housekeeping and building control which have been enforced in Britain during the postwar period, discrepancies would be even greater. Questions of money apart, local authorities vary in their frame of mind, usually reflecting their political majority.

Local education authorities, according to the 1944 Education Act, can draw up their own plans for implementing that act, and have great freedom to experiment in various ways. However, they must satisfy the Secretary of State for Education and Science (formerly Minister) that their plans cover all foreseeable needs of all sections of their population at all ages and levels. The LEAs are not compelled to provide all the opportunities themselves; but they must see that they are provided, and that they are either wholly maintained from taxation or so aided that no one is deprived of opportunity on financial grounds. Equalization arrangements thus assure that poorer districts do just as well as prosperous ones. On the other hand, the control possibilities inherent in "satisfying the Minister" (who has power over the central purse) have been used in the past to *prevent* the implementation of LEA schemes for fully comprehensive schools (in 1954, under the Conservative administration of Winston Churchill). Correspondingly in 1965, a Labour Secretary of State for Education and Science issued a national directive to the effect that all LEAs must supply information within a year showing in what way the now official policy of comprehensive schools would be implemented. A continuing tussle can be expected between the advocates of total local independence and those concerned with implementing nationally desirable policies in an increasingly mobile Britain. In fact, LEAs catering to more than two thirds of the child population had already introduced comprehensive or near-comprehensive schooling into their plans before the 1965 directive was issued.

Local education authorities employ teachers; the central Department of Education and Science does not. LEAs also recommend curricula and methods; but the final determination of curriculum is left to a considerable degree to the head teachers of schools. There is nothing equal to the centralized direction of these matters which one finds in American school districts, and there is no exact equivalent of the American school superintendent. Local and ministry inspectors, like American "supervisors" in theory, are advisers and expediters. They cannot really order anyone to do anything, and they do not behave as though they wanted to.

In any case, beyond pointing to the practice of exemplary schools and teachers, there is no norm or desirable end to which they could officially point. There are no official syllabuses, not even at the local level. To a certain extent, the university-linked but effectively self-regulating examination boards (which operate school-leaving examinations) do impose certain curricular requirements; they have been accused of exercising a stranglehold on the upper level of academically-oriented schools. But it should be stressed that even here the majority of the examiners are school teachers, who have the remedy if they choose to use it. Since 1965, a quite new kind of Certificate of Secondary Education has been offered at a lower level of attainment (suitable for the average-to-good pupil about the age of 16), to be administered at grass roots level under the teachers' control, with 14 regional coordinating boards.

However, the whole question of educational policy and of reorientating schools generally is being reviewed in a totally altered perspective—not just in the light of curriculum study, the study of how we learn, and similar educational considerations, but in the light of national economic planning. Indeed, one has to consider the evolutionary prospects of Europe as a whole. During the 1960s, all Western European countries have been greatly concerned, for example, about the shared development of their science, technology, and basic supporting research. So intricate and costly are the demands of "big science" alone—both financially and in terms of personnel—that they can hardly be met at the national level, but must be internationally conceived and implemented. European cooperation for atomic research (in Geneva, at the European Center for Nuclear Research, for instance) is but one example of international interdependence of the functional kind that seldom comes under political dispute. Economic and manpower considerations, and studies of such socially cataclysmic phenomena as migration and the advent of automation, come more to the fore every year. They therefore make preindustrial levels of decentralized administration seem archaic, and introduce special problems for Britain.

Among the necessities for Britain is a reappraisal of the value of decentralized responsibility as seen in schools. Although the head teacher has, as we said, huge powers of decision about the curriculum, devolution of authority goes deeper than this. Almost every subject specialist may draw up his own syllabus or prescribe his own preferred books and methods within a generously permissive outer framework. There is nothing to guarantee that such a teacher appreciates the implications of curriculum research, methodological experiments, or the subtler forms of reorientation which are penetrating all thoughts about education.

A Schools Council for Curriculum and Examinations, representing all educational interests but with teachers in the majority, was set up in 1964 to advise the Department of Education and Science. It operates with an annual budget of over £1 million for research and experiment. Without directive powers, the Schools Council has nevertheless important prestige in indicating suitable directions, while the Secretary of State for Education and Science could assume directive powers. There has been a belated, but impressive, commitment to large-scale educational research at the national level. The research is sponsored not only by official bodies, such as the Schools Council and government itself, but by charities such as the Nuffield and the Gulbenkian Foundations which have aided basic enquiries or specifically scholastic research.

In 1964–1965 alone, public expenditure on education (not counting private payments) amounted to £1,459,000,000 in England and Wales, representing 13.5 percent of all public expenditure. It is not surprising, therefore, that a sensible direction and on-the-spot efficiency should be sought by whatever means research can reveal. Public expenditure on education is expected to increase by almost one-third over the years 1965–1970, with corresponding implications for manpower distribution (not only of teachers, but including teachers) and for effective use of all skilled personnel. It is not surprising that the Department of Education and Science increasingly sees education within the framework of the National Plan, if not so obviously or officially as in France. This trend is fraught with implications for amateur activity at grass roots level. Where any teacher or school board is concerned, such activity is not *self*-determination for *them* but the orientation of children's lives for the next generation.

Moreover, there are manifest limits to local competence, whether amateur or expert judgment is used. The expanding demand for higher education, for expensive technical plant, extracurricular reinforcement and all kinds of follow-up services, re-emphasizes local limitations with every passing month. No lives are to be lived locally any more, and none can be determined locally.

The British government relied heavily on long-term statistical extrapolations in predicting the development of higher education after 1963; and for some years before this edition was published, careful preparations had been made for a large-scale "computable model" of educational needs for a generation or so ahead—not theoretical, but practical. Such quantitative projections, far from being utopian, have previously erred on the side of underestimating growth. Demand mushrooms even more.

Inseparable from strictly educational thought for the future (already costing more than £1 million a year in Schools Council researches alone), are the deliberations of related bodies. A Social Science Research Council was established in 1965. Likewise, the National Research Development Council fosters postgraduate studies, and there is an Advisory Council for Technology. All these careful enquiries, destined to develop strongly and form a kind of contextually sensitive matrix for educational growth, must be set within the wider housekeeping of the National Plan sustained by the National Economic Development Corporation. It should not be supposed that such research-based growth is socialistic or confined to Britain. In their several ways, the great industries and commercial enterprises are finding their bearings and reorienting themselves, not in an insular way, but in line with trends throughout Europe and the world at large. In education itself, the international survey of educational achievement (IEA) associated with UNESCO, the comparative work of the Council of Europe, and the developmental studies of the Organization for Economic Cooperation and Development (OECD) all remind us constantly of dynamic, international trends—indeed necessities. How can the last third of the twentieth century, therefore, be ruled solely by the considerations and apparatus of the 1930s? Yet this we must continue to use, and introduce the future through today's administration.

In Britain there is not the same divorce between teaching and educational administration that is familiar to some other countries. Inspectors and administrative officers are recruited from among the more successful teachers. Inspectors, by their very nature, become aware of enterprising teaching, and so are able to contribute practical common sense and progressive thought in their visits. They also draw up advisory pamphlets which the Department of Education and Science publishes. The local authorities get the benefit of this service too, because the inspectors advise them also, and sit in on a large number of advisory committees. The LEAs have their own national organization in an Association of Education Committees, and their chief education officers are in close touch with one another. Of course, some are less progressive and generous than others, but the moral pressure to modernize is great. As a last resort, the central government (through the Department of Education and Science) could withhold its contribution to local expenses.

Thus the British system of central control over minimum standards is powerful though gentlemanly. It permits widespread local variation and personal experiment, but leaves no loophole for slackers. This paradoxical tolerance, indeed encouragement, of local initiative—combined with an insistence on the public interest—has tended to cut down reliance on direction from above, and to increase both the amount of *permissive* legislation and the rather polite advisory services. In favorable circumstances this state of affairs encourages a strong sense of personal as well as local responsibility; but its virtue, like many others, has an associated vice—that of inconsistency and hesitation. The organizational habits of centuries become a state of mind. There is little point in bossing a Briton. Before he will budge, you usually have to show him the logic of the move and produce some pragmatic sanction for it. This is not merely the constant message of his educational arrangements; it is the only justification for their present jumble. However, this is at last being sorted out, just as railways and roads have had to be. We can remind ourselves that these, too, were once under local or private control.

It is characteristic that educational law does not compel parents to send their children to school; they are compelled to secure them a proper education between the ages of 5 and 15 (16 after 1970). But it is also characteristic that children do not merely go to school; they are most faithful in attendance. The absentee problem familiar elsewhere is almost nonexistent in Great Britain. If, however, parents persisted in neglecting their children's education (which in practically every case would be by nonattendance at school), the children could be taken away temporarily as "in need of care and protection," and the parents could be fined or even sent to prison. Of course, the minimum insistence on education permits parents to employ tutors (if they are rich enough), to send their children to private establishments, or to avail themselves of the publicly provided schools. Private or partly private education flourishes to an extent unfamiliar in most other countries (including the autonomous Dominions of the British Commonwealth). This is particularly true of England, and in England is especially true of the comparatively wealthy. Some private schools are of exceptionally high quality; but some are, to say the least, no match for the publicly provided schools. There is increasing impatience with the present disparity of school opportunities, frequently leading to different social futures and different prospects in higher education. This range is wider, perhaps, than in any other democratic country. Sometimes it is a matter of superior schooling; more often than not such social differentiation bears little relation to the intrinsic merits of the schooling given or of the children thus differentiated.

On the other hand, geographic or economic background does not usually affect a child's access to first-class education in the publicly provided schools, though in 1963 the Newsom Report (*Half Our Future*) stirred the national conscience by revealing social handicaps which permanently blemish educational prospects. Apart from local amelioration, a national reappraisal has had to be made, to make sure not only that oportunity is potentially there but that it is provided on equal terms. One important consideration is that teachers everywhere receive the same basic rates of pay. Awards are made above the minimum for higher academic qualifications, for experience, for special responsibility, and so on. But these awards are nationally agreed upon between the representatives of the LEAs and the teachers' unions, and are enforced on all local authorities. In London and other large cities with heavy urban expenses, an agreed supplement is paid. Therefore it does not matter very much whether a school is in a village or a city; there is the same opportunity for teachers with good qualifications. In fact, some heavily industrialized and smoky cities are finding it increasingly difficult to get teachers.

At one time, teachers were paid according to the type of school in which they were employed. Now all teachers in publicly provided schools are paid the same according to their qualifications and responsibility. So it would be possible, for example, for a Ph.D. to be financially as well off in an infant school as in the upper classes of a grammar school (academic high school). Of course, other considerations usually attract teachers to their appropriate level. The main advantage of the present arrangement is that social distinctions between junior and secondary school work, and between work in the various kinds of secondary school, have been largely removed. Higher salaries, of course, are paid in institutions of higher learning, such as colleges of education, technical colleges, and universities. But here again the rates payable for the type of institution are normally paid throughout the country. It is an axiom of British educational thought that every child should have access to the education for which he seems qualified by "age, ability, and aptitude," and that differences of origin and present circumstances shall be no handicap. Educational opportunity is now open to all up to and beyond the university, and entrance is open to all professions.

This is a remarkable transformation from what can be remembered by many people. Until 1902, local school boards were not strictly entitled to offer education beyond the elementary stage at public expense, although many of them did. The meager higher opportunities thus afforded were in the higher classes of elementary school premises. Some school boards were not at all eager to spend money. They had been created in 1870 in order to fill the gaps in elementary education provided until then by religious denominations receiving direct government grants for the building, improvement, and extension of schools. The first of these grants was paid in 1833, and the amounts had been gradually increased until, in 1870, the Church of England maintained elementary schools in all towns and most villages. The nonconformist and Roman Catholic churches also had numerous schools.

At that period public opinion could not consider any education worthwhile if it did not have a firm doctrinal basis offered by convinced, practicing Christians. The Church of England's firm grip on public education, however, (amounting to a monopoly in many small townships) caused so much dissatisfaction among other Christian sects that the latter eventually supported a campaign for nonsectarian public schooling financed by taxation. The resulting 1870 Act was a compromise, however. It let the churches retain the schools they had before the law was passed; yet it established "school boards" to supplement Church education, and not to supersede it. Thus the country was covered with a patchwork provision. Voluntary (church) activity had provided as much as it could, or thought fit; the deficiencies were made good by local school boards. Board schools were fully financed out of local taxes ("rates"). Church schools at first received no such help, though after 1891 they had support from central taxation.

Elementary education was not made free everywhere at first, because to forbid fees would have put church congregations in bankruptcy, especially where there were many children. Partly for this reason, and partly because of misguided tenderness toward "parental rights," compulsory school attendance was not universally imposed until 1880, although most local school boards had bylaws requiring it. Even then, compulsory attendance was for only five years, from ages 5 to 10, though here again some local boards were more progressive. By 1891, elementary education was generally free, and the token fees (about twopence a week) had nearly all been discontinued. This jumble of hesitant reforms exemplified British "muddling through" in education. Those who suffered were the children.

Only in 1902 was a coordinated national school system secured. In that year, newly constituted local education authorities were required to make sure that elementary, secondary, and higher education was available in their areas. To make sure it was also accessible, the authorities were empowered to pay fees and grant scholarships.

Thus public secondary schools, linking the elementary schools with the universities and the professions, were established in England for the first time. There had already been similar schools in Wales for 13 years, and for a much longer period in Scotland. France had had them for almost a century. Other European countries had left England far behind. In fact it has been said that the expanded elementary education provided by the Act of 1870 was demanded as much by the requirements of modern industry as by any humane considerations. Also, that the 1902 Act's extension of a higher provision with tax support was similarly called for by fear of European and American competition. Undoubtedly, skilled workmen and clerks were being imported from abroad. British economy had been cushioned against competition by the fact that early industrialization was mainly a British invention. Overseas markets were captured, and foreign investments on a vast scale gave the manufacturers and merchants an easy living that prevented them from seeing future needs clearly. Education on a much more thoroughgoing scale was one of the investments necessary. The many private or partly private secondary schools were not sufficiently numerous or available.

It would be unfair to leave the impression that only bread-and-butter considerations brought about an improvement in British education. From the very beginning of the nineteenth century the churches had been actively extending elementary education as a work of charity, keeping children off the noisome streets of factory towns, and still more, from day-long labor in factories and mines. But what these schools offered did not fully serve worldly ambitions. Self-help organizations of many types among the working people themselves had pressed for education—not merely elementary, but up to and including the university level. This voluntary provision, however, was severely limited by the difficulty of getting it after an arduous day's work, and by the lack of systematic preparation for university and professional examinations. All British universities and skilled professions are exacting in their admission requirements.

The 1902 Act was revolutionary, even though some of its proposals had been set before Parliament as long ago as 1833. The revolution it has brought about is seen more clearly when we look at its results about half a century later. British society is transformed. Voluntary effort (nowadays called private enterprise in economic circles) is no longer trusted alone to provide the nation's requirements. There is still much more private initiative in British tax-aided education than in American, for instance; but it is brought under vigilant public supervision and regulation, and is increasingly appraised by national criteria of attainment and need. Voluntary effort is not so much curbed as prodded. If it does not move nimbly or skillfully enough it is superseded. This is seldom done by suppression; the public provision is raised in quality and extended in scope so as to make other arrangements unnecessary. At the same time, pressure is mounting to prevent private funds from being a disguised way of buying privilege in later life. Of course, to remove this possibility altogether would be a superhuman task. Unfair advantage is still perpetuated by private schools; but the extent to which children can now mature with equal chances would have seemed impossible a generation ago.

The term "elementary school" is no longer used, because it was associated with a type of schooling kept deliberately inferior. Children have free primary education (to 11); free secondary education (11 to

15, as a minimum, or to 18 if they wish and show ability); free university education if they satisfy university entrance requirements and do not come from prosperous homes; and free admission to all technical and commercial careers. No financial barrier stands in the way of an able child. Admission to higher education in a university, college of science and technology, and most technical and art colleges, almost invariably secures the student a scholarship for free tuition and substantial or complete maintenance during the period of study. Where wealthier parents make a contribution that usually approximates roughly to the cost of supporting the student at home. This aspect of financial support (so far granted automatically as a right) inevitably makes the over-all expansion of higher education a more burdensome public liability in Britain than in any other noncommunist country. It also, in part, explains British preoccupation with university admission standards. In fact, the huge and continuing expansion of tertiary education seems bound to introduce budgetary problems that may necessitate a reappraisal of grant policy.

Inseparable from the school provision is that offered by the social services. The national health service assures everyone complete medical attention (hospitalization, surgical, dental, ophthalmic, and psychological services) from the beginning to the end of his life. This service is like the school provision in that everyone pays taxes for it, but no one (physician or patient) is required to take part in it. 95 percent of all doctors and over 80 percent of the population do participate, however. Patients choose their own doctor. No one is denied full health opportunities by his own or his parents' poverty. Children get vitamin foods and school meals at subsidized prices, or free if necessary. In cases of real hardship they can even get free clothing. All these advantages, though dreamed of, must have seemed remote at the beginning of this century. There is no genuine, ascertainable need not catered to in the attempt to provide every child with everything needed for full development—at home, in school, or in special services for the handicapped. A generation ago it was still possible to see children whose education suffered severely because they were undernourished or diseased. Now the schools are full of healthy, well-cared-for youngsters. Homes are also much more responsible places than they were in 1902.

The grudging nature of most early provision for popular education and health has made all parties in Britain now determined to secure comprehensive facilities. Differences arise only over questions of how much, by whom, and in what circumstances social services can be best provided. Voluntary efforts in the past prepared the way for national schemes; but they were unequally distributed, spasmodic, and incapable of securing fair opportunities for all. Past inconsistencies also account for the survival of serious difficulties in education.

Among the problems that still defy solution is the future of the many kinds of private school and denominational tax-supported schools. The vast majority of the latter are Church of England; a large number are Roman Catholic; a few belong to other denominations, and a handful are Jewish. The teachers in almost all cases are lay persons; but Catholic schools are sometimes taught by nuns, brothers, or priests. Church schools were paramount before 1870. They were denied support from local taxes after 1870, though they could still sometimes get per capita grants from central funds. However, the Act of 1902 enabled them to draw all their running expenses (though not the cost of initial building or maintaining the premises) from local taxation ("rates"). All recognized church schools—those that were called elementary schools before 1944—catering to children of compulsory school age, benefit in this way. Their teachers get the same salaries as other local authority teachers, but they are usually appointed by the local clergy with or without advice. In nearly every case, they belong to the appropriate denomination.

Church secondary schools that cater to children between the ages of 11 and 18, and offer a rather more advanced type of education, can also benefit in this way. They must apply for status as an "aided" school, and show that they are doing the same kind of job as a local authority secondary school of the same type—with the additional characteristic of being religious. In many of these church schools (especially the Catholic schools, of course) the administrative staff and many of the teachers are nuns, brothers, or priests. The religious authorities who engage them use the same academic and professional criteria as the LEA. Where such an arrangement is made, the tuition, like that in the local authorities' own schools, is free. The Catholic community, and some members of the Church of England, think this partial support is unfair in view of the rising costs of building. Yet over the years the proportion of denominational school costs paid by taxation must amount to at least 90 percent over all. It may actually reach 95 percent even when the church's original purchase of the school site and buildings, and their external maintenance, are included.

Furthermore, a number of church schools which were in process of reorganization in 1944 (and called "special agreement" schools) received up to 75 percent of the physical costs of that reorganization. This privilege was extended on a large scale to meet subsequent reorganization of church schools that required new building. Reorganization was specially needed at the secondary level. In 1966, building grants, up to 80 percent henceforward, were made available to *all new* voluntary schools. It was made clear at the time that this offer terminated the piecemeal adjustment that had taken place within the framework of the 1944 Act, and that any further raising of the issue would very likely bring into question the whole 1944 religious compromise. Whereas once the Church of England was the main controller and spokesman for voluntary schools, the growing indifference of Protestants has now left Roman Catholics as the chief crusaders. There is an increasing tendency, however, to view schools in a national perspective of educational need. This has stiffened resistance to what once seemed domestic or parochial rights appropriate to a system of limited, local enterprise. However, the very small proportion of total costs which the churches still have to bear is felt by their members to be an intolerable burden. Voluntary schools total about 10,000 of the 29,000 tax-maintained schools, with between 20 and 25 percent of the children.

Some other church schools (nearly all primary, and nearly all Church of England) have preferred what is called "controlled" status under the 1944 Act. They get the local education authority to pay *all* their costs in return for handing over their buildings. The LEA will then appoint all teachers, except that, for the appointment of the head teacher and of "reserved" teachers whose job it is to offer denominational instruction, the LEA will consult the foundation managers of the school. Such denominational instruction is then given for two periods a week.

In Scotland the arrangements for denominational schools are quite different from those in England. Since 1918, all church schools have been under the management of local education authorities, which maintain them and select and pay their teachers. Safeguards are given to protect their denominational character and the sectarian character of their staffs. Religious education is not inspected. In practice this means that more primary schools in Scotland have strong church associations, being either Protestant (mainly Presbyterian) or Catholic. In Holland a similar arrangement prevails, except that there is a third group of schools—the secular. Dutch educators complain that their country is being increasingly divided into three camps—a complaint that is certainly justified.

A number of church schools in England and Wales take advantage of other arrangements open to private secondary schools generally, whether religious or not. They are able to ask the Ministry of Education to recognize and aid them as "direct grant schools." Nonsectarian trust foundations are the usual recipients of this recognition, which is granted only if the schools are not conducted for profit, have a high standard of secondary education and premises, and give a proportion (at least a quarter) of their places to children who pay no fees. "Direct grant schools" may also be required to allow the local education authority to fill a further quarter of their places with children for whom it affords free places by paying their fees to the school. Even ordinary fee-payers must be of a high standard. In 1943, there were 232 such schools; in 1950, there were 164. In 1966, there were 179 direct grant grammar schools—the number having grown because of the inclusion of some previously independent schools. In fact, 63 of the well-known "Public Schools" to be described later are direct grant grammar schools.

The majority of schools in the category of "direct grant" were not primarily intended to be denominational schools. They were once exclusive secondary schools catering to wealthier children, though they now admit an increasing number of free-place children. However, it must be admitted that the "snob value" of these schools is noticeable. They are often able to take their pick of the bright children applying for admission. In addition, they are sometimes able to afford better facilities and smaller classes than the schools maintained by the local authorities. Finally, they sometimes attract better qualified or more enterprising teachers who have their eye on improved prospects of promotion. The majority of these schools are no longer associated with the Church of England, though at the time of their foundation it was probably assumed that most "respectable" citizens were.

In discussing this last category we passed from the strictly denominational classification to the partly supported independent or semi-independent schools. These originally attracted public support from taxes, because they were once the only schools offering secondary education at a reasonable rate. The Ministry of Education thus indirectly made good the lack of publicly provided schools. But this does not apply today. The justification for such categories was historic; the inequalities are in the present. Local education authorities can also assist schools for particular educational purposes. As a rule, the acceptance of public money means being under some public control; this is normally limited to providing a certain proportion of free places to children who have attended public primary schools. We must question whether all these semi-independent and socially attractive alternatives can be financed in their present form alongside the public system, if they "cream off" children—and teachers—for social or intellectual reasons from the publicly maintained grammar schools (academic high schools), and thus impair their development. It is paradoxical that, without their present support from taxation, few direct grant schools could continue to exist; and certainly most of their pupils would be "priced out" if economic fees had to be charged to maintain independence.

Other than the schools receiving partial tax support, there are the completely independent schools financed entirely by fees or by ancient foundations. They number about 5000 and have 500,000 pupils, of whom 10 percent are over 15 years old. A small minority of these schools enjoy international fame, and rightly. Examples of the great Public Schools are Eton, Harrow, and Winchester, which are not at all public but very exclusive and expensive. Many independent schools are comparable only to the publicly maintained grammar school. Indeed, the majority perhaps are not nearly so good. They are actually genteel alternatives to the grammar school or to the secondary modern school, accommodating children who have not been catered to by the tax-supported institutions. A large number are, in fact, primary schools (though it would be a bold man who said so!), preparing boys and girls for the minor Public Schools. Most of these "preparatory" schools are undistinguished, but on the whole they do a useful job. Independent schools receive no tax support (with rare exceptions of a merely token kind) and, until 1957, they were not inspected by the Ministry of Education unless they invited inspection so as to secure "recognition as efficient." A number of them did so for prestige. Yet the independent schools are of really great importance in Britain's social system. In prosperous London suburbs, and among the elite of the provincial towns, they have a high popularity because they impart a socially desirable accent to their young charges, because they prepare children in appropriate subjects for the examinations that admit them to Public Schools, and because they often have smaller classes than the publicly provided primary schools. The importance of the southern English accent, and of examinations, in British life will be dealt with shortly.

It is a matter of historic interest worth mentioning here that the Public Schools got their name because they were once what it implies, being monastic foundations intended for the education of the less wealthy. However, instead of being ladders for all, and leading poor boys to a career in the Church or the professions, they have in recent centuries been the preserve of the governing classes. As late as 1962, over 40 percent of the students at Oxford University and 60 percent of those at Cambridge University (thus enjoying a socially favorable start in public life) had been to boarding schools of this type. Indeed, one Oxford college recently had 75 percent of its student body from such schools. Public Schools' importance can be shown in another way. If we interpret the term "Public School" broadly, roughly 12 percent of all grammar (academic) school pupils are in them, including 20 percent of all those in the "sixth form" (top classes); while approximately 20 percent of all university entrants come from them. About one third of all the highest posts in industry and commerce are held by "old boys" of Public Schools, and about two thirds of those in the learned professions.

During the nineteenth century, the majority of the present Public Schools were founded in order to cater to the sons of rising manufacturers and merchants. Reformed by such crusaders as Arnold of Rugby, and Thring of Uppingham, they have provided a thorough though sometimes formal preparation for the more respectable professions. Perhaps more than any other instrument, the Public Schools account for the astonishing absorptive capacity of the privileged upper middle classes, especially in England. The ruling class will generally accept anyone who can make the grade and conform to the exacting requirements of the "approved type." Among these are possession of the southern English accent (not native to any part of the country, but polished as a class index) and an habitual confident elegance. These are, at least in the intentions of Public School educators, only the external tokens of strength of character, of what psychologists (but not economists) call socialization, and of cultivated sensibility. It is important not to underestimate the high standards of teaching, study, sportmanship, and service in these schools. Their academic requirements for admission are severe; their regime is strict, often Spartan. Their fees are high (not much below an average employee's yearly wage), for a child's annual schooling and residence. Scholarships are few.[3] Several proposals, such as the Fleming scheme, have from time to time suggested that some scholarships should be made available to the poorest children. It is not surprising that the combination of high academic and social standards, strong insistence on "character" and careful home backgrounds, has given the Public Schools immense prestige. The fact that nearly all these schools—and all the most famous—are boarding establishments gives close control over personal development. Many people still assume that leadership and personal integrity can only be developed in these schools, or according to their fashion. Though rather less than 3 percent[4] of British children go to

---

[3] Direct fees at the time of writing averaged between £450 and £550 per annum, and many additional costs (clothing for example, and games requirements) must be reckoned in. Thus Public Schools are out of range for all but the top 10 percent of incomes—if so many. Since 1960, LEAs have agreed to pay for a few of their children to attend Public Schools, priority being given to children with both parents abroad or with adverse home circumstances.

[4] In 1961 the headmaster of Eton (who should know) said that 6000 boys annually out of 300,000 reaching the age of thirteen went to Public Schools, that is 2 percent. Professor H. C. Dent about the same time estimated the proportion as 3 percent of the whole secondary school population, a figure that tallies with the above.

such schools, their access to positions of wealth and influence is conspicuously easier than for others.

In particular, we must notice that the ordinary English "grammar" school (that is, the really public academic high school) has been shaped by the example of the Public Schools. Some grammar day schools are so ancient that they antedate most residential Public Schools, which grew up in their present form to attract the children of administrators and well-to-do people from all over the country; and there have always existed some day grammar schools for the children of the locally successful. Therefore when tax supported secondary schools were introduced in 1902 it was not surprising that they were given an ancient name and some features of the Public Schools, which were themselves increasing greatly in number to serve the newly rich. The chief executor of the 1902 Act, Sir Robert Morant, was of Public School type to the marrow. During the last quarter of a century before publicly provided secondary schools actually arrived, however, many expected that they would be of a much more technical or directly prevocational kind. That was the direction of public demand and also what manufacturers envisaged. Yet the prestige of Public Schools, and of the older grammar schools, was such that the newer academic public secondary schools are not only officially called "grammar schools" but also copy their organization of "houses," prefects, school loyalty, team spirit, and so on. To an astonishing degree this has enabled the products of the public grammar school to compete academically with Public School products in the struggle for university and professional places. But it has also resulted in much frustration and perhaps misdirection of effort.

It is of the greatest importance for an understanding of British educational problems to appreciate the long unchallenged sanctity of all that the Public Schools stand for. This type of boarding school is, after all, the characteristic British contribution to educational thought and school organization. It is not claiming too much if we say that preoccupation with character-training and self-discipline, through teamwork within a rather narrow horizon of social obligation, has been the hallmark of these schools; it has been prized by such different observers as the founders of New England "preparatory schools" and the more recent founders of Soviet boarding schools. Such schools, furthermore, changed the meaning of the English word "sport" from bed-play, and hunting, and rumbustious gambling contests, to a gentlemanly recognition that "the game's the thing," with emphasis on team discipline, but without too much zeal for victory as long as "fair play" is maintained.

The commercialization of sport, international sporting events with national prestige at stake, and the wide reinterpretation of amateurish

British upper-class interests in a world that puts the benefits of industrialization to a richer social use than its first beneficiaries intended—all
these developments have brought into question the complacent assumptions underpinning and buttressing the Public School concept.
The heyday of the Public School as a "self-evident" ethos (as distinct
from an advantageous lever) ran from the 1870s to the 1930s. Most of
its teachers and many of the public still believe in that ethos. This is
why there have been persistent attempts to link the Public Schools
somehow with opportunities for the "most deserving" boys and girls
from the really public schools maintained by taxes. This is still the
serious program of some Public School headmasters. But the widespread tendency to reassess all institutions in a broader perspective of
social justice and efficiency portends great changes.

In addition to any voluntary moves already made by the Public
Schools themselves (especially after the admission of boys and girls
on tax-aided scholarships became legally or administratively possible),
the question of associating the Public Schools closely with the public
system has been in the air for many years. An intention to "incor-
porate" them into the public system was announced before the Labour
Party was returned to office in 1964. With an increased majority in
1966, that intention seems nearer fulfillment, especially as a Public
Schools Commission was set up the previous year for the express
purpose of integrating the 277 Public Schools into the national system.[5] The report of the commission (due in 1967) will bring to mind
the Clarendon Commission of 1861–1864, which resulted in the Public
Schools Act of 1868. This act reformed the constitutions of nine great
Public Schools, and provided for the "wider representation of national
interests"—as they were then conceived by the ruling classes. Certainly,
those responsible for the Public Schools are now at pains to show that
they serve, and can even more bountifully serve, the public interest;
but the average onlooker is skeptical. Nevertheless, the indirect public
influence on Public Schools has been profound.

As always happens everywhere, those more recently emancipated
from social and economic disadvantage aspire to the conspicuous tokens
of success. It is difficult for newcomers to discern the differences of
social context, of professional orientation, and indeed of historic and
economic circumstance that make their own case different. Society has
been and is still being revolutionized, but not its legends or its holy

---

[5] No exact definition of the term "Public School" is possible. Recognition of this status
is self-perpetuating, as it depends upon admission to the Headmasters' Conference, the
Governing Bodies' Association, or the Governing Bodies of Girls' Schools' Association.
This sounds informal enough, but admission is rigidly controlled, and attained only after
strict scrutiny.

symbols. What sociologists call "social distance," therefore, is still measured in Britain largely by old-fashioned criteria different from those in America. In the very top bracket one includes not only the titled nobility (which nowadays may include industrialists, successful administrators, and former trade union officials), but members of the learned professions, such as university professors. Universities are exclusive, and their faculties highly esteemed. The big men of local industry and commerce frequently stand rather lower in public estimation. Prosperous provincial manufacturers and storekeepers may even now be socially equated with teachers in good schools, although their incomes are much larger. Recent public opinion polls and broadcast discussions still bear out what professional sociologists say, though "Americanization" of social criteria is taking place. We may say that the way an Englishman speaks and moves is much more likely to affect his immediate social mobility than the amount of money in his own or his father's account. Speech alone is a significant social ticket. The vital importance of socially "good" schools is thus enhanced.

Of course, there are subtleties, as there are in all class distinctions. Local speech in the British Isles shows strong differences in pronunciation, idiom, and intonation. Much would at first be unintelligible to anyone who knew only "standard English," and the more vigorous local peculiarities would long defy an outsider's understanding. (Nothing is said here about the different *languages,* such as Welsh, which is the medium of instruction in Wales for children whose mother tongue it is, or Gaelic, or Irish. Attention is paid only to variants of English.) As a kind of compromise between the extremes of dialect and the central norm of standard English, most towns of any size have a distinctive speech of their own. Citizens distinguished in the local hierarchy have progressed furthest from local idiosyncrasies. In some occupations a cosmopolitan English accent is not so strictly called for as in others. A Church of England clergyman, a lawyer, and a doctor must generally "speak well"; their children certainly must. Secondary school teachers also speak well, as a rule, though not necessarily if they teach science subjects. Factory owners need not. So it goes on.

Some local speech survivals are less welcome than others. A Scottish accent of medium strength is something of a distinction, an Irish one much less so. Ambitious Welshmen are careful to change their vowels, but some surviving Welsh intonation is not unattractive. A strong Lancashire, Yorkshire, or Midlands color is a downright social drawback for the ambitious, however, even in those very regions; in London, and in high academic or administrative posts generally, it is even more so. These absurd but cherished talismans profoundly affect geographic and, still more, social mobility—much more than in Germany, for instance. We cannot separate from them the high prestige (and effective social importance) of the Public Schools and others that are semiprivate. At the moment, considerations of speech and social punctilio are perhaps the biggest hindrance to a wider acceptance of common schools for all children. So powerfully do social intangibles become educational facts.

Having sketched in the background of influential forces still at work, we can proceed to a more formal examination of the school system in England and Wales. Scottish methods are different in certain important respects. In England and Wales, compulsory free schooling begins at the commencement of the half-year after a child reaches the age of 5. There are three terms a year, each of about thirteen weeks. Twelve weeks' holiday is usual, generally divided into six weeks in the summer, three weeks at Christmas, and three at Easter. (Winter in Britain is mild, spring is early, and summer is cool. A favorite joke is that Britain has no climate, only weather.) Schools have a five-day week, usually from nine o'clock to three-thirty or four with an hour's dinner break at midday and two shorter breaks in the morning and afternoon sessions. Local school authorities have complete discretion to arrange all these matters. It is also usual to have a short midterm break of perhaps two days in each of the three terms. Physical education is an essential part of the curriculum and, in addition, there may be one or two games afternoons a week. In most schools, except those for very young children, extracurricular activity is encouraged. In the "grammar" schools (academic high schools) this is specially vigorous, and highly prized as a formative influence. A British school is certainly not a place for instruction only.

All the same, the school means business. A child beginning school soon after his fifth birthday starts straight away to learn. There is no official program or method. The head and assistant teachers do what seems best, and adjust themselves to the children's needs as much as possible. Young children are grouped according to ability and speed. By their sixth birthday they are usually able to read simple books and do elementary sums. They write without hesitation, sometimes in script. In addition, they paint, sing, dance, and become acquainted with each other and the world about them. The infant schools (5 to 7) and junior schools (7 to 11) are usually the most progressive parts of the British system; they are bright and cheerful places, and up-to-date methods are now usual. Unfortunately, the postwar increase in the birthrate, the heavy cost of reconstruction, the worsened international situation, and the shortage of teachers have led to classes that are much too large. Forty (and sometimes even fifty) pupils are found in one class. Schools also have a playground, a place to assemble, and a place for meals and exercise. Books, stationery, and other necessities are provided.

The work begun in the first school year is consolidated and improved in subsequent years. By comparison with some other countries the pace is rapid; but it is certainly not forced. When a child is about 11 (that is, in his sixth year) he is doing work comparable with that of the seventh grade (perhaps higher), of most American schools. The average standard of proficiency is high. By this time the pupil-teacher relationship has become more formal. This is partly because it is traditional, partly because people think it works out better, and partly because of the long-standing selection for secondary education at about the age of 11.

Here again huge changes are anticipated, as the adoption of a comprehensive secondary school system (that is, one catering to the various abilities of all children in one establishment) is now official policy. A much-discussed circular was sent to LEAs in 1965, requiring them to inform the Secretary of State for Education and Science one year later how they proposed to implement reorganization along comprehensive lines. In order to make use of existing school buildings and other local opportunities, and to meet local needs, a variety of organizational patterns was authorized in advance. No doubt was left as to the over-all requirement. The traditional "break at eleven" from primary to secondary education, which was formalized in 1944 when some form of secondary school was first provided for all, has also become less inevitable now that the age of transfer may vary to accommodate local experiments. For example some systems have already been modified from 9 to 13 to provide a three-tier range of schools—5–9, 9–13, and 13–16—before 16 becomes the minimum school-leaving age in 1970; and the 1967 Plowden Report proposed three phases: 5 to 8; 8 to 12 or perhaps 13; 13 to 16. Varied experiments are likely. LEAs need latitude to make the best use of buildings now available.

In any case, long before the "comprehensive school" circular, many LEAs had already introduced schemes of comprehensive or near-comprehensive reorganization, and a great many more had voluntarily planned to do so. As has been said, some two thirds of all the children in England and Wales had thus been planned for, or already accommodated. A fair number of LEA systems had already moved over towards a two-tier secondary school structure. These had all children between 11 and 14 years of age in a lower-secondary school (often called a high school) with no permanent or marked differentiation, and followed this with either self-selection or counseled selection. The prototype of such reorganizations in Britain was the Leicestershire Plan, which in one form or another had been followed by a large number of authorities. It will be seen that there is a resemblance to the "observation cycle" of France and the *scuola media* or "middle school" of Italy. A number of such changes have been proceeding in parallel in several European countries. They have the administrative advantage of using existing buildings for a junior or a senior secondary school, where the appropriate type of teacher can be used to best effect. In Britain all such modifications of the secondary school structure until 1966 had perforce to include a break at the age of 11.

Because buildings last a long time, and ideas are often just as firmly structured, it is important to give a condensed account of the system still usually practiced in England and Wales. This system came into effect under the 1944 Act, which guaranteed "secondary education for all"—but differentiated into two or three types of parallel school according to the children's age, attainment, and supposed aptitude. The notion of any once-and-for-all diagnosis has come under heavy criticism from scientists, sociologists, teachers and parents. In 1944 such an "objective" prognosis at the age of 10 or 11 was welcomed by many, on the ground that it was fairer than the criterion of wealth or social ambition which hitherto had been more influential, even though there had been an "educational ladder" before then for children who could pass a scholarship examination.

After 1944 the emphasis was supposed to be not on passing an examination for privilege, but on selection according to the child's merit and needs. Nevertheless, the promised "parity of esteem" for the distinct kinds of secondary school was never attained. Children, parents, and teachers were too conscious of the diagnosis and its implications. In any case, the influence of school, home, and other circumstances was reflected in the knowledge tested, and in the child's performance —no matter how "objective" the examination. Besides, the tests have been criticized for their content, methods, and the narrow spectrum of personality tested. So the "eleven plus" diagnosis earned a bad name in many quarters. On the other hand, there has never been any rigid "eleven plus" examination or selection method. Local authorities have always been able to choose as they wished, within obvious limits. Some abandoned the "eleven plus" long ago, selecting by other means— parental choice, teachers' advice, school records. However, some form of selection is still usual—even where comprehensive schools have been established. It typically includes intelligence tests (more suspect now), attainment tests, critical compositions, and tests in arithmetic. Reference is usually (sometimes exclusively) made to the child's school record card. Parental choice, too, is weighed.

However it is done, children in the publicly provided school system are all transferred to a secondary school at the age of 11 (or 12 after the Plowden Report, or exceptionally at 13). At one time, the term "secondary" signified simply a more privileged school with a curriculum leading to the university or the professions—an old-style grammar school. Now it refers to public provision of any type between the ages of 11 and 18 or 19. Three main types of school were recognized after 1944: "grammar" or academic; technical; and "secondary modern." Some remarks have already been made about grammar schools. The grammar school offers systematic preparation for university, technical, and commercial occupations in a wide range, but it also sets a high standard of personal and civic responsibility. Work is earnest, but so are the numerous and diligently followed activities. In addition to games and athletics, we usually find debating clubs, concerts, and dramatic presentations of good quality. Art and singing are taken by everyone. Competence in self-expression and public speaking are expected and trained for, though not as well as on the continent, where oral repetition of homework and oral examinations ensure great proficiency in the spoken word. There is usually an orchestra. Science clubs and naturalists' societies, stamp and chess clubs, camping, scouting, and similar organizations—all these are common. Nowadays foreign travel is often organized on a voluntary basis, and many pupils have pen-friends abroad with whom they correspond in French or German. Life in a grammar school is very busy indeed.

School subjects, though not so exactingly pursued as they are in France (where they tend to exclude extracurricular activities of any kind) are numerous and serious. Nearly all pupils take the same subjects at first, though there is increasing specialization as they advance. In the first "form" of a typical grammar school (ages 11 to 12) the pupils begin learning algebra and geometry, a foreign language, and either general science or elementary biology. They also take English (which includes "speech," drama, and so on), history, geography, music, physical education, and nondenominational (but Christian) religious knowledge. Children may elect not to take this last subject if their parents object. A second foreign language is begun in the second year, as a rule; in the third year a third language may be added. The third year also marks the beginning of physics, or chemistry, or biology, or a combination of these; in mathematics, trigonometry may be added. Girls may also include domestic science and boys some workshop skill, usually woodwork.

What has just been described may seem a formidable program, but a close scrutiny reveals that not so many subjects are continuously and simultaneously studied to the final school-leaving examinations as on the continent, or even in Scotland. It is generally assumed in England and Wales that in order to learn subjects or basic skills efficiently, something else must be dropped. Early specialization is therefore the characteristic of English education—one which has been taken for granted in many official reports. Specialization is ostensibly for the sake of higher standards, especially from the age of 13 or 14 on. But (overlooking the greater spread of interests covered by the continental curricula) can we always say that the attainment of English school-leaving is as high as that in France or Germany in the individual subjects—especially on the literary side? Clearly not. The English apologia points to character-training, extracurricular interests, sport, and all the other things so integral to school life in England. There is a point here, but the English are having to think more internationally and less amateurishly. Therefore international comparisons and penetrating curriculum study are combining to question complacency in British education.

Is it really true that so many pupils are "not much good at languages" or in some way second-best at mathematics or science—at any rate to the extent of "dropping" parts of the syllabus? Every pupil retains core subjects such as English, history, and mathematics at least until 16 or so in a grammar school. Are the other subjects which make up a modern citizen's viability in adult life to be "dropped" so readily —perhaps because of idleness, poor learning methods, timetable difficulties, or even just because specialization is unquestioned?

To present a fair picture we should stress that what is said here about subject-dropping and specialization refers mainly to the study of subjects for examinations, for which the attainment level is really high. Such specialization in the "sixth form" (top classes) may be particularly marked in the sciences. It should be mentioned that science and mathematics form a larger proportion of school curricula in Britain than in the United States, being comparable in this respect with programs in the Soviet Union—though not for every child, as must be the case in the USSR. Some unexamined subjects and activities always accompany the subjects of specialized study for any British examination, at least until the first public examination described below. There is often narrowness in the formal studies of the last two or three years of a grammar school course before 18 or 19, not altogether relieved by "minority time" studies or extracurricular interests.

Partly for this reason, a number of LEAs have been experimenting with "sixth form colleges." These are likely to be found in areas where a common school accommodates children to the age of about 16 and the first examination level of the General Certificate of Education, with more specialized courses later in the same school or in different establishments. Alternatively, such a "college" may constitute the sixth form of a grammar school absorbing many pupils from various secondary schools. The Department of Education and Science has deliberately fostered imaginative experiment in a number of pilot schools to meet a variety of contextual or structural requirements. In any case, some developing features are clear. A more collegiate kind of atmosphere of deep study leavened by wider human contacts and a certain independence of research (in place of formal teaching) can certainly be found in any such school, no matter whether it is a "sixth-form college" separated from a grammar school or a "sixth-form unit" maintaining an indissoluble union with one.

Such educational opportunities also exist, in fact, at the lower end of some colleges of further education. These are often called "technical colleges," and their main function is to provide a lower-than-university complement of education and training normally begun at the age of 18. Such colleges often have a large junior department operating at approximately sixth-form level, and overlapping the sixth form work of the grammar schools in some fields, especially for students who have left secondary schools around the age of 16. This parenthetical information is necessary to fill out the picture of upper-secondary opportunity, even though it means anticipating the bulk of information to be given later on such colleges.

In a growing number of districts, the majority of grammar school pupils stay until they are 18—the age level of final examinations. A smaller proportion (again growing) of pupils in other types of school remain also. In terms of absolute numbers, but not proportionally, the majority of those staying on until 18 are now outside grammar schools. This fact illustrates two things: the growing strength of comprehensive schools (or the more ambitious secondary schools of other types), and the flexibility of arrangements mitigating the supposed "finality" of a selection about the age of 11. As one would expect, the tendency to stay on until 18 and to develop studies beyond school is greater in those school systems where academic segregation is less noticeable. However, in some industrial towns with a high rate of well-paid employment, there is still a tendency for too many able children to leave school and get jobs. This may be attributable to alienation of sympathy on the children's part or their parents'; it may also call into question the scholastic methods they have experienced. In any case, there is no need for children to be lost to further education, though the record of "staying power" in part-time further education is as disappointing in Britain as it is in most countries.

We have been talking about the pursuit of subjects at a level appropriate to many or most American colleges, and sometimes beyond. When we look at Japan we shall see that the level of most European upper-secondary work would, in that country, be classified as of "university" rank (not even with the slightly junior imputation associated with the word "college" in the United States). Therefore we must not swallow statistics of higher education (or anything else) whole, without discerning what is included in the definition, and what its significance is in the context where it occurs. What has been questioned so far in the British scene is not so much the attainment level but the complexion of interests fostered in schools, and the justification of those interests in terms of the pupils' future world connections.

The main school examinations are for the General Certificate of Education, which has two levels: "Ordinary" at about 16, on a fairly broad base, and "Advanced" at about 18, with close specialization. Questions are set and marked externally by examining boards operated by the universities. At least half, and often more, of the examiners are teachers. They draw up syllabuses on which the examination will be based. Schools are profoundly influenced by these syllabuses, which in a language, for example, may prescribe certain authors for detailed study. It is true that head or even assistant teachers can get a paper set on any subject, or on any special aspect of a subject, particularly developed in their school; but few avail themselves of this facility even though the additional cost is negligible. As has been said before, the choice of a school's curriculum is left almost entirely to the school itself. The influence of external examinations keeps them all up to standard, and to some extent restricts modifications in the curriculum, though it need not do so. Despite many attempts in recent years to minimize concentration on examinations, there is no doubt that the results attained in them have an enormous influence on future careers —at least in the initial stages. What is said here about grammar schools may apply equally to the "grammar" sections of comprehensive schools.

It will be of interest to suggest the standards attained, though that is rash. One 16-year-old boy or girl would take English as a required subject, and might add mathematics, physics, chemistry, biology, history (or perhaps geography), and French. Another might choose history, geography, mathematics, French, Latin, and Greek, in addition to English literature and language. These are not unusual cases. Other combinations are possible in a wide range. By the time 18-year-old pupils take the Advanced Level of the General Certificate of Education, their subjects can often be compared with those in the senior year of the average American college (where students are around 22). In recent years, many British teachers of classes at the Advanced Level have begun using American *college* textbooks. These are often admirably produced, and are in some ways especially useful for review or consolidation because their material is arranged in a different way.

This tendency is particularly true of biology and physics books, such as those prepared for the (American) National Science Foundation. The teachers in question assume that, as it is in the British idiom, "college" is a synonym for an academic high school (that is, a British grammar school). Unfortunately, these books are usually too expensive for the British pocket.

Not even this level of attainment will guarantee pupils the opportunity of entering a British university to *begin* a course, however. British universities are highly specialized places, concerned with a restricted range of academic interests, and preparing only for the highest grades of a few professions. The manifold services offered by American universities, for example, are provided by other institutions in Britain.

It should be noted that nothing is implied in my remarks about the comparative *personal* worth of the education offered in Britain and in the United States. Comments on standards of attainment may touch a tender spot, but they do not say everything. A country like Britain, which has limited natural resources and must earn abroad by its skill at least half the food it eats, just cannot afford extravagances with time. "If you don't earn, you don't eat" is a lesson that has been dinned into British heads incessantly in the postwar years. Standards of skill and knowledge can hardly be abandoned without disaster. Industry, no less than the universities, demands ever higher and higher attainment. On the other hand, some industries requiring the highest skill nowadays prefer to have a broadly based school foundation, and look for such qualities as initiative or enterprise (not to speak of a sympathetic awareness of the world at large). Thus they come closer to the needs of citizenship, too. The critical problem inside the grammar school, therefore, is how to decide between specialization and flexibility. It is not beyond human ingenuity to foster understanding of worldwide problems and deep human issues even when specialized studies are followed within a restricted field. But there are manifest dangers which need particular attention—and not just in the grammar school, where many attempts are already made to widen interests and develop human concern. The very important Crowther Report[6] dealt with these problems, and contained excellent information about the evolution of British schools for this age range. I do not, however, accept some of its more conservative conclusions.

The grammar school, which has become the pivotal point of most British skill and enterprise in the twentieth century, has its own special

---

[6] Crowther and others, *Fifteen to Eighteen*. H. M. Stationery Office, London. 1959–1960, 2 vols.

problems. It has not changed enough with the times, either with regard to the range of subjects covered or in relation to social attitudes. It certainly has its own special type of narrowness. For example, segregation is usual—not between people of different color (for that would be both illegal and shocking in Britain), but between boys and girls. Relatively few grammar schools are coeducational, though most primary schools and secondary modern schools are. The ancient Public Schools and grammar schools were for boys only, and girls' education was an afterthought. The ancient fashion still prevails in today's grammar schools, and plenty of reasons are given to justify it. Also, it is usual to expect boys (or girls) to wear clothing of a distinctive type. This cuts out vulgar ostentation and also sloppiness, but it may cramp individuality. Many schools now permit older girls, especially in the sixth form, to wear their own choice of clothing. Some boys' schools adopt a similar policy, but a "school uniform" is customary.

A "school uniform" in Britain, of course, bears no resemblance to the genuine military-style uniform worn by Soviet or Japanese schoolboys, which in turn was derived from Napoleon's intention to provide a civilian army of educated men for national strength. In Britain, it is just a matter of sober, neat clothing of a standardized pattern and color. Not all schools adopt one, but it is interesting to note that the general improvement of status in all kinds of nongrammar secondary school has usually been contemporary with the adoption of a school uniform. Another advantage is that it helps parents' budgeting.

Yet the fostering of *esprit de corps* by this method is also associated with the spirit of the "old school tie." There is no doubt that people in grammar schools or the "grammar" sections of comprehensive schools have felt socially as well as intellectually superior, on the whole. They represent between 20 and 25 percent of the children sorted out at the age of 11. Some local authorities have always selected a much higher proportion of children for grammar school placement, and this fact indicates once more the uncertainties of selection at this age. Attention to manners and speech, as well as the very real difference made to professional prospects, make most parents eager for their children to be selected for grammar schools or similar academic opportunities elsewhere. Although parents can express a preference, only a few can be satisfied. Several noteworthy results must be mentioned. Parents of children around 11 tend to become very anxious about selection procedures (and so do the children themselves). Some parents have their children coached, and others send their children to "preparatory schools" (private junior schools) instead of to the public junior schools, though they seldom do much better. Finally, a number of those disappointed by the selection send their children to fee-charging independent grammar schools, where admission requirements may be lower. This practice is growing. A number of the latter schools are run by religious organizations; others are commercial ventures with no religious affiliation.

Public Schools such as Eton and Winchester, and a large number less well known, have their own selection examination, of a more conventional kind. Pupils take these examinations at the age of thirteen. The tests include papers in Latin and French, and in fairly advanced mathematics. Therefore it would normally be very difficult for a child from an ordinary tax-supported school to compete, even if his parents could afford the fees. To serve these requirements, a large number of "preparatory schools," not tax-supported, are found in prosperous suburbs. Since the usual pattern of selection followed after 1944 virtually made the free grammar school the main preserve of juvenile intelligence (at least, as indicated by tests), many preparatory schools also made a point of preparing children for the "eleven plus" examinations as well as for the Public Schools' "common entrance."

All these considerations, in more or less articulate form, have been brought home to parents whose little 11-year-old boy or girl is faced with selection procedures. There has been a crescendo of protests—against the ordeal, against its restrictive influence on the junior school, against unreliability in the selection, and against its finality (despite marginal adjustment up to the age of 13 or even 16 or 18). The protesters have become more influential as their number has included many who, before the war, could have paid fees to get their children (of a lower intellectual or attainment level) into grammar schools that are now free. University professors, heads of schools, and professional men find their children excluded. Influence and money count for nothing, except so far as children from wealthier and professional homes are more likely to do well in an impartial examination. In fact, the agitation and frustration of many middle-class parents has helped, as much as anything else, the general veering of opinion toward acceptance of the comprehensive pattern of schooling. This has been irrespective of political associations, or the fear of lowering standards as some overseas comprehensive schools are generally believed to have done. For some years to come, however, it is obvious that the interim survival of many tripartite school systems, or internal divisions within a comprehensive school, will continue to raise anxious questions about most children aged 10—for the selection has always preceded transfer at 11.

The sort of anxiety felt by parents and many teachers (to say nothing of the poor children themselves) is indicated by the fact that they, and the local education authorities as well, are often aware of a "pecking order" of prospects, not only in the junior schools but between the grammar schools themselves. This latter "merit grading" is based upon university prospects afterwards. Selection procedures are now known to be fallible, or restricted in their purview of scholastic potential. Yet the mere placing of children in an alleged order of merit, combined with the slight latitude for parental preference (allowed under the 1944 Education Act), has resulted in children being enrolled in grammar schools at some distance from their own districts or towns, though of course within the same local authority area. Meanwhile, other children with brighter (or duller) prognosis at 11 are brought in from other towns or districts. School buses are unusual in Britain, but those who have to travel far receive free passes for ordinary public transportation. Thus, between eight and nine o'clock on school days, it is still possible to see great numbers of children in different colors of uniform criss-crossing each other's paths or "commuting" in opposite directions—all because of school selection. The whole, immensely valuable concept of a "neighborhood school," with its educative links that transcend academic or career considerations, has been largely ignored in England.

What is said here about a "pecking order" of grammar schools applies even more rigidly in their relationship to other kinds of secondary schools. These remarkable peculiarities (almost entirely absent from other civilized countries) have been accentuated by the post-1944 determination to eliminate favoritism derived from parental position, and to substitute instead an assessment of the child's supposed merits. However, the fallibility of tests, the narrowness of the field of personality under review, the ignoring of contextual factors affecting any child's performance in a test (as well as his later development or downfall) raise grave doubts. So does the insensibility involved in the process, and the bland arrogance of supposing we know all the qualities and interests that any secondary school should try to select children for. All this has led to impatience with selection in many countries simultaneously. Though we are discussing Britain, the same discussions are appropriate to much selection on a world front. Much the same conclusions are being reached in one European country after another, as they have already been reached in North America and the British Commonwealth.

It is rightly assumed that protests would not have been so energetic if the alternatives to the grammar school had enjoyed that "parity of esteem" so cheerfully anticipated at the time of the 1944 Act. This happy state was not reached, though remarkable progress was made. There are several reasons for social and educational distinctions. Before 1944, the old elementary school carried the stigma of lower status, being intended for the laboring poor. It often used wretched buildings, a few of which are still in use as junior schools or secondary modern schools. It was "creamed off" by scholarship awards. Its teachers were worse trained and worse paid than those in grammar schools. As the effective life of a teacher is some forty years, it is obvious that many of those still in service in nongrammar schools date from the pre-1944 period. Although many are exemplary in their social attitudes, in their teaching ability, and in their good will, it would be rash to say this of them all. It cannot be claimed that the older teachers, on the average, are as well-informed as the younger ones who have come into the schools from the universities since equalization of pay made such service more attractive. The best of the secondary modern schools have managed to combine some of the general educational advantages (though not the academic standards) of the grammar school with greater resourcefulness. More money, however, has been spent on grammar schools for the number of pupils involved, both on capital equipment, such as laboratories, and on books and teachers. And in any case, careful analysis shows that good jobs, if not already taken by people from the great Public Schools, continue to go to grammar school pupils, or to candidates from "grammar" streams in any other sort of school.

It is not too much to say that the secondary modern school has always suffered from an unofficial downgrading. Teachers and administrators protest against such a statement; but parents and politicians make no secret of the common opinion. The Newsom Report of 1963 showed that opinion to be based on fact in all too many cases. The status of the better secondary modern schools has been rising very slowly, partly again because of examinations. Sometimes pupils take the very same examinations for the General Certificate of Education as grammar school pupils; usually more commercial examinations are taken, and a most important innovation is the school-based and regionalized Certificate of Secondary Education (CSE) already referred to. This examines at a lower level and on a broader front about the age of 16. But must it always be a case of salvation by certificate? Some teachers complain of another straitjacket; if so, they are tying the cords themselves. The new system is flexible, the incentive value is great, and in the world of tomorrow the entirely unqualified man or woman will find it hard to win a good place. Even so, not every child will get a certificate; and no examination can measure the whole of education—or the personality.

In British circumstances, perhaps more than in most other advanced countries, we must remind ourselves that these discussions do not take place in a vacuum. Alongside the schools in the public sector we must measure the immense prestige and the powerful career prognosis of the private sector, and the semiprivate schools (such as the direct grant schools). These cannot simply be rubbed out for legal and institutional reasons, even if one were blind to their many excellences, some of which have filtered down into the publicly provided sector. In less than forty years after tax aid to secondary schools in 1902 success in public examinations in many respects equated the publicity provided grammar schools with the Public Schools on academic grounds, and caused many of the latter to change their policy in favor of less sport and more serious study. Certificates and the like may be no more than talismans; but far less substantial emblems have evoked the rivalry of human beings throughout the ages and seem likely to go on doing so. It is something if genuine equivalence can be recognized where it truly exists, and if a fair basis for competition can be provided. Recruitment must also take place on a much broader front than has hitherto been imagined. That is what a comprehensive school policy is intended to provide now, and what it was hoped the secondary modern school would offer after 1944.

At the present crossroads of decision and development, it seems appropriate to consider what a good secondary modern school has been and still is. In some ways, though not often in the excellence of its buildings or in the money available, a progressive secondary modern school can be compared with the ordinary small American high school. Academic standards are generally similar, though activities are not. There is an attempt at the same orientation toward a happy and responsible life at work and in society. It has not become the "people's school" in popular affection, even though more than two thirds of the population have been attending it. It might have a better chance of becoming such when the projected raising of the school-leaving age to 16 takes place. Before then, however, it seems likely that in most cases the "secondary modern school" as such may have faded into something else, either by incorporation into a fully comprehensive school system covering ages 11 to 18, or by the maturing of plans which associate various "streams" of children or school departments into new units until the age of 16. In any case, it seems likely that the less fortunate connotations of the phrase "secondary modern" will be avoided. The term is already avoided in many districts, a simple "secondary" being substituted. This has been not only a change of name but a recognition that mergers have taken place—sometimes between secondary modern schools and technical schools, sometimes even with "grammar type" courses or schools. Evolution has been rapid during recent decades. Consequently, any isolated secondary modern school suffers from a historical hangover, and from unfavorable comparisons. Some of these had their origin partly in factual differences of standard and partly in somewhat fictitious differences (such as those of speech and mannerism). The social stratification which is exemplified by the grammar-secondary modern distinction is the most hotly debated issue in British education today. Scotland, with its common schools, found its own historic way out of this difficulty; but England and Wales are not quite ready with their solution.

A third kind of secondary school envisaged in the 1944 Act has certainly been successful in some towns and cities. This is the secondary technical school, arising out of the junior technical schools that have existed since about 1905. Such schools (now often merged with grammar schools or closely parallel to them) have recruited boys and a few girls about the age of 13, sometimes at 11. They have normally admitted bright children who did not do quite well enough in the selection procedures to enter grammar schools. Their evocation and practically-linked studies have often served to win success for these supposedly second-best children in a way that grammar school courses would not have done. It is safe to make this surmise because the success ratio of secondary technical schools (or the secondary technical department in a combined school) has been unusually good.

In deciding what to do with boys and girls staying on until 16, particularly if they do not take kindly to the bookish studies on which more "verbal" children can thrive, the example of the secondary technical school may be potent. Such schools during recent decades have not predestined any boy or girl to a manual or lowly career. On the contrary, they have stressed that aspect of generalized perspectives, or "polyvalence" or "polytechnical education," which continental neighbors proclaim as an invention or a Marxist verity. The Germans, the Danes, and more recently the French have learned how to combine general education with vocational training on a large scale for boys and girls over the age of 14. The British knew that before, but they did not develop on any large scale the good work they had begun so long ago, despite the existence of thriving secondary technical schools and the suggestion in several laws or reports that such work-linked or life-linked education could become better developed. Perhaps the "gentleman ideal" is to blame; but the gentlemen now have their backs to the wall, and the continental example may show that the white-coated technician or supervisor (not to say the technologist) is as respectable a member of a nation's educated citizenry as the literary man. However, in view of the structural changes now going on in Britain, it seems unlikely that separate secondary technical schools will persist for very long—except perhaps as upper-secondary schools beginning after 14 or 15 like the *collèges d'enseignement technique* and *collèges du second cycle* in France.

The 1944 Act's almost unintentional division of secondary schools into three types (the tripartite system of grammar, secondary technical, and secondary modern schools) really had its origin in historical accident and in social and economic stratification. Yet it actually resulted in a widespread belief that there are really three types of mind— bookish, technical, and practical. References are made to these in legislation and supporting official reports; and of course the educational psychologists busied themselves finding tests with which to recognize them. Fortunately, this oddly schizophrenic psychology is now largely discredited, but some university chairs of education or psychology have been earned by this kind of exercise. Such stalwarts of the test began to repent a generation ago in the light of better social and comparative evidence, and now the majority are converted. Many of the schools and school populations docketed by these people long ago still persist, beset with teachers or politicians convinced of the old dispensation; but the merging and blending previously described has been hazing the outlines for a long time.

Multilateral schools (that is, several schools or departments on one campus), bilateral schools, and comprehensive schools have all been possible under the widely permissive legislation of England and Wales. They have recommended themselves for one functional reason or another (and sometimes from social or political rather than strictly pedagogical justification). Then came the Leicestershire reform, which transferred all 11-year-olds to the nearest secondary school without a test, keeping them there until 14 or 15. It allowed further transfer to a grammar school—again without tests, but on condition that parents promised to let the child stay until at least 16. A much larger proportion than usual did so. Education in general was belived to be better served; and examination or other successes were conspicuous among many children whom the older system would have rejected. These developments during more than 20 years after 1944 (which had been widely copied even in Conservative LEAs), logically prepared the way for the comprehensive type of secondary provision. Why then was there such distaste for the comprehensive school as seen in the United States, the Soviet Union, Sweden, and several parts of the Commonwealth? The answer must be mainly found in the preceding parts of this chapter, not in logic.

A few rural areas in England and Wales have had comprehensive or near-comprehensive schools for a long time, usually for reasons of economy. For a similar reason, schools built in recent years in several new towns or suburbs have been constructed either as comprehensive schools or with that possible use in mind. In any case, more recently constructed schools do not make the same class distinction architecturally as would once have seemed inevitable. British unreadiness for the comprehensive solution to many educational problems must be

attributed to class distinctions still pervading the whole of social encounter, to the very different levels of attainment and evocation found
in Britain's existing schools, and—let us whisper it—to extremely unflattering judgments made on American comprehensive schools. Most
European champions of the common school have had to fight against
such unfavorable comparisons, mostly made by people ignorant of the
fact that American schools have been geared to quite different purposes
from those of Europe, and had also been running in low gear, academically speaking, between 1930 and 1955. Not even the smear of "socialism" attached to common schools has been such a handicap as "guilt
by association" with the United States, before that country's recent
transformation of its schools.[7] That kind of taunt is beginning to count
for less, but countries dependent for their very life on imports and
skills cannot run the risk of lowered educational standards.

In Scotland the common school for all children has been traditional,
though not in a way that gives them all equal consideration. Scottish
schools have always tended to be formal, and to push academic children
and academic subjects forward even if this has snubbed other interests
and children with other possibilities. The teachers have urged promising scholars toward the university, which has always been the reward
of a larger proportion than in England; but the slower and less bookish
pupils have been somewhat neglected. Englishmen know the high regard Scots have for education, and their conspicuous success in getting
top jobs in England. Scottish experience has not been called in support
of English comprehensive schools, however, because Scottish practice
in the smaller towns was not "comprehensive" in the European or
American sense. Indeed, large Scottish towns have English-style selective grammar schools or "academies."

It is probable that home experiments, and the example of the
Scandinavian countries and other communities with high educational
standards, would have led before long to general acceptance of the
comprehensive pattern. But British conditions do not favor a clean
sweep of the board, not even after 1965-1966. There are too many
alternative private enterprises that might spoil prospects. Centuries
of experiment have also sanctified certain values in school life that will
not be abandoned lightly. Besides, it is altogether unrealistic in British
circumstances to ignore the incalculable influence of the Public Schools
which extends far beyond their own domain. The comparative egalitarianism of modern Britain has been achieved by the expansion of
privilege through competitive opportunity. When Britons talk about

---

[7] The implied reference is to Professor L. A. Cremin's *The Transformation of the School*
(1962).

equality of opportunity, they usually mean an impartial competition. The Public Schools, with their specially favorable staffing ratio, their manifest scholastic advantages, and still more, the less definable intangibles that secure their possessors' success in all the "interview situations" with which British life abounds—are still in a paramount competitive position. This is a factor no champion of the people can ignore when he is thinking of how to reconstruct what Americans and Canadians call public schools—that is, those supported by taxation. It is, therefore, not surprising that the development of comprehensive schools will be hedged about with all kinds of safeguards for the many excellent qualities that the publicly maintained grammar schools have already displayed.

It is for this reason that the Commission on the Public Schools (1965–1967) is so important, though it is immediately concerned only with schools attended by some 3 percent of the population. The pursuit of excellence—with equal access—is as powerful an objective in England as in France, though with a different idiom. It is a matter of bread and butter. On the other hand, so much excellence of so many varieties has been hitherto ignored or underdeveloped. Therefore school reforms and the abolition of archaic prerogatives must keep in step with developing opportunities at all levels—especially in higher education.

The term "higher education" in the United Kingdom has been traditionally applied to universities only. It has not applied, as a rule, to work of university standard which may be undertaken elsewhere. So it was rather revolutionary of the Robbins Committee, which produced a momentous report on *Higher Education* in 1963, to include the higher ranges of technological and managerial education and also some of the work undertaken in colleges of further education and teachers' colleges—provided it reached the same level as that of the 25 British universities that had existed until that time.

We can take the Robbins recommendations in due course, beginning with a description of what was in force at the time. In 1962, there were 25 British universities, several with constituent colleges that are widely separated (like the University of Wales), or federally grouped (like the University of London). The Universities of Oxford and Cambridge also have a collegiate federal structure. Of the colleges making up the University of London, several are big enough to match or outstrip most of the provincial universities, and many of them have all the faculties or academic departments that any autonomous university might have. Indeed, most British universities are small by world standards. London, the biggest, has about 30,000 students. The universities have concentrated on careful recruitment, with as much corporate life and personal contact as possible. They accept students already well qualified and highly specialized at the level where many American colleges break off. Most of the professional subjects taught in American universities are not featured in the British, but are trained for in other institutions that do not graduate students but award professional *diplomas,* which are not recognized as equivalent to a university degree. This situation continues even after the reforms initiated by the Robbins Report.

At the time of the report's publication, four additional universities had been designated in parts of the country hitherto not well served with universities. In fact, there have been ten entirely new regular universities founded since the end of World War II. This does not include the official elevation of several existing institutions to university status for excellence in the technological field. To found a university requires the concurrence of government in a "royal charter," subject of course to satisfying those academic requirements which exploratory enquiries can appraise. In other words, everyone must be sure about general equivalence of standards, though not about identity of norms or of curricula.

Once formally established, a university receives financial support through the University Grants Committee—a body consisting of university representatives and highly respected laymen. The funds at the disposal of the University Grants Committee come from the Treasury, and are administered with an eye on proved need—offset by whatever endowments, benefactions, fees, or other revenues the several universities can lay their hands on. Only about 11 percent of the universities' income is derived from student fees, and most of the rest (all in some cases) is from taxation. Therefore—apart from questions of standard—universities cannot be founded lightly. On the contrary, each new establishment means a heavy drain on tax resources, not only for obvious instructional and research expenses, but because students will be maintained at public expense. A student admitted to higher education (or, for that matter, to the lower ranges called further education) receives free tuition and, generally, a substantial or complete maintenance grant, according to his parents' financial position.

In these circumstances it seems strange to insist that there are no state universities in Britain. In the strict sense, all are private though publicly financed for the most part. They are autonomous. The state may recognize their degrees for various purposes (as with doctors and teachers); but determination of curricula, standards, and the like rests with the universities themselves. This kind of academic freedom is essential, though in view of the financial burden they represent, there have from time to time been murmurs about requiring them to be more accountable financially. No governmental or local authority control is exercised over the universities—apart from founding new ones, or recognizing older institutions, or (indirectly) setting certain funds at the disposal of a university for specific purposes. "After Robbins" this has been influential; but the autonomy of universities remains. By a system of "external examiners" mutually exchanged, the universities maintain approximately equal standards. Salaries of university teachers are practically uniform throughout the country, with a small addition for those in London. So when a Briton talks about a "university" he is quite clear about what is meant.

In the Robbins Report it was anticipated that, as institutions "grew up" to the university level, they would become autonomous institutions like the older-type universities. Because of subsequent government decisions, this has not happened, unless (like the former colleges of advanced technology which had long been working at university level without being named universities) they have formally received a royal charter and come under the dispensation of the University Grants Committee. Thus, what is called a "binary system" of higher education has grown up—the autonomous sector of true universities, and the sector which is still under the control of the local authorities' administration. The latter includes technical colleges and teachers' colleges (formerly called training colleges, and now generally called colleges of education). This division does not necessarily cast aspersions on standards, but it suggests that not all the work of such institutions is of real "higher education" level in the stricter sense. Universities award their own degrees. The other kinds of higher or further education may provide courses leading to degrees, but in this case the degrees are awarded by a Council for National Academic Awards (set up in consequence of the Robbins Report). Students also may take the examinations of the University of London "externally," graduating on exactly the same footing as internal candidates.

An official list at the end of 1965 showed 35 universities in England (counting the new technological universities), 6 in Scotland, and 7 university-level institutions in Wales (of which 6 were really colleges of the University of Wales). Since that time another university has been founded at Stirling, in Scotland, and one more has been designated for the northeast of England. This makes 44 autonomous universities. It is unlikely that the number will increase for at least a decade, in order to consolidate development in the recently established institutions, and concentrate the student populations. Even counting the constituent colleges in Wales as one university, and omitting the proposed university in the northeast, the above list shows 46 universities on the plane supervised by the University Grants Committee in England, Wales, and Scotland. In 1962 there were 25, all told; before World War II there were 16.

This shows to what extent the government of the day, and subsequent administrations, have seen fit to implement the Robbins recommendations. In 1962 there were 123,000 university students—roughly double the prewar figure. At the time of the report, in 1963, there were 130,000 in universities; 55,000 in colleges of education; 31,000 in "further education"—all full-time students, and all capable of being considered under the Robbins terms of reference as part of "higher education" in the British sense. By the same criteria, the total figure was expected to rise from an over-all 216,000 in 1963 to a total of 392,000 in 1973, and a total of 506,000 in 1980 (of whom 350,000 would be in universities). Expansion to the present date has exceeded the Robbins expectations, and this has been achieved without loss of standards. Indeed, during the past few years careful appraisal seems to show that standards are improving, not deteriorating. Even so, a few of the universities are becoming more experimental in the type of student they admit, at least as far as formal admission requirements go.

The normal pattern of admission is for secondary school pupils who are likely to get good marks in at least two of the three or four subjects of specialization at the Advanced Level of the General Certificate of Education to apply through a Universities Central Council for Admissions. The pupils list the universities of their choice in order of preference. Interviews are held at the universities, and places are offered to candidates subject to their attaining the required standard. Some colleges in a few universities have their own admissions test in addition. Interviews and school recommendations count for a lot, but a Scholastic Aptitude Test and other objective criteria are currently under consideration.

Courses leading to university degrees usually last for three years, occasionally four. Medical degrees take much longer. All universities are coeducational, and all provide for postgraduate research. A very high standard of serious, independent, and critical study is prerequisite to a degree, with a great deal of wide and deep reading. Critical independence is indeed fostered much earlier by the essay-type written work always expected in a grammar school. ("True-false" answers are extremely rare in British education except for diagnostic tests at an elementary stage.) Students' final performance in degree examinations is categorized into classes. A "first class" demands a magnificent performance and an outstanding intellect. It stands its possessor in good stead for many years, if not throughout life. British students, receiving grants, are thus discouraged from trying to "earn their way through college," which would be impossible because of the required study (to say nothing of lower wages than in North America). Until recently, higher degrees in British universities were difficult to attain, demanding long periods of independent work. For example, a Ph.D. in Education from the University of London took six years of full-time study after the first degree, or 10 years of part-time research. Hence a doctorate is still a mark of real distinction even among the members of a university teaching staff. Since about 1965, the minimum time required for some higher degrees has been shortened, so that it is possible to obtain a master's degree in some fields in one year of full-time study (but not, for example, in a year's professional preparation as a future teacher). A Ph.D. is a notable achievement, not a basic certification for the university's teaching strength. A D.Lit. or D.Sc. is a still higher award, based upon substantial publications.

Graduate studies are a regular part of any university's provision. At the University of London, for example, postgraduate students numbered more than 28 percent of the enrollment at the time of writing. But this is unusually high. It is not the custom to hive students off to a graduate school for this work, though the Robbins Report anticipated that there would be "special institutes for scientific and technological education and research" at this level (called SISTERS from their initials). This has not been followed up, because of the belief that there must be a continuum of research throughout the whole of any university's life. In some instances, however, where higher studies in the scientific and technological field appeared to be lacking, postgraduate colleges have been set up—as at Oxford. Normally, such work takes place in established institutions, though many regret the failure to implement this part of the Robbins proposals. Commonwealth and other overseas students form a large part of the intake into higher education, together averaging over 10 percent of the whole. London's Commonwealth proportion accounts for 10.3 percent of total enrollment, while foreign students add another 8.2 percent. A large number of these are postgraduate students, or are in law or medicine. Women number fewer than one third of most universities' enrollments, though their proportion is growing.

In Britain a large array of certificates and diplomas adjudicated by leading professional organizations, or granted by colleges of further education (and occasionally by universities), takes the place of the majority of degrees awarded in American professional colleges. A British university degree is usually a more advanced award, based on a larger body of fundamental knowledge. It does not always indicate (even in the more technological subjects) that much attention has been paid to the application of research to the daily problems of life and industry, whereas the professional diplomas do. Bankers, accountants, surveyors, architects, and journalists are not usually graduates. The possessor of a university degree was traditionally expected to look toward continuing inquiry and research, or administration, rather than be occupied with the practical on-the-job adjustments that increasingly become his lot after graduation now. The old assumptions are changing, however, especially in "sandwich" courses or in relation to them. New universities (and some departments of older ones) now maintain close links with the world of industry and commerce.

Though no colleges of advanced technology were, strictly speaking, technological universities before 1965, they already had many features of such institutions. They enjoyed, for example, a wide measure of autonomy, receiving direct grants from the Ministry of Education instead of being dependent upon local resources. Their students were of university caliber, and after taking the Diploma in Technology (the award made on the satisfactory conclusion of one out of more than 100 different courses) they could proceed to postgraduate studies in a university, or to more "applied" research under guidance for three years. The latter could lead to higher qualifications—even degrees. At this level, interchange of university and CAT students and teaching staff was common. Though the Diploma in Technology was not instituted until 1955, it quickly had a marked influence on ordinary university courses in science and technology, in which fields some two thirds of all university degrees were already awarded. Moreover, for such *postgraduate* diploma courses as that in Management Studies (established in 1960), university and CAT graduates or diploma holders were combined.

The Diploma in Technology has now been given full graduate status as a bachelor's degree (B.Sc.), and a free flow between other substantial diploma courses and higher degree courses is possible in both directions. This is especially so under the dispensation of the Council for National Academic Awards, a body set up in 1964 to grant degrees from B.A. or B.Sc. to Ph.D. level. After the present transitional period, it seems certain that many awards hitherto called "diplomas" are likely to be reconstituted and renamed "degrees." Their content is evolving rapidly to meet new industrial needs, not to mention the expansion of knowledge and the increasing academic competence of the major colleges on which so much finance and interest is being lavished. Indeed, technological higher education now seems to be the favored child, though some of the newer universities showing liveliness in sociological studies may be similarly indulged.

Some of these high level technological or managerial courses are followed on a full-time basis; but a large and perhaps increasing number are "sandwich" courses. That is, to say, either periods are spent alternatively in college and in industry, or else a preparatory year in industry is followed by a full-time college or university course and then rounded off by another year in industry. A majority of courses following the first pattern last for four years, though a substantial minority extend for four and a half or five years. A few similar courses can be concluded in three full-time years in college which must, however, be followed by a further year's full-time industrial training. The over-all time spent is about the same. That is the organizational plan of the former Dip. Tech. courses in the former colleges of advanced technology (now B.Sc. courses in the universities of technology). In 1964, there were 10,000 students in that category, who are now counted as university students. In addition, during 1965–1966 over 4000 students were enrolled in 89 courses for the new degrees of the new Council for National Academic Awards (CNAA), studying in 39 colleges formally recognized for this purpose. (That number is being extended.)

When, before Robbins, there were ten colleges of advanced technology, they were already operating on a lofty plane. A condition of their work was that it should be exclusively on the university level. Since they have been formally chartered as universities, their promotion has perhaps left a gap. Even before that happened there had existed five "national colleges" specializing in particular technologies, and enjoying considerable university-like independence under their own boards of management. But they were, so to speak, "monotechnics." At a somewhat lower level, and on a broader base, there were 25 "regional colleges of technology" overlapping the university level. These have formed the basis of new "polytechnics" (see p. 148). Still lower down, but well in the range of tertiary education and including some university-level work, are some 500 institutions officially ranked as "major" but which may be called "technical colleges," "colleges of technology," or "colleges of further education"; of these about 350 offer full-time study. In them there are about 120,000 full-time students, 565,000 part-time day students, and nearly 700,000 students for evening only.

Clearly there is a pyramidal structure here, with a flow of talent and opportunity; but it has become necessary to rationalize the system somewhat so as to make the best use of opportunities, of plant, and of personnel. Not all the work of the colleges just described has been at university level, if we use British criteria. None of the colleges, other than the former CATs, have been granted that distinction, even though they now offer genuine degree courses under the dispensation of the Council for National Academic Awards. They also award very many diplomas. For example, there are Higher National Diplomas (HND) in a variety of technologies or professions which are awarded after "sandwich courses" and substantial attainment, officially said to "approach that of a university pass degree" (that is, not quite of the honors standard now usually insisted on in universities). In the 1965–1966 academic year, there were 8000 students preparing for HNDs. At a lower level, but substantial enough to give a preliminary qualification to a civil engineer, for example, comes the Higher National Certificate or HNC, prepared for in 175 colleges. (I say "preliminary" because most professional organizations confer full recognition only after experience and further examinations.)

This is all quite confusing even for an Englishman, though he can without too much difficulty distinguish the main outlines. There was a risk that these might become further blurred because one of the indications of Robbins was that colleges would be encouraged to try out their ambitions academically. However, to rationalize matters it was announced in 1966 that most degree-level work outside the universities and colleges of education would be concentrated in some 30 "polytechnics" designated for that purpose. In consequence, we can see that they are, so to speak, the partial inheritors of the colleges of advanced technology, though they are not to be confined to degree-level work as these were. In fact, they are comprehensive academic communities "to complement the universities and the colleges of education" on the side of technology, commercial careers, and the like, now that the former CATs have established themselves at a higher level and will inevitably become more research-oriented.

The establishment of "polytechnics" has not escaped criticism from those principals and college teachers in other places who looked forward to satisfying their ambitions according to the Robbins formula. (And that, in its notion of a pyramidal structure with an upward flow of talent is reminiscent of Sidney Webb's ideas more than half a century before in Britain, or Tappan's in the United States.) The reason given for concentrating degree-level work and apparatus was the husbanding of strength for greater effort and efficiency. All advanced countries with rapid development of higher education show the same tendency to develop and bluntly recognize a hierarchical structure within higher education itself. The California Master Plan of 1960, mentioned in the chapter on the United States, is a case in point—only one of several in that country. But the mention of California reminds us that the British officially-used phrase "comprehensive academic community" is, itself, reminiscent of the catchword "multiversity" which has been applied to the University of California. While conserving the exclusive dignities of the universities (whether old-style, new-style or technologically reoriented), the British seem to be responding on the higher education plane to the ever mounting content and ever expanding range of modern occupational training—and also to the widening range of talent coming up from high ability ranges in new-style secondary schools.

In any case, it is obvious that even before the reforms of the past decade, British "technical colleges," of whatever rank, have been doing a heavy volume of work comparable with that in the *Technische Hochschulen* (technological universities) of Germany, or in colleges and graduate schools of American universities. Yet until the past few years they have not in any way received recognition as universities in Britain. This unofficial disdain is not peculiar to Britain; it is fully representative of nearly all the world. Sometimes, to be fair, the very utilitarian concentration of attention on *training*, or on knowledge of a rather narrow kind, has contributed to the "two cultures" mentalities (that is, on both sides) which have really deepened ignorance and hardened insensibility on the part of both scientists and literary people. The latter have claimed to be the "humanists." The other college people have tried to become "humanists" by adding a "liberal" jam or sandwich-spread to their bread and butter. In fact, something of this sort was required of colleges of advanced technology in Britain, as well as their American counterparts. In the long run, however, the humanizing perspective or sensibility can be given in and through vocationally linked studies, as in a doctor's preparation or that of a teacher. Certainly this is one of the areas in which the Soviet Union can claim some modest success.[8] The gradual development of this and comparable university-like features in British "further education" is one of the cares of a Further Education Staff College, and several regional advisory boards as well as the advisory councils at central government level.

The huge reconstruction of British technical education at the higher levels, which gathered pace from 1956 onward, has more recently taken under review such ill-defined areas as that between school and further education, either in colleges or in apprenticeships. Britain has no "junior colleges," though notable proposals for them have been made in recent years, entirely superseding such notions as those relating to "county colleges" expressed in the 1944 Education Act. Moreover, the link between school and vocational training, mostly in part-time courses, is unsatisfactory and wasteful. Nearly half a million students (mostly part-time) were recently struggling through a bewildering labyrinth of courses, examinations, and qualifications. Not only is there heavy wastage, itself a consequence of poor counseling; there is also

---

[8] This and some of the other problems of "higher" or "further" education (structurally, functionally, and in terms of perspective) are reviewed in my *World Perspectives in Education* (1962), Chap. 8.

imperfect account taken of the extension and variety of secondary education in many new forms which might lead straight on to further education. Those trained are still only a small proportion of those who, in the interests of industrial efficiency, ought to be. The link between schools and technical training is, accordingly, in full process of being tightened.

An Industrial Training Act was passed in 1964. Since then 11 training boards have been set up for different industries, and a further 20 or so will be created within a few years. The boards have statutory powers to raise funds by a percentage levy on a firm's payroll, according to the demands and resources of an industry. In the case of engineering the rate is about 2.5 percent. Firms which show that they have good training schemes are reimbursed, even to the full amount of the tax. The whole purpose of the new program is to encourage firms to do their own training if possible, but not enough care has yet been taken to make sure that the boys and girls really do have the opportunity for attending training courses. Nor is the educational balance of such training courses absolutely assured so far. To make sure of that, further responsibilities may be placed upon the colleges of further education ("technical colleges").

Some readers may be wondering why nothing has been said so far about the education and training of teachers. One reason is that in Britain most of the preparation of teachers does not altogether count as higher education—not yet at any rate—though it is on a level at least comparable with that of American counterparts and is also, in various ways, kept under the scrutiny and protection of university boards of studies. On the other hand, teachers' education does not count as a sort of secondary education—as it does in many parts of the world, notably continental European countries. Nor is it "further education" in the narrow, quasi-vocational sense. In Britain it is a hybrid, with more affinity to higher education, into which it merges at its upper level. That is specially true since Robbins, for that report included the colleges of education (as they are now called, instead of "training colleges" as formerly) squarely within the framework of higher education.

It is often said with justification that the higher education systems of the world can be subjected to a preliminary diagnosis by asking one question: whether they include the preparation of teachers on the university plane or not. From the answer to that question many collateral conclusions may be drawn about a whole range of attitudes and courses.[9] By that criterion Britain cannot be safely categorized. In Britain, the theoretical and practical elements of a teacher's prepara-

[9] See my *World Perspectives in Education,* Chap. 9, for some of these problems.

tion are distributed between the university departments of education (for graduate teachers), university "schools of education" or "institutes" of education" embracing a number of associated colleges of education (especially for academic purposes), and the colleges of education themselves (especially for less academic and more practical studies). The whole system is in a state of rapid evolution, for which the main tendencies seem quite clear. Let us therefore start with the existing situation.

Teachers' education and training may generally be undertaken in one of two ways. The majority of teachers are admitted to three-year colleges of education (formerly training colleges) after good performance in the General Certificate of Education at Advanced Level in a grammar school. These colleges teach "subjects" of the ordinary academic type, as well as pedagogical subjects such as psychology and history of education, and they pay much attention to sound teaching methods. A teacher's certificate (not a degree) is awarded on the results of the final examination. This is conducted not by the state, but by a university with which the training college is associated for this purpose; but at the end of a probationary year the certificated teacher is "recognized" by the Department of Education and Science. Colleges of Education, following the Robbins Report, also provide for an expanding minority of students new four-year courses combining, with the professional training, a degree (B.Ed.) of the university with whose School of Education they are associated. Some able students may transfer to ordinary university studies in mid-course. Many colleges have long wished to develop their "university" aspect; and in the rapid growth of further and higher education at present underway in Britain this ambition may come closer to fulfillment, though most teachers with certificates teach in junior or secondary schools of the less academic type.

Students who wish to become teachers in academic (that is, grammar) schools or departments must normally go to the university and get a degree of the usual arts or science type, and follow this with a year's professional course in the education department of a university. Such a year consists of practical training and theoretical studies. It leads to a teacher's diploma or postgraduate certificate (not a master's degree). For a master's or higher degree in education (as in any other subject), a longer course of postgraduate study involving research is required. For permission to embark on it, a second postgraduate diploma is usually a prerequisite.

It will be noted that a distinction is made between the teachers in grammar schools or departments (who have a longer and more difficult professional education), and the teachers in other schools. There is this further separation, that before 1970 graduates need not strictly to have more than the ordinary academic degree without professional follow-up. On the other hand, as we have seen, all teachers have had a sound grammar school education or its academic equivalent before going on to college and university. This makes impossible the cleavage that is implicit in the older continental pattern of recruitment from different types of secondary school for the two sections of the teaching profession. Moreover, an increasing number of university graduates have for some years found their way into teaching in schools or "streams" of the nongrammar types. This, with the equality of basic pay, helps to alter the internal social structure of the teaching profession in Britain. Moreover, the universities' "Institutes (or Schools) of Education" are in special relationship with the colleges of education in their areas, keeping up their standards with advisory boards, and undertaking the work of examination, which they share with the colleges' teaching staff.

The other kind of segregation from which teachers can suffer—namely, isolation from those who have pursued "liberal arts" or graduate studies—does not apply to graduate teachers in Britain. They start out with just the same sort of university education as the other professions, and they have very often done equally well or better in the same university examinations. They are encouraged to pursue researches and attain postgraduate awards in their original academic fields as well as in "education." Moreover, those who impart their professional education to them, and those who supervise or administer their work, can usually claim real academic competence of the best university character in non-education subjects, as well as sound experience in schools and their associated problems. This academic strength is steadily increasing, because of ever closer association between colleges and universities, and also because of involvement in research projects of a fundamental or applied kind which are now developed both officially and privately. The idea of a pedagogical ghetto, isolated behind a hedge of "professionalism," would be anathema both to the colleges of education and to the universities. The association of the colleges with universities has been strengthened notably since 1963, but it has a firm foundation in the Institutes of Education established soon after 1944.

Another kind of possible isolation seems to be precluded by a very recent development of teacher-preparation (sometimes on a sandwich basis) in the new technological universities, and also by the provision of some courses for teachers in colleges of technology at a somewhat lower level. Day by day such future teachers rub shoulders with colleagues who are very practically engaged in workaday affairs. Moreover, the association of some teacher-preparation with the training of social workers—at least for informative and theoretical studies—revives an old proposal of the McNair Report of 1944, and at the same time comes closer to meeting the Newsom suggestion of 1963 that teachers should pay more attention to the social aspects of their professional life.

Teachers are encouraged to undertake a fair amount of in-service training and refresher courses. These may be provided by the Institutes of Education (now more often called Schools of Education) or by the local education authorities, or the central Department of Education and Science. A great effort has been made recently to involve teachers more and more in active research or experimental work, most conspicuously in the teaching of science and mathematics, but equally as soundly in the teaching of almost all topics and ranges of children.

Leaving the formal side of after-school education, we come to a large if amorphous proliferation of "adult education." Britain has long been rich in courses provided by the University Extension movement (from 1867 on), by the Workers' Educational Association (from 1903 on), and by numerous voluntary organizations. In addition, local education authorities provide a range of opportunities from the humblest to the highest level for people who come out of general interest. In American terminology these are noncredit courses; that is, they do not count toward degrees. Yet that has never seemed a drawback. In some cases the universities' Departments of Extra-Mural Studies offer the incentive of nonvocational diplomas. One or two such departments now run televised programs, some of which lead more systematically to the obtaining of certificates and may, in time, lead on to university degrees. In fact, it is the declared intention of the Department of Education and Science to develop this kind of systematic study in a "University of the Air," which would doubtless bear some resemblance to the practice familiar in the United States and in Japan.

Before going on to mention broadcasting generally, it should be explained that, under the 1944 Act, all LEAs are required to make sure that in their areas a full educational range of everything that may be reasonably needed is available to residents. They are not required to provide it themselves, though many of them have truly worked wonders. In support of their own endeavors, or perhaps because their adult students prefer it that way, nearly all of them support financially and in other ways the work of Workers' Educational Association and the universities' Extra-Mural Departments when those operate in their local areas. The Department of Education and Science also assists financially such "responsible bodies" as the Workers' Educational Association and Extra-Mural Departments. Cooperation is exceedingly smooth.

The British Broadcasting Corporation (BBC) is a national system. It is financed out of public funds collected in the form of a small license fee from each radio owner. There are no advertisements. The BBC's affairs are administered by a largely independent body of experts representing public affairs, entertainment, and the arts and sciences. Programs are generally of a good standard. Set periods are devoted to school broadcasts by radio, and similar programs for adults. Teachers' and children's pamphlets are issued in connection with this service. Three main programs are provided, with regional variations. The "Third Program" regularly provides talks of a university standard for adults, as well as music and plays of the highest quality. There is also a BBC television service and an independent television system. School television began only in 1957, but is now assiduously used and universal. The Inner London Education Authority has its own school television service. Needless to say, all other kinds of audio-visual aids, language laboratories, and other mechanical aids are widely used. Several universities operate closed circuit TV systems.

Intellectual and civic life in Britain is also enriched by such officially sponsored but largely self-regulating bodies as the Arts Council (to promote music, the arts, and associated interests) and the National Foundation for Educational Research. A distinctive feature of Britain is the number and variety of tax-supported organizations operating in the public interest and under close public scrutiny, but with an effective measure of independence and self-determination. In addition to those, and on top of services connected directly with schools, there are also official organizations like the Youth Service (catering to the leisure of young people between the ages of 15 and 20), which is organized by the Ministry of Education in association with the LEAs, and the Youth Employment Service, which acknowledges young people's need for help in securing satisfactory and beneficial employment.

It will be recognized that although the United Kingdom is in many ways a near-socialist republic, committed to what its critics call the welfare state and what its supporters call the social services program, it is still custom-bound and strongly conservative in very many respects. The "rights of man" are not talked about; they are acted upon. Life to most overseas visitors seems very orderly and polite and loyal. Crimes of violence, drunkenness, and the like have greatly increased again in recent years; but still they are proportionally little worse than they were fifty years ago. Policemen are not armed. There are no flags in British schools except in the cupboard for rare display, and there is no daily declaration of allegiance. Strangely enough, there is always a "corporate act of worship" and there is also religious instruction of an agreed nondenominational kind (except in church schools). Pupils can withdraw from both of these on conscientious grounds. Yet surveys

made in 1957 showed that only 14 percent of all denominations go to
church on Sunday; 70 percent believed in God (but only 41 percent in a
personal God); and 85 percent believed that Christians need not go to
church. Church attendance, Bible reading, and formal observance are
taken less seriously nowadays. On the other hand, there remains some
reliable indication of religious interest, though usually of a theologically
imprecise kind, which has to coexist with a growing disrgard of what
orthodox Christians believe to be the correct sexual code. A 1966 survey of the population as a whole indicated that less than one-third
never go to a church at all; 42 percent go for weddings, Christmas, or
Easter; and more than 25 percent go between one and four times a
month. Yet when we recognize that Catholics, for instance, must be in
that 25 percent, others do not show up too well. If we confine our attention to young people, we see that two thirds of young people under 16
never attend church or Sunday school.

It is sometimes said to be in consequence of this that young people's
sexual code is much slacker than it was. Despite firm acceptance of the
traditional Christian code of sexual belief in many quarters, those
norms are more disregarded than formerly, challenged by an increasing
percentage of the young. At least that is true of older adolescents and
young adults, not least when they become students in higher education, although it is questionable whether out-and-out promiscuity is
as common as sometimes alleged. Premarital continence is openly
stated by many young people "going steady" to be as unjustifiable as
it may be irksome. Christians very often equate "morality" with sexual
punctilio, and no parent takes kindly to the thought that his or her
children may be having sexual experience whether dishonorable or
perhaps "honorable." Therefore we tend to condemn, perhaps with
good reason; but it should be remembered that the young people themselves may condemn us for the immorality of social injustice, or nuclear
weapons, or just for our hypocrisy as "whited sepulchres." Many have
also been stupidly deprived of their educational birthright. In some
respects they have lively consciences, sensitive to world disasters such
as famine and ignorance. Any such topic brings a lively response in
discussion and action.

In any case, so many rigidities of an unquestionably unacceptable
kind have had to be softened down in Britain during the past generation
that it is not surprising if young people (and their elders sometimes)
behave like the proverbial adolescent boy of the upper classes a century
ago. People read enough to know of Victorian humbug and Edwardian
irresponsibility. Change is so fast during the present phase of a non-
violent social revolution, and young people feel a need to find their
own frontiers. In any case, the export of loud British bands and lively

teenage fashions should not lead observers to identify prominently
displayed eccentricities as the norm. Though it is true that higher
living standards make people of all ages less willing to put up with
dictation or standardization—and, therefore, more reluctant to work
hard for meager rewards, it should not be forgotten that Britain exports
16 percent of its gross national product in order to live, has the biggest
computer industry outside the United States, and has a most impressive record of inventions and personal services.

These remarks do not justify complacency, but the immense turn-
about exemplified by the educational transformation described in
the present chapter indicates that Britons are businesslike. However, they tend to underplay the enormous social, technological and
educational revolution which is going on under anyone's eyes. They do
not altogether like it, though they know it must happen. All Western
European countries (and many others) are undergoing astonishing
change, as the full social logic of the Industrial Revolution overtakes
them; but amid deep attachments to tradition or ancient forms such as
Britain cherishes, every radical innovation looks like a betrayal of
something rather holy, though no one may know why. Habits of conscience (indeed nonsensical scruples) play tricks that sometimes hold
up progress, sometimes make for real stability.

What are the controls? Custom and self-regulation, through the
many types of association and belonging that every Briton takes for
granted. One of these is the school, with its strong emphasis on character strengthening, though far less socialization goes on than in
American schools, the emphasis being on responsible personality. "Student government" of the American type is also very rare indeed; one
way or another the prefect and "house" systems, and all the numerous
societies, communicate a similar message in a more paternalistic way.
Parents and teachers expect and get considerable respect. Education
at school and home is not "child-centered"; in the better homes and
schools children are given "equal consideration in equal circumstances."
There is still much loosening-up to do, however, and a need for more
diversity with subtler reaction to a changing world. The old social
structure (with its injustices) and the old international situation (with
its imperial advantages) are changing faster than habits. The schools'
increased opportunities are bringing about a social revolution, but
many of their assumptions remain conservative.

Some time-honored criteria need to be changed. The premium on
certain kinds of ability, on certain "gentlemanly" subjects and mannerisms, on certain professions—all this needs re-evaluation in a transformed social and international context. "Character training" of the
old-fashioned defensive (or "stuffed shirt") type can well be replaced

by an informed and active social responsibility. In some ways this change has begun, but it needs to be speeded up, systematized, and also communicated to that majority who previously had little dynamic character training in school. The old constraints that made conventional proprieties seem inevitable are now relaxed. It would be a pity if emancipation brought no positive opportunities for learning civic and personal responsibility.

Honesty demands the admission that, as an official document said before the 1944 Education Act, most British children still suffer (to use a photographic metaphor) from being underexposed, underdeveloped, and underfixed educationally. British education is not popular in the strict sense of the word. Too many people slip through its meshes affected only didactically; too few find much relationship with their lives; too many think of it as restrictive or childish. By contrast with other English-speaking countries, British schools (and still more their social consequences) often seem complacent and unevocative.

If ever the old school patterns had a real and persistent virtue in themselves (as distinct from the homes where they were cherished) they cannot automatically diffuse virtue to a wider population now in a world that has altered so much. For educational no less than hard economic reasons, much more understanding and responsibility will have to be rehearsed in workaday situations—in relation to jobs, on the job, and through the job. Jobs are still considered altogether too much in terms of knowledge, proficiency, and examination-type excellence—whether we are thinking of plumbers or professors of Greek and Latin. Therefore personality, citizenship, and broader humanity tend to be either taken for granted or developed in a purely hortative way (as in old-style adult education classes). This is a danger particularly acute in Britain, for at least two reasons. British society is so rich in manifold types of "belonging," in venerable public and private associations—each with its own system of rehearsal in public or private virtues—that decency and human dignity seem to happen naturally without cultivation. But the old-fashioned matrices of social decency need to be replaced or modernized. The second reason is that even now it is often assumed that the more admirable characteristics of man belong to a special class of society, and can probably not be associated with "common" people engaged in "common" pursuits at work or play. Only a few diehards dare to put such thoughts in words, but the schools often exemplify them in stratification, isolationism, or other-worldliness.

Now that a vast proportion of Britons, previously underprivileged, are not only "in the money" but determined to show themselves as good as their neighbors, it is urgently necessary to repudiate the old suspicion that they are essentially inferior or uncultivable because they do not display certain kinds of intellectual nimbleness. It is equally necessary to call for, and reward more fully, a really responsible co-partnership in industry and public affairs. Millions of Britons and hundreds of their towns still show deep scars of former contemptuous treatment and near-servitude. It is difficult for them not to feel hostility and a "two nations" attitude toward the privileged, especially as "parity of esteem" and "equality of access" are still so far from being achieved in the nation's schools. If the schools could really become the people's institutions, linked effectively with the learning of a job or other daily preoccupations, and leading to a fairer range of the professions, more would be done to combine "cultural" considerations, "gentlemanly" attitudes, and civic responsibility with the interests of what are still sometimes called "working class" children.

External history and internal social change have brought about a revolution in Britain more radical than some countries have achieved with bloody cataclysms. Some have been swept into totalitarianism for less. Others have been driven to reactionary conservatism. British habits of "muddling through" have made it possible to retain what seems to be the "best of the old" amidst a desperate struggle to come up to date. Britain's attempt to establish social justice is orderly and likely to succeed; though for efficiency, no less than social justice, some downright alteration of the school system is long overdue. The schools of Britain are the chief instruments of social change—more so than in most countries. But only a radical alteration of the school's orientation, as well as of their practices, can help a formerly imperial and hierarchical country to live effectively in its present circumstances. Britain needs an alert and coordinated adjustment (itself flexible and changing) to the world which she has done so much to transform—economically, socially, scientifically, and politically.

5

THE UNITED STATES | A NATION
OF AMERICA | ON WHEELS

The United States has been aptly described as "the great experiment."
It is a nation very largely made by conscious human contrivance. The
building of it during nearly two centuries has been in accordance with
plans originally devised for universal human betterment—though, of
course, nature and chance and human vagaries have all helped to baffle
the calculator. Nevertheless, as things stand, the United States is a
nation second to none in international power, superior to all in its
material standards of living, and probably fourth in the size of its
population (180 million in 1961, expected to reach 200 million in the
1980s). Only China, India, and the Soviet Union are more populous.

If it were not that its educational devices and its history have welded
a passionate nationhood, the United States might be a loose federation.
Its territories are vast. The area of the continental United States is
over 3,500,000 square miles, little short of that of the whole of Europe.
If the moon could be imagined as a disk laid flat on the map of the

United States, the Atlantic and the Pacific coastal states would be well exposed at the sides. The northern states have severe winters, during which the farmers gaze for months on a lonely white landscape dotted at rare intervals with clustered farm buildings. In the South, at the very same time, the roses are in bloom on New Year's Day, and the streets are lined with date palms. Between the near-tropical splendors of the Gulf Coast and the northern silences there is almost every imaginable type of terrain—gentle green lands like England, huge mountain areas where great forests are smoky with mist, plains of vast extent, the Rocky Mountains bare and wild enough for the moon itself, extensive and fantastic deserts, mangrove swamps that are the homes of ibis and alligator, and the Pacific pines and orange groves. It is not surprising that even without conscious encouragement the settlers who struggled out into this remarkably diverse country developed strong regional characteristics. The mere winning of a livelihood must so often have been a fight for self-vindication. In such circumstances men are bound to work out their own way, and if they were refugees from other people's dictation (as so many of the settlers were) autonomy and self-sufficiency were doubly valued.

As though the lessons of sheer survival were not enough, the men and women who made North America their home very often brought with them systems of religious or secular government that were schools of self-sufficiency also. Except in the oldest colonies, settled by Englishmen, congregational types of parish regulation and of civil jurisdiction were transplanted from England to a freedom for development that they had never fully known at home. Self-determination became not merely customary, but a right and a virtue. Indeed, even the oldest colonies with their hierarchical and regal administrations championed universal claims for unrestricted self-government and self-development when the time came for a breakaway. To this very day this is the core of America's message for the future, her central legend. And the legend is supported by facts. There are not merely fifty sovereign states; there is a most thoroughgoing decentralization of authority even in towns and villages. These are called cities in the American idiom when they are incorporated, though by British standards the majority of these self-governing communities are very small. Certain powers are reserved to counties, as in Britain, but the over-all tendency is to encourage decentralization wherever possible.

Among modern and fully developed nations, the United States is the supreme example of a decentralized system. This characteristic applies particularly to school arrangements. Each state is sovereign in regard to education. It determines the length of compulsory schooling, makes its own school laws, sets standards for teacher training and re-

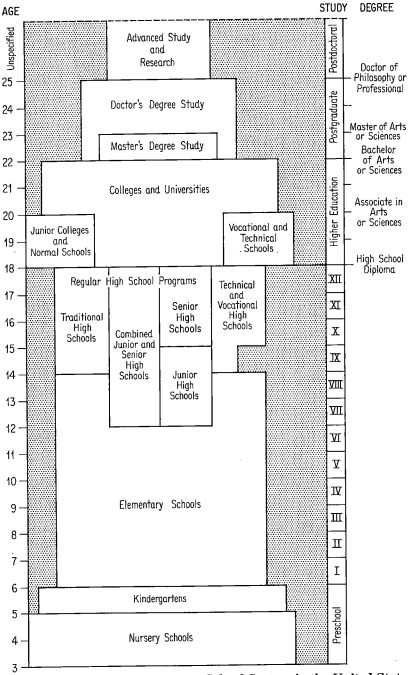

AGE

Unspecified

25
24
23
22
21
20
19
18
17
16
15
14
13
12
11
10
9
8
7
6
5
4
3

Advanced Study and Research

Doctor's Degree Study

Master's Degree Study

Colleges and Universities

Junior Colleges and Normal Schools

Vocational and Technical Schools

Regular High School Programs

Technical and Vocational High Schools

Traditional High Schools

Combined Junior and Senior High Schools

Senior High Schools

Junior High Schools

Elementary Schools

Kindergartens

Nursery Schools

STUDY   DEGREE

Postdoctoral

Doctor of Philosophy or Professional

Postgraduate

Master of Arts or Sciences

Bachelor of Arts or Sciences

Higher Education

Associate in Arts or Sciences

High School Diploma

XII
XI
X
IX
VIII
VII
VI
V
IV
III
II
I

Preschool

School System in the United States

cruitment, and so on. Yet these definitions may be considered the outside boundaries which, though strictly enforced, permit local initiative to enjoy a great deal of latitude. A city usually has its own school system, which it pays for substantially out of its own revenues; it can go far beyond the minimum requirements of state legislation in what it demands and provides; it can set its own curriculum and make ordinances of a very detailed and independent kind. Unincorporated communities are regulated by school district or county boards. Two states, Delaware and Hawaii, have a unitary state system. The size and resources of all these education authorities vary greatly. The City of New York, for example, legislates for many more children than there are in the whole country of Denmark, and in an equally centralized way. Within the very same state, however, there were also 7912 responsible school districts in 1937, some of them much poorer in ideas as well as in resources.

Since then, as over the whole country, "consolidation" for school purposes has proceeded rapidly, so that by 1960 the number of fully responsible school districts in New York State was reduced to 596. Discrepancies are still amazing within nearly every state; but this is only to be expected where self-determination is so highly prized. In 1950, there were 40,605 school districts in the United States; in 1967, about 27,000. Many do not maintain high schools, however, and fewer still have college facilities. For various reasons of interdependence, such as basic financial help and scholarship awards, greater reliance on centralized direction has been growing in recent decades. There are also many unofficial sources of centralizing influence—quite apart from relationships with state or federal government—and some of these will be mentioned later.

As compared with those of Britain, schools themselves have small powers of autonomy. The curriculum is determined already; the principal is responsible to the city (or county or district) superintendent for the administration of the state education law and local ordinances. On the other hand, parents have very much more say in the running of schools and policy-making for schools than they have in any other country. The American school is very much a folk institution. From the earliest days it has been intended to respect the ideas (religious or secular) of its community and to further their material ambitions. It is not the channel of officially correct enlightenment that the school is supposed to be in France; neither is it an instrument for the dispensing of norms and graces from the upper classes, as it was traditionally in Britain. The American school has long been an extension into the future of the working community itself, with its plans for satisfactory jobs and for public prosperity and comfort. At the same time, it is also imbued with the hallowed purpose of self-determination. It is a place where children are given more thought and latitude than they enjoy in any other school system. The somewhat contradictory influences of the community and of the individual's own growth requirements are discernible in any American school to a marked degree.

The basic facts of the American school system are simply told and impressive in their plain assumptions. It is expected that every ordinary child will attend a public school close to his home, moving on from elementary school to high school at a later stage without examination, together with all the other boys and girls who went to school with him. They are likely to stay in the same high school together until about the age of 18, and nowadays a significant proportion will go on to a further stage of education, called "higher education" in the United States. That will include opportunities for general education, together with optional courses in vocationally linked or preprofessional education. Admission to some form of this "higher education" (which should not be identified with other countries' provision of the same name) is normally secured by possession of the school-leaving certificate. Public primary and secondary education are free; higher education is usually not, but is seldom beyond the means of an average-income family and is increasingly accessible through scholarships, loans, or other facilities.

A remarkable American assumption is that in formal education people are not "thrown out" as they are in many countries; nor do they quit of their own accord with any readiness. The onward flow of attendance is amazing. Elementary schools nearly all begin at the age of 6, and high school may begin at the age of 14 (old-style) or 12 (newer and now dominating style). In the latter pattern, high school is usually divided into two halves; junior high school (12 to 15) and senior high school (15 to 18). The school is a neighborhood center of interest, closely associated with parental support if not control, and is an integral part of community life. The public school reflects this community aspect in everything that happens within its walls or around it. The young children are welcomed into a community and encouraged to make their own. As the children mature, they are initiated into many sectors of American life (such as self-government), and as far as possible whatever they study or learn about is given a social perspective. Insofar as educators can contrive, the school is metaphorically "all windows" or "all doors"; and in most of the schools the intellectual and personal atmosphere prevailing reflects this pedagogical assumption. The big question whether educators have succeeded in their intensions has been pressed home in recent years; but of the intention there has hardly ever been little doubt. American educators by their child-study, and by the technology of educational organization, have done very much for the schools of every country in the world.

Some children do not attend the public school. The majority of these go elsewhere for sectarian reasons. They are predominantly Roman Catholics, though schools of other denominations are to found—Jewish or belonging to the larger Protestant denominations in large cities, but sometimes adhering to tiny religious communities in the countryside. Such parochial schools (as religious schools are generally called) do not receive tax support, though this constitutional separation of religious institutions from the public schools' tax advantages has been a subject of recurring controversy. The traditional American assumption, however, has been that "the people's schools" are local, free, and secular community extensions of the home.

The typical American school (though it is dangerous to talk in such terms of a land so diverse) is a bright and cheerful place. With their generous supply of impressive pictures, the American information services have familiarized the world with how the schools look in any go-ahead city (and that is what each American community considers itself). There is certainly an American flag; in fact, one may be displayed in each classroom. Well-fed children in a gay variety of clothes —all the more informal because the interior is very warm—evidently feel that the school is their very own place. Mobile desks and chairs facilitate rearrangements for group work and other types of "sharing" (a hallowed word). Books are very well illustrated and expensively produced; their contents are directly related to problems within the child's daily interests. They are usually weighty in the literal sense only. There is practically no suggestion anywhere that they represent authority. Nor does the typical teacher, if it comes to that. The school is a place where a community of children is housed, with suitable personnel to help them realize themselves in their world, and with suitable aids of other sorts. In their material aspect the classrooms are often lavish, including not merely pictures and wall charts (many devised by the children themselves), but radio, films, and television in the bigger schools. Considering the generosity with which these audio-visual aids are provided, a European is sometimes surprised at the relative lack of apparatus for children to use in a search for knowledge (that is, microscopes or lenses or simple scientific apparatus). This comment is still true despite the great enrichment of interest, and the generous funds available, under the provisions of the National Defense Education Act of 1958, or the very encouraging financial and advisory support offered subsequently by state or federal legislation and the learned foundations. There is, however, abundant provision of wood and metal and automobile workshops in schools of any size for older children, and home economics for girls is efficiently and gracefully taught.

In this very point of contrast with many European schools we find something distinctively American. A twofold emphasis prevails in the United States: practice in skills directed toward visible and practical ends; and a suggestion that manipulations enjoyed (as in a constructional workshop) have a near-absolute merit in themselves, irrespective of whether they contribute to human knowledge and happiness or not. Europeans are struck by these assumptions in schools and teachers of all types. Under American conditions they are more to be expected, quite apart from the prevalence of Dewey-sponsored philosophy and methods. Indeed, one may say that Dewey was a spokesman and philosophical planner for the basic assumptions of the typical American school. Regard for knowledge is often limited to its instrumental value —not a bad notion if we take a farsighted and comprehensive view of human problems. The criterion for its usefulness must be conceived in children's terms; and the children must find their own pace and their own way into the future. These have been the clarion calls of the great European educations from Rabelais through Comenius and on; but they have received their fullest (though sometimes travestied) realization in the American school. Paradoxically, it might be maintained that the Americans are the only true Europeans—the only people who have so far carried out the great traditions of the West with the richness and universality that industrialization has made possible. It certainly seems that these aims, socially speaking if not always scholastically, come nearest to realization in the best of American schools. Why should this be?

It is impossible to give simple reasons. It is certainly not because Americans care more for education than do others. In some ways they do; but foreign visitors usually believe the opposite when they see what American schools do. Nor is it because Americans spend more money on education than others; in proportion to their incomes they certainly did not until recently, at any rate. Even now, with an average of above $450 spent annually on every child in the public schools, it is doubtful whether that sum takes proportionately more out of the brimming national income than the school expenditure of other advanced nations. (Underdeveloped countries are sometimes driven to invest proportionately more in education.) One of the main motivating factors behind the astonishing fiscal allocations to education which have taken place in the United States since about 1958 has been the realization that

American financial commitment to school investment was not keeping pace with the national need at home or the country's international development as one of the two leading world powers.

Yet well within the parental lifetimes of many people who still have children at school, these were not the kinds of consideration that seemed to matter in any evaluation of the apparently flourishing school system. In the eyes of most parents and almost all teachers, the schools of the United States seemed, until recently, to be almost self-evidently admirable, an example to the world. Busy and happy places most of them undoubtedly were, if present-day questions of purpose and orientation or achievement were not too searchingly pressed. How did it come about that Americans so successfully established their school system as one that was child-centered and "progressive?" Do they love their children more? It would be rash to claim so. It is certainly true that most Americans, living in a rich and still incompletely exploited country, feel they can well afford to spare the time and resources necessary for their type of education in a way that no other nation could— just as they can throw away longer cigarette butts and waste more food and use up automobiles faster than other nations. But why should they wish to? There is no need to hazard a complete answer that would be false anyway. But some suggestions are offered by a glance at American history and America's industrial prospects.

The American settler's eye has always been away from the past and turned toward the future. The prevailing inclination has always been away from absolute authority and toward some pragmatically justified solution for today, and perhaps for tomorrow. "Universals" and "absolutes" often faded in the rigors of forest and frontier life. We should remember that these hard conditions have not altogether disappeared now, and that they are actual memories of thousands if not millions of grandparents. They still live in the anti-intellectualism of most small provincial cities. Moreover, the conditions of westward expansion— achieved by generations of spasmodic migration at walking pace, from scarcely established settlements out into an unknown challenge— created and re-created opportunities for women and children, no less than for men, to show themselves equal in practical use as well as in personal value. Accuracy of shooting, skill with the ax and plough, toughness in the face of acute physical distress—all these things superseded old-style parental and governmental authority. They left no room for a leisured class making "culture" its playground or badge of office. They also made more tenuous the old interpretations of churches, and made new dispensations seem not merely inevitable but right. Criteria of immediate expediency must often have been the only law in many pioneer settlements. It would not have been surprising if cynical ruthlessness had become the characteristic of American society—which after all is a very new and relatively untried thing outside the older Atlantic settlements. Instead, the traditional British experience that self-government is responsible government, and the often consciously religious sense of a "manifest destiny" that was missionary, added a leaven of self-righteousness to practical considerations. This has from time to time resulted in wild extravagances of course. The long-term results have included both a keen concern that children should be brought up to be useful and civilized, and a feeling that the children's frontiers should not necessarily be the same as that facing the parents at present.

Moreover, the inclusion of many non-American and non-British immigrants in the pioneer settlements dotted at immense intervals over this vast land strengthened the conviction that the future belonged especially to the children now brought up to be Americans in a country strange to the parents. Conditions for growing up were at least unfamiliar. On the whole, they were more evocative and richer in rewards than the parents had known in their day, though they were sometimes very much worse, as is seen in the conspicuous degeneration of some mountain communities derived principally from those of the purest English stock. Even now, the sense of an ever-moving frontier, and of a horizon of limitless possibilities, is a most infectious experience for the visitor welcomed to an American community. Indeed, the very richness and reality of that welcome has a bearing on Americans' attitude to education. There is room for you, even with your odd speech and odder ways. If you can "make out" you will be all right, too. This sounds as though there is no need to conform, and in some ways there is great freedom from such a requirement. It is necessary, nonetheless, to stress in advance the reverse or compensatory side of American life, which is one of the most highly socialized patterns on earth. Insofar as we are considering the effect on children's relationships with their elders, we have to note the extraordinary degree of self-determination of self-justification permitted to the children and, indeed, expected of them.

This theme could be pursued at length, but we have to pass on to the influence of monumental mechanization in a land already abundant in natural resources—so rich, in fact, that the production of food is widely restricted by government subsidies. Each hour worked in the United States produces more goods than anywhere else on earth. This is not individually true of all Americans in all their occupations, of course, but it is true on the average. The amount of mechanization, and its intricacy, have become a byword throughout the world. American pure science has a glorious record of its own in recent years, although Americans are much more successful in the application of scientific discoveries to practical problems. Britain pioneered the world of industrialization; Germany and other European nations have been in the forefront of pure scientific research. Until recently, only a few of the great leaders in this field have been American by birth; but no country has been so overwhelmingly successful in turning its own and other people's discoveries to the production of material abundance. This is partly due to the blessings of geography and the quirks of history; but credit must ·also be given to the restless ingenuity of Americans, native born and immigrant, in making more things mechanically—and, therefore, more cheaply in the long run.

Unlike India and similar nations where excessive manpower, combined with land shortage and lack of capital, make mechanization a prospect full of problems, the United States is constantly concerned with underconsumption of its brimming production. Sales campaigns daily and by every conceivable means urge Americans to use more or at any rate to buy more of everything. So they do. American economists truly tell us that their whole economy is geared to reckless consumption, if not to waste. In an almost closed economy that is nearly independent of imports and exports, no immediate harm is felt at home; but there are many and varied social results which directly or indirectly affect the educational pattern. Some of these must be postponed for later consideration; but one aspect at least is of present importance.

In the present state of American "know-how," a very extensive adoption of automation would offer no serious mechanical or managerial problems. Yet it is very unlikely to take place in the immediate future. Why? Because even now there is little need for young people to go to work at an early age or to earn their way in the world. It is increasingly anticipated that young men and women need not be professionally qualified before the age of 25 or thereabouts. Even now the chances of their holding down a really skilled job in a post of responsibility are postponed year by year. That is not to say that adult Americans do not work hard—they do indeed, but their final involvement in occupations at normal adult American status is perceptibly later as time goes on. Excellent wages can be earned anyway, in unskilled or semiskilled positions if necessary. If automation were allowed to reach its full logic, it is difficult to forecast the outcome in the United States. Though nothing like full-scale automation has been introduced into any industry or commercial enterprise yet, the yearly advance of what we might call the prototechnology of automation throws more unskilled people out of work, and makes it harder for the modestly qualified to compete for good employment.

Aside from any question of competence, the steadily improving

standard of living also accentuates the personal demand for education
—particularly at college or postsecondary level. At the same time, the
social distance between the well-educated and the dropout stretches.
Thus, both from inclination and ambition, and also because of the
changing structure of occupations as technology advances, the American people are demanding more from their schools than almost any
other nation—and that demand is steadily growing. As things are now,
the schools are unmistakably faced with a custodial (rather than a
training) problem that is unfamiliar in other countries. Indeed, many
Americans have remarked that the custodial responsibility is passing
over into the college (post-secondary) phase, which is already achieved
by about 35 percent of the population, and will undoubtedly be reached
by many more. The difficulty is not that of getting boys and girls ready
professionally in the shortest possible time—so that they can help with
the national housekeeping; it might, until recently, have been somewhat unkindly described as that of keeping young Americans happily
and rather profitably occupied as long as possible before getting them
ready. American abundance, it was long thought, could well afford this
kind of parental indulgence. Parents were proud that it was so. Criticisms of American education based upon its slow progress (at any rate
in the typical school) miss an important educational assumption, and
also underestimate the interplay of economic and scholastic considerations which are vital to a fair interpretation of any educational system.

As late as 1956 and 1957, the few Americans who had already been
criticizing low scholastic standards, or a lack of national purpose in education, were considered to be reactionaries or indeed unrealistic by the
majority of parents and teachers, who did not hesitate to declare that
those calling for a more efficient school system were merely harking
back to European norms—or else scaremongers trading in trumped-up
stories about questionable Soviet achievements. In fact, however, as
Professor L. A. Cremin has pointed out in *The Transformation of the
School,* the American resuscitation of real learning and genuinely educative activity would have taken place "had the Russian Sputnik never
illuminated the Western pedagogical skies"; for the unquestioning
adulation of "progressivism" had doomed itself through its own follies
by 1955 at the latest—if only people could see it. Very few lay persons
or general practitioners of education then could, unfortunately, despite
an ever-growing American criticism of American schools' practice, and
of college of education doctrines then in vogue.[1]

---

[1] For an account and analysis of such criticism at this formative period of American
educational history, see my *Society, Schools and Progress in the USA* (1965), especially
pp. 112–117, 165–166, and 168–172.

In the years since 1957, however, Americans themselves have accelerated and broadened the critical enquiries with which a minority among them had seemed to support criticism from outside. Evidence of Soviet technical progress stung discerning Americans like a challenge; reliance to anything like the previous extent on foreign-born or foreign-educated researchers and instructors might be a security risk; and such home-based criticism as that contained in the writings of Dr. J. B. Conant raised many questions about equality of opportunity and the quality of much ·publicly supported schooling. The National Defense Education Act of 1958, by its very title and orientation, aroused the country to the implementation of its domestic and international responsibilities. The magnificent achievements of the space research programs have in recent years enthused the youth of America as well as educational leaders—all the more tellingly because of initial anxieties. From inside the United States it seems as though the great ferment going on—with evidences of increasing competition, "higher horizons," and national merit scholarship awards—is rapidly transforming the educational system.

This may indeed be the consequence over an extended period of time; but short of a national disaster any radical and overall revision of such a diverse agglomeration of localized experiments seems unlikely in the extreme. At any rate, for the youngest Americans, the schools seem to retain their national characteristics. As late as July 29, 1962, the *New York Times* reported a survey of elementary school textbooks under the significant title "Baby Talk," and complained of the proven deterioration of English in college students.

It is perhaps more difficult to achieve a representative national appraisal in the United States than in any other country. The material signs of prosperity encourage complacency, especially when words like "advanced" are used, with their sometimes unmerited overtones of qualitative assessment rather than quantitative measurement. This is particularly marked in school statistics. Is an "hour" or a "year" of any significance at all, unless the time spent is profitably spent on something · that matters? During the pre-1955 period it was already true that on average Americans spent more time over their schooling than the people of any other country. Since that time practically the whole American people has become aware what serious shortcomings were allowed to go unchecked (though quantitatively counted as "hours" or "students") during those years of unconcern for real learning and real purpose at the personal or social level. Since what passed for "progressivism" collapsed during the years 1955–1958 (a period which we shall later survey in more detail), it has still remained difficult for Americans to know America—and above all to appraise American edu-

:ation—for several reasons which continue to hinder clear perception. One of these is the brilliance of American technological exploitation)f national intellectual power at the top level, and also exploitation of vhat Europeans call "the brain drain" of intellectuals imported from)ther places at the pinnacle of their research achievement. The finance)ehind American research, and the incomparable advantages some- ;imes made available in equipment and opportunity (all financially)ased), exercise an enormous pull on scholars outside the United States. In addition, it must be fairly said (as I have already done elsewhere) that the intellectual encounter that can be made at the top level on a very few American campuses may be more stimulating and rewarding than academic life anywhere else. But to say so is to talk about a plane)f existence more remote from many an American college than are the iniversities of Europe. Overlooking this vital distinction, simple but patriotic Americans may believe that the lofty pinnacles of their :ountry are only a little above the foothills pr plateau from which they rise—as happens to inexperienced mountain climbers everywhere. The highly creditable fact that access really is open in the long run to the eager striver who survives all the gruelling exercises of the upward climb, makes many people believe they have reached the same eleva- tion—especially as the same names are used across the country to describe vastly different attainments.

The extreme decentralization of the United States is another con- fusing factor bedeviling American judgment. The sense of nationhood is strong; also, Americans can expect to find the same commodities on sale, and the same material services, wherever they go. The colleges of education and the mammoth textbook enterprises seem to use a universal language. All middle-class parents (and that means nearly everyone) want "college" for their children—so colleges and high schools and kindergartens or anything else may appear to be supplied on a conveyor belt. Yet every parent, stopping to think, knows that that is not the case. Colleges vary vastly, because school achievement varies vastly. Districts vary in resources of material and intellectual kinds; and motivation and quality vary, too. So do the states, though not quite so markedly; yet the five states with the lowest incomes in 1965 spent only $276 per pupil, less than half the average of the five richest states.

That sounds plain enough talk; but the less statistical talk of quality speaks more plainly than ever to those experienced enough to under- stand what is meant. The lower down the scale you go, and the more localized the observations of those passing judgment, the more likely you are to find complacent satisfaction combined with a happy belief that the "satisfactoriness" envisaged usually prevails over the whole

of the intensely differentiated United States. Indeed, when we consider the unparalleled decentralization of the United States, it becomes
astonishing that such a high average of educational attainment has been
reached—if we judge by world averages in far less favored countries.
That is not the criterion by which Americans have ever judged their
living standards, machines, or homes in this century. But school has
been sheltered from outside life, not least during the heyday of "life
adjustment." Though a critical corner is being turned in the decisions
now being made for American education, it is still safe to represent the
average American school as the relatively unruffled place which most
parents and teachers want it to be.

School is still a sort of oasis, a happy land shielded from the stresses
and competitions of adult life—a children's garden in more senses than
Froebel's *Kindergarten* was ever expected to be. Latter-day prosperity
combined with the love and promise for children that are traditional
in America have made the modern American school a wonderful place
in every material way. Observers from other countries will find much
to profit by. They will also find every school a playground of paradox
such as they have not encountered elsewhere, for the simple reason
that no other country's schools are either as experimental or as favored
as those in the United States. Some detailed instances of paradox will
be examined later. It is important to emphasize here that although the
American school is very "realistic" in terms of child-centered education as a rule, it postpones the child's realization that the world is not
child-centered or even (with all respect) America-centered. Gone are
the frightening bugbears of other countries (examinations, corporal
punishment, child labor, and so on); but perplexities of a different kind
may be detected, as we shall see.

In the United States the effects of school life are more marked than
elsewhere, for several reasons. The building of the American nation
into an independent federation was a prescholastic task; but the assimilation of millions of immigrants' children (a problem just as difficult today as previously), and the establishment of a technologically
advanced society, were the responsibility of American schools and colleges. American education has had more to do than most other public
systems, not least because of the remarkable mobility of the American
scene.

Another reason is that even at the college or university level it is
usual to speak of "school." If an Englishman asks which school you
went to, he is quizzing you about whether Eton or Winchester or some
other Public School can claim credit for you. By the same question an
American is asking you which university you enjoyed. In the United
States, moreover, that is a friendly and not a snobbish question (as it

would tend to be in Britain), because it is assumed that you went to college anyway. Soon after World War II one third of the then adult population had finished high school (that is, they had stayed on until 18 years old); nowadays about 95 percent of the children are in school from ages 6 to 17 or 18. In towns of any size, a third of these or more will sooner or later get to college. Perhaps a higher proportion will have a little experience of it. The terms "college" and "university" are regularly used as synonyms in the United States, and both are included under the comprehensive term "school." This significant extension of use for "school" indicates a continuation of juvenile guardianship not found in other countries' universities. Therefore "school" in America covers a much larger proportion of the population for a much longer period than elsewhere.

Moreover, for the reasons already outlined, school is from the very beginning a place where children find their own way of life in their own community, and where the psychological compulsion is away from elders' authority and leadership. Socialization (in the psychologists' sense) is extremely marked, not only because it is inevitable in the circumstances but also because parents wish it to happen too. Some schools have observation rooms with a one-way screen, behind which parents and other observers can watch progress. Needless to say, mothers have many questions to ask, but the first one in nearly every case concerns junior's sociability. It would be absurd to make much of this inquiry if it were not followed up to the very end of school life by similar anxieties.

Without exactly setting out to deliberately do so, the American school pays enormous attention to "community mobilization" at the junior level. In certain spheres of socialization the American school is bound to take priority. We have already remarked on the need felt by many immigrants' children for emancipation into the new world of which they will be citizens. Long-settled countries with innumerable normative mannerisms, and manifold rehearsal systems in public life, do not need to have overt standardization programs like the Americanization which extends down from the level of adult immigrants to every newcomer in the American school. Every school day begins with a salute to the American flag and a declaration of loyalty. This little ceremonial, at first embarrassing to a visitor who takes loyalty for granted, is not attended to perfunctorily but with some solemnity.

Seen dispassionately, it shows once again the community emphasis of American schooling, which is brought out again daily, if not hourly, by many activities involving corporate work, in elective pupil bodies organizing particular aspects of school work and play, and in a remarkable concern lest any child be unusual. Until Sputnik, many parents worried lest any child appeared intellectually outstanding, though there were no inhibitions about being especially good on the sports field. However, inadequacy in the more glamorous sports is not by any means total failure in the bid for popularity, because all kinds of opportunities are provided for each child to be at least in some thing the king of the hour. The pace and scope of school life are skillfully regulated to minimize any appearance of competition, at any rate on anything like a non-American scale. In spite of what Americans believe to be a great increase in competition recently, their system has still to be described (in comparison with other countries) as one generally lacking serious competition inside schools or as between schools. This is true despite wide differences in standards, for differences may be ignored or unappreciated. Some diminution of competition may be a needed corrective in a society that is economically so competitive and sets its social sights so high. But it makes a school's pace seem laggard by a European standard, and it often makes children's behavior seem lackadaisical. Many Americans do not use such a critical word. They see what the foreigner sees but they approve. However, growing numbers are increasingly worried by what they feel to be a lowering of intellectual levels, a devitalizing of initiative, and the risk of uniformity. These are charges that ring strangely in the land of independence and enterprise, and we shall have to examine them more closely in due course.

The American school has innumerable successes to attribute to this very process of assimilation. Children of all types of orientation and from very unequal social backgrounds are taken in to receive a new and promising status. The hardships and perhaps coarseness of the older America are being effaced by an easygoing gentleness in personal relations. To this is added the very real chance of social mobility through access to an unlimited range of jobs. Children whose forebears, less than a hundred years ago, were red-necked frontiersmen in a one-street wooden town (or perhaps even in this century thought a thirty-mile journey an occasion for a three-day visit) are now cosmopolitan Americans with a world of opportunity open to their confidence. Ethnic, religious, and social backgrounds are little handicap to those of European stock. That is more than could be said in most countries of Europe. Moreover, Americans as a rule are tolerant and generous. They are characterized by a real if not always logical reverence for the great human principles of the Renaissance and the Enlightenment. In some ways they are the only true Europeans. The American common school can claim the credit for that.

That is why "the little red schoolhouse" has a place of real affection in American legend. This is no mere nostalgia for childhood; it is also a record of appreciation for an institution that, like the trundling covered wagons and the railroad, has made modern America possible. Those who observe the United States from outside, or even from the big cities, should not imagine that the schools of today are all huge and glossy. The average size of American schools is probably around 400 or 500 children, though in all large towns and cities schools with 2000 children and more are now common. An uncountable number of American schools are still literally of the "red schoolhouse" type, and in most of the states it is easy to find schools that have only one teacher for all the children. The impressively empty countryside that surprises any European is thinly populated with little settlements whose children mainly attend small schools. The automobile and the school bus are slowly transforming school-going; but even in a populous and rich state like California a postwar report revealed as many schools of what Europeans would consider a "village one-room" type as of any other. Of course, their total population was small compared with that attending consolidated country schools or city institutions. Consolidation is a growing practice. The yard of most country schools now shows a row of old-style yellow buses waiting throughout the day to take home the children they rounded up that morning. It is characteristic of American assumptions that in some areas these buses are driven by senior schoolboys. The traffic in the vicinity of schools (even in busy towns) is also normally regulated by the children themselves; they wear distinctive white helmets and other insignia.

The consolidation of schools is more economical in teachers' salaries, in heating, and in other expenses; but above all it gives the children in remoter areas a much better chance of effective and lengthy education than they would otherwise have. School attendance is sometimes very difficult to enforce in the poorer rural areas. Some school district authorities are far from being as diligent as the rest in attending to this matter. Moreover, even if children are brought to school, the educational opportunity set before them varies considerably in extent and quality. Local committees decide fairly freely how much money they are able (or willing) to spend on education. In 1950, over 70 percent of school districts gave the school board the right to levy *its own* taxes, 34 percent were financially independent, and another 22 percent were independent in taxation and budgeting, though partly dependent in other ways. States usually make some gesture toward equalization by subsidizing the poorer areas, yet great inequality prevails. This is one of the major problems in American education, which post-1958 legislation at the federal level is attempting to solve.

Cities acting as manufacturing or trading centers, and thus serving a rural territory as a local metropolis, very often have much better education facilities than their supporting hinterland. Indeed, within any urban area living off a single economic complex, we may find several "cities" that are educationally independent and are endowed with schools of different quality because local tax resources and policy vary. Sometimes this variation depends on the social class or ethnic composition of the population, though not always. In no modern nation is it possible to find greater inequality of access to education from different localities. This is one of the penalties to be paid for such complete decentralization.

It is always a source of astonishment to people outside the United States that public school systems in the favored residential districts outside Chicago, Detroit, Boston, or Cleveland (for example) manifest most of the characteristics of private schools elsewhere. It is true that they are "public" in the sense of being maintained by that section of "the people" who are privileged enough to live locally, and that the schools are open to all local residents, as a rule. But effective zoning of one sort or another in a land of commuters often enables a community to boast that it has "the best school system in the United States," or in its own state. Preferential salary rates, experimental and career opportunities, or even ephemeral fame make the educational provision extremely disparate. Indeed, the mischances of residential fashion can make a district's school level fluctuate violently within a single decade. In 1959, F. M. Hechinger said: "The American school as we know it today does not offer anything resembling fair and equal opportunities." [2] Since that time discrepancies have grown, not diminished, though this fact is usually overlooked or disguised from "the people."

Responsible officials and legislators in every state do their best to "level up"; but there are limits beyond which it is nearly impossible to drive American local sentiment, especially as it is institutionalized in local politics. Education is a political matter not only in the sense that it is a matter of universal public demand, but also because American devotion to "Jacksonian" or "grass roots" democracy causes many offices (such as school superintendent) to be elective in many districts, even though most foreigners think this notion as crazy as the idea of having elected engineers or elected physicians. In Britain, for example, educational officials are professional, though they are closely supervised by the "watchdog" lay committees who finally determine policy. But then rural districts in the United States may also have elected judges, elected tax assessors, and so on. It all goes to show how firm is the

---

[2] F. M. Hechinger, *The Big Red Schoolhouse*. New York: Doubleday & Company, Inc., 1959.

belief that schools must be not only under electoral supervision but directly under electoral (that is, parental) manipulation.

In practice it does not appear that children altogether gain from this Jacksonian approach; at any rate in poor communities. Many schools certainly lack the enviable facilities of better placed neighbors. Teachers' salaries vary enormously, not only between states but sometimes inside a single state. In 1965–1966, the average per annum school salary in California was $8000; in New York State it was $7700; in South Dakota $4650; in Mississippi $4190. In 1960, the extremes were about two thousand dollars for beginners in some rural states to over ten thousand dollars for fully qualified men in some eastern high schools. In fact, the high school teacher in a prosperous district may be paid notably more than university teachers in other parts of the country, while in an extremely favored suburb of a prosperous city it is not unknown for high school teachers to draw such good salaries that they are unwilling to take up university appointments in the same city. Apart from salary discrepancies (with all that they may entail), there are different requirements for recognition as trained teachers, different pension and promotion prospects, different ratings in the local pecking order. The absence of uniform arrangements in these relatively uncontroversial matters means that the standards of professional skill and academic knowledge vary too, even from district to neighboring district. That is without taking account of the rural backwaters and downtown slums whose condition prompted the remedial legislation of 1963 and subsequently, which we shall later review in this chapter.

American parents are normally free from the sort of anxieties that plague British parents, for example. The typical family, enjoying middle-class standards of affluence, lives in a town well served by schools. In fact, before any neighborhood is built, sites are set aside for publicly provided and maintained schools. They can be seen marked on ordinary local maps by those wondering about the location of their new house. Every child, it is assumed, will go to the school in his neighborhood. It will probably be as good as the next one in the same district or town. At least, that is the traditional expectation, though we shall soon see that this may need to be modified. At any rate, little question arises of additional private expense in search of a superior accent or other desirable social badges. It would be foolish, though, to underestimate the significant growth of private schooling in recent years—especially that which is nonsectarian, and not particularly linked with color problems either. Of course, snobbery exists as in all human institutions; but it is trivial by other countries' standards as a rule, being mainly confined to differences in clothes and in family automobiles.

However, fine houses are the latest status symbol in the United States; and if present tendencies continue they will certainly affect the choice of residence (and, therefore, in many cases, school district) greatly. They will accentuate a notable tendency to differentiate the quality of tax-supported schooling according to the parents' income and social position, inextricably bound up as these are with questions of housing. Indeed, growing post-Sputnik anxieties are making the best-informed parents directly relate their choice of residence to the proved existence of "good" (that is, more demandingly academic) schools in the neighborhood. The ever-growing "commuting" distance traveled from home to work makes it just as easy to colonize a good school area as to colonize the perimeter of a country club or golf course, which cynics often say amounts to one and the same area. Moreover, the consciousness of different (and, therefore, competitively or socially desirable) standards of academic attainment in the nation's highest universities has also made parents more desirous than ever of having to find schools which are "good" academically; because, to do them credit, the really distinguished universities are more concerned nowadays to recruit talent rather than wealth. While they become more egalitarian in recruitment, they inadvertently prompt parents to become more selective of their residence in terms of school advantages at the preuniversity stage. This means choosing favored districts, or perhaps sending Junior to a well-known private school during his senior high school years—a practice that is on the increase.

Not many parents are wealthy enough, however, to satisfy such ambitions and, in any case, the overwhelming majority do not have the information or criteria by which to judge scholastic merits or demerits. After all, the same names and mannerisms, and the same amount of time for various activities, may equally characterize quite distinct kinds of school provision. Therefore the typical American school is, and will doubtless continue to be, the neighborhood school. The sort of open or hidden inquiry about *"which* school?" that is usual in England would be either incomprehensible or disgraceful. The number of private schools in America (that is, excluding the parochial schools which in most respects resemble public schools) is small, though growing significantly. The public schools afford as high a standard of intellectual life as most Americans want. Otherwise they would do far more about them—under American conditions of school management they have every opportunity to do so. As it is, the schools offer a higher standard of social apprenticeship than any other country can boast. That is not to say that many things—personal, social, and academic— could not be improved without doing violence to American susceptibilities; it is simply to indicate that the American child, on the whole, benefits greatly by attending his local school rather than any other. The outstanding American child, over a wide range of talents, can usually win through to any desired distinction with the additional gain of a real understanding of what other people's qualities and problems are.

Although Americans are great churchgoers (about 80 percent of them being regular attenders at church), the public schools are all secular. In some states a minimal amount of Bible reading is permitted, but this is unusual. The private schools (including the denominational or parochial schools, a high proportion of which are Catholic) enroll only about 14 percent of the children. It should be noted that the number in private schools rose from 10 to 14 percent in not much more than a decade, perhaps on social and academic grounds as much as religious. This is a reflection of dissatisfaction, therefore, and of willingness to pay for something better; for private schools receive no direct tax aid for their programs, buildings, or equipment. Indirect aid *may* be obtained for special purposes under the Elementary and Secondary Education Act of 1965 or the National Defense Education Act (1958), but under strict public control and within defined limits. Otherwise the constitutional separation of Church and State is rigidly enforced; some districts refuse public transportation to parochial schools.

At the same time, all kinds of inquiries are made in casual conversation about a visitor's religion, as the assumption is that he will have religious beliefs, or at any rate observances, that he will not mind discussing—as in other countries one discusses hats or favorite sports. It is perhaps an indication of American community pressure that this conformity-of-belonging is so keenly sought, though no one seems to mind what you belong to. In other countries with mixed religious communities, questions about one's personal position in regard to them are often felt to be in the same category as questions about family relationships—suited only to the circle of closest intimacy, and therefore avoided. Advertisements in American papers and in subway trains assume that you will link all kinds of ambitions and commodities with church membership. The critical and most indicative words are perhaps "membership" and "corporate life." A great deal of life goes on around the churches. In comparison with other countries, less is said and perhaps less is felt about *being* and believing. As far as the average American child's school is concerned, however, religion is an entirely private matter. There is not, as now in Japan and formerly in France, an attempt to instruct the young in the principles of morality on a secular basis as part of the curriculum. But the stress of community example is powerful. This can have its negative as well as its constructive side, and will be worth examining again when we consider adolescence.

The usual age for beginning school in the United States is 6, although kindergartens exist in many places for children under this age. Many preschool opportunities have been provided in slums and other depressed areas in recent years under what is called the "Head Start Program" initiated by the Economic Opportunity Act of 1964, or reinforced through its agency. Seven of the 50 states require children to attend for eight years; 33 for nine years; 5 for ten years; 3 for eleven years; and 1 for twelve years. These are the legal minimums. As we have seen, most children attend for about 12 years, and many longer. On the other hand, in many areas the attendance of rural children, white as well as colored, is still not really satisfactory though it has greatly improved with the provision of good consolidated schools to which they are conveyed without charge by bus. The number of days in the year on which attendance is required varies a good deal, sometimes for climatic reasons. In the Deep South, for example, temperatures in May (when school finishes) and October (when it recommences) are stifling. Again, a lot depends on the energy and concern of the local officials. The average number of days attended has grown in the past 50 years from 99 to 156 each year. In Britain the figure is nearer 200; but the climate there is unusually temperate (if cool), and in a crowded island there are no real problems of distance.

Boys and girls attend the same school not just in the lowest classes but throughout. Americans are always surprised to learn that segregation of the sexes is common in Britain, and are puzzled to know why. No real problems of any sort—either social or educational—can be fairly attributed to common schooling, and there are many gains. In most northern areas and an increasing number of southern districts, no formal or systematic attempt is made to keep colored children out of any particular public school. Until recently, 17 of the then 48 states legally required the separation of whites and Negroes not only in schools but in public transport and many other places. Several of these states, all in the South, and not usually distinguished by a high standard of education, expressed their determination to resist United States Supreme Court orders which declare this segregation to be unconstitutional even if a semblance is maintained of granting Negroes "separate but equal" opportunity. The most important of these orders was published on May 17, 1954. Long before that time the process of allowing Negroes to enroll in hitherto white schools, instead of in inevitably inferior Negro schools, had gathered momentum. After 1954, many school districts even in the South announced their intention of complying, and integration has in most such cases been achieved with little disturbance. The Negro cannot yet be said to have equal access to education even in the North; but during the hundred years since slavery, and especially during the past generation, the position of Negro children has been transformed with surprising speed. In 1940, Negroes were undoubtedly the majority of the two million American children between 6 and 15 who were outside any school. Most Americans are now eager that Negro children should have an equal chance, though subtle social distinctions are still maintained in many places by human frailty and selfishness. Equalization has undoubtedly made great progress, but it still has far to go. Not surprisingly, many Americans in socially advantageous positions would greatly prefer the equalizing of opportunity to begin in schools where their own children do not go.

Colored people are predominantly poorer than whites. Some are quite wealthy, and there is a small but expanding Negro middle class; yet the total of those who do not live in very poor districts is still small. It follows that even without formal segregation many colored children will be in schools that are almost entirely Negro. Dwellers in slums and ghettoes throughout the world find that their children suffer during school life from lack of contact with a better or more promising social world. Reports published by the City of New York in 1964 and 1965 showed that in (unofficially) segregated schools in the metropolitan area, there was a two-year lag in school attainment on average, and half the schools were worse than that. By contrast, 94 percent of white schools were at normal levels. Recordings of IQ by tests intended for white children showed not a single underprivileged school where the mean IQ score at sixth grade (age 12) was the normal 100; and almost two thirds of the schools came between 85 IQ and 94 IQ averages. Furthermore, evidence of dropouts, disease, delinquency, and other troubles have been mounting to shake the complacency of some, and to spur the already alerted consciences of many more.

"Buck-passing" from one autonomous district to another has sometimes been the cause of neglect in the past. Now whole urban areas like New York, Chicago, and Los Angeles have earned great respect by a frank avowal of their problems; while under the impetus of the Civil Rights Act of 1964 (primarily concerned to guarantee voting opportunities), a great reforming movement gathered strength. A further civil rights bill, introduced in 1966, sought to cover practically all aspects of equality not assured or enforced elsewhere. This meant particular reference to housing and education. Some educational misfortunes affecting colored people had been in part provided for, in principle, by the Economic Opportunity Act just referred to, by the Vocational Education Act of 1963, and by a whole labyrinth of bureaus and agencies supported by federal legislation or states' initiative. (In

fact, it is sometimes alleged that there are too many agencies—a complaint frequently appearing in the leading journals, but that just shows
the extent of public committedness.)[3]

Public concern and assistance are not quite the same thing as un-
stinted private support for the measures proposed. Though discrimination against the poor and handicapped of any complexion piles up
social evils for the future, people do this sort of thing everywhere. In
the United States it is particularly tempting to do so, because it is so
easy. The recognizable badges of discrimination are distinctive; pigmen-
tation, features, and accent are used to discriminate against Negroes,
Japanese, Poles, Jews, Puerto Ricans, and other members of the community—even though American born. Moreover, the district system of
schooling makes it easy for well-to-do parents to send their children to
school in communities where the unwelcome ones are "priced out" or
even illegally kept out by the "gentleman's agreements" of house-
agents.

It is no service to American education or to American civic ideals
to pretend that these things do not happen on an extensive scale. It
is fairer to record that even so they are neither representative nor in
keeping with what Americans officially and unofficially recognize as
the ideals of their way of life. In fact, discrimination of all sorts is a
diminishing factor in the United States even in respect to the Negro,
as anyone can see by comparing present practice with the customs
of a generation ago. In connection with this tendency we should stress
the assimilative force of the schools' formal and informal socialization
process. It is obviously very important for the children of Poles, Germans, Swedes, Italians, and so on to be indistinguishable Americans.
The same is true for the children of any less favored economic group.
The common school is a remarkable instrument of social mobility for
them; for the United States as a whole it is the indispensable instrument of "the great experiment" of nation building. Those who feel
misgiving about some of its intellectual standards ignore the multiple
emphases of the school (which is not the single-purpose instrument
of some other nations), and they also forget that American intellectual
standards have not merely advanced considerably during the past
century but have done so on a very wide front.

In 1909, 57.8 percent of the children in thirty-seven of the biggest
cities in the USA were of foreign-born parentage, and from very different levels of social attainment. These have now all become viable Amer-

---

[3] For more details about the problems of segregation and the remedies adopted, see my
Society, Schools and Progress in the USA (1965), pp. 70–85. For a review of similar "barriers in education" elsewhere, see Chap. 13 in *World Perspectives in Education* (1962).

ican parents or grandparents—to say nothing of smaller proportions of immigrants spread throughout the other reception centers of this hospitable land. Between 1900 and 1920, over 14 million immigrants entered. In the postwar period up to the present day there has also been a huge influx of Puerto Ricans (who are technically Americans but Spanish-speaking and culturally very different), while Mexicans have thronged into California and French-speaking Canadians are numerous in New England. The task of maintaining the assimilative process without losing standards has been monumental; yet standards are improving, and the tendency to prolong education has been marked. When comparing American schools with those of settled European countries these are some of the handicapping factors which must be borne in mind. Of course, Americans are not now prepared to cushion themselves with such considerations but are positively planning a national renascence in education.

While it is important to bear in mind that there is no federal Ministry of Education, and that the national administration has no control over education (which is a state and local matter), there is nevertheless a strongly national character about most schools in the United States. We must not underestimate either official or unofficial all-American influences in education. A crescendo of federal legislation started with veterans' affairs during World War II. It gathered strength after the National Defense Education Act of 1958 by rewarding local initiative, encouraging science and foreign language study, and by research contracts and scholarships. By specific grants (such as the $10 million a year dedicated to the study and treatment of delinquency) it has advanced particular projects. Indeed, if we care to look back beyond the post-1917 legislation and even the land grants which followed the Civil War, we can always find some healthy encouragement to education by the administration in Washington. The United States Department of Health, Education, and Welfare has no directive powers whatever as far as the general school systems of the country are concerned; but, in addition to sponsoring such important projects as cardiovascular research, it supplies a vast quantity of world-oriented educational advice which may or not be utilized by those directly responsible for teaching or school administration. More information about the United States, not to mention other countries, is something that many "grass roots" administrators and teachers really need.

Moreover, the National Education Association, the teachers' colleges and interested departments of universities, and the extremely influential educational publishers of the United States combine with the above statutory bodies to perform many (or most) of the advisory functions of a Ministry of Education—at any rate in such a permissive country as the United Kingdom. Responsibility for advice and guidance in relation to educational practice and policy is hard to pin down in the United States, but there is no doubt that that guidance is given. The city and district superintendents in a progressive state were shown by Dr. Henry Brickell,[4] in 1961, to have been quietly responsible for much more educational advance than the university departments of education. Some of the most thoroughgoing recommendations for reform in recent years are the result of government research grants for individual inquiries or team investigators. Some are already inducing great changes, especially in curriculum reform, learning and teaching methods, and the like.

It is these local and piecemeal changes which the ordinary American sees most prominently. Thus parents and teachers may be convinced that change is still on the old empirical pattern. But the crux of present decisions is something national in quite a different way from the old nationally recognizable faith in "grass roots." It is concerned with the possibility of formulating and implementing a consistent national over-all policy for today and tomorrow in a world that has brought us all within a four-minute risk of thermonuclear destruction. Indeed, peace is assurable not by strong-arm rocket-oriented studies, but by the ability to contribute permanently to the full development of human abilities *everywhere* by evolving an educational system in tune with the twentieth century. For Americans that must be a nationwide appraisal, with a full appreciation of the nation's international context. For the first time in American history that appraisal and policy-making are taking place.

The pivotal importance of these events may best be seen by putting them into historical perspective. The role of all-American decision, and the parts variously played by voluntary organizations, states, and Congress can thus be seen in evolution. In textbooks on American education, and among American teachers, it has long been fashionable to underplay the contributory importance of immense federal funds laid at the disposal of states, districts, and group interests in education. These have included huge tracts of land—more than seven times the area of England. They have continued through federal aid to agricultural and vocational education, adult education, home economics, higher education, veterans' and other scholarships, with all kinds of "pump-priming" additions during the past century. That says nothing of indirect aid through federal subsidies to agriculture, the lumber industry, roads, flood control, irrigation, and direct assistance to states for noneducational purposes (because the determination of educa-

---

[4] H. M. Brickell, *Organizing New York State for Educational Change,* Albany, 1961.

tional need and purpose has been constitutionally left to the individual states). A foreigner is staggered at the discovery of all this disbursement from central funds, which has put into some states five times as much as federal taxation ever takes out—even currently, without taking account of the land grants which founded many school systems and have both founded and sustained the higher education enterprises of many states.

Not only was the contributory role of the federal government under-played in all this (though the disbursement of all those federal shots-in-the-arm caused the United States Office of Education to grow from a statistics-collecting bureau to a powerful financial agency which could issue some very shrewd and influential proposals for education), but the part of the officially responsible states themselves also was often mini-mized because of the devolution of responsibility to all the autonomous districts, cities, or counties. Into this power vacuum the teachers' pro-fessional agencies and the nationally persuasive bodies like the great publishers swept with all their force. Some universities, like Chicago, and Teachers College at Columbia University, acted like missionary centers. The National Education Association (the teachers' chief organization) achieved formative power. Its *Principles of Second-ary Education* (1918) made old-fashioned "subject" interests seem discreditable. In 1938, the same body under its newer name as the Progressive Education Association, published an eight-year study in several volumes, indicating that the "traditional college entrance re-quirements were unwarranted"—even at that ebb tide. But, as Pro-fessor Cremin has shown, by 1955 the tide had begun to turn and the teachers' association reverted to its old name.

Already at that time a number of selective schools and university admission programs had begun to look for, and to husband, both talent and diligence. An awareness of the country's international interests was reflected in the establishment of the National Science Foundation in 1950. (By 1965 its annual budget, from government support, was $408 million.) The Talented Youth Project was organized in 1953, and the National Merit Award scheme about the same time. A few active critics of previous complacency, such as Dr. J. B. Conant, had tried to bring federal interest into higher gear, but not too obviously because the word "federal" is still frightening. President Eisenhower called a highly respectable White House Conference on Education in 1955, to be (as Americans say) "inspirational." No question of federal aid was on the agenda, though a few radical teachers were known to be think-ing of it. In fact, however, the Conference discussed it and approved; but nothing effectively happened just then. Some college presidents visited the Soviet Union in 1955–1956 and openly stated on their re-turn what American intelligence services knew to be true: that Soviet achievements in mathematics, the sciences, and education generally were a national threat to the United States. Their own country, they declared to a largely disbelieving audience, must really improve its standards—and quickly.

The disgust with which this contention was received (vivid in my own memory of American campuses that year) soon turned to dismay when the first Soviet Sputnik sailed successfully overhead, in October 1957. It was followed by other manifestations of great achievement. The first general American reaction was to catch up technically, but to keep the atmosphere of the schools as Dewey was alleged to have wished it. (Most people forgot Dewey's critics, and forgot that Dewey himself had fallen out with the "progressivists" and objected to Dewey-ism.)[5] But the psychological cleansing of purpose had already taken place among serious students of education, and at the level of the federal government.

In 1958, the National Defense Education Act was passed after difficulty; but the word "defense" was important in its acceptance. By 1963, the federal appropriation for education under this act was approximately $1 billion 500 million—to be distributed, of course, through state agencies for ordinary school and college purposes (thus respecting state sovereignty in educational matters), but also under direct contractual arrangements with universities, foundations, and research projects. In 1963, the NDEA was extended for another five years, thus doubling the amount. In the same year a Higher Education Facilities Act made available $1 billion 195 million in matching grants to develop universities, colleges, and technical education. This act was described as the most significant single step since the first Morrill Act of 1862; but the National Defense Education Act was perhaps a greater pivot in principle. In the same year, 1963, the Vocational Education Act extended similar provision on behalf of those suffering from "socio-economic handicaps." In 1964, an Interagency Committee on Education was set up under the leadership of Francis Keppel, formerly Dean of the Graduate School of Education at Harvard University, with the intention at last of coordinating the many endeavors and establishing some consistent priorities.

Keppel himself, enjoying the confidence of Dr. Conant, went on record in 1963 at a National Congress of Parents and Teachers as pleading for "the making of national educational policy" which was "not a spectator sport." In 1964, Dr. Conant's book *Shaping Educa-*

---

[5] John Dewey declared that his followers "could not see their idol for the incense they sent up." (A personal communication from Mrs. John Dewey to the author.)

tional Policy proposed an "Interstate Commission for Planning a Nationwide Education Policy." There already existed, as a matter of fact, a United States Educational Policies Commission, and Dr. Conant was a member, but something more governmental and less advisory was evidently in his mind—and in the commission's. In June 1964, the existing commission published a memorandum on *The Educational Responsibilities of the Federal Government,* urging "categorical" or directly specific aid to projects thought to be nationally desirable, instead of giving it as hitherto simply to institutions or autonomous bodies without specific direction.

Something of this sort has already been happening. The United States government now provides more than 75 percent of all expenditure on research in universities, and concentrates almost four fifths of that on 20 of the universities in the country. Indeed, the federal government now supports 60 percent of *all* those undertaking research and development in the United States.[6] At a humbler level too, the work of the Economic Opportunity Act of 1964 is noteworthy in its purpose and method: "to increase the prosperity of all ... because for the first time in our history it is possible to conquer poverty," and to do so largely by means of educational supplements and improvements. The aim was to build the Great Society, not to bolster the little red schoolhouse.

In 1965, a second White House Conference on Education was a much more purposeful affair than the one 10 years before. It proposed the creation of federal organs of greater strength, with an Assistant Secretary at Cabinet level to coordinate policy and execution. The move began with the appointment of Keppel, who resigned a year later. The size of the enterprise is indicated by the President's own figures (March 1, 1966), in which he proposed for the coming financial year "a total Federal investment in education and training ... in excess of $10 billion—a threefold increase since 1961."[7] The legislation already mentioned in this and foregoing paragraphs is not the whole muster of measures giving purpose to national education. The truly historic landmark was the Elementary and Secondary Education Act of 1965, reaching out to wherever need was felt in any of the states. Furthermore, some previous assistance for education had already induced eager Americans everywhere to seek their own direct links with

---

[6] The Killian Committee's Report, July 1964.
[7] Eighty-ninth Congress, second session; House of Representatives; Doc. no. 395. (To avoid international ambiguity, the sum mentioned may be expressed as $10,000 million. In British English, "one billion" means a million millions).

the Office of Education's beneficence—and presumably its powers of focussing policy. There is no doubt at all in the Presidential Message just quoted, or in a similar one on January 12, 1965, of the intention to "focus" and concentrate on the national priorities there spelled out.

The whole national enterprise itself is seen in international perspective. An International Education Act of 1966 proposes to allot vast sums (perhaps $500 million) "to strengthen international studies and research in the United States." At least part of this investment would undoubtedly be devoted to comparative research into other nations' educational development, and to whatever lessons might be derived from that for the national development of education in the United States. The formal, official statement in support of the bill drew attention to the formative contribution of the universities to national development.

It is in relation to all this high-level commitment that anyone might surmise some trends in American educational policy. "We march in a campaign which can have no retreats, no truce, no end, only new victories." The President's ringing words may not always bring the particular appropriations of money he expects (as he was disappointed over the Teaching Corps mentioned later in this chapter); nor will all approved plans mature as successes in actual practice (as befell some of the arrangements made for the domestic Youth Corps). Yet a national campaign has been launched which already makes the Morrill Acts' land grants look like chicken feed, though they were destined to alter the complexion of the whole world's universities for evermore, mainly by establishing a broader base of intake and interests. Not many people thought so at the time, and few have realized the connection now—even at this moment when universities everywhere are being transformed as a long-term consequence of those days.

Within the United States itself, the consequences of the federal change of role which has been taking place since 1958 (or before) are still beyond the surmise of most people. In popular esteem the rich flow at the top is simply the topping on the cake. Its leavening effect may be suspected or welcomed; it is seldom clearly worked out. Nearly all the American teachers or parents one talks to think of this momentous shift in movement as only an enrichment of a school system that will otherwise provide the same service and the same kind of welcome as before. Of course, the American people are sovereign in politics, and locally autonomous in many ways that foreigners are not. But external events and comparisons may impose on the United States a kind of reconsideration for which many Americans are ready but which most of those "at grass roots level" can scarcely realize. The most important consideration of all is that Americans shall be free to make their own future, by having the effective power to do so.[8] With schools as they were in the 1930s or even the 1950s, that was not the case.

Apart from questions of orientation and national purpose (vital though these are), the smooth management of the nation's educational enterprise and expenses alone required businesslike coordination and managerial planning, just like any other nationwide business. (American business now plans for 10, 20, or even more years ahead—so much so that in a recent year delegates from the central institute of planning in Moscow came to see how that was done.) After all, the questions of supplying a wholesome commodity are immense. One quarter of the whole population is "at school." High school attendance has grown eighteenfold since the beginning of the century, six times faster than the population, while college enrollments have increased eightyfold in the same time. Each one of these changes has transcended the boundaries of some old-time school district, and of all the states in turn. Americans are the most mobile people on earth. All their commodities, communications, and services are now supplied on an all-America basis. Even regionally, the growth of nine huge metropolitan complexes has redistributed the effective seats of power, attachment, and thought for the future. The supply of books and broadcasting, and the logic of "Big Science" and technological development, are obviously conceived in nationwide terms, according to the scale and scope of the late twentieth century. The old story of "our schools" is still told in horse-and-buggy terms, though quadrupled federal aid covered 12.5 percent of all costs by 1966.

At the same time, it must never be forgotton by the student of American education that the states (not the USA) are sovereign, and that sovereignty is further devolved in practice. People speak of federal "aid"—not of prodding, much less of control. The states could well "interpose" their rights in the face of federal intervention—even if the federal government had constitutional rights in education, as it technically has not. All this immense new educational enterprise is technically conceived either as "welfare" of the people, or as "defense" of the nation, or sometimes as "civil rights." Of course, it is all these things; and if the interpretation were really pushed very hard no one knows what decisions might not be reached. So far, the crisis of decision has been avoided, for the old realms of sovereignty have been scrupulously respected—even in such a thorny national and international problem as civil rights.

A conspicuous change of heart among the people most shrewdly concerned with American education has, however, tended to bypass

---

[8] Americans' freedom to mold their future in terms of education is reviewed in *Society, Schools and Progess in the USA,* Chaps. 2 and 7.

much legal punctilio. Under the National Defense Education Act and its subsequent extensions, individuals and associations have reached out for federal aid from behind the localized entrenchments. Research planning is on a nationwide basis. In the antipoverty campaign and in the struggle to diminish the causes of delinquency or social incompetence, "welfare" considerations have come very close to "education" throughout all the states and cities, and indeed have been identified with it. What of the millions of American children and other disadvantaged persons who cannot reach out? What of all those parents, teachers, and sometimes rulers who do not know, or do not fully measure, the extent of their own backwardness by national or international criteria? A shattering crisis of conscience has seized the United States. The suddenness of its force can be seen from the fact that all the massive legislation mentioned in the past few pages has been passed since the first edition of this book. Indeed, the crisis here referred to is masked for many people even now by the excellent and undisturbed supply of education's "business as usual."

Most of the 32 million children in over 100,000 public elementary schools would still find a familiar atmosphere wherever they went throughout the United States. That is not to say that the organization and curriculum are uniform—far from it. In fact, the division of school life into phases varies widely. The older style was to have eight years (or grades) of elementary (grade or grammar) school between the ages of 6 and 14. This was increasingly extended by high school to an average age of 18. In very many school districts this 8–4 pattern, or a variant of it, is in vogue; but an increasing tendency is to have six years of elementary school followed by three years of junior high school and three of senior high school. Sometimes the same district will have variations within its single system.

Children move around from school to school, and from district to district, without disadvantage. Americans are surely the most mobile of mankind. The overwhelming majority of the world's automobiles are on the roads of the United States. It is said that if every car in America were filled by the inhabitants, there would still be an empty space in each one. What was, within living memory, a full day's trip by cart or wagon may be less than an hour's journey by automobile today. It is nothing for "commuters" to travel by car up to a hundred miles in a daily round trip from home to their place of work. I myself have taught university classes starting at eight o'clock that included students who had traveled over 120 miles that morning and several others who came more than 50 miles. "Commuting" is a daily experience for millions of Americans. It is also a common practice to change homes at frequent intervals. During the period following World

War II, the average length of time spent in one house by the typical American family was two years. Though this is still generally true, a yearly or even more frequent house change is about the average in southern California.

It is not unusual for the opening gambit in a conversation to be an inquiry about where you are from. This is notoriously true of Texans and Westerners, but it would be quite appropriate in many other parts of the United States. The growth of California is exceptional; the 1950 census showed a 53.3 percent rise in population over that of 1940. The 1950 figure was an 86.5 percent increase over the 1930 census return. Since 1950 the rapid rate of development has been further accelerated. The rate of migration to California is exceptional, but it is only a latter-day example of a tendency for westward movement that has been characteristic of America. The covered wagon, the railroad, and the automobile represent a crescendo of traffic whose bulk is as portentous as its rapid movement. Nowadays air travel is commonplace and cheap. For example, in 1962 it was possible to travel the 2800-mile air journey San Francisco-Dallas-New York for less than $174. In these circumstances, Americans and their children move around with astonishing facility. This has a direct bearing on their expectation of school life and urban living generally.

Parents, children, and teachers expect to find close similarity between the *n*th grade in any two cities. Though they do not always strike it lucky (or unlucky), they usually find what they expect. Standardization is, of course, more marked in the towns than in the rural areas. Divergence is perhaps more often a mark of backwardness, however, than of advance, except in those rich and progressive cities which pay their teachers high salaries. The teachers themselves are perhaps unwittingly responsible for much of this standardization, because the majority of them have been trained in a 4-year teachers' college, or in a special "college of education" on a university campus. The teachers' colleges are usually recognized as of university rank and give university-style degrees, but they are seldom truly accorded that recognition by the more reputable universities or even accepted as equals by the other "colleges" or departments which go to make up the same university. The characteristic feature of most teachers' colleges (though not of the best) is the tremendous time allotted to courses on how to teach this or that subject, how to administer this or that activity, how to cope with this or that problem. "Education" is broken down into a multiplicity of separate, stylized courses. Books in huge and often profitable abundance are produced to suit them. Consequently, degrees in which the candidate has "majored" in "education" are seldom as highly thought of as other degrees, and there is a tendency not to say too much about them. It is not the undergraduates who are chiefly to blame for a somewhat un-critical attitude, though they must take their share of reproof. The staff of many education colleges are chiefly responsible, and those who prepare and publish and prescribe *"the book for the course"*—a concept unimaginable in universities outside the New World. Fortu-nately, some of the more radically reforming colleges and universities are at last heeding the crescendo of American criticism and good ex-ample, and a growing number invite foreign professors and advisers to assist them in the necessary reorientation. Among the most notable comments on the poor educational standard of much of the American teaching profession in recent years is that of Dr. Conant in *The Edu-cation of American Teachers* (1963), a book which has been widely heeded.

The kind of social ostracism faced by many "education" people on university campuses may break down if some of his recommendations are followed. Prominent among these, of course, are his earlier sup-positions that high school work must be strengthened; then at college level he proposes that such subjects as sociology, psychology, and other social sciences be taught by real specialists in this field (without the prefix or suffix "education"), together with really academic studies like those followed in any other university-level course. Only about 20 per-cent of teachers "come from colleges that can be clearly designated teachers' colleges,"[9] but that does not prevent the unofficial isolation on campus of the departments or colleges which are most closely asso-ciated with the preparation of teachers. Furthermore, a large number of former "state teachers' colleges" are now "state colleges" or "state universities" which do not stand high in the hierarchy. Under the Cali-fornia Master Plan of 1960, all the higher institutions of that state were graded officially into three main categories: the campuses of the Uni-versity of California taking the top 12.5 percent of high school gradu-ates; the state colleges (formerly teachers' colleges for the most part) taking the best of those with lower qualifications; and the junior col-leges taking any Californian who graduates from high school. A similar policy has already been adopted in a few other states, and is under con-sideration by more, if only because it prevents claims for expansion and research funds from unworthy institutions. If Dr. Conant's recom-mendations are followed, however, especially as exemplified in the Harvard Master of Arts in Teaching program (MAT), high school teachers will be drawn from the graduates of good university depart-ments with high personal attainment records. Furthermore, they will have degrees awarded by the whole university, not just from the college

---

[9] J. B. Conant, *The Education of American Teachers,* p. 74.

of education which may form part of one. Indeed, it is true already that on the best campuses this regrettable isolation is breaking down. In any case, graduates from a 4-year teachers' college can always move on to higher studies outside "education" as well as in it. As things are now, upwards of 60 percent of all candidates for the master's degree are teachers or future teachers pursuing courses in specialized "education" departments.

There are practical considerations, as well as reasons of esteem, why isolation should discontinue. The administrators have been responsible for much innovation and rethinking in education, as Dr. Brickell showed. Then the great studies of the learning process by such people as Professors Skinner and Bruner have taken place in the regular university departments, not in "education." Curriculum studies, machine-aided learning, better teaching methods, and better teacher education generally have been fostered and studied by university "nonprofessional" departments, by the great foundations, or by the "biological sciences" and "physical science" study committees. These are able to speak of the intrinsic requirements and interests of the subject matter, or the learner, instead of concentrating on abstractions of theoretical methodology. That sort of craze brought teacher training (called "teacher education") into disrepute.

Just as children move around with their parents, so it is common for students to spend their four undergraduate years and any further years of graduate study in different colleges. It is undoubtedly educative in itself to move around, and to learn to adjust to different circumstances if that requires some responsible reaction to events and teaching or some control of circumstances. Adjustment-by-compliance is a frequent risk all too seldom recognized in American schools. Also, the sheer mass of students thronging every American institution requires some conveyor belt handling. For example, examination answers are often machine-marked. There is a temptation for educational administrators (a different and somewhat superior profession to that of teaching) to streamline and equate until the whole thing ticks over like a well-conducted factory designed to turn out a standard product. Many Americans are extremely outspoken critics of this tendency. Some problems arising will be reviewed in detail later. Here we are more concerned with the standardizing effect on the elementary and high school, and on the intellectual and social prospects of the young Americans who experience their "life adjustment" there.

As we have seen, children in the United States enjoy in some ways a finer opportunity for self-differentiation than children in other countries. That is one aspect of the American legend. On the other hand, Americanization, group work and adjustment, and the influence of

administrators, teachers, and books bring about a socialization unparalleled outside the communist countries. I hope to show later how
close are the assumptions of many responsible American educators to
those acceptable in the Soviet Union. Readers will decide for themselves if this is good or bad. Some well-known and highly patriotic
American books, however, give the impression that only the American
school is "democratic," that democracy can only be established by its
means, and that democracy is also its inevitable result. It would be a
great help to clear thinking on American virtues and achievements if
a distinction were drawn more often between the central and humane
inspiration of the American "myth," its actual embodiment in programs which have advanced the material lot of so many millions, and
the merely accidental features introduced by mass production. Through
such a distinction it should be possible to make a more critical appraisal
of the many virtues and comparatively few weaknesses of American
schooling. It is a wholesome thought to remember that Ortega y Gasset
in *The Revolt of the Masses* declared that what Europeans called
"Americanization" was simply the result of mechanization. It would
be a pity if Americans themselves got the impression that their sole
merit consisted of being a "nation on wheels." The wheels are meant
to "take them places." The destination and the delights of the journey
should be a matter of responsible choice and not of further automatism.
Therefore it is no treachery to the American way of life to reserve praise
for features that well deserve it. After all, American self-criticism is
the most virulent of any.

Linked with the influence of the schools is the special character of
American city life. The older cities in the East often retain features
that reveal a European origin and preindustrial assumptions about
living. But as you move farther westward the cities are obviously much
newer creations that have served the direct purpose of exploiting and
distributing America's resources in as straightforward a way as possible. They are nearly all built or rebuilt on a squared plan, with the
streets at right angles. The majority of the towns and cities west of the
Appalachians are less than a hundred years old in any effective urban
sense, and a surprising number have mushroomed up since the advent
of the automobile. Communications are streamlined, provided you are
not a foreigner or too poor to have a car (and that applies to very few
indeed). By contrast with Europe, there is a remarkable sameness about
American cities, not so much in their geographic layout as in the
stylized nature of their assumptions and their services. Most of these
are now geared to the automobile and the problems of parking. In the
older part of a city you will find stores, supermarkets, eating places,
garages almost exactly like those anywhere else in the United States.

There is the same standardized service or lack of it. In the newer neighborhoods you will find very large shopping centers in which most of the space is reserved for cars whose owners do a round of quick shopping at small branches of the big downtown stores or at chain stores. Either there or elsewhere there are drive-in movies, drive-in eating places, drive-in banks—even drive-in library facilities. Shops are very often to be found open until late in the evening. Eating places (not the convivial cafés or pubs of Europe) can be found open at any time. In big cities the traffic never seems to stop. People are always dashing around, "going places," and getting things. The simple foreigner will be forgiven for wondering if they ever have time to *be* anything, or even to do or have anything that is not engineered or "laid out."

If you want to relax you can go out to a movie, or go home to the television set, or read the paper. For more than 90 percent of Americans this last is a local paper—though almost certainly manipulated by a chain. On the average, it will devote little more than a quarter of its abundant space to news that is not provincial or even downright local. For many small-town American newspapers the United States and its government hardly exist, except as sources of news about crimes or "love life" or unwelcome taxes and regulations. The world outside the United States is a place of un-American activities. It is much better to crowd it out with page upon page of lavish advertisements or even with "funnies." Whether printed or on the radio or televised, advertisements tell you what to buy, eat, and use; how to "have it now" on increasingly easy terms; what things you and your family must have to be modern or American; how to enjoy life; how to have your food and yet avoid the calories; even how to "enjoy your fun." Whatever it is you want you must have a lot of it, have it now, and have it typically. Also, everybody must have it.

The spread of urban and mechanized assumptions is not confined to cities as Europeans understand the term. Small villages with one street have their little replica of the big city, which is glamorized rather as tractors and engines were hymned in early Soviet days as the heralds of human advance. Indeed, it is no longer necessary to have a city to enjoy these urban delights. Old-style concentrated cities relied on the railroad, coal and iron power, heavy industries; new-style urbanization is a much more diffused thing, as we see when looking at the new industrial life of the South. There is a permeation of the countryside with small enterprises that rely on electricity, motor transport, and natural fuels piped in underground from as far away as Texas. When every home already has or aspires to central heating, refrigeration, a car, telephone, radio and television, and the whole battery of marvelous kitchen gadgets and prepared foods, it is not surprising that in education, too, every American child comes to expect "the whole works." Everyone must have it, and have it now.

It is an everlasting credit to American determination and skill that so many children do have educational opportunity. The colossal task of supplying it, at what looks like a uniform standard, is even more gigantic when we consider the geographic difficulties, the very uneven resources, and the obstinate independence of so many local interests. Under the circumstances, a preoccupation with near-uniformity under the guise of "the American way of life" or "democracy" is easy to condone. Any foreigner who has experienced the freedom, generosity, and forward look of American education will fully appreciate its actual achievements to date and its dynamic promise for the future. Every other country has much to learn from it. But Americans as a whole are very self-critical in private, and now their criticisms do not spare American education if they have some understanding of what goes on in other countries. That is why so many powerful programs are afoot for the reform of American teacher-training, and why progressive colleges take up the study of Comparative Education. This should, however, be a critical and not a self-congratulatory exercise. The time has come for the United States to reach toward greater perfection in education by a greater use of differentiation and qualitative criteria, which have markedly increased since 1959.

Indeed since about 1955, questions of quality and wasted talent have received insistent attention in the United States—so much so that it is impossible here to refer representatively to the literature on this theme. But it is true to say that until the end of that decade effective action based upon such misgivings was neither widespread nor popular, though hundreds of thousands of students have since gained thereby. Such ventures as the Talented Youth Project (organized in 1953), the Advanced Placement Programs (which had long admitted able students to shorter university courses), and the National Merit Scholarship scheme were once sharply criticized by some professional educators as "un-American"—by implication if not in those terms. Even the introduction of specialist teachers (for example, for art or music) is still hotly resisted by influential teachers' groups. Slowly, however, the general expectation from a high school course has been raised, the process being helped by various schemes of accreditation for university admission qualifications and above all by the College Entrance Examination Board in New York. A summary of relevant inquiries and experiments is contained in the Board's publication *The Search for Talent*.[10]

A typical elementary school curriculum in the United States gives

---

[10] New York College Entrance Examination Board, *The Search for Talent,* 1960.

children lessons in arithmetic and English (which will normally appear as several different subjects—reading and literature; language arts and listening; speaking; spelling; writing), in health, in physical education, in social studies, and in music. Children over the age of 12, if still in elementary school, usually take up additional subjects with a practical core of interest such as home economics or "industrial arts." Neither of these last two is purely manipulative, but links a good deal of general information to the practical activity. On the whole, by comparison with any other advanced country, actual competence in the school subjects is somewhat meager. Many parents have long been aware of this, as was shown in the 1950s by the ready sales of books with such disturbing titles as *Why Johnny Can't Read* and *Quackery in the Public Schools*. The vast majority, however, were blissfully content until the first Sputnik set educators by the ears, and the challenge had to be met.

Parents take an incessant and active interest in the public school, which enjoys the support of parental advice and gifts of apparatus or gadgets. Children's needs and even their preferences are individually discussed; the children themselves very often help to regulate progress, and will "share the difficulties" of their weaker brethren. Though work is frequently done in groups, there is little formal "streaming" or "homogeneous grouping" if it can be avoided. Promotion from grade to grade officially depends on satisfactory completion of a year's work; in fact, the child's schoolwork must be unusually bad (perhaps through result of absence) to make him repeat a grade. There are practically no real examinations as other countries understand them, and the standard by which a child is usually graded is his own average expectation. Not only is there reluctance to let nimble wits run ahead, but in some places there has been unwillingness to recognize the special needs of backward children. However, these "exceptional children," as they are called, now get careful attention from teachers who have specialized in their problems, and American remedial work in these areas is outstanding.

For the sake of contrast with other countries (which is not altogether satisfactory) most American schools may still be described as comparatively indifferent to subjects, to academic accuracy, and to progress at any given speed—so as to complete a curriculum (like those determined in other countries by economic considerations or ministerial prescription). Even hard facts are given secondary importance by many teachers. They are much more eager to have cheerful children developing "wholesome social relationships," "evaluating" and discussing daily experiences, and understanding their role in society as they see it. In achieving these aims the schools are phenomenally successful, and most of the children are quite delightful to know; but astronomical delinquency figures make many wonder if enough is expected of children, and if they are sufficiently occupied and "committed" to develop a sense of purpose.

Nearly every American child goes on to high school from elementary school at an age between 12 and 14. Of more than 30,000 high schools, 84 percent are free public schools. Many of these public high schools are in rural districts which have been handicapped by isolation and smallness, but increasing trends in consolidation and mobility are improving this situation. The children "graduate" at around 18. At one time this graduation entailed a very serious examination rightly supposed to be a challenge to the unusually able pupil who was honored by a certificate, if successful, and with the glory of a cap and gown. Now nearly everyone remaining in school can expect to graduate. However, it was estimated in 1965 that in the ensuing decade one out of every three American pupils would leave high school before graduating,[11] very often because of discouraging family circumstances. And surveys show that "dropouts" are usually doomed to a lifetime of low level jobs and spasmodic unemployment, if not worse; so exacting is the American labor market in its schooling requirements. Later opportunities to graduate at high-school level are now more widespread.

The typical high school is coeducational and completely comprehensive. Future lawyers, doctors, and clergymen are classmates with future mechanics, shopgirls, and farmers. This is because the schools normally allow a wide range of elective subjects in the upper grades. An attempt is made in most cases to ensure that a child has a really broad education, either by grouping electives in suitable patterns or by "counseling." A school of any size has one or more counselors or other ancillary educators whose job it is to personalize relationships for the children and to advise them on problems.

There is no doubt, however, that much of the counseling is done by ambitious parents who persuade their children to choose the "college preparatory" type of subject, such as mathematics, languages, and science. For these there is now some very good federally provided equipment. On the other hand, rather slow-learning children, and those with worse advice or less farsighted parents, can and often do choose very practical subjects with an immediate sales value. These include not only such subjects as bookkeeping, agriculture, journalism, and auto mechanics, but even bricklaying, plastering, shoe repairing, and hairdressing in extreme cases. In poor areas, especially in the segregated "separate but equal" Negro schools, the proportion of practical subjects taken grows. In other words, selection by social class or future is dis-

---

[11] President's Message to Congress, January 12, 1965.

cernible, but we must note (a) that these children are still at school and subjected to a wide range of humanizing influences when many other nations' children would be hard at work, and (b) that in association with these practical subjects it is often possible to develop both personal qualities and really sound understanding of conventional subjects.

Home economics and "industrial arts" are usually, though not always, admirably taught and studied. Moreover, a great deal of subject interchange occurs. Your future teacher or doctor may include "shop" (that is, mechanical work or carpentry) and home economics in the round of school subjects. Some of these may be taken for only one year, or even half a year. American history and some form of literature are the only subjects all pupils will take, though the core curriculum of general interest subjects has had a wide vogue.

On the other hand, it is rather misleading to talk as though children's futures were settled. The majority of them come very late to specialization. Many of them do not know even after high school graduation what they will ultimately become. This has its severe drawbacks, but it has the great advantage that many of them have a very wide range of future callings still open to them.

Among the obvious disadvantages to such a system, which is not only comprehensive but usually "unstreamed" into differing grades of ability, was the longstanding reluctance to make a challenging opportunity for the really bright or eager child. Another has been that of securing full attention for the profitable if somewhat unpopular subjects, such as mathematics. This is aggravated by the acute shortage of specialist teachers, who are drawn off by higher pay elsewhere. But even if the teachers were there, the intrinsic difficulties of a free choice would raise problems. It was stated in 1954–1955 by the United States Office of Education that 23 percent of the high schools in the country did not offer courses in the basic sciences or in mathematics. Though this statement could easily give the wrong impression, (because the figure of 23 percent really refers to small rural schools catering to only about 6 percent of the total high school population), it does suggest a wider neglect of the very subjects that are basic to the future of a technological society. Furthermore, the National Science Foundation in 1961 showed that many high school teachers assigned to teach mathematics and the sciences had "hardly more than a bowing acquaintance" with the subjects taught.[12]

General science, physics, chemistry, and biology—to say nothing of foreign languages and information about foreign countries—do not come high in the popularity poll. When they are taken, it is still usually

---

[12] J. B. Conant, in *The Reporter,* December 3, 1964.

at a very elementary level, despite the availability of absolutely first-class American texts for those willing to bestir themselves, especially at college level where so much high-school slackness must now be remedied. Though "enriched" and presumably more demanding programs now appear more frequently and prominently, foreign observers should not expect anything very spectacular in most cases. They might class such programs as "normal"; though if the present example of some federally-prompted intensification prevails, the standards of the whole country might alter conspicuously. Many districts, however, and whole states, remain unconcerned and unaware; and all too many professional educators are complacent.

Therefore it is not surprising that in his school subjects the young American is still usually two years (or even more in special cases) behind his European counterpart. Many subjects must, in fact, be postponed until college, though in Europe a standard in them would be required before there could be any possibility of entry into college. An extreme critic of American standards, R. M. Hutchins, once declared that early in the twentieth century every young person holding the leaving certificate of the French *lycée,* a German *Gymnasium,* or an Italian *liceo* had acquired, at the age of 18, after 12 years:

> approximately as much knowledge of subject matter as three modern college (i.e., university) graduates together will have acquired in the United States after 16 years' schooling, at about age 22. If a college student in America specializes in mathematics he will have arrived at the age of 22 at such branches as differential and integral calculus, analytical geometry, and differential equations. The fundamentals of most of these fields were, however, known to 18-year-old graduates of the old-fashioned European secondary schools, who also knew equally well three other subjects at least: Latin, Greek, and their native tongue.[13]

Every outside observer, like the American Dr. Hutchins, experiences continual shock from contrasts of this kind. There are signs that better informed Americans generally are feeling them too. The more reputable universities are becoming increasingly selective on the grounds of attainment. Many firms offering scholarships at the university level are insisting on certain minimums before awarding them, and in some cases are unable to find takers for what they offer. Recent comparisons like the 1967 *International Study of Achievement in Mathematics* are making patriotic and sympathetic American leaders wonder if too little has been expected of the high school in the way of solid work. Once they have left school, Americans work very hard indeed—and at a pace which it is almost exhausting for some foreigners merely to observe. But

---

[13] R. M. Hutchins, *The Conflict in Education,* New York: Harper & Row, 1953, p. 38.

for many American children, the shock of the career world's competitive ruthlessness is postponed until they leave college at the age of 22.

Still, criteria of attainment are not the only valid ones to apply to
a folk institution not altogether designed for the purposes of intellectual training. Much attention is paid to socializing activities in
groups of every conceivable kind. A surprisingly frequent word for a
democratic country is the ever-recurring "leadership." On the other
hand, much trouble is taken to ensure that everyone can hope to be a
leader in something (as long as he is not too radical or intellectual). The
very wide range of interests and skills found in the normal large school
secures a high standard of work in such things as school newspapers,
celebration pageants, and so on. Moreover, very many children have
some experience of paid vacation work during their summer holidays,
or travel widely. The American child usually "knows his way around,"
and is confident that he can get where he wants to go. Perhaps most
other educated children in the world are deficient in this sense of ad-
venture and personal dignity. On the other hand, these admirable
qualities in the American child might be enriched if combined with a
greater readiness to learn. Such readiness may indeed be induced by the
"sales pressure," not only of educators but even of advertisers, who no
longer commiserate with "eggheads" but glamorize them. That is a
great change.

In addition to the public high schools, more than four thousand
private high schools enroll nearly 1,500,000 children. This is about 14
percent of the high school population. Most of them are denominational
schools, but a few resemble the English Public Schools in demanding
very high fees and in specially preparing their students for the universities. The influence of the "college preparatory" school and of the
"Ivy League" university in securing privilege for a few is much stronger
than Americans care to realize, but is nothing like so powerful in this
matter as the English Public School. For one thing, the ordinary high
school is the training ground for most of America's really successful
men and women. Secondly, the inquiries of selectors are much more
directly concerned with present excellence than with antecedents of
parental position and one's own school. Thirdly, society itself in the
United States does not exclusively venerate particular occupations,
but tends to have a real admiration for any boy or girl who makes good.
Lastly, the standard of the ordinary high school (taking in everyone,
and not just the 20 or 25 percent of the population formerly found in
the English grammar school) is recognizably similar to that of nearly
all American private schools, though it must be admitted that some
of these are impressive by any standard. A few cities (New York, for
example) are experimenting with advanced public schools for espe-

cially gifted children, and some universities help to speed up progress for such people in ordinary high schools by admitting them very early if they have reached an appropriate standard. This is the Advanced Placement Program.

The next stage after high school, and following naturally from it, is "college." That word and "university" are practically synonymous in the United States. More than 2600 colleges enroll about 6 million students. Enrollments are officially expected to reach 9 million by 1975, presumably including postgraduate students. The majority of colleges are coeducational and many are state-supported or city institutions. A large number of these charge no tuition fees to residents of the state, and the fees of the other publicly-maintained institutions are often very small when taken in relation to American earning power. Any high school graduate has the opportunity to enter a university, though not any university, if he can pay the fees requested. In considering a candidate's admissibility, we must bear several criteria in mind: the standards (voluntarily) imposed by College Entrance Board examinations and by other boards seeking to promote higher attainment levels; the inducements offered by selective scholarships; the California Master Plan and other grading schemes; and the "prerequisites" demanded by the more selective colleges in the Directory of Colleges or their prospectus. Many students earn their way through college by securing employment either in the college (for example, as a waiter, switchboard operator, gardener, or clerical assistant), or outside. Some find it possible to earn enough in the long summer vacation to pay most of the cost (including residence) of an inexpensive university; but this means hard work. Sometimes college timetables are arranged on a sort of shift system—partly to accommodate those who come in before or after a half-day's employment, partly to accommodate married students who alternate studies with baby-sitting and other domestic chores, and partly to cope with the enormous numbers of students. The drop-out rate, however, is very large indeed.

It is obvious from this description that a representative American university is unlike anything of the same name anywhere else in the world, except perhaps in postwar Japan, the Philippines, and other spheres of American influence. The standards of academic work required in Europe and Asia would be unattainable in these circumstances. But then, the American college is not intended to do the work that the world's universities consider to be their special distinction. It is not so selective of intellectual quality, taking in about one third of the population of university age, and in some districts more. In some cities with "junior colleges" (that is, to age 20), the majority go. College is, therefore, not so specialized a place, not only because it has to follow a comparatively unspecialized high school, but because it has itself a much broader base of study for the individual student. Many courses are on a level familiar in foreign high (or selective secondary) schools. They may indeed be much lower than that, though, as is proved by the still frequent provision of remedial reading courses and elementary mathematics or comparable basic subjects during the freshman year of a state college or university. The range of the typical college includes many courses that would be prepared for by less grandly named schools in other countries, or even by professional apprenticeships not given the name of "school" at all. Such colleges freely award degrees in subjects that would be doubtfully awarded a much lower certificate elsewhere. Far less emphasis is placed on independent, critical study than in foreign universities, and far more emphasis is placed on attendance at lectures. Of these there is often a heavy and somewhat repetitious load.

Foreign professors generally find American students too docile for their taste—a surprising thing in the land of liberty. More importance is attached to terminal grades and "credit hours" than to searching examinations or critical reading as expected of students everywhere outside North America; and not even the most loyal champion of the representative American campus could claim that the extracurricular pursuits of undergraduates effectively supply real, critical compensation for intracurricular passivity. The students' whole experience (very often with only "objective" answers in any tests they have undergone) has all too frequently left them unschooled in criticism or detachment, and often left them unprepared with the basic knowledge. Their university career does not always help them. The more advanced or graduate students will often work methodically, for example, at "term papers" or essays which must be abundantly documented with annotations and sources; but there is so much of the archivist and so little of the scholar in them that they will not infrequently ask an instructor whether "research" or "original work" is required! Outside North America such a distinction would be quite meaningless. In extreme cases it is easy to get by with only the professors' handouts or the "book for the course," and one can hear idle or perversely able students swear that they "never cracked a book." However, increasingly selective admission requirements and the competitive recruitment of talent (indeed, of already developed talent) are already aggravating the academic and social distance between the prestige-enjoying minority of colleges and the still complacent majority. Many small "liberal arts" colleges and the highly selective "prestige" colleges have long set very high standards.

This is the negative side to a massive achievement. Though Americans persist in saying these young men and women are in "higher education" and, therefore, to be compared with university students in other lands, they thus put them at an absurd and unnecessary disadvantage. The majority of American college students are getting something that is not available to most of their foreign counterparts —a taste of the elements of academic learning, and a foothold on the ladder of social esteem and advancement that is elsewhere restricted to the learned professions. Everybody in the United States must have this chance; so all professions, more or less, must be "learned" and suitable for a university degree. This is an exaggeration of American regard for the romance of learned status; but like all caricatures it bears a recognizable likeness. Nursing, accounting, catering, local government service, advertising, commerce, and journalism are typical graduate careers in America, though not elsewhere.

An extended period of general education is afforded young Americans by the special characteristics of their undergraduate life. This usually consists of four years in a "liberal arts college" or its equivalent, though a growing proportion of students now major in "applied" subjects such as business administration and commerce. In 1961 these were the major fields of interest of 12 percent of all American first degrees. So many students want to have some college experience (preferably at little expense and near home) that an increasing number of junior colleges start them off for the years 18 to 20. There are now over 500 of these, many of them also serving as community education centers for the adults of the neighborhood. Graduates of teachers' colleges, or those who are halfway to graduation after two years in a junior college, can proceed to further study in universities at the appropriate level. Because they have not really specialized so far, even at the age of 22 with a bachelor's degree, students are frequently able to begin genuinely professional training (for the master's degree) in one of their previous subjects or a new one in "graduate school." Of over 2600 "colleges," about 150 are officially listed as "universities" proper—that is to say, institutions with graduate schools and research facilities. These could be more truly compared with the universities, technical colleges, and commercial institutions of Europe in their intellectual and professional standards. Although only a relatively small proportion of Americans enroll in a graduate professional school, it probably represents more than 10 percent—at least twice as high a percentage as reach comparable standards in Britain.

At this level, too, "teaching fellowships" and other ladders to the academic life encourage many a young scholar of talent to persevere with his research and serve a university apprenticeship under very favorable conditions. The library and research facilities available in the better American universities, and indeed in some departments of many which are not so distinguished, are outstanding by any international standard. For such exceptional young academics, too, careful teaching and patient guidance are provided—often on a friendly and stimulating seminar basis that can put to shame the struggling isolation of researchers in many of the world's universities. However, we must remember that here we are considering the minority of university research students, and not the typical undergraduate or, indeed, the typical "master's" candidate. Many students complain of remoteness.

If we except many of the masters and doctors degrees in "education," American higher degrees are very often comparable with similar degrees in Europe, at any rate in the more selective and exclusive American universities. Graduate schools often have a sound and searching professional curriculum. It is impressive to find that although a bachelor's degree obtained by a scientist, for example, may be little more advanced than a *baccalauréat, Abitur,* or General Certificate of Education at Advanced Level, the doctorate is very often quite up to the standard of a Ph.D. in Britain. This cannot, however, be said of colleges in general. Yale, Harvard, and Princeton and some other notable institutions are magnificent universities by any standard. The great technological universities are models for the world. Many other research institutes and universities have outstanding specialist departments that attract the cream of America and academicians from all over the world by their incomparable resources. (American salaries have something to do with it, too!) But this cannot justify an unreflecting and blanket defense of what passes for higher learning in many places.

It is especially important to make this point in connection with an increasing tendency to parade scholarship under the trappings of annotation and documentation drawn from any sources that seem appropriate. This particular fad was rejected in large measure by most of the universities of the Old World toward the end of the nineteenth century, when the heavy artillery of German professors bombarding each other over the interpretation of classical texts was shown to contribute so little to real insight or humanity. The almost compulsive scholium of overdocumented yet often unreflective "library research" now so common in those American university departments uncertain of their academic respectability (particularly in the great search for quality since 1957) should not be taken as proving the presence of critical scholarship. It can actually be a token of a "climate of disintegration" (to borrow an expression used by Professor Ulich in describing the decline of creativity in the medieval University of Paris); it cer-

tainly may inhibit not only creativity by indeed original interpretation.[14] Sober, well-grounded scholarship needs no salesmanship; it
would fare better with less counting of documentation and doctorates.[15]

One understandable consequence of the prodigality and experimental diversity of American higher education, particularly, is that
many leading scholars who ought to know better are tempted to make
pronouncements based upon the institutions and departments they
know, and then suppose they have made universally valid declarations.
No other country has quite this problem because no other has quite
this diversity or such chasms. The author has made seven extended
study and teaching visits to the United States, and has had the advantage of participating in two nationwide surveys and one international
evaluation of American higher education by unimpeachable American scholars. He has also benefited by numerous well-informed
but down-to-earth discussions in nearly all parts of the country—not
to mention meticulous preparatory inquiry and continuous follow-up
research. Yet nothing is more common than to encounter pseudocomparisons or defensive manifestoes put out by self-confident professors who are just not effective students of *their own* system. As the
National Defense Education Act and other reform laws showed, such
ostrich techniques neither serve the United States nor truly represent
the wishes of well-informed Americans.

It is fairer to America and a more genuine appreciation of its genius
to admit that a college education is still, for most of its recipients, a
social experience more than an experience of work and scholarship.
On the typical American campus young men and women destined for
all kinds of profession, and of many different origins, mix freely to
discuss their responses to many of life's problems. Normally, the faculty
(that is, the academic staff) consider it their duty to be accessible to the
students for all kinds of consultation. In addition, a "dean of men" and a
"dean of women" are in charge of the general well-being of the future
citizens of one of the most fluid societies on earth. Medical and psychological services are also available, and vocational counselors help with
careers. It is also of great value to most young people to make personal
contact with real scholars and the originators of progress. Perhaps this

---

[14] R. Ulich, *The Education of Nations.* Cambridge, Mass.: Harvard University Press,
1961, pp. 27 on; see also my *World Perspectives in Education,* pp. 38–39 and 173–174, for
a fuller examination of these techniques in relation to the encouragement of scholarship.
[15] "The farther down in the university hierarchy, the larger the proportion of (those
who believe they) both *could* and *should* . . . expand doctoral enrollments . . . within present
faculties and without lowering standards." (B. Berelson, *Graduate Education in the United
States* (1960), pp. 101–102.

splendid opportunity would be appreciated more if all students realized that knowledge of facts and a willingness to undertake independent inquiry into original sources are essential constituents of a proper discussion. In a small minority of universities or colleges, and in some enterprising (but as yet untypical) departments of others, this realization has been achieved. In speaking of Denmark we noted the value of the folk high school as a kind of retreat house conceived in secular terms. In America the campus is not quite that, but it serves a comparable purpose in some ways, and it similarly mixes up young men and women drawn from different localities.

Of course, the extremely lively campus life is an integral part of a college education. It is not quite as crazy as the films show, but near-professional football and basketball (mainly pursued by student athletes recruited for this very purpose and with little regard for other qualities) are a staple ingredient of the typical college. Many functional societies and a large number of fraternities and sororities (often associated with professional interests) claim the attention of students. Some of them are socially exclusive, but that is not typical. Initiation into a fraternity is a kind of blend between a religious service and a Greek drama. It is often taken seriously despite that, because belonging to a fraternity is very important. There is a comparative lack of the literary, political, philosophical and generally skeptical clubs familiar to European students. If anything, the faculty are more intellectually and socially critical than the typical student of today.

A somewhat disturbing indication of this was brought home to me in 1955 (and five later university assignments). In lectures on social philosophy and a comparison of educational ideas, I noticed that the traditional liberal assumptions of the Western world rang somewhat strange for American students (mainly graduates). So I joined forces with professors of philosophy and related subjects to draw up questionnaires and test discussion topics. These revealed among students a marked reluctance to recognize the basic claims of individuals and minorities in a multiple society. They showed fear of encouraging marked individual differences, even in complementary kinds of difference; they showed strong reliance on "leadership" and other kinds of worship for big men or "experts"; they certainly revealed an absence of real concern for separate and responsible personal reactions. In America this all sounds peculiarly ironical. It may be added here that nothing was said or directly implied in these questions about Negroes or communism. On the contrary, when notions directly quoted from communist sources or when details of educational or corporate activity in communist countries were tried on these graduate Americans, they were found to be more familiar and acceptable than most of the contrary notions of liberal Western democracies—the notions, that is to say, of the American founding fathers and of those who throughout the ages have championed the rights of man.

Once again, my implied criticism is no attack on American institutions. It is one more indication of the impact of mechanization and of industrialized relationships on democratic notions of personal dignity and responsibility. It is only more remarkable for being so clear in the one country founded on charters of human liberty, and dedicated to progress. Modern abundance is, of course, based upon the mass production of standardized wares. Commodities and opportunities are produced that way—even schools and books; but men's minds and freedoms are of different stuff.

One feature of American social life, which is also conspicuous at school, never fails to impress foreigners. It is the emancipation of women to something more than equal status. The American woman has not merely caught up with men; she has achieved her own special dignity and prerogative beyond those accorded to men, so that in some ways she is a "man plus." It is an unforgettable experience to attend a business or professional women's gathering, and to note factory managers, real estate agents, scientists, doctors, lawyers, and even ministers there. They are not all young, either—many must, in fact, have had their professional education at a time when their European sisters were struggling to claim something beyond a mere rudimentary schooling.

It would be a mistake to attribute feminine advance to the schools, though they have certainly helped a really American advance to gather momentum. From the earliest pioneers days women have been at a premium. Simple shortage, combined with abundant opportunities for self-vindication (and for mobility or escape) perhaps gave women in frontier settlements stronger claims to equal consideration than women have had anywhere else. These unspoken but real ingredients in the background have long been rationalized, so that Americans take them as "natural." But they do not need to go too far back in their own history to find college coeducation mentioned as a sort of utopian madness. Now coeducation is almost the only conceivable method, from kindergarten to research.

In circumstances of complete freedom and abundant proximity, American girls have long had an opportunity to get to know boys well. They go about with them freely as companions, flirt with them, and go through all the preliminaries of love with no public disapproval. On the contrary, Americans probably do not know how amazed most foreigners are at the extent and frequency of this adolescent play, though the American example in this matter has been assiduously taught to the rest of the world by exported films and packaged television shows. In these, of course, the seamier side is portrayed, together with a hefty dose of quite unrepresentative violence. Nevertheless, the ordinary campus actuality still amazes foreigners. What Americans feel is degeneracy in Sweden and Britain is often thought in those countries to be Americanization. Much juvenile American clothing itself may seem naïvely, and therefore innocently, indecent. On the other hand, foreigners seldom realize how vital a part all this is of the American legendary virtues of self-recognition, self-expression, freedom of choice, freedom to find one's own frontier and so on, all in the rather unique circumstances of their long preadult tutelage.

For modern Americans this dance of the sexes is not merely permitted; it is, in their own idiom, a "must." The near-universal practice of "dating" ensures that girls and boys learn a personal and social routine that is of the greatest importance to self-adjustment. It is both a token of personal acceptability and the means to further acceptance by the group. Boy-girl relationships, though certainly not a formality or inhibited, are highly stylized. They come under close supervision (seldom with an eye to disapproval) by parents, elders, and also one's peers. They are prompted by advertisements, by one's sisters and brethren in sororities and fraternities. Parents can be as anxious as the adolescents themselves if a week, and above all a week-end, goes by without "dates." Dating could in large measure be describable to foreigners as parent-sponsored.

Since about 1945 a marked change has come about in the pattern of dating. Whereas for at least a generation it had been supposed that boys and girls would have a succession of different dates, ringing the changes perhaps twice a week, the custom has grown up of "going steady"—not just as a direct preliminary to marriage, but in the very early teens also. I have often heard highly respectable matrons warmly defend their own adolescent practice of successional dating as an experience which not merely brought them into contact with a wide circle of friends of both sexes but also allowed them more clearly to discern personal virtues from merely masculine attractions. By the same token, these people view with regret the change of fashion which prompts twelve- and thirteen-year-olds to ask their parents how soon they should "go steady." Of course many parents are anxious about such premature "going steady" both for obvious reasons and because they are reluctant that their youngsters should form an inexperienced attachment to an unsuitable companion. The youngsters themselves, even under the age of 14, have keenly examined me about comparable practices in other countries when I have invited "any questions" during visits to their classes.

It might be supposed that going steady would imply a less socialized form of juvenile courtship than successional dating. That is not really so. The rules are elaborately, if tacitly, drawn up by one's contemporaries; performance is often thrashed out in a sort of open confession in sororities and other clubs, and there are many books to advise, some soundly. It is still too early to form firm judgment, but young people are marrying earlier. Many are married in college; some leave high school to marry. This might have happened anyway. The outside observer should be content to observe rather than judge this American innovation in juvenile freedom. Although at the time of the first edition of this book in 1958 the phenomenon described above could have been named as typically American, it has since then become more common in many other countries (particularly Britain). The question of young love and early marriage is hedged in with all kinds of economic and social problems; but the juvenile expectation or dream is surely there. It is interesting (though not altogether profitable) to speculate how much of this change is directly attributable to popular records, films, and television suggestions—for these are the voice of America most avidly listened to abroad—educational and political differences notwithstanding. Or, how much is due to a worldwide change of a subtler kind in the expectation of youth, now more than ever cooped up in school and having its powers and desires denied an adult fulfillment. But that raises questions of social reorganization, of working challenges, and of significant participation in the exacting struggles of adults, while we are simply thinking of youth's emotions.

Like every human innovation, early dating brings its attendant problems. Despite Hollywood and canned television, American adolescents are neither more salacious nor more depraved than those in other places. It must be said that most of them are well poised and very agreeable indeed. But greater freedom (as in Britain, for example) permits a more overt disregard for the older proprieties among most; it would be very hard to say if it causes more wickedness, because in the heyday of real wickedness it is often fashionable to hide it. Dating also stimulates a higher expectation of marriage and a readier dissatisfaction if things do not come up to it. This brings about more divorces; but once again it would be hard to say if, by the same token, it blemishes more marriages than were imperfect in previous generations. By all accounts, however, it does provoke marked anxieties about being up to standard, true to type, and so on. On the basis of American statistical surveys and spontaneous comment by Americans whom I have addressed on this topic, I feel that anxiety about conforming is perhaps more marked in premarital relationships than in any other potentially socializing activity. All over the world freedom between men and women is growing, as a necessary consequence of permitting women to be judged by male standards. It is usually, however, a freedom (like religion or politics) that seeks a relatively unsocialized and private area for its fullest development. All sexual behavior is more socially determined than anyone cares to admit; but manifest American socialization in this matter often surprises well-informed foreign observers.

This last comparison once again raises the important question whether the American pattern of living is not also the "shape of things to come" in other countries. If Americanization, as most other people see it, is almost indistinguishable from industrialization and urbanization, it is most important that others should study its blessings and pitfalls with their own future in view. In fact, few cultures have had a wider publicity at any time. Not merely are American examples (and not always the best ones) broadcast through the world by books, film, and advertising; they are also implicit in programs of technical and economic aid—even in the very instruments and staffing arrangements that help modern industrialization to run smoothly. Truly we may say that modern American assumptions are built into modern technology, which in one way or another is as full of educative suggestions and rehearsal systems as the round of daily school and life at home. Whether these assumptions are the same as those consciously striven for by parents, teachers, and educators is another question—one that it is crucial for Americans no less than foreign observers to answer. An increasing number of significant American publications reveal profound misgivings on this score.

Why should it be so important to decide whether modern "Americanization" is automatic or a matter of consciously chosen values? The whole philosophical foundation of the American republic is one of European liberalism nourished in an atmosphere of free growth, free experiment, and tolerance for others. The "great experiment" of all time has been the building of a nursery for individual human enterprise amidst abundance—not in conditions of uniformity or automatism but in conditions that assure the basic minimums of social justice and economic sufficiency. As a matter of principle rather than of actual practice, these "inalienable rights" are the very heart of American education in schools, in homes, in public life. It is American insistence on equality without identity, on differences that can be complementary, on accepting qualities as "right" if they can justify themselves pragmatically, that have differentiated the American way from pure intellectualism in the past and from Soviet-style standardization in the present. It seems of primary importance that the same distinction should be made now. The private decisions of American life are front-page news for the world. They may in fact be decisions for the rest of mankind.

Well over half the human race is yellow or brown, and a considerable proportion of the rest are black. Most of them are still literally hungry a large part of the time. Even liberty and the rights of man take a secondary place in their preoccupations. Industrialization seems the god that will rescue them from servitude and poverty. They know America not as the land of liberty but as the Mecca of abundance. Yet by the same token the USSR is also remarkable. Its stupendous machine is just at the beginning of its work, and also in an imperfectly exploited territory. Marxist preaching of equality and democracy (which may be "double talk") in any case means little to those who have never understood democracy. But Russian technological excellence, Russian raising of living standards for tens of millions, Russian standards in scholarship and research are likely to be persuasive messengers even where no communist has infiltrated. In our next chapter we shall consider some of these redoubtable achievements. Only the enemies of our type of democracy waste time denying them. To round off this chapter we have to ask once more what it is that essentially differentiates the Western way from the Marxist, and what are the problems that this examination poses for Americans.

The essential difference is the claim and the guarantee for a full and self-determining life for each person irrespective of origin, race, sex, or belief. It is written in glowing terms in the preamble to the Declaration of Independence, and also in the preamble to the United Nations Charter. Americans need to decide whether their colossal achievements so far can be added to by reconsideration of children's access to education and well-being throughout the highly decentralized and unequally equipped territories of the United States. Arrangements that suited the thirteen colonies and the English villages before them may not be suited to today. Though this fact has little to do directly with domestic American decisions, hundreds of millions of black and brown eyes are watching all over the world. In addition, Americans must decide whether the youthful delights of the American schools can also permit the brilliant, or simply different, American child to enrich himself and his country more fully and more quickly than at present, even with the help of all the post-1958 legislation, the national programs, and the great foundations. In the field of science this is already an urgent question. It is also a basic problem in social philosophy.

The whole complex of problems arising out of industrialization, urban life, and automation is transforming the educational arena in the United States. As a pioneer in this field, the United States is bound to make critical decisions which will affect the whole world. I said earlier that automation's full force is being checked; yet in the decade ending 1957, factory output was increased by exactly 50 percent with an increase in factory workers of only 2 percent. Farm output was increased by 20 percent, with an actual decrease of 25 percent in the number of workers. Since then, change and productivity have accelerated. The problems of life's tempo, of how much a profession itself is educative, of leisure, of "custodial" education are all bound up with this development. Mankind has never before really needed a conscious solution to this range of questions before, because technological and social change has been piecemeal and evolutionary. Now it is impossible to "let things happen" for, as we have seen, the machine can take over control and produce a state of pretotalitarian standardization, or, at any rate, the passive receptor-mentality which is equally demoralizing.

Therefore the outside world, already heavily indebted to Americans for technical aid and much material assistance, looks anxiously toward the development of another kind of "know-how." The material aid given by the United States is without precedent in history. Readiness to help mankind in education (as distinct from technique) is made manifest by all the scholarships awarded to foreigners, by all the grants given by American foundations to foreign institutions of learning, and by fundamental education projects throughout the underdeveloped lands of the world. Not even the most cynical could whisper that these activities are designed only to defend America, though they certainly help in that direction.

Americans increasingly recognize that civilization and the humane solution of recurring human problems (like health) must be available to *all* mankind if they are to be firmly enjoyed by any of mankind. But no technique for living—not even the American prescription—can be exported like a "package deal." Every solution needs to be worked over repeatedly *in its own context* and studied in the light of comparable experiments. For this reason, the slower insights of the Old World may still have valid suggestions to make to those shaping the New. Indeed, they may help that still newer world to shape itself where a choice must somehow be made between the Old World, the New World, and the advancing techniques of their totalitarian competitors.

The choice will be easier for the rest of the world, and for Americans themselves, now that Americans are taking stock realistically of the immense achievements of their country and its educational system within the present century. The greatest of these has been the determination to provide a high all-round minimum standard of education and consumption. The deliberate, and well-informed, intention to build a Great Society, based upon the eradication of disadvantage by means of education, is one of the most remarkable manifestoes of human endeavor that mankind has ever known. Indeed it is not only a manifesto, but a sober program for action which already lies with the compass of American technology, if not always of popular realization and decision. Not everything is admirable, to be sure; but of what human institution could that be said?

Take another example, this time of a noneducational achievement. Within a field of endeavor which is universally regarded as being distinctively American, the colossal superhighways accelerating motor traffic across the continent, and the less spectacular but equally admirable highways which preceded them, are revolutionary creations of this century if not the present generation. Yet it now seems so inevitable to think of American life as based on them that no one thinks of boasting about them and comparable achievements in the way that Russians boast about their spectacular technological advances, or as foreign scholars pay tribute to Japan's rapid modernization after the Meiji Restoration in 1868. That road system, and that technology *are* America, as we see life in the United States now, though in the period of "dirt roads" during the 1920s and later they would have seemed unimaginably revolutionary. The revolutions of one generation become the commonplaces of the next. The role of world leadership has fallen upon the United States somewhat unexpectedly, but it is nevertheless a direct consequence of revolutionary advance in some fields of ingenuity and enterprise. That advance did not come from regarding the status quo as sacrosanct. Neither can education now become static or base itself on familiar norms.

The United States now stands particularly at a world crossroads of educational decision. The whole period since 1945, and especially since 1958, has been marked by an unprecedented stocktaking of previous deficiencies and inequalities. Keppel wrote of *The Necessary Revolution in American Education* (1966). Many others reproach "educators" who, for two decades or more, reduced the level and purpose of the nation's educational upsurge, often by the punctilio of "process" and "methodology," but more often by isolating "progressivism" from the true progress that sharper eyes could already see under way in the more advanced parts of the national endeavor. Sometimes plain ignorance was to blame; but this can be remedied by the careful study of Comparative Education as a *basically analytical* assessment of systems at work. Comparative studies help us to work over problems which may seem local and peculiar, but which (like all great poetry and music) communicate something of universal value and edification. Thus, peculiarly foreign systems are not just so many statistical items or factors or solutions, important though these may be. Those systems are significant parts of the human drama in which we are involved, to be studied for their universal import and indeed for their relevance to the very place where the observer is undertaking his study.

Comparative studies of any kind, if they graduate beyond mere academic tourism, obviously include certain hypotheses from the very first examination of the "foreign" object in relation to the observer's own counterpart. Those working hypotheses, with any luck, will be either challenged or, at least, made to justify themselves. A few improvements at home may seem to be indicated by what is seen abroad. More important than that is the realization that so many educational phenomena are relative to a time or place, to a stage of development, to the kind of apparatus used, or to the purposes envisaged. Not everything can be written off as merely "relative," however. In these days of interdependence many things are more complementary to each other— more like constituent parts of any person's or country's decisions. The whole virtue of democracy—of equality-with-difference as we see it between men and women, and in all the interchanges of our pluralistic modern society—is in the acknowledgement of complementariness. No one person, no team, no theory or method is wholly right; but all when added up may indicate a fruitful line of decision in education as in every other respect. The whole world is at a crisis of decision in the use of education to construct a better society, not just in one country's prospects but with an eye to a better society all round. The existence of that is ultimately the condition of well-being anywhere.

In the tumultuous self-evaluation of the United States, therefore, the most farsighted of Americans are aware of the critical importance to the world of their domestic decisions. They are also aware of the domestic relevance to them of the world's decisions. The radical boldness that made Americans part with European assumptions, when technologically produced abundance made another estimation of mankind seem possible and desirable, can once more bring about a reassessment of their own interwar values and of mechanistic shibboleths in school practice. Recent developments have shown these to be but technical phases in the nation's historical development. So America's world responsibilities in education are no longer a matter of generous disbursement only, or an unprofitable one-way traffic; they inhere quite as much in that stocktaking process which loyal Americans so assidu-

6

THE SOVIET UNION | THE CLAIMS OF COMMUNISM

The Union of Soviet Socialist Republics covers about one sixth of the earth. A glance at the map of Europe and Asia shows that the heart of that land mass is comprised by the Soviet Union, with free Europe and the Indian peninsula and Japan seeming like dissident fringes, and all the rest of temporarily indeterminate status. China, though separate and hostile, is politically akin. India, though not too friendly, is impressed. Japanese opinions and emotions are torn between the Soviet Union to the west and the United States to the east. This picture of Asia and Europe is roughly as the Soviet citizen sees it.

The present area of the Union's territory is over 8,500,000 square miles. The population in 1962 was estimated to be roughly 218 million. This figure means that there are perhaps four Soviet citizens to every three Americans, or for every one Briton. Nearly 70 percent of this population is in Europe, although less than a quarter of the Soviet territories are there. The vast and still mostly undeveloped resources in Asia place the Soviet Union in approximately the same position of "unlimited possibilities" as the United States enjoyed in the early days of the republic. The population is increasing rapidly. Industrial and urban development might be compared with that in Canada—but on a vast and radically planned scale.

The 15 Union republics and 22 autonomous republics of the USSR are not a federation like Canada or Australia; nor do they possess in practice those "state's rights" so cherished in the USA. For governmental purposes there is tight centralization, but in some aspects of education and in cultural matters the regionalism of the USSR can still be strongly felt. Only general education (not vocational or higher instruction) is administered by the several republics, and even then Communist party centralization makes for uniformity. A little more than half of the whole population either speak or easily understand the Russian language (for the Soviet Union is essentially based upon the territories of the Tsarist Russian Empire), and the Russian republic (RSFSR) is, of course, the most populous and influential of all. But up to 180 languages are spoken in the Union. Several are of Turkic affinity, being spoken by 11 percent of the population. Of the others, some have ancient literatures, whereas several had no proper grammar or even alphabet until after the Soviet Revolution in 1917. Although Russian is the prestige language, and although no educated Soviet citizen is likely to lack real proficiency in it, it is possible to find vigorous linguistic and cultural nationalism throughout the constituent republics in all except the political field. For example, at Tiflis, in Soviet Georgia, students can proceed from infancy to the university through the medium of their mother tongue. It is not possible, however, to go so far in the regional tongue everywhere, and therefore Russian is taught to every Soviet child as the international language of technology and higher cultural opportunity.

Though it is natural and convenient for us to talk about "Russia," it is far more helpful to our understanding if we remember that the Union of Soviet Socialist Republics means something far more emotionally gratifying to millions of its subjects than Russia ever did. Under tsarist rule the minority territories, especially in Asia, were like colonies of Moscow. Though Russian is gathering strength as the international tongue (and rightly so), and though Russification and Sovietization still go on (especially in the economic and technical fields), we blind ourselves to the truth if we do not recognize that the linguistic, racial, and cultural minorities are generally proud to identify themselves in enthusiasm with the Soviet Union. The faces that look up with pride to the remarkable phenomena of Soviet science in the heavens include millions of Mongoloid features or aquiline Turkish

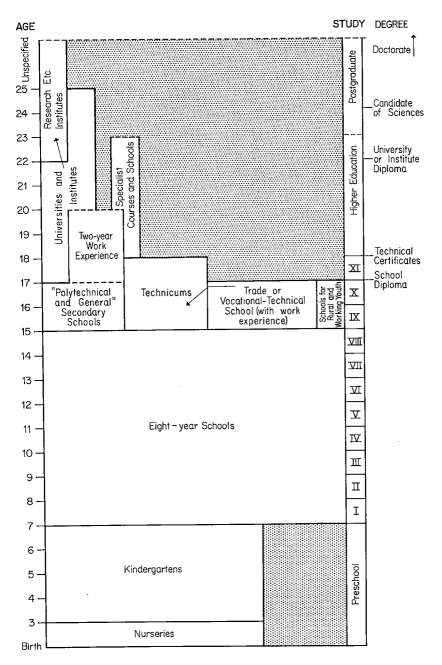

School System in the Soviet Union

219

types—the faces of children who know that they are not despised for being different, and whose enthusiasm is proportionate to the change that has come about within their parents' lifetime. The Soviet system has opened up the universe to them.

That is why the startling success of the first artificial satellite, in October 1957, was such a triumphant vindication of Soviet education in the eyes of Soviet citizens. Its solid evidence was a sort of cement for identification. If tractors and dams have been hymned, how much more Sputnik? The flight around the moon, and the highly successful space flights of other kinds, have reinforced this pride. It is a mistake for us outsiders to think that practical or material considerations alone are involved in such triumphs (though these are of huge importance).

Two other aspects must be constantly borne in mind, one psychological or social, the other ideological. The psychological or social victory so richly prized in Soviet education inheres in the knowledge that an extremely vigorous and arduous school system evidently justifies itself—not only in being successful at the top but in the broad social basis of its recruitment, enlisting the capabilities of nations and classes once thought to be of inferior caliber. The ideological triumph which the Communist party leaders capitalize on is associated with their belief that all human progress can be "scientifically" studied and planned in accordance with perennially valid principles; material and scientific progress therefore confers conceptual justification on the orthodoxy of the new interpretation. The sense of being right, of having a genuinely new civilization to offer—based upon a truer philosophy and deeper interpretation of humanity—this a conviction extremely widely and sincerely felt throughout the Soviet world and its satellite fringe. We do not accept these views, of course; but we are guilty of the most crass purblindness if we do not recognize their widespread existence, their fervor, and their evocative or cultural power. More than any other nation, perhaps, the Soviet Union is "sold on education" both for its manifest results and also for its inner virtues.

It follows from what has already been said that the republics and peoples making up the present Soviet Union differed profoundly in their degree of advancement at the time of the Revolution. It has been fashionable in most Western circles to suppose that most of the Russian Empire was backward anyway, and became perhaps more retrograde after 1917. This is ridiculous. The Soviet achievement has really been to bring the eastern and southern regions up to and beyond the former standards of its own western republics, where most of the population were in a state of education comparable perhaps with that of much of the Austrian Empire or certainly present-day Spain and Portugal.

The well-educated people even before 1917 were cosmopolitan gentry and scholars like those of other countries. Despite large-scale emigration and liquidation, the majority of these stayed behind under the new regime. The oldest people with whom one discussed the revolutionary changes of recent years (for example, the "Khrushchev reforms") in the Moscow of the early 1960s were brought up under the tsarist regime, and in its schools and universities. But this must not obscure the magnitude of Soviet changes. Though Russia proper had a long tradition of scholarship even in science, technology, and the arts in its schools (so much so that the United States was glad to copy),[1] nevertheless there were grave inequalities of education and opportunity within Russia itself, and in most of the former imperial provinces there was real backwardness. The Russian revolutionaries themselves, in the early days, seem to have agreed with Marx that the Russian Empire was the last place in which communism could be expected to triumph. Germany or Britain, with their high industrialization and their urban proletariat, seemed to be much likelier ground.

In the chaos, famines, pestilences, civil wars, and foreign interventions which followed the 1917 revolution and persisted until at least 1922 there seemed little chance of building up a new and educated nation with any prospect of economic stability. Foreign capital was withdrawn, and trade was at a standstill. Many of these terrible misfortunes persisted until the late 1920s. Moreover, in World War II the Soviet Union sustained more severe losses and damage than any other country. Yet despite a poor start and all kinds of interruptions, the Soviet educational recovery was such that, by 1955, the USSR was turning out 60,000 university graduates a year in engineering, compared with 22,000 in the United States and 3000 in Great Britain. Since then the pace of technological learning has accelerated. Engineers are not everybody, of course; but these figures are paralleled in other Soviet education activity—and the quality is without any doubt very high. Americans equate Soviet "diplomas" with their own "master's" standards. In 1963–1964 there were 331,000 diplomas and 12,000 higher degrees.

Making all allowance for the fact that a higher proportion of Soviet diplomas and degrees are in engineering and technological subjects, we are still left with the conclusion that Soviet educational achievements are phenomenal. They are already outstripping the prowess of the free

---

[1] The Rensselaer Polytechnic Institute in New York State was widely known for its following of the Russian example. Professor Cremin closely links the American development of technical training (indeed the whole "progressive movement") with the impact made by Russian technical education at the Philadelphia Centennial Exhibition of 1876. (L. A. Cremin, *The Transformation of the School,* Chap. 2.)

world and the West. It is not yet a generation since Soviet educational standards, in all except a few favored areas, were judged by observers to be regrettably low. How has all this change come about, and what lies behind it? We must not make the mistake of supposing that educational advance has only been at the highest level, and that the lower grades have been neglected. Illiteracy, formerly very widespread, has almost entirely disappeared not only from the younger generation but from among the old people also. Boys and girls do not merely go to school (nowadays more than forty-two million under 15), they also tend to stay on. By 1955 over three quarters of a million finished their tenth year of intensive schooling, after a decade of postwar reconstruction.

In that year it was confidently expected that by 1960 between two and three million children every year would reach the school year before university entrance. (The corresponding figure then estimated for the United States was 1,700,000; that for the United Kingdom was 70,000.) In fact, so successfully was this goal pursued (without being actually reached), and so strongly academic was the schooling provided, that changes were introduced in 1958 and subsequent years to divert the majority of children away from the universities and other formal higher education. About the same time, increasing competition and an academic bottleneck created difficulties that are reviewed later in this chapter. Since 1958–1959, much education, though general, has turned away from universities and toward work-linked education or technicians' careers. This change of emphasis does not necessarily curtail *education,* though it diversifies *schooling* and career prospects. It certainly makes some concessions to scholastic ineptitude or plain dullness; but the reiterated and well-argued dedication of Communist educators to a high standard of genuine all-round education (within the confines of fidelity to their faith) leaves no doubt of their intentions, or of their positive planning to elevate and not debase the academic and cultural level of all their peoples. Just what does it all mean in terms of children, teachers, and parents?

Though the peoples of the Soviet Union have their long-standing local ideals, the mass propaganda of the government officials and of the Party has substantially produced a new ideal for Soviet youth. Children are very much to the fore, smiling in photographs, and cheerful in reality. Like Junior in the United States, young Ivan is expected to be well-fed, husky, and "normal." He must be, and usually is, public spirited. The future belongs to him, and he is expected to play a great part in developing it through participation in many juvenile activities. Many of these, like some American youth programs, subtly wean the young people from the folkways of their parents; as a rule they are far more thoroughly manipulated than in America. The Party sees to that, whereas in America the public mores and community expectations are less direct or effective in their socialization. Russian children are well disciplined, by their peers as much as by their elders. They will not get far, even in youth organizations, unless they are good at school work, for example. A private as well as a public passion for education possesses Soviet citizens, and is very noticeable even in young people. The Soviet system has offered it to them in abundance, and the Soviet system (which seems good to them) is the only one they know.

Obviously, the emotions that different types of Soviet citizens experience when they think of their country and its system cannot be altogether the same. For one thing, Soviet territories extend from the Arctic wastes, barely clad with stunted bushes, down through the forests and wheat plains to the Black Sea and the Caspian shores, where tea and rice and palms are grown. The distances the other way are far greater, spanning the earth from the Baltic to the Sea of Japan. The country, in its physical diversity as well as in its climatic fluctuations, is one of extremes. Extremes of wealth and poverty, privilege and servitude prevailed within living memory under the tsarist regime. Only two or three forces made for real unity—the centralized bureaucracy of the imperial government; the difficulty of free communication with the outside world; and the sense of "being right" indulged in by rulers and clergy under the dispensation of the Orthodox Church. It will be obvious that the peculiarities of the Soviet government of today have evolved in large measure from the special features of Russian imperial rule. The methods and mystique of godless communism are very like those of "Holy Russia." But added to the traditional emotions there are others of a very significant kind which are skillfully reinforced by up-to-date application of sound psychological principles in the best Soviet schools, and are cultivated especially in the controlled creativity of the youth movements. In recent years there has also been plenty of opportunity outside the schools for ordinary observers to see the material improvements which their economy has made, and the still more spectacular achievements in the heavens.

Despite present harshness, and a standard of living lower than that of continental Europe (to say nothing of Britain and America), most Russians and most other Soviet citizens are conspicuously better off than their parents and grandparents. Their material living and working conditions are much better, on the average. The absence of real freedom is not felt by those who have never known it. Indoctrination is not much different. The differences mainly result from the highly mechanized controls exercised by propagandists and supervisors in these latter days, and from a scarcity of those private oases of free thought and discussion once available to liberals and the "intelligentsia." It is obvious, however, that since Stalin's death more latitude is being successfully claimed. In fact, the change in intellectual climate between 1960 and 1964 alone was astonishing to the author; and that "loosening up" within the Marxist framework has been more marked still in other communist countries. Indeed, a Czechoslovak education book in 1966 urged the study of western European school systems and educational ideas!

If we are to try and understand how the average Soviet citizen feels about his country's achievements and controls, we have to concentrate first of all on his material gains and still more on the material promises held out to him. Party privilege, party interference, and universal regimentation are not so much resented (being historically familiar) as some other things are appreciated: the abolition of hereditary castes and privileges, the closing in of economic extremes, the offer of first-class opportunities in education and careers. Moreover, noncommunist observers have frequently commented on the exhilaration often sensed in gatherings of Soviet youth. It seems they feel they are working together for a future which they can make for posterity if not for themselves. Youth is required to contribute to the future, practically and culturally. It is helped, in so doing, to realize an inward happiness and sense of personal fulfillment in "the collective"—one that can only be compared in fairness to a religious sense elsewhere. This sense of dedication has been described as a "YMCA" feeling.

Comparison with religious feelings and aims is not made lightly. Lenin once said: "The whole of education and up-bringing shall be directed to their training in communist *morals*." Youth organizations of all kinds carefully watch over the behavior not only of their members but of their neighborhood. They discourage slack and dirty habits (including smoking). They vie with each other in "socialist pledges" to maintain the proprieties, order, and productivity. So do the trade unions, neighborhood associations, and so on. All this is officially encouraged by the Party, of course; but in large measure it also seems to arise from eager cooperation. The communist faith, and also the practical business of social reorganization, are served by dedicated bands not altogether dissimilar in spirit from Catholic guilds and sodalities, except that the Soviet organizations ramify in their activities throughout the whole of civic and industrial life—including adult activities. Hence all those quasi-voluntary "brigades" engaged on civic projects, or on the tidiness campaigns which make Soviet streets, public buildings, and transport so immaculate. The overall cultivation of civic and personal sensibility and commitment adds more to the aims of education than most school systems have imparted—except religious schools and the English Public Schools, which were studied by the

Russians for possible suggestions they might offer for the cultivation of communism in Soviet boarding schools.

A comparable "forward look" is discernible among young people in less developed areas of the United States, and still more in western Canada. There they often endure harder conditions and more loneliness than they are accustomed to, though the material rewards are greater; but the sense of a beckoning future is one of the strongest experiences of their lives. In the Soviet Union the "virgin lands" of the eastern territories exercise a similar pull; and if it is not a physical horizon that beckons, there is a promised millennium. Undoubtedly there is drabness and sometimes dreariness in Soviet schools, fashions, and cities; but observers should not underestimate the contentment and perhaps enthusiasm with which people generally support a regime that is planning a better future for them. (For that, after all, is the way *they* have been taught to look at it.)[2]

The essence of Marxism is in its suggestion that the future is scientifically controllable through an understanding and manipulation of the rules of economic progress. It teaches that ideas, emotions, and political experiences are only a manifestation of the environment as it controls human development; the environment itself, according to Marxism, can be bettered by improving the methods of production and distribution and the sources of driving power. For a well-brought-up communist this is no mere matter of management, but turns upon an ideologically correct interpretation of accurately known "scientific laws" included in the canon of Marxist writing and currently reviewed by the Party for their contemporary significance.

Two points should be noted here, one continental European and the other with religious overtones. Most continental languages do not make a clear distinction between "science" of an empirical Anglo-Saxon kind and "academic studies" of a near-philosophical or speculative kind. Thus one speaks of "science" in terms which include the arts, literary studies, and philosophy. Therefore Marxist speculations and writings are describable as "scientific," just as medicine and space technology are. The second point is that the Leninist role of the Party as the contemporary guardian of Marxist-Leninist infallibility is strangely reminiscent of the role once claimed by the Orthodox Church or claimed by other churches now. The big difference is that churches confine their official interest to faith and morals. The Party also has control of the

---

[2] Values and priorities can be regulated in somewhat unexpected ways. At the end of 1964, a 75-gram bar of chocolate (roughly four ounces) cost 1.20 rubles ($1.20). A seven-inch LP record of Rachmaninov's Second Concerto cost one ruble ($1.00). But then, the chocolate's wrapper had a poem printed on it! (The record would have cost three or four times as much in England.)

material development of the economy, the educational system, and the reconstruction of power resources and communications for improving the standard of living. Its achievements are very persuasive—more so than any theoretical propaganda.

The young Soviet citizen sees plenty of evidence of such improvement around him. Questioning and disquiet come less naturally to him than they would to an American or a Briton. They seem like questioning the basic principles of faith—always a difficult and lonely thing to do. If we appreciate how the Soviet peoples have been "sold" the Marxist assumptions of dialectical materialism, and if we also bear in mind the authoritarian and self-righteous patterns of pre-Soviet Russian life, we shall be better able to understand the hold that the present Soviet upbringing maintains over its young people.[3] They also usually feel they know how their bread is buttered; many feel near-religious dedication; and in any case the outside world is pictured as less advanced or hostile.

The educators, and most of the private persons we meet in communist countries, impress us by their sincerity and dedication to the personal development of the young people with whom they are concerned. Yet it would be naïve to suppose that all the advances in production and education achieved by communist governments are prompted by more tender concern for individual citizens than mark the business world or the politicians of capitalist countries. In fact, during the ruthless revolutionary days which latter-day communists in Europe like to think of as a nightmare now gone away, the present constructive "certainty" which makes Soviet educators blandly believe they possess the whole prescription for the future had perforce to give way to harsh, practical decisions. According to an extreme environmentalist view, individuals are little better than puppets or manifestations of the economic pattern; it is that which you are trying to manage. If personalities are difficult, they can be altered or put out of the way, much as we might train a tree to a desired shape or even uproot it. The "cult of personality" is adjudged to be a defect not only when it entails a glorification of Stalin or another fallen deity, but also when it attempts to justify personal claims by you or me. One crazy revolutionary (Tkachev) in the early days suggested exterminating everyone over the age of 25, so that a clean start could be made. This criminal brainstorm was only a *reductio ad absurdum* of a then widespread attitude— in shaping the future it might be necessary to disregard not merely many people but even whole generations. Instead of disregarding them,

[3] For a closer look at these and related aspects, see "The Concept of Ideology in Communist Education," in *Communist Education* (ed. E. J. King), 1963.

however, Soviet planners and educators from the very beginning sought to reshape the older citizens into a favorable matrix for the future. Only the intractable were exiled or liquidated. Techniques of influencing people had not been developed to their present expertise, and time was short. After a while the system could be left to take care of itself except in unusual circumstances. In any case, the rulers concentrated on the young and on re-education.

The "bourgeois" institution of marriage was among the first to be attacked by Soviet leaders, for three reasons: it perpetuated the continuous cultural exchange between parents and children, cemented by emotional ties; it was linked with the inheritance and accumulation of property; and its taboos were associated with religion. Therefore the importance of marriage was minimized, and divorce became for a time a mere matter of form-filling. Casual relations and abortions were encouraged—though they are now very strongly discouraged. The Church and its workers were persecuted. However, children were well attended to—not just by parents but overwhelmingly by the state. Crèches, nurseries, and the like took care of babies while their parents worked, as nearly all of them still do; and schools, too, took away not merely the duties but also the authority of parents. An abundance of preschool and extracurricular care for children is still characteristic of all communist countries.

In the mid-1920s, the emphasis was on emancipation and equality. Women became equal to men, and received identical treatment in official matters. Children, too, were made to feel real partners in their own and public development—of no less consequence than parents and teachers, whom they were not afraid to defy and criticize or even denounce if need be. This was the phase of Soviet thinking exemplified by the story of Pavlik Morozov, a twelve-year-old "pioneer" who denounced his own father as an "enemy of the people." The father was condemned to death, and the boy widely acclaimed as an example for all young citizens. During those days army distinctions were reduced to a minimum too, and officers did not receive salutes or special uniforms. School subjects, books, and timetables were adopted and discarded by children in the most "progressive" way. Until the early 1930s, children sometimes chose their own teachers. There were no formal examinations, and the standards and curriculums were those that seemed justified locally by "life adjustment." Pupils could expect to advance from grade to grade each year in accordance with their own personal standard, and those who wished to proceed to higher institutions could do so without having to satisfy predetermined criteria. This pattern of organization was thought at the time to reflect contemporary American methods. For a long time John Dewey was a great favorite in the Soviet Union, and he in turn reciprocated that admiration—as we can see in his writings. (Those relevant to the Soviet Union are collected in *John Dewey's Impressions,* 1929 [ed. W. W. Brickman, 1964].) The only formal barrier to advanced education in those days was being the child of a former aristocrat, professional person, priest, or other suspected opponent of the regime.

As part of self-determination, education was before 1933 entrusted altogether to the constituent republics. There was no federal Ministry of Education. Centralized control was limited to that implied by the power and solidarity of the Communist Party. Local notions and needs determined what should be taught, and children were encouraged to plan and regulate their own school life. Though there was a shortage of schools and teachers, and though fees were still charged in schools (which did not have compulsory attendance until 1930), there were good opportunities for young workers and older, underprivileged people to attend evening schools. These attempted to give them a "middle school" (that is, American high school) training and even to offer them university studies. Obviously the system could not work; it was bound to result in gross lowering of standards, and in an assumption that everyone had as good judgment as anyone else. (Soviet educators hold that everyone, given the right opportunity, is equally educable.) Anti-intellectualism was rife. Of immediate practical concern was the poor quality of workmanship in the Soviet factories and in agriculture.

Low standards in practical matters were rather surprising. Ever since the eighth Communist Party Congress in 1919, the new pattern of proletarian education had included much experimenting with the "work school." The idea of learning about life, and of developing personal culture through work was recommended by Marx in 1848, and further recommended by N. K. Krupskaya (Lenin's wife) in her very influential writing from 1917 onward. At its best, the "work school," as developed by Georg Kerschensteiner in Germany, may be compared with the very finest of the "industrial arts" programs of the United States. In the Soviet Union it had long been popular on account of its orientation and name, but by the 1930s it was obvious that it was not helping toward the successful education or industrialization of the Union. Lenin had, of course, been an avowed admirer of this and other "American" methods; but Stalin had already struggled to power, and in 1928 the first Five-Year Plan was proclaimed, to begin the following year. It was marked at every level by increasing centralized control and by its great thoroughness. By implication, of course, the old slapdash methods of education, which had served well enough during the period of casting off shackles, were doomed. Dewey fell out of favor at the same time, and all other "American methods." Thus we come to the end of the first important phase of Soviet education (from 1917 until about 1929) and pass on to the second.

During the second period, the years from 1929 until about 1935 were spent on the consolidation of elementary education, and the years from 1935 until about 1941 were devoted to the stiffening and coordination of intermediate and higher education—all with a view to the strengthening of Soviet power and the establishment of an efficient hierarchy in industry and government. Less, rather than more, concern seems to have been felt for the interests of persons and subgroups in Soviet society—a tendency paralleled by Stalin's ruthless collectivization of farms and industries, and his suppression of local cultures (though he himself was not a Russian, and spoke the language with a strong Georgian accent until the end of his days.

At this point it is helpful to explain a few simple terms used in writing about Soviet education. Until 1959, the *four-year school* meant the elementary school period from the beginning of attendance (at seven years of age) until eleven. Village schools were usually of this character, and many still are. The *seven-year school* meant the elementary four years with an additional three years spent either in the same establishment or (frequently) in another building which might be in a larger village or convenient center. The *ten-year school* meant a provision for the whole period between the ages of 7 and 17 or later.

Since 1959, the term *eight-year school* has been used for the "general education" years until 15. That is the basic elementary school covering the compulsory period of attendance. In ordinary speech and sometimes in notices, the word "middle" is frequently used of the same school in Russia. In any such connection it must be distinguished from a different use of the word "middle" in other European schools, for in western Europe that term usually signifies a newly contrived combined lower-secondary school of a comprehensive type roughly comparable with the American junior high school—at least in its age range (from about 11 to 14 or 15). But it will be noted that the basic Soviet school covering the eight years from 7 to 15 does, in fact, cover the period of lower secondary schooling; and sometimes in Soviet statistics it is counted as an "incomplete secondary school." In recent years the word "polytechnical" has been officially added to its Russian name—not to indicate *vocational* training, but to remind hearers that the school is a polyvalent one giving a wide view of "production" (that is, elementary technological awareness) and a "positive attitude" to the modernization of the Soviet Union.

Between about 1959 and 1964, the term *ten-year school* was replaced by a new pattern of organization that extended the school period by one year (giving an *eleven-year school*), so as to include much practical working experience for the children during school time. (More will be said about this later.) But the scheme was not a success in actual practice; so the eleven-year school was abandoned, and a return was made to a ten-year school in the 1964–1965 school year.

This means that for about 67 percent the secondary school phase is now completed in two years on top of the eight-year general education school, and the important school-leaving certificate can be achieved then. About 15 percent do not continue in a "general" secondary school of this type, but go at 15 to a three- or four-year *technicum* which reaches the same scholastic standard as the general secondary school academically, while adding thereto a very systematic vocational preparation at what might be generally called "technician" level. A third group of boys and girls (about 18 percent) leave regular school at the age of 15, but they usually go on to combined work-and-instruction for varying periods up to three more years in what used to be called "labor reserve schools" and are now called "trade schools" or "vocational schools." Thus there is a tripartite differentiation after the age of 15; but there is none of the finality associated in some other countries with such distinctions, because of two features. First, it is believed that the educational process is continuous for all "workers," whether in trade schools or general secondary schools after 15; second, interchange is encouraged. Attendance until 17 will be compulsory in 1970.

At this stage it is worth emphasizing two other points. Soviet schools, like nearly all continental systems, make a child repeat a grade if performance is not satisfactory. Therefore, many have had 10 years at school without completing ten-year school. The second point is that although they may complete ten years or any other specified number of years of "school," the children may not have been attending formal classroom instruction in conventional subjects during the whole of that time. Even during the most typically Stalinist period, the last three years might be spent (and certainly were for the less "academically" suitable children) on projects closely associated with work, and particularly linked with the current Five-Year Plan. It was during this period that the "labor reserve schools" and "trade schools," [4] with very utilitarian instruction linked with basic general education, became firmly established to guide future thinking about adolescents' scholastic potentiality. As many Americans, most Russians like to have practical consequences from schooling. Much more even than Americans (especially in the later stages of education), they like to present basic prin-

---

[4] It must not be supposed that the attainment level in these schools was necessarily low. Major Gagarin, the world's first spaceman, was trained as a youth in one of these "labor reserve schools" before passing on to higher technical training.

ciples in relation to utility and action. Soviet children and their parents are particularly responsive to this form of presentation. The over-strong emphasis on academic talents and attainments before 1958 was itself utilitarian—part of the determined drive to produce top-level scientists and administrators in unprecedented abundance.

Having, therefore, outlined the present structure of Soviet primary and secondary schools, we can postpone our examination of what comes above these in order to revert to our historical analysis of how the pattern grew up; for this throws some light on the real significance of alterations in recent years. The process has been one of continuous evolution and adaptation, partly caused by changes in Soviet leadership, but still more necessitated by the development of Soviet technology—and indeed by the very success of the Soviet schools and universities themselves. Let us then go back to the period soon after 1930, still within the first Five-Year Plan, while the Communist Party's economic planning under Stalin's tight hand was systematizing the instruction given in elementary and secondary schools, so as to make the Soviet Union a technologically advanced nation.

To initiate the second phase of Soviet educational development, after 1930 school became compulsory from eight to twelve years in rural areas, and in towns from 8 to 15. At first, there were too few schools and too few teachers, but compulsory education was soon reasonably effective. The old "self-determining" methods were promptly abandoned, and by 1936 were nonexistent. Teachers were reinforced in their traditional authority. Textbooks had to be used systematically, and became official. Each word and each definition in every book was, henceforth, scrutinized with the utmost care on ideological grounds as well as for accuracy. Pupils were ordered to work hard in school, or leave and work hard outside. The "work school" idea was left out of general education, to become the lot of less successful children after the age of 14. Under Stalin, far less was heard in "middle school" (that is, American high school or British grammar school) about "polytechnical" education. Proper attention to *subjects* was insisted on; and the traditional "liberal" ingredients of European schools (except the classics) were restored to the curriculum.

A federal "Committee for Higher Technological Education," established in 1933 (later a Federal Ministry of Higher and Technological Education), has maintained strict control over higher education ever since. It, therefore, effectively controls the academic curriculum immediately preceding higher education. (In 1965, for the first time, a USSR Ministry of Education was set up. Other ministries control different aspects of further education (for example, agriculture). The research and planning of the Soviet Academy of Sciences, of the current

State Plan, and of the Party all systematize the aims and functioning of higher education and everything below it. The researches and publications of the Academy of Pedagogical Sciences of the *Russian* federal republic (not the Soviet Union) are also increasingly influential in directing school developments throughout the USSR.

It should not be imagined, either, that school is for juveniles only. Extensive adult-education programs accompany it, sometimes undertaken by school children and young students as well as by their elders. Elaborate and highly successful campaigns have swept illiteracy out of farms and factories. The Soviet people are avid readers, and in some ways perpetual students of a sort that Western Europeans find it hard to understand. Therefore museums, planetariums, and the general harping on "culture" are really popular manifestations, and not just hackneyed gestures. That is not to say that everyone is always satisfied with communist handouts, but the general zest for educational opportunity expects "culture" from somebody, and the Communists have full control.

In 1944–1945 the period of compulsory attendance was changed to begin at 7 years, and to last until fourteen for those in the country, and until 17 for those in towns and cities. It was planned to make a 10-year comprehensive school period compulsory by 1960; but the new law of December 24, 1958, did not do that. Instead, it introduced a third phase of Soviet education whose story we shall pick up later; but that third phase was made possible and desirable by the formalizing successes of the second, on which we should continue to concentrate for the time being. The second phase of Soviet educational development secured universal elementary schooling, ensured substantial "middle" schooling, and made the Soviet Union one of the most thoroughly schooled of nations. During the second phase, special care was taken to ensure that village children went to school. It was a step toward the intended industrialization of agriculture itself, as well as a means of preparing more workers for urban industries.

The "middle school" or "general" period still reflects Stalin's formalization. Its curriculum includes much mathematics, physics, and chemistry in addition to history, geography, physical education, Russian, and foreign languages. (About half the children in the Soviet Union learn English.) The going is hard, the presentation formal; but progress is sound and steady. Children attend school six days a week, if we include their organized activities in school time. (By this I mean officially sponsored participation in youth movements and the more instructional kind of "circles" or clubs—without counting more recreational activities.) Before the 1958 reforms, some hours of "socially useful labor" were already required every week and this continues.

Children often devote their Sundays to quasi-voluntary work in the public interests—in harvesting, or in work brigades keeping the town or parks tidy, or similar operations. Yet they have spent 32 hours already under instruction, and they have a great deal of homework to do—not to speak of youth organization activities. (In the elementary school there are 24 hours a week of classroom instruction.)

We should remember the Russians' previous heritage of agricultural history when many of their ancestors were serfs. There is habitual emphasis on work followed by more work, just as in the United States the popular picture of the young American at work on the farm or in the kitchen or garage is an honorable one. In the old days, most Russians had the children of the petty gentry, the clergy, and the educated classes lording it over them while they worked; they now, therefore, do not mind so much what appears to us the dull insistence on work as a means to emancipation, to good jobs, and to the tickets to the theater and ballet that once were others' prerogatives. Where many of us would flag they still seem enthusiastic. Most parents are at work every day, and partly for this reason school holidays are still short. This does not seem literally true when we learn that the schools are closed during June, July, and August (except for the final examination classes, whose ordeal takes up nearly the whole of June), and that there are two-week vacations also at New Year and in the spring. But the school buildings are constantly used for youth clubs and other extracurricular activities, in which the teachers help for long periods. There are also camps, harvest work, and other kinds of "socialist reconstruction" to claim the children's energies, quite apart from directly academic studies undertaken either privately or in association with a Pioneer House. Many, or most, urban children now spend up to three months under looser supervision in camps (organized by Party youth groups, or by trade unions and so on). These are often at the seaside or by lakes or in forests. An increasing number, too, spend their six-day week in boarding schools, going home only on Sundays. Leisure, school and home are linked. Performance is so important that marks are publicly announced. It is impossible to do well in social life or in the Party without a good scholastic record. The children are under supervision and subject to prodding all the time in more ways than we might suppose.

Control is ensured not only in the schools themselves, but in the actual or virtual monopoly of books (including the hero stories that have replaced many of our nursery tales), in the censorship of newspapers and radio and films, and through the various youth organizations. It is impossible to avoid the constant "plugging" of the Party norm. This is all the more effective in the absence of alternative influences. Just think what our city life would be like without advertisements constantly urging us to buy this or that, to conform to some fashion, or to dream of something gorgeous beyond our proper expectations! Soviet propagandists in particular point somewhat primly to their own freedom from "sexy" advertising and other "decadent" influences that might distract or demoralize the young. All radio and television programs (which seem to continue incessantly) are also vehicles of approved enlightenment and taste. It is really surprising that there are so many concessions to popular preference—in the circumstances! Only a very small percentage of Soviet citizens are members of the Communist Party, for that is a real privilege often keenly sought after as a steppingstone to promotion. It cannot be achieved without a careful scrutiny, about the age of 27. In order to be acceptable to the party, or in order to be admitted to responsible membership of the Pioneers (ages 9 or 10 to 14 or 15) and *Komsomol* (Young Communist League, from 15 upward), boys and girls must not only live exemplary Party lives but be able to prove excellent performance in school or factory. When candidates are proposed for office, one of the first questions concerns marks in examinations.

Even outside party affiliation, the prestige attached to the work of these youth organizations is enormous. They offer all the community services available to young people in other countries. They also provide facilities for sports and extracurricular activities of an academic kind. Some additional instruction is given, and especially such things as foreign language clubs attract the participation of young people who are not communists. The real emphasis of communist education is, in fact, placed on activities outside school. In school, the dreary brown tunic with a black pinafore worn by girls may be relieved only by the red scarf of the Pioneers. One way and another it is not surprising that 90 percent or so of the children wish to belong. Many who are not admitted to real party status nevertheless take part in the activities of these organizations.

This general pattern of elaborate control through school and party was confirmed during the Stalin period, and deviation was ruthlessly eradicated. A fair number of intellectuals who had weathered earlier storms found the means to escape from the Soviet Union. Some of these have written about intellectual standards and behavior in Soviet schools and universities during the admittedly chaotic inception of the second educational period—when young teachers and students who had grown up during the 1920s were passing into adult life. Their memories are doubtless true; yet they are certainly not a true picture of the period immediately before World War II, and they are still less true of today. The rigidity and vigor of formal schooling under Stalin's control has really established the structure as we see it today, though with some modifications in policy and practice. Some of these are intentional, and others were introduced almost willy-nilly from wartime experience. The German attack on the Soviet Union, in 1941, meant the abandoning of all but the war effort. Teachers were withdrawn from schools; many pupils were drafted for work of national service; women took over still more of the professions. Tuition fees which had been abolished were reintroduced in 1940–1941. They were not removed from higher (that is, university or "institute") education again until the end of 1956.

The third and present phase of Soviet educational history could perhaps be dated from the end of the war in 1945, but it is probably truer to see the postwar period until well after Stalin's death, in 1953, as one of reclaiming what had been lost, and as a fuller development of the plans enforced immediately before the war. Thus this period was one of restoring and consolidating the second phase, which really persisted until 1958 and what in that year were proclaimed as the "Khrushchev reforms." In Stalin's time purges and party maneuvers were not allowed to affect the general building-up of a heartlessly efficient training at school, at work, and in public organizations of a well-disciplined and well-informed totalitarian citizenry. A new political aristocracy arose, and these and the economic heroes were given rich personal rewards; but for the rest there was little expectation of diversified opportunities through school, any more than there was decentralization of control. "Frills" of all kinds were embargoed; there was a shortage of consumer goods, and a denial of variety in everything from classrooms to clothes. Therefore, although the late Stalin period may be characterized by the mass production of "capital" goods for the future in the shape of numerous well-trained scientists, as well as in vast development schemes, the present or third phase of education can be described as beginning only after Stalin's death.

Since 1953 there has been a natural reaction against many activities associated with Stalin. Old plans have been cautiously and then more generally revived. Controlled experiments of many kinds are taking place. The greatest is the radical school reform of 1958, differeniating pupils between 3 school types (of which we shall speak later) after the age of 15. The supply of top technologists and researchers is well assured, and more technicians are needed. The "polytechnic" idea is being revived in all education; training for automation and its consequences is beginning; boarding schools are named as "the schools of the future"; and much attention is given to education for a Communist millennium instead of the mere "socialism" of the present.

The overcrowding of schools adds to the importance of extracurricular work. Numerous schools visited very recently in Moscow, Len-

ingrad, Baku, and elsewhere were on a two-shift system. A school building may be an elementary school in the morning and a middle school in
the afternoon, or vice versa. The premises are in continuous use. The
simple fact introduces another aspect of Soviet school life—the standardization of presentation. Young children and adolescents are expected
to use the same desks and classroom arrangements. Also, the great emphasis on the theoretical and social (that is, dialectical materialist)
study of physics, for example, is not matched so far by a full provision
for practical work at this stage. Standardization is such that there is a
completely undifferentiated school program from the Baltic to the
Pacific, except that in Lithuania and Georgia, for example, the "ten-
year school" may take 11 years because of difficulties of learning additional languages. All pupils take the same subjects. Beginning in the
first year with Russian language and literature (or the mother tongue)
for 13 hours, with mathematics, physical education, singing, and some
practical work, they eventually reach a grand total of seventeen subjects in which they have received instruction. In an article published in
February 1957, Dr. George Counts of Columbia University calculated
that the ten-year school offered 9962 hours of classroom instruction,
some 10 percent more than a Canadian child got in 12 years of school.
This, in turn, is more than the American average. We must add to it
the strong extracurricular influences at work.

   Children do not have a choice of subjects, though there is specialization at university and "technicum" or college level. All secondary
school teachers are specialists, and responsible in detail for the "correct" presentation of their specialty. Methods officially approved at
one time are changed at another, and subjects such as history or biology
are re-edited from time to time. There are no private or independent
schools; no religious teaching is permitted in schools. Schools are prevented from having much individual self-consciousness, quite apart
from party considerations, by the fact that they have numbers and not
names as a rule. They are all coeducational, and apart from the period
of paramilitary training for boys, and that of domestic science for girls,
there is no basic differentiation in the curriculum, either between boys
and girls or between children of varying interests and abilities. Superficial modifications may be found; for example, a majority of children
aged 12 and over learn English, while others learn French or other
languages. Supplementation for the slowest and brightest children (and
for esthetic taste or practical skill) is abundantly supplied in the youth
organizations.

   A high standard of proficiency and diligence is demanded by the children's own "collective will for advance" no less than by the teachers.
The children are taught in groups—*never* selected according to ability—

in which the forward ones help their slower brethren. As much as is consonant with predetermined standards, children are made responsible for the organization of their progress through the curriculum. Character training of a somewhat puritanical austerity is very much part of the school's atmosphere. No experimentation in education is permitted at the individual school or class level, though there have been very many carefully controlled official experiments which may affect a few schools or hundreds; and there are many research institutions at the highest level. In particular, the Institute of Defectology, in Moscow, has paid special attention to remedial reconstruction of a child's learning environment. It claims good results with those who, in some other countries, would be considered hardly educable, or at any rate unsuited to a bookish education.

Though there is no selection for schools before 15, nor any "homogeneous grouping" into streams of equal ability, there are state grade examinations at the end of the fourth, eighth, and final years; there were also yearly examinations until 1957. Children whose performance is not satisfactory are kept back. If they repeatedly fail their grades they may then be sent to a special school. Learning includes much memory work and repetition of facts. On the other hand, the subjects are presented as scientifically as possible. For example, in the learning of English, student-teachers who have never been outside Russia acquire a sound intonation and perfect accent by means of oral diagrams, intonation graphs, and records. They also undertake a comparative study of Verner's law and learn Old English. In personal contact they are found to have a remarkable command of the language, which they are eager to use in discussion. English is perhaps the third language they have learned. In schools a similar, though less advanced, technique is used.

Fees were abolished again after World War II (even from higher education in 1956); but education at the middle-school level is not entirely without cost to parents. They must pay for books and stationery; and children wear a sort of uniform, which must be paid for if possible. On the other hand, differences of social and economic origin, and those of race or color, are not allowed to handicap the promising Soviet child. (An exception must be made for the kinder consideration given to party officials' children for selection into universities.)

A typical lesson observed recently may be described as follows. A teacher gave an almost unbroken lecture for about 45 minutes, with but little feeling for his class. He was a purveyor of information, and a subsequent assessor of pupils' achievement. (There was a slight variation in this technique for science and languages; but even then little give-and-take took place.) During the lesson a child was called up to show his homework. He wrote on the board for several minutes. The

others watched silently, with hands clasped on their desks. A mark
was given on a five-point scale. This was recorded with much public
interest. Teachers who push on fast may make things difficult for about
a third of the children, and nearly impossible for the slowest third. If
teachers are slower, bright children may be bored, but will find plenty
to occupy them at the Pioneer House (school subjects as well as recreation). Russian children aged 16 or 17 are about British "ordinary level
certificate" standard in knowledge, though below it in practical work
in science subjects. This means that, in knowledge, they can be more
than favorably compared with most average American high school
graduates. That is a fairer comparison, for the Russian school is, like
the American, a "common school." We should note here that the classroom atmosphere and promotion system just described are still entirely characteristic of those European continental schools in which
progressive methods have not taken hold.

Countries with great educational arrears to make up, or with difficulties arising from geography or a shortage of teachers, often rely
more strongly than others on standardization and official programs.
This "keeping up to the mark" is of service to the ill-informed or un-
imaginative teacher, especially if he is isolated. It is found, for example,
in Australia and parts of Canada, and is at the basis of the French insistence on a unified program for city and hamlet. It is in marked contrast to the practice of many American states which give people high-
school teaching certificates without specifying what subjects they are to
teach, and without making sure that they have a sound enough background for the various duties they may be called upon to undertake.
English certification is much more lackadaisical still. But at least it
may be assumed that the teachers have had a sound grammar school
complement followed by specialized academic "subjects" (as well as
"how to do it") in college or university. As a complete contrast to Soviet
uniformity, we may refer to a publication of the Fund for the Advancement of Education, *Teachers for Tomorrow*.[5] It said that 49 percent of
American high schools did not then offer a foreign language, that 23
percent taught no physics or chemistry to anyone, and that 24 percent
taught no geometry. In the Soviet Union these subjects are taught
universally as the basis for a Soviet child's understanding of the material world; but they are also of very practical value to Soviet statesmanship and technological advance. Mathematics and science subjects take
up nearly 40 percent of a middle-school pupil's time.

When the "seven-year school" was the most that the ordinary child
could hope for, the threat of possible rejection in the seventh year was

---

[5] Fund for the Advancement of Education, *Teachers for Tomorrow*. 1955.

of great importance in keeping up the tempo of work. Now gradual differentiation by abilities demonstrated in lessons or "life-linkage" before 15 is equally important. Performance at 17 or 18 is more critical still. Once, all students obtaining middle-school certificates could enter higher education. More recently, only "gold medalists" with outstanding results could be sure of admittance. Now even these prodigies have to submit to tests and interviews. Those chosen immediately for universities and higher institutes are the top 20 percent of an already selected group. The 1958 reform law required all others (that is, 80 percent of the academic school graduates then aged 18) to take jobs of any sort for two years before entering higher education—if they were qualified for that. Many thus begin their university work with evening instruction or correspondence courses. Again the best of this latter group may be admitted to full-time study about the age of 19 or 20. But at present, half the students in higher education are on a part-time basis, and of these a large proportion continue so. Courses then take a minimum of six years instead of the usual five, or five years in place of four for lower qualifications.

Whether Soviet educators are making a virtue out of necessity or not it is impossible to say; but there is no doubt that an extensive development of part-time higher education is official policy. Officials have been heard to say that this is good for the character of the worker-student (as well as perhaps good for the economy); and certainly some students themselves seem to prefer part-time study combined with work, which gives them an income far better than that obtainable on student grants. But in trying to assess Soviet practice and achievement, one must always bear in mind that high standards of attainment and diligence are required; that very skillful part-time students can "make the grade" into full-time study with an appropriate grant; that the whole business of part-time study is inseparable from considerations of quality, because the brightest students are entitled by full-time study anyway; and that throughout all branches of tertiary (that is, postsecondary) education of every kind, there is elaborate provision for correspondence (and television or radio courses and part-time instruction), supplemented by occasional full-time conferences and generous leaves-of-absence for taking examinations.

What is more, Soviet full-time higher education generally includes some practically oriented studies, such as the "diploma project," which may be related to a current problem of technique or production in the way that engineering studies are in a number of countries. In complement to this tendency of the universities and institutes themselves, there is a marked extension of "factory colleges" or instruction-on-the-job of both a technical and a general kind—at all kinds of level. So there is not at all the same cleavage between "work" and "study" that has been traditionally found in noncommunist countries. In order to give a truer perspective to our own view of the matter, we should remember the establishment of "sandwich-type" courses in higher education in the United Kingdom, and the tendency everywhere to relate post-graduate research at any rate to some practical interest of industry, commerce, or government.

Moreover, we shall draw naïve conclusions if we fail to take note of the increasing selectivity of all Soviet education. Just as work experience before the age of 15 is a valuable indicator of suitability for this or that future career (particularly when combined with class records daily reckoned from one to five marks for every piece of work done), so the two-year work requirement now imposed upon the great majority of even the more academic 17-year-olds is a sort of filter too. Only the best and most persistent are likely to get straight into university or institute at 17; and only the most diligent and deserving of the others will go full time into higher education at 19 or so after their compulsory two-year work stint (from which the "brightest" have already been exempt). It is no secret that the most famous of institutions (like Moscow State University or the Kalinin Polytechnic in Leningrad) add special requirements to those normally exacted from students admitted to other centers of higher education. Most notable has been the widely proclaimed establishment in recent years of Akademgorodok, or University City, near Novosibirsk in Siberia. This city of learning and research, with all its supporting schools at the secondary level and its lofty provision for the arts, is perhaps not the pinnacle of Soviet learning; but it is certainly an example to the world of the deliberate use of one kind of productive enterprise (that of learning) for the service of a whole, vast country. The personnel recruited there are outstanding. Other academic cities of the same sort may follow.

In connection with this careful husbanding of brainpower and diligent learning we should remember once again the work of the youth organizations in supplementing the learning opportunities of the bright child. Through the youth organizations, future Soviet citizens can pursue additional or more varied courses in languages, mathematics, sciences, and the arts. They are also encouraged to take part in academic competitions at a local, regional, and all-Union level—the so-called "Olympiads." And everywhere there are the "honor mentions" of able boys and girls or diligent workers who have merited the applause of their peers. The strange thing is that amid this cultivation of excellence there is so much sense of a peer status.

The selection at 17 years of age is, therefore, relentless. No fees are charged in higher education, and most students get scholarships or grants, which are conditional upon progress. Only the best scholarship holders have quite enough to live on, though; the others need supplementation from their "work experience." University students proper have many advantages, especially in relation to the housing shortages and other hardships of Soviet urban life. They are exempted from military service at least temporarily. They work very hard for the five-year course, but they once again are enthused by a sense of future promise. Though the number of university and institute (college) places is proportionately higher than in most other countries, it is not enough to meet the demand. Add to this the fact that Soviet public opinion is in favor of intellectual distinction—so much so that people (nonstudents) read textbooks freely on public conveyances—and it becomes easier to appreciate how much it matters to be excellent. Some indication of this same esteem is given by the relatively high status of teachers. Engineers and miners or those who work in dangerous occupations are given the highest rewards. University teachers and researchers, followed by other teachers, come next. The medical profession, consisting largely of women auxiliaries to specialists and researchers, come about fifth. The whole of public opinion thus supports a systematic attention to work and intellectual training.

So much, then, for the academic type of upper-secondary school and the prospects of transition from it to higher education. What of the other alternatives after 15? It seems best to begin with the provision made for the average and below-average pupil. When a seven-year school life was still normal for all but a few pupils, many quite able but nonacademic children thereafter entered the labor reserve schools already mentioned. Instituted during 1940 to train a million boys for major industries, they were immediately popular. The war halved their numbers, but until 1959 they still trained hundreds of thousands of teen-age boys and girls for one to three years, making them skilled workers. Many such schools were residential, with tuition, board, and clothing provided by the state—especially for war orphans and refugees. These schools are now called trade schools or vocational-technical schools (*remeslennoye uchilishche*), and offer a tough utilitarian course to boys and girls who have finished the eight-year general program. Though they offer a basic nonvocational supplement too, they do not yet complete the ten-year school curriculum to the extent of reaching a certificate. For this, bright children are urged to go on to the next stage in day or evening study. (It should be noted that trade schools may actually be on factory or farm premises.)

A technical or "specialized secondary" school (*tekhnicheskoye uchilishche* or technicum) is in a higher intellectual category than the last named school. It offers either a three-year course (usually, but sometimes longer) to 15-year old entrants, or a shorter course to 17-year-olds with a middle-school certificate. For the former group the "technicum" offers training as a medium-skill specialist, together with a general education up to university entrance level. For the latter, it gives technical training and preparation for intermediate management positions and the like. In 1955, *Izvestiya* declared[6] that half the students then in technicums had previously completed the ten-year school course. Until 1959 the proportion of entrants with a complete secondary education increased. There is an exacting entrance examination. In 1966, 3.3 million students were in technicums.

On completion of the course, students may apply to universities or institutes, and about 5 percent are admitted; but the technicum itself is the "college" for music, ballet, art, nursing, medical auxiliary work, and much ordinary teaching, as well as for technical skills, business administration, journalism, and the like. Some 3500 technicums in 1965 trained more than 2 million students for well over a thousand distinct careers. They include thoroughgoing practical experience "on the job" during their later years. A "factory college" beginning at this, or a comparable level, was also initiated in 1960. Foreign observers should not underestimate the importance or attainment level of this "intermediate" kind of further education, which, to say the least, overlaps much that is called "higher" education in some other countries, as the professions mentioned above indicate. At the present moment, a new and extended range of higher technicums is being planned, for students who have completed the full 10-year school period.

An interesting sidelight is thrown on the academic standing and social prospects of schools in this range by the fact that, in some rapidly industrializing districts in some communist countries there is a tendency for boys to go into the technicum as an alternative rather than the more formal academic school after the age of 15, so girls may predominate in the latter. This is surprising anyway; it is the more surprising when we recollect that, in the Soviet Union, engineering and similar professions have been successfully colonized by women.

In addition to these school-day preparations for the lower and intermediate ranks of the vocational hierarchy, there are many supplementary offerings. Not only are there evening high schools and extramural courses; it is also possible to make use of a wide range of correspondence courses. It is largely by means of evening opportunities and of factory schools that illiteracy and ignorance among older people have been combated. Trade unions, cooperatives, collective farms, and commu-

---

[6] See A. G. Korol, *Soviet Education for Science and Technology,* Boston: Massachusetts Institute of Technology, 1957, pp. 101 and 127.

nity organizations all have a share in them. The Communist Party also covers the country with a network of propaganda centers which hand out much general information on the side. Library and museum services have always been vigorously developed by the Soviet government. Ballet, theater, music and opera are generously subsidized, and immensely popular.

It follows from the description of technicums given above that the old European division of the teaching profession into two or more parts has for the time being been accepted by the Soviet government, though there are many signs of change. Abolishing illiteracy and universalizing elementary education demanded many teachers immediately. Now there are more than seven times as many teachers as existed in 1914. Until 1957 some teachers' technicums offered a four-year course from the age of 14 (or 2 years after completion of the 10-year school). Since that year, elementary school teachers have been trained in four-year pedagogical institutions or technicums. They enter at 17 or 19 years of age. There is an admission examination and the course is hard; yet the leaving certificate does not count as graduation. Such teachers are never specialists. They teach all subjects in the first four school years, and move up year by year with the children. They are paid on a basis of four periods a day, for six days a week. In-service training is common, and the best èlementary teachers are urged to proceed to higher pedagogical institutes of university standing, where since 1958–1959 more than 1000 places are reserved for them. This is said to be the goal in all teacher training for the future.

The higher pedagogical institutes just referred to are part of the higher education system. Over 700 specialized *institutes* (or colleges of advanced technological education) in the USSR run parallel to the universities,[7] in some cases exceeding the prestige of the latter. Their difference lies in more specialized or "applied" courses. Not all the buildings are impressive architecturally; but they are often superbly equipped and have magnificent library facilities, with numerous copies of individual titles and dozens of photostat copies of current learned periodicals from all over the world. So in attending a pedagogical institute a

---

[7] Some discrepancy is sometimes found in the numbers given for Soviet higher institutions because of differences in placing them within foreign-imposed categories. It therefore seems convenient to use American sources, particularly the work of Seymour M. Rosen and his colleagues in *Part-time Education in the USSR* (1965), *Higher Education in the USSR* (1963), and a supplement for 1965 in *Significant Aspects of Soviet Education* (all published by the U. S. Department of Health, Education and Welfare). The most recent overall figure for Soviet institutions of higher education at European university level is 739, including the universities. (The majority of these also run part-time and correspondence courses, as well as full-time.) In 1964–1965, total enrollments were 3,600,000.

future teacher shares an experience comparable to that of most Soviet graduates, the vast majority of whom were institute students. There are also general universities (40 in 1961), with over 200,000 students. Moscow and Leningrad universities each have more than 20,000, and enjoy all-Union prestige, though each of the separate republics has at least one university fostering its regional culture as well as serving utilitarian purposes. Students in all higher education (except advanced theoretical scientists and mathematicians), must now take some courses in education. A good supply of excellent scholars thus enters teaching. Since 1960, courses in pedagogical institutes have been extended to five years—like those in other institutes and universities. Teachers trained in them are specialists serving the academic 15–17 classes and other senior grades in the middle-school. An increasing number, however, are found lower down in the age range and also in more practical subjects.

Many institutes can be compared for subject intensity with American graduate schools, or the Honors specialization of British universities and specialized research institutes. On conclusion of the course, the student obtains a "diploma." The term should not be misunderstood; it may be equated with an American master's degree or a British Honors degree—and not just in terms of technical knowledge. Eyewitness evidence and personal encounter leave no doubt of the extremely high quality of Soviet students. About 60 percent of them are technologists (compared with 56 percent in Britain and 25 percent in the USA); more than 40 percent are engineers of some sort.

Specialized in its application and orientation though Soviet higher education usually is, nothing could be further from the truth than to suppose that its alumni are little better than supertechnicians. Those institutes or courses devoted directly to the humanities can boast a degree of scholarship and sensibility not to be dismissed lightly.[8] It has, in fact, been greatly admired throughout the civilized world— no slight recommendation when we reflect on the isolation Soviet scholars have had to endure, imposed by restrictions at home no less than abroad. Moreover, the average level of all-round cultural development manifested by Soviet specialists is admirable. What other countries have worried about as a "two cultures" cleavage is less apparent in the Soviet Union in consequence.

Testimony to the excellence of Soviet higher education has come from many sources in recent years, but none has been more striking

---

[8] See D. Grant, ed. *The Humanities in Soviet Higher Education,* Toronto: University of Toronto Press, 1960, and C. L. Wrenn, *"Higher Education"* in *Communist Education,* ed. E. J. King. London: Methuen; and Indianapolis: Bobbs-Merrill, 1963.

than that of Lord Robbins,[9] who gave his name to the Robbins report issued in 1963 by the committee on higher educational reform that visited the United States, France, West Germany, and the Netherlands before proceeding to the USSR. He declared that he had "tremendous respect" for the way in which the Russians had combined quality with quantity in education. Some non-Russian observers are foolishly misled by the names of Soviet qualifications, above all, the "diploma." Non-Russian comparisons will remind us that in several western European countries a "diploma engineer" is the most highly qualified of engineers. Incidentally, in this field, Soviet higher institutions have in several years been training as many technologists as the rest of the world put together. Of course, the more settled economy of the United States or Western Europe could not absorb 60,000 graduate engineers a year simply as engineers; but the expanding development of the Soviet Union and its friends can. Moreover, it certainly does no harm to the government and administration of a country if such people are employed in a nonengineering capacity. After all, graduates in the classics and other nonadministrative fields are widely employed in official capacities. Why not more people with a "polytechnical" background?

One area where Soviet studies might be severely criticized by people from the Anglo-Saxon world is that of the social sciences and other empirical fields of like nature. There are economists, of course, but they tend to be unempirical because they are working within a Marxist framework of "scientific prediction." The same circumscription makes social surveys of an autonomous kind seem somehow heretical to a Russian. Yet there are noticeable changes. "Management" was once considered to be a purely bourgeois interest; now it is officially encouraged as a systematic study in its own right. Social surveys of a somewhat "Western" complexion seem to be developing. A team of Soviet experts has been to the United States to learn how to plan in the superplanning way which directs the future of the country of private enterprise. Educators are now studying not only "foreign educational systems," as they used to, but Comparative Education as a systematic review of educational dynamics in a variety of *complementary* contexts. All of this is much more empirical and unscriptural than communist education and statecraft was in the recent past.

The whole educational system of the USSR is in full evolution; nothing is changing faster than technical and higher education. Conventional distinctions between subjects, or "levels," are being superseded by new arrangements—always to make the most of the human,

---

[9] Interview reported in the London *Times,* June 12, 1962.

scientific, and productive potential. Elaborate research and careful discussions are going on, to implement the plan of "10-year school for all" by 1970, with new forms of intermediate technical education. Graduates in each specialization are trained in numbers anticipated to suit the State Plan; and on graduation they can be directed to particular jobs for three years, after which they are free to move elsewhere. Not only directive powers, but financial and promotion incentives too, ensure the full deployment of skilled resources. Teachers (especially in higher education) are well paid and highly esteemed, though there is a moderate teacher shortage there too, because other sectors of the economy are expanding and paying more. This fact should be assessed against a world background of severe teacher shortage. In the USSR, not only ideology and patriotism, but sheer industrial realism, make leaders of the country's enterprises realize that education is an investment that can never be skimped. Much attention is also paid to higher education in the arts. There are 47 special institutions of this kind, for music, visual arts, theater, and cinema.

No real difference is made between women's and men's access to the professions. Some 25 percent of the engineers, about one third of the physicists, and 75 percent of the doctors are women. There have been women generals. Coeducation is once again the rule, as it was until 1939, when it was discontinued during the war years.

Since Stalin's death there has been a crescendo of interest in "polytechnicization." This includes a return to the old idea that work or a career prospect gives life-interest and realism; it also suggests that a truer perspective on all life is given through working experience, especially when oriented toward the communist millennium in which all will be workers together, giving according to differentiated abilities and receiving according to need. (The crusading value of this slogan is everywhere evident in the USSR.) Polytechnicization, therefore, has its moral and aesthetic side as well as utility. It is absurd to represent it as disguised "child labor." Though it certainly entails hard work, there is little doubt of its evocative success—for the average child at any rate. General as well as technical education is obviously secured, and children seem to like it. About two-thirds or more of them above the age of 15 are now trained indirectly for occupations while receiving a general education; yet the formal content of the *schooling* received by many of the remaining one third during their vocational training years is as substantial as if they had been in a Stalin-style 10-year school—and indeed may go well beyond it. For the 67 percent or so selected for "polytechnical and general" courses between 15 and 17, there is still some work experience in school workshop or public enterprise before leaving school. The 1958–1959 reforms made a great feature of setting part-time experience in the factory or on the farm; but it did not work out well in practice, so the 1964 return to a shorter school life over-all cut "outside" work considerably. Some working experience is continued, however, and special school-work centers have been set up in Moscow and elsewhere. Moreover, all except a minority of university or institute entrants have now had two years' full-time working experience beforehand. They are said to be much better students in consequence, in terms of learning as well as of character.

Why has there been all this experiment with work-experience? Has it all been for reasons of pure utility? Hardly, to judge by the disgruntled comments of some factory managers who had youngsters thrust upon them! It was not the exploitation of child labor, which could have been much better done anyway. Serious educational and administrative reasons weighed heavily in making the new changes, as well as a wish to return to the old genuinely communist principle of making education and life into a sort of polytechnical continuum, as Krupskaya and Marx wished. (Even the noncommunist Robert Owen had outlined kindred proposals in 1813–1816, and had tried to make them work in Britain and the United States. But Soviet educators do not like you to say too much about that.) We can see the immediate justification for altering Stalin's overacademic curriculum by looking at its results.

The undoubted bottleneck in the approaches to Soviet higher education before 1958 certainly made diversion of would-be students necessary on merely numerical grounds; the hangover of European disdain for "dirty hands" occupations was felt even in Russia. Such bourgeois immorality obstructed the building of a collective spirit, of course; but it also was a nuisance when technicians, maintenance men and supervisory people were needed rather than more pioneers of research or teachers—abundantly supplied by the ten-year school. Middle-grade occupations are those predominantly needed by contemporary society, and even more by the automated world of tomorrow. Soviet society is as planned as its economy. A Marxist must believe that patterns of production and distribution provide not simply the material basis for life, but its very roles and perceptions; they are, therefore, the stuff of culture and the web of sensibilities. This is much nearer to medieval Christianity, and to Dewey, than the nineteenth-century traditions of European schooling. Stalin's formalization of the curriculum of the ten-year school, therefore, through the foundation of Soviet technological triumphs, was a reversion to continental (but noncommunist) assumptions and also a departure from the "American" ideas Lenin had admired. De-Stalinization reintroduced more "learning-by-doing"; it also combined what had become necessary for the next stage of industrialization with what was thought socially desirable as the next step toward communist culture. Previous ad hoc attempts to retrain academic half-successes for practical work were not popular or satisfactory, as this one is.

One universal reason for inattention and absenteeism among older school children is boredom. The inclusion of subjects of more obviously practical value, especially when the training is given residentially away from home, will probably help to cut down the uneasiness and disaffection of youth. The Soviet Union, like most other nations now, has its problems of juvenile delinquency and the type of borderline behavior that not long ago produced beatniks and hot-rodders in the United States and Teddy boys in England. No one is so likely to be a public nuisance as a young person whose abundant energies are unabsorbed while his ambitions are frustrated.

It is a mistake to imagine that polytechnicization need necessarily be a whittling-down of the liberalizing possibilities of education. If more insight or conviction is gained by linking studies with practical considerations, well and good. Yet, however praiseworthy the plan may conceivably be, the sudden change found the teachers unprepared. They have been, as we have seen, trained as specialists eager to be correct; they were at a loss to know how to be correct in an application of their studies that was unfamiliar to them. Still, sudden about-faces are part of Soviet history, and no doubt teachers will both survive and comply in due course.

The outside observer is more interested to discover what underlies the initiation of this third phase of Soviet education. First it was laissez-faire and self-determination; next it was the austere formalities of the European curriculum, but with a much stronger scientific content; now we are witnessing the development of a "polytechnical" and more socialized move toward communism. "Socialism today—Communism tomorrow!" is a familiar slogan. "Children, think, speak, and work like communists!" can be seen in many classrooms and workshops. "The task of our school is the creation of a new communist humanity" does not ring so strangely in eastern Europe as the more work-oriented new variants upon the reiterated theme of "Study, study, study as Lenin studied." Lathes and other equipment, some quite elaborate, now appear in Pioneer houses and recreation centers more obviously than before. The same evocation to "school" is given a more workaday complexion in this way.

Other changes inside the Soviet Union may perhaps be associated with this one. In the disorientation and jockeying for place that followed Stalin's death, western European liberals tried to discern a stirring of independence that might have loosened the shackles of communist dictatorship. Undoubtedly, something of the sort seems to have occurred. There have been violent repressions in East Germany. Poland seems to have come as close to emulating Tito as her Soviet masters were prepared to allow. Hungary went too far in the direction of liberalism, and was ruthlessly quashed with violence and bloodshed. Such violent eradication of "counterrevolution" is quite in keeping with communist philosophy, but what prompted this anxiety abroad was perhaps an inner disturbance at home. It has been credibly said that the communist regime's ideological hold over its own youth was at stake. Much emphasis has been placed since 1956 on the establishment of increased numbers of boarding schools, presumably for greater control and discipline. Stress has also been laid since 1958 on the disciplinary value of work.

Reference has already been made to the difficulties experienced by school-leavers in getting into higher education. At the universities and colleges themselves it has become fashionable to cultivate independent attitudes, read "dangerous" books, discuss heterodox ideas, and generally to become "decadent." In free countries this sort of puppy-play is no more than a trial of strength against what is old and traditional. In the Soviet Union it could be a challenge to the communist way. The affected Western European clothes and hot jazz records of the *stilyagi* (Teddy boys, beatniks) are certainly more than a matter for critical cartoons in the comic papers now; the Soviet authorities go out of their way to denounce the disaffection of these youths. Dissatisfaction has probably not so far reached the stage of serious disaffection, however; and some criticism or heterodoxy (at any rate in poetry and music, and perhaps in the interpretation of the Marxist canon in relation to similar things) can apparently be accepted. Striking evidence of this is shown in open debates in Soviet periodicals, and still more in the visits of Yevgeny Yevtushenko and other "angry young men" to Western capitals.

Yet undergraduate excesses must not be considered in isolation. At the working-class, less intellectual level in the Soviet Union, there has been hooliganism, delinquency, and "even religion!" Even in the communist world, opportunities and rewards are evidently so unequal that a kind of brutal repudiation occurs. Sometimes there is good reason for frustration. That is no doubt why, after Stalin's death, a considerable decentralization of management—or at least a devolution of responsibility under the central, watchful eye of Moscow—has been initiated. As one writer put it, the immense beehive of Moscow bureaucracy has been overturned. The safe jobs are no more. Managers are to be more effective and responsible in their sphere. Remote control can evidently become too remote. We may be sure that the dispersal of industrial responsibility is not only for strategic reasons. It is at least partly caused by a need for greater public contentment. Admittedly, it coincides with an announced determination to open up the east and north more effectively. The twentieth Congress of the Communist Party in 1956 published plans for the irrigation of large stretches of arid land in Asia. There has long been a movement of the young people to the "virgin lands" either before or immediately after their college careers. This migration is semivoluntary, and those who participate usually find it a rewarding experience. From the point of view of the top administrators, it must undoubtedly be a safety valve also.

Communist orthodoxy had in the past clamped down on literary and artistic deviation as though it were political sacrilege. In recent years there have been unprecedented strayings from the party line. By 1960, university professors could publicly listen, without fear, to broadcasts in English from British and American radio stations—not just in their homes but in the faculty clubs. Strangers meeting casually in bars and public places would freely discuss such programs, either initiating a conversation or willingly taking part in one when started. They clearly had read and listened widely. They also took anticommunist visitors to their homes, though 1957 was the first year that teachers had been permitted to do so. As said previously, this "loosening up" process is continuing.

It is impossible to state, or even to guess, what the future will be, at any rate in the matter of politics or of liberal evolution in literature and art. One thing is quite certain: the controls are still there. The Soviet Union is planning the full development of her vast federated empire with every foreseeable human device. Every day sees the building up of vast capital resources and the founding of real human wealth —good land conservation, fine crops, material advantages. This, of course, could well be done without communism; but it so happens that those doing it now are communists, and claim they do it because they are communists. The masters of the Soviet Union are able to lend technical assistance to countries in desperate need of it. They would probably do so even if it meant injustice to thousands of their own citizens, and perhaps this does result. However, the technical and educational prowess of the Soviet system is now so well established as to be beyond controversy; it is unremittingly watched by the governments of the United States, of the Commonwealth countries, of every free nation. It is the envy (or the lodestar) of emergent territories.

A writer on social and educational backgrounds will not meddle with political futures; but since 1957 Soviet leaders have repeatedly declared that the Soviet Union's "inexorable" technological advance toward a higher standard of living for the world was a more potent weapon in her armory than all the nuclear weapons ingenuity could devise. Most of the world is too backward, hungry, and ignorant to be fastidious. It sees real advance in science, technology, and production; it sees educational advance far beyond the dreams of man half a century ago; it cannot stop to consider the political price because it has no experience of freedom whereby to measure what has been surrendered. The only effective counterblast of noncommunist nations is to show that, in equal circumstances, they can achieve an equal or superior excellence which will spill over all the same material abundance—together with a richer political, social, and personal experience.

To sum up, what does living in the Soviet system mean to its millions of men, women, and children? To outsiders it seems in some ways a gray and repressive life. Congested housing, mainly poor quality consumer goods at high prices, regimentation, dull fashions, and conventional art—these are what we see, even if we forget the grim political side. What does it matter that full-time working hours are being steadily reduced to a *maximum* of 40 a week, with the aim of 35 before long? What is it to outside observers that Soviet maternity leave is now 112 days of paid absence, or that sick workers get holidays in fine hotels in the Crimea? Outsiders miss the subtle taste of freedom. But then we are judging by inappropriate criteria—our own, and not theirs. Those who, for example, are accustomed to being packed like sardines inside Indian trains, or to riding on the top in the dust and heat, do not object to third-class travel in European trains. They may think it luxury. So it is with the Soviet citizen, as a rule. But education is, fortunately, a discontenting thing in itself—and at its best a potent source of "divine discontent." It is to be hoped that the evolution we have experienced, and that Russian liberals experienced in the past, may repeat itself. Whether this happens or not will certainly be decided in part by the educational and technological successes of the noncommunist world. It also depends on international education.

In this chapter every attempt has been made to point out the comparative austerity, if not drabness, of private expectations in the Soviet Union. But people who are living in what they feel to be an emergency out of which they will triumphantly emerge, will often put up with the rationing of what we consider essentials but they consider desirable luxuries. Therefore what we think of life in the Soviet Union is irrelevant; the only sensible criterion is what Soviet citizens and their neighbors think. The neighbors are very important in this case. They are more than half of mankind. Much of what they see under the hammer and sickle seems more attractive than their own present lot even now. As Soviet productivity approaches American productivity, and American-style material abundance comes closer to the reach of the hungry world, the growing admiration for Soviet technology will know no bounds. Education on the Soviet plan is recognized as the foundation for Russian development.

Many of those neighbors who see plainly the perils of communist authoritarianism are harried by their own extreme underdevelopment. They have seldom been helped very much by noncommunists—at any rate until recently. The United States has been outstandingly generous, and other Western nations too; yet embarrassing evils remain. There is great underproduction of food in the world, and bad distribution of what is grown. Part of this imperfection arises from the inability of poor nations to buy other people's surplus—or even their waste. They cannot acquire purchasing power until they develop industrially or build services (such as shipping, works of art, precision engineering, or mercantile and administrative skill) that other nations want to buy. None of this can happen without educational developments, preferably very inexpensive developments.

In this connection the world role of Soviet education is of extreme significance. The first stage in education is having enough to eat. Then a man must have a home for his family, and keep them free from starvation and disease. It is a vital step when it no longer becomes necessary for a whole family to labor relentlessly from dawn to dusk (or longer) in primitive agriculture or some noisome factory. Repressive class stratification can be questioned. So can its supporting superstitions. Even half an hour a day to one's self is a humanizing instrument of the greatest importance—a chance for self-recognition, for conversation, for cooperation. Modest promises with simple, practical results are powerfully persuasive.

The most remarkable item of knowledge for anyone is that he is a man and that he matters. To attain this beginning of self-help all kinds of simple reforms are helpful: a more prolific strain of seed, a finer breed of cattle, a better marketing organization. Even a different pattern of hoe can be educative if it allows its user to stand upright and talk to his fellows instead of being crouched almost double like a beast. When we think of present needs in education for a very large part of mankind we are thinking of life at this elementary level. Perhaps a quarter of mankind, though above this utterly depressed status, are still barely at subsistence level. Providing them with an effective chance of further advancement depends on the skill of their governments in securing the benefits of modern technology and the opportunities for more education. The future of education depends on a material change now; children cannot go to school if they are exhausted in the fields or the kitchen.

To appreciate the importance of the Soviet Union's influence in world affairs, therefore, especially in its cultural influence on desperately poor countries, we have to feel as vividly as possible what it means to have a neighbor who has recently and with difficulty done all these wonderful things, and apparently made them available both to its own subjects and to others, irrespective of nationality and color. Our own objections to the Soviet system then seem trivial, compared with the multiple gains held out by using Soviet methods. In wartime, as we ourselves have seen, even convinced liberals and democrats accept curtailment of freedoms and privileges. Greater things are at stake, things upon which peacetime privileges and opportunities are based. For the majority of mankind, the mere acquisition of the material basis for what we call civilized living is still a long way off. The winning of it is a war more desperate than we have ever known, because it is lifelong and merciless.

Empires, besides inflicting certain injustices, have also shown formerly subject peoples what riches can be envied and now, in these latter days, be obtained by emulating western technological and scholastic excellence. Those very empires have passed on to their subjects the educational and administrative foundations necessary for the building of indigenous progressive societies. But it is not surprising that, where a speedy and gallant emancipation has not been permitted to former subjects, there should remain an impatience of occidental hegemony and a doubt whether democracy really means what it is supposed to do. All the nations with many overseas representatives export some poor specimens along with their worthier examples.

Those who want success quickly, therefore, and who want it without the seeming wastefulness of inequality and "muddling through," are usually attracted toward a planned rather than an evolutionary society. Not even Soviet harshness in some respects seems less humane than destitution and former repression. The things that seem central and fundamentally objectionable in a communist or near-communist system when we look at it, may seem to others merely an accidental disadvantage, like fumes and heat from a highly productive furnace.

Material development is of prime educational importance. That is why agencies like UNESCO devote such energies to fundamental education, food production, the elements of government and commercial administration. The Colombo Plan for the development of south and southeast Asia is another agency of paramount educational importance, on a world view. The unprecedented generosity of the United States government in the postwar period has helped the painful stages of pioneer industrialization or agricultural reform in many countries. Capital investment by private persons and corporations is also of great value; yet it needs to be done with extreme sensitivity if it is not to be misconstrued as "economic imperialism." Not one of these activities can be effectively assessed without reference to the influence of the Soviet Union as a potential alternative, or China as another.

The position of China is difficult and peculiar. It is far too vast a subject to treat here. But communist history is mainly repeating itself, at least in public works and in schools. There is immediate concentration on capital development. Major works of reconstruction are undertaken. Communications by rail, road, and cable are being revolutionized. Rivers are being spanned for the first time, and power resources are being exploited with great speed. Schooling is groomed (or desperately trimmed, as in 1965–1966) to serve immediate technological and political ends. Its recipients are obviously enthusiastic and prepared to tolerate hardship. They work hard in return for the benefits. Uniformity or regimentation is so little resented that it is patriotic and cooperative to wear blue overalls. The neat blue suits and blue caps of Chinese delegates in Moscow used to present as sobering an appearance as the clerical garb of a latter-day Puritan; but they have vanished. The Chinese, besides being the most populous nation on earth, are also proud and unpredictable. Recent Chinese policies show their old independence leading them along a road of socialist development deviant from that approved by Moscow, and bitterly opposed to it.

To return to the USSR, we should carefully consider Soviet educational achievements not only in terms of material abundance or military strength (important though these are for the moment), but also in terms of a new view of human potentiality, especially as that may appear to hitherto underdeveloped countries. That is to say, we must heed Soviet claims to have produced not only an efficient technological apparatus but a new and fairer prescription for civilization, with a more fully developed conscience and sensibility as well as opportunities for a rich life. For this, no less, is what Soviet educators mean when they talk of a communist society. We shut our eyes to the inner driving force (and the "sales value") of Soviet education if we limit our appraisal to plain politics and economics. Economic improvement and social justice are the bait dangled by communist propagandists before the underdeveloped people outside. Inside the Soviet Union it is very widely felt, in addition, that the present stage of development has made Soviet citizens more civilized than those in capitalist countries, and that the next stage is one of even greater intellectual, esthetic, and moral perfection.

How much this program owes to ancient Russian messianism, how much to religious orthodoxy, how much to Marxist ideology, and how much simply to a firm commitment to education is a problem we should ponder. Alexander Kerensky, who was displaced by Lenin in

1917, declared in 1966 (at the age of 85) his belief in the continuity of the Russian character and civilization—of which communism was but a phase. Yet it is a European phase—in part a consequence of Byzantine Christianity and of the Industrial Revolution—in part an educational pattern.

How far might that pattern be usable elsewhere? How might it develop in the Soviet Union itself, as the nations comprising that federation achieve a higher standard of living and a lower sense of urgency? But rather than venture here upon a purely speculative and hazardous study that could not in any case be profitably undertaken in a small compass, it would be better to consider the case of India. India has similar economic difficulties in some respects; she also has a vast and mounting population. For the first time she is able to control her own destiny as in independent country. The solutions with which she is experimenting may ultimately be of supreme importance to Asia and Africa, and in turn to mankind.

7

INDIA | DEVELOPMENT AND DEMOCRACY

A hundred years ago it did not seem altogether likely that either the United States or the Russian Empire would be in a position of paramount world leadership within a century. In some ways, despite their real achievements, they must have seemed rather like the relatively undeveloped countries of our own day such as Brazil or Argentina; their future had so many uncertainties. Looking forward from our own time we can not be sure what countries will ultimately have most lessons to offer mankind, even though we can see that some (like Canada) are likely to have a future of great material prosperity. The present position of a country like Canada represents one extreme of the human situation—a vast territory with riches still to be developed, and a small but enterprising population. In these circumstances there is ample opportunity for continuing and improving on the education successes of either the United States or the Soviet Union. From this standpoint, their educational problems and responses might seem to have some affinity.

But when we turn to such a country as India, we feel unable to forecast either prosperity or world leadership. The land is so poor, the population so vast, and the present situation so depressing. On the other hand, our own nineteenth-century forebears were unable to foresee our world, and we may be making just as serious mistakes in our own calculations. It is stupid to see the future in contemporary terms. It is also misleading to judge other people's educational problems by our own frame of reference. The children of India are undoubtedly being taught in schools and universities. They will be trained in fields and factories and offices. But to see the crux of Indian education we have to look beyond these familar institutions and come down to fundamentals which we take for granted, but which in India are suddenly revealed as demanding all the educational skill we can muster.

It is time for us to consider children on a different plane of reality. The whole world's problems of food and population, of class, of superstition, of poverty and disease are gathered together in the Indian peninsula in an acute form. (Most references to India in this chapter might also be applied with minor variations to Pakistan.) The solutions which India can achieve for these ancient problems may well place her among the nations which have most benefited mankind. We must also reflect that no human community so far has effectively suggested how to safeguard the old "liberal" or "rounded" humanities in a world that is increasingly specialized, industrialized, urbanized, and proletarian. This is a matter in which India feels vitally concerned. Any solution she can even tentatively suggest will help to save the health and sanity of mankind. The educational and economic problems of India seem at first glance to be in another world from our own; but in truth they epitomize the ancient terrors of mankind, and they may also comprise its future.

No country is more in need of radical reshaping than India, for several reasons. India, although the seat of the Hindu way of life for thousands of years, achieved a new beginning only in 1947. She then ceased to be a dependent part of the British Empire, and became instead a self-governing member of the Commonwealth of Nations like Canada. She was the first nonwhite dominion, and the first republic to stay in the Commonwealth. India had never previously been united, except under British rule, and even then several princely states had large autonomy. Though Pakistan broke away as a self-contained Muslim federation in two parts, the remaining territories of the republic of India survived as a great nation knowing unitary existence for the first time. It now consists of 16 states and some smaller, centrally administered territories.

Yet it was not only its newness that faced India with a challenge. She has many profound problems, each grave enough to be urgently critical in its own right, but each even more complicated by being bound up with the others. The first is that India has the lowest standard of living in the world—and that far below the comprehension of those who have only experienced destitution in Europe. There is just not enough food to fend off starvation from time to time, not to think of health or (even more remotely) prosperity. The majority of Indians know what it is like to be hungry—not merely in the sense of missing a familiar meal or two, but in the sense of being undernourished to the point of disease and the risk of death. Nothing happens on a small scale in India —great droughts, great floods, burning heats, and torrential monsoons are aggravated by plagues and hostile insects or animals. When your peasantry are skirting subsistence level, or when you are sinking all in a cash crop, any one of these visitations can bring irreparable disaster.

In case this sounds like an exaggeration, let us point up the information with a few hard facts. In 1960, the per capita income in India was only £21 ($58.00) a year. Some 49 percent of all mankind lives in countries where the average annual income is less than £25 ($70.00) a year, as in India, China, Ethiopia, and Indonesia. Thus the Indians are more representative of the human race in that respect than any nation hitherto discussed in this book. Indians (who are mainly vegetarians, but would in any case be short of animal protein because of poverty) eat only seven pounds of fish or meat products every year, whereas the average Briton eats 179 pounds and the average American 214 pounds. Amidst all this poverty, the Indian economy is being made to invest 9 percent of its gross national product; but foreign experts think it will have to invest 15 percent in order to keep India solvent and free from starvation.

Food shortage is not a simple risk unconnected with other things. It is immediately bound up with the problem of overpopulation. Since the reader first started on this chapter, some thirty or forty new Indians have been born. India is one of the most outstandingly prolific countries in the world. It is estimated that in 1800 there were about 50 million inhabitants, roughly the same as the present population of the British Isles; in 1951 there were rather more than 359 million. The 1961 census showed that the population had risen by more than 82 million. Moreover, we should add to India's total of 438 million the 85 or 90 million in Pakistan if we are to assess the increase over the Indian peninsula as a whole. India's third economic plan for 1961–1966 reckoned on more than 8 million additional mouths per annum to be fed; but that figure was exceeded. A yearly increase of 2.5 percent is an anxiety,

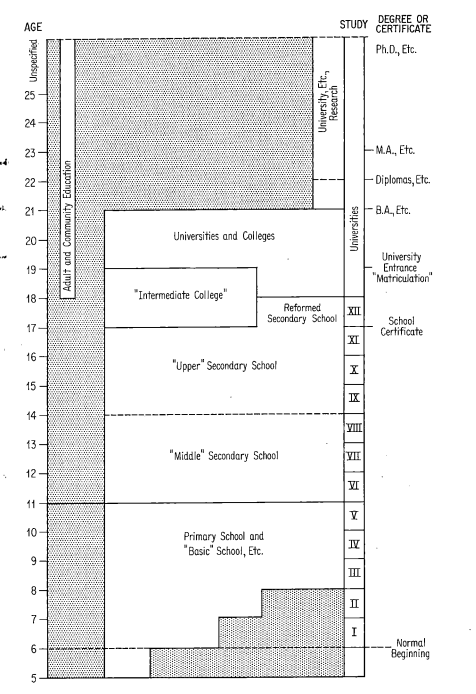

School System in India

when there is already insufficient food to go round for the most meager standard of living. This calculation says nothing of other social needs such as health and education.

Too many babies are not the only problem. Because of starvation, malnutrition, disease, and other misfortunes, India long had an almost incredible mortality rate. No Indian baby could expect to live much more than 20 years in the not-too-distant past. Advances in the control of malaria and other tropical diseases have increased life expectancy by more than 10 years in a comparatively short time. More mouths to feed! Fewer deaths in childbirth! Longer parenthood! So the spiral rises.

Rising population is not a problem confined to India, or to Asia. It is most rapid in South America; but as the population of Asia is so immense now, the actual increase there fast outstrips that anywhere else. It is worth reflecting on these figures. Out of a total world population of well over 3,300 million people, nearly half are found in China, the Indian peninsula, and Ceylon. The world population is *increasing* by 80 persons every minute; some 170 babies are born, and only 90 people die. The total human race counts 120,000 more than yesterday, and at least 43 million more than at this time last year. At this rate the number of human beings will be doubled by the end of the century. In fact, with medical advance, the rate is already being stepped up, because the death rate is being quickly lowered while the birth rate stays fairly steady at 34 per thousand per annum. India, in particular, is a country where a diminished death rate is likely to increase the population enormously. It was the reduction of the death rate, even more than large Victorian families, that brought about the sudden increase of population in nineteenth-century England. In India the increase has been appropriately called an explosion.

Before considering the measures taken to cope with this and related problems, it will be as well to complete our picture of the total situation. The total area of the Indian peninsula is about half that of the United States' mainland territories; there are roughly 1,265,000 square miles in India, and 365,000 in Pakistan. Yet the Indians and Pakistanis outnumber Americans by nearly three to one. There are no external resources, few raw materials such as minerals, little industrialization, and little expectation from trade. Much of the land is exhausted by centuries of cropping, and some is desert or mountain.

The Indians so densely crowding this large country live for the most part (85 percent) in villages, which number about half a million or more. The majority of them are self-contained units, where subsistence agriculture meagerly supports peasant families and innumerable small craftsmen serving rural and domestic needs. Jawaharlal Nehru once estimated the total of these underemployed and penurious crafts-men as 100 million. Their earnings are unbelievably small; but they are higher than those of the peasants, for whom it is a comparatively rare thing to handle money. Even then that is usually in coins worth a mere fraction of a penny. Anywhere in India one can see people endlessly walking about on the off-chance of being hired. In the great cities many just sit or lie around hopelessly. Urbanization in India is already a run-away problem, without the support and supplements that have made up Indian life for millennia. Though village life is hard, and fraught with incessant labor, it has traditionally enfolded the population in the security of the Hindu way of life. The very caste system helped to en-sure easy acceptance of status for the present in the hope of promotion in another life. To us it seems deplorably unjust; but then we should re-flect what human beings have endured without much or any complaint in the interests of stability. Security is a basic human need. When it is associated with religions it is sometimes encouraged as "resignation."

The Hindu way of life is not so much enjoined by religious dictation as practiced out of habit. In addition to the influence of example itself, the tradition of oral instruction is very strong in the villages to this day, and this is a powerful force in education (sometimes very conservative) that must be reckoned with in our assessment of other methods of in-struction. In a village, respect for the *guru,* or wise man, may be para-mount. Besides, rural people everywhere (especially in a preliterate state) set great store by proverbs, riddles, and the like. The rules of Indian life are those evolved for self-sufficient and isolated villages. For example, the veneration of the cow originated in an unwillingness to kill or harm the constant supplier of milk and butter and cheese. After its natural death the animal yielded hide and other products anyway. To this day the life of the village is regulated by ancient custom and the rural round of ceremonial, linked with crops and ani-mals. Its pivot is the local temple or shrines.

Secular life moves round the well or pond (usually contaminated), and the local stores. The villages are feebly linked with each other and the outside world by earth tracks or muddy roads; along them the pace of communication is that of the oxcart or the pedestrian. When epi-demics and natural disasters took an unchecked toll, the population did not increase beyond the native resources. Now there are far too many hands to till and harvest crops for the landowner, and far too many mouths to feed. Though this is widely true, and likely to remain so for a long period, the establishment of industries in some areas during the 1950s and 1960s has led to local shortages of adult agricultural labor. This change is sometimes a disadvantage to children, who must help out; and it does often help to raise living standards appreciably for those who remain. In the old days the crops were consumed locally. Now modernization has made familiar the notion of the cash crop, garnered and sold for profit (not the villagers') in some distant town. Less stays behind, and the standard of living is worsened, at least by comparison with that of others.

Though toil is relentless from dawn to dusk, the human surplus is such that many are unoccupied. Between about 1951 and 1955, four million new jobs were found; but in the same years natural increase added another seven million to those looking for jobs. It is obvious that unemployment and underemployment depress wages to an almost incredibly low level. To give an example: elementary school teachers are paid much higher wages than the average, but in 1955 some of them received eight rupees ($1.50 or 10 shillings) a *month* as wages in rural districts. However, properly qualified teachers now earn about ten times that amount. The huge population and ensuing cheapness cause human muscles to be used where Western people would hardly credit. It is much cheaper to use manpower to empty wagons of railway ballast, or to carry baskets of earth from excavations, or even to carry massive steel girders, than to use machinery. Thousands, including women, can be seen helping to pile up a railway embankment or working on a housing site. The conveyer belt of India is a human chain. Recently 12,000 workers were employed on one double-tier bridge in China, and between 100,000 and 200,000 manual workers were engaged in laying a single stretch of railway track. A similar labor situation is typical of India.

Though ruinous strain and muscular effort are so often demanded, human energy has frequently been sapped by malaria and malnutrition. Weakness and cheapness have made it no uncommon sight to see two men digging with one spade—one to press the blade in the ground, and another to pull on a cord for leverage. Men, women, and children work together in order to scratch a living. Some are refused access to these scanty means of livelihood because they are restricted to certain occupations by their caste (hereditary class). Thus, several different workers will be required to do the jobs involved in running a house, or selling articles in an urban store. In villages or small towns, occupations are often minutely marked off by caste limitations, partly to maintain a meager opportunity of getting some job, though a trivial one. Some people belong to no caste, and are left to do the filthiest jobs such as attending to sanitation, which is of the most rudimentary kind. Such outcaste people were formerly called "untouchable." Though untouchability is now illegal, many village people keep up the old forms of segregation. Those discriminated against, for example, are not allowed to approach the village well for water, but have to get a higher-caste person to draw it for them. Hindu religious custom forbids a high-caste person to eat food contaminated by low-caste or "untouchable" people. Even their shadow is enough to make food unclean. Though "untouchability" is disappearing, it remains an extreme illustration of the low value generally put on poor human beings—who compose the great majority in India.

It is therefore clear that the low standard of living cannot be considered apart from the problem of overpopulation. Even if there were enough food to go around, the wage structure is not such as to enable workers to buy enough. Nor are there enough jobs to provide wages of any kind, no matter how miserable. Any prospect of industrialization is also bound to raise the question of reducing the demand for crude labor still further below the level of that now available. On the other hand, India needs better health, more skills to turn into cash, more money for capital development, more industries. None of these aims can be realized without improved education. Here again the population problem appears. The number of literate Indians has been rising for some time; yet the *proportion* of these actually decreased in relation to the whole for several years.

In India's circumstances effective information about health and nutrition and better crops is of more immediate significance than literacy. People who have learned to read soon forget about it if they have no books or lack the time or energy to read them; but basic education in the skills of health and community well-being is likely to last. It will bear fruit cumulatively. Unfortunately, it may also result in more babies. It is obvious that one fundamental step must be the limitation of India's fertility; but Indians are so poor that the cheapest known contraceptive is at present too dear for those who need it most. It is sometimes said that it is cheaper simply to have babies if the mother can, and to let the mother or the baby (or both) die if she cannot. Puerperal deaths from various causes are still appallingly frequent —a consequence partly of economic destitution and malnutrition, but also of feeble education. "Basic education" in the subjects of domestic and agricultural interest can easily precede formal schooling (and eventually lead to it), especially in a country like India where the communication of wisdom relies so much on oral instruction. But it is not always easy to secure sympathy in the villages for suitable instructors from the towns. The facts may all be known, and the opportunities for improvement available; yet they may all be ignored.

Supposing reliable means of family limitation were available without cost, it would still be necessary to bring information and carry conviction. It is necessary that the information should seem to matter, and that it should be properly used. We take it for granted that it matters

to reduce the strain on young women, to save life, to improve standards
of education and social prestige, to save India from self-suffocation.
But that shows how little we appreciate the problem. We fail to have
insight in exactly the same way as an Indian would if he were to advise
us to reduce our road deaths (more numerous than those in a typical
war of recent years) by abandoning private motoring or reducing speed.
To many an Indian peasant it does not seem unusual or unnatural that
there should be so many babies. Sons are honorable and necessary. It
seems inevitable that women should begin to have them at an age when
all our girls are in school, and that near-starvation and degradation
should be the consequences. Every leading Indian educator and states-
man is committed to campaigning for contraception; but first factual
knowledge and social education must be widespread enough so that
population control will seem important. The most significant point of
contact for this education would be among young women and girls; but
here we find grave difficulties.

The social status of girls is low. They are usually expected to bring a
dowry—a great nuisance to their fathers; and then after marriage they
traditionally belong neither to themselves nor to their childhood home
but to their husband's family. In these circumstances it is not surprising that only progressive parents bother much about education for
girls even if they get as far as sending their sons regularly to school.
The status of woman as a mere appendage to a man's life was traditionally recognized by the practice of *sati* (now stamped out, though
with difficulty). This custom required widows to burn themselves to
death on the funeral pyre of their husbands. Girls and women in India
now have a much brighter future to look forward to. A great many not
only go to school but actually become university professors, scientists,
and diplomats. However, life in the villages is exceedingly slow to
change. Western ideas of feminine emancipation seem to belong to
another world, or an alien religion or a remote caste. Well-educated
and progressive Indian men often find it difficult to find an acceptably
educated wife. We can imagine how much harder it will be to communicate emancipated ideas, like those of controlling a family's future,
to women whose whole life expectation has been one of trailing behind.
However, we must look on the bright side, and note that in some parts
of India, as in Ceylon and other countries not too different, the education of girls is rapidly becoming a familiar practice. With the nationwide extension of compulsory schooling (not achieved yet), a better
chance of social reform will be secured.

We foreigners must not interpret too naïvely the signs we sometimes
see of educational improvements for girls. The results may be admirable
in the long run but the motivation is still sometimes primitive. One of

the greatest disgraces for an Indian family has always been to be left
with unmarried daughters. Therefore prosperous parents of lower or
middle class will frequently give a daughter some extended schooling
so that they can arrange a better marriage for her. That is to say, the
whole family (and not the mere girl) will thus obtain a more profitable
investment. Such perspicacity is more often shown too if the girl in
question happens to be a bit darker than usual, or has other disadvantages. Girls in these circumstances may have their education continued
later too (under orders) by their husband's families, for the same socio-
economic reasons and not out of personal consideration. Maneuvers
of this kind are particularly common among those prosperous and
highly placed enough to be able to go to college and university. It is
ironic to think that many Indian women graduates in western Europe
and the United States owe their chances to such inegalitarian prompting. Lack of equal consideration is also abundantly shown in the many
household and family demands placed upon Indian women, who must
undertake them in addition to their career responsibilities or onerous
studies. So the mere experience of education and the unfolding of
career prospects other than the traditional ones do not in themselves
automatically emancipate Indian women or change their status greatly.
It follows from what we observe in these highly exceptional women
that the educational and social prospects for ordinary girls in India
still leave much to be desired.

At this point we must observe that no educational or cultural change
can ever take place without profoundly altering the social context.
Many hallowed ideas have to be challenged. It may be necessary, and
often is, to alienate the generations from each other. We may begin
our experiments on a small-scale and tentative basis; but sooner or
later the whole social system will be leavened or challenged. It is not
so disturbing a process when the historic background is such that the
shocks can be absorbed, or when social advance has already proceeded
so far that an evolutionary and free society is flexible enough for
further, easy change. But when a tradition-bound country like India
becomes involved, it is necessary for those who supervise reform to
take an exceedingly long view and to maintain a detailed and comprehensive vigilance. Otherwise frightful rifts will gape, uprootedness
and bewilderment will be found everywhere, and existing resources
will be dissipated before new ones can be developed.

India has so little in the way of economic reserves, so little educated
capital on which she can draw, that the strictest budgeting and planning must be maintained. Therefore it is not surprising that one of the
first acts of the new government was the establishment of a Planning
Commission, and that India is making her way toward a better future

through a series of Five-Year Plans. Though education in India is a state responsibility and not a federally administered activity, nevertheless the Central Advisory Board of Education exercises great influence, and the All-India Council for Technical Education is planning scientific and technological training on a wide scale. Only thus can the domestic and personal problems we have considered be tackled in accordance with India's prospects of evolution. Change must be realistic in terms of the resources and opportunities available. Indian lack of realism in planning is a byword in India itself; one official plan after another has repeated the recommendations of its predecessor.

The difficulties reviewed so far can be listed as follows: those arising from India's recent emancipation, and from her newness as a sovereign nation; those provoked by the need for forward evolution without the chaos that might result from a sudden disruption of the old systems of social rehearsal; problems of social inequality; those caused by an acute shortage of capital and the terrible destitution of India's people; those of a rapidly growing population in a land so crowded that men are cheap; the low status of women; and general ignorance and superstition. This is a formidable enough list, but we have not finished yet. There are also to be considered the disadvantages of geography and climate; problems arising from food habits (associated with religious beliefs); acute language difficulties; outmoded ideas about schooling and the aims of education; and finally anxieties about the political future of the country, especially in relation to democracy at home and to peace abroad. It would be a desperate situation for any nation to have to clean up.[1] It is a particular testimony to India's determination and resourcefulness that so much headway has already been made. We can proceed to examine plans and progress, not according to the logic of India's needs, but in the order that seems simplest for our purposes in this chapter.

Hinduism has been the main framework of Indian life and values for many centuries. Nearly all Indian leaders of note, though determined to win for their country the material opportunities that are enjoyed by western countries, and which depend on western education, are also eager to retain many of the virtues and graces of the Hindu way of life. Therefore it was a very bold decision to declare India a secular state. Such a declaration does not mean that it is an atheist state, or for that

---

[1] The social, economic, and technological problems of India and other developing countries are reviewed in my *World Perspectives in Education,* Chaps. 4, 5, and 13, with particular reference to educational development and culture conflicts. A seventeen-nation UNESCO conference at Karachi, in 1960, concluded that to provide universal free and compulsory education for South and Southeast Asia would cost $64,000 million (£22,860 million) over a twenty-year period.

matter indifferent. It signifies only that the state takes no part in religious controversies. It will require no views and forbid no views on religious matters. This is in contrast with Pakistan (which at first officially proclaimed itself an Islamic state), with Indonesia (also founded on Islam) and with Burma (Buddhist). Hinduism is one of the most tolerant and assimilative of religions; yet it was considered safer for the people as a whole to declare India secular. Thus we may hope that the sectarian disputes which disrupt many countries, and have frequently resulted in massacres in many parts of the world, may be avoided. On the positive side we may hope also that the reform of the caste system and of food habits will be made easier. Some 85 percent of Indians are Hindus by faith; about 10 percent are Muslim, including former ministers of education and the current President; 2 percent are Christian; 2 percent are Sikhs; and approximately one percent are Jains, Buddhists, Parsees, Jews, and so on.

To anyone reflecting on the acute shortages which bedevil India, it always seems strange that cattle (which are sacred in Hindu belief) ramble about unmolested and are only very imperfectly used. They may be seen interrupting the traffic in big cities; they eat much-needed crops; they are not bred systematically for dairy utility; and their meat is just wasted though it is greatly needed as a source of protein. Indians vary in what they will eat; but the majority are vegetarians living on a very poor diet. Yet their religion does not actually forbid them to eat meat, and those who come to cool countries like Britain can be persuaded to build up their resistance with meat, even with beef and veal. Pandit Nehru, the former prime minister of India, never scrupled to make clear his contempt for the veneration of the cow. Secular-minded Indians do not hesitate to point out the paradoxes of Indian regard for the sacred animal. Emaciated, diseased and entirely abandoned cattle can be seen everywhere. They may live for 20 years, reproducing scrawny progeny to no purpose; but no one wants to kill a single one, and the traffic may be in a turmoil because of homeless animals whose owners have turned them loose. Some states positively forbid the slaughter of cattle. Yet lusty buffaloes could be killed, and can give a good supply of milk as well as meat if needed. "We worship the cow, but we look after the buffalo," an Indian has been heard to observe. At the cattle census of 1960, the approximate total number of cows and bulls was 176 million, with an additional 51 million buffalo. That makes up a quarter of the world's cattle population—about one cow or buffalo for every two inhabitants, and reproducing at about the same rate. The poor quality of many of these animals is shown by the fact that the average consumption of milk by Indians is pathetically low by world standards (estimated to be 15 centiliters a year). Officials of the Food and Agriculture Organization of the United Nations know well enough what to advise: cull the cattle, select for milk production, and eventually use the meat; for as things are, animals of all kinds are believed to consume more food than India imports.

However, the cow is more than a religious emblem; it is also strongly felt by some politicians to be a symbol of nationalism. Everyone knows too that it is a token of Hinduism versus any other religion—of no small significance in the "community"-conscious world of the Indian (we would say, "sectarian" world in this connection). Besides, strong and genuine religious scruples must be overcome by anyone taking such a step. The onlooker sympathetic to India's future can only be patient and hope that a very important food reform will one day be achieved. After all, at one time it was considered shameful (if not sinful) to leave one's village—still more to cross the sea to another land, or to eat in the company of unbelievers and outcastes such as Christians and westerners. International travel helps to convince Hindus that such notions and customs are not really essential to their religion's ethos, but more in the nature of symbols that can be dispensed with in due course. Habit dies hard, though.

Also the monkey population of India is also absolutely enormous, and eats or wastes huge quantities of food desperately needed by human beings. Monkeys are sacred, and must not be killed. They are not even driven off as they might be. It has been officially estimated that one third of the total harvest is lost each year in India mainly because of animal consumption or damage. In 1965 it was said that a total rat population estimated at 2,400 millions consumed 12 million tons of food annually; yet Indian respect for all life makes campaigns against even nonsacred animals (though the rat is occasionally revered) a thorny matter for any would-be reformer. Apart from the conspicuous hindrance to progress constituted by beliefs about cows and monkeys, there are many other items of religious conviction or habit that need to be adjusted to the times. Some of these are conspicuous, like those of caste; some are more subtle and difficult to cope with. As we have seen, untouchability is now illegal, and it is difficult to imagine how the development of industrialization could possibly allow the caste system to survive. After all, the essential characteristic of industrialization is the standardization and interchangeability of services and parts. In India, industrialization will be a potent agent for democracy if it does not result in an uprooted and irresponsible proletariat unschooled in the positive performances of an educated democracy. In that event the urban population would undoubtedly be a ready prey for totalitarian ideas. The delicate balance to be maintained between old rigidity and new chaos exemplifies the difficulties besetting Indian statesmanship. In the matter under review, secularism seems essential: yet careful cultivation of genuine, humane values in a new social matrix will also be as necessary as it is unprecedented.

Also associated with caste status and religious scruples is the method of distributing and cultivating the land. A great deal of land has been redistributed and entrusted to new ownership (or cultivation) after the expropriation of great landlords, who were often absentees from their estates. The next stage will be the establishment of a more self-sufficient peasantry, well educated in a range of technical skills transcending caste limitations, and with a balanced diet now denied to them by religious habits. It will also be highly desirable to secure the economic future for such peasants by organizing cooperatives for marketing, for the purchasing of requirements, and for insurance. Before these desiderata can be achieved, a great deal of education will be necessary. On the other hand, the gradual establishment of self-help organizations for agrarian reform will perhaps be the most promising vehicle of elementary education in responsible citizenship as well as in factual information. Indeed, an appreciation of this possibility was the mainspring of Gandhi's plans for "basic education." He urged the cultivation of "head and hand" together. UNESCO programs are very similar.

Reforms of the kind just mentioned seem inevitable in the case of India; yet they are all too easily stigmatized by the ill-informed as irreligious and socialistic. They are certainly not irreligious, though they combat superstition which the ignorant confuse with religion. Undoubtedly they are socialistic. It is difficult to see what else could happen in the special circumstances of Indian difficulties. Not a penny can be wasted, so that the whole process must be publicly regulated in the best interests of all. There is no private capital available for investment on the scale required, and India has so far not enough external trade. On the other hand, Indian planning is a bulwark against precommunist chaos.[2] If India were to become communist, something like two thirds of the human race would be under the red flag, and the chances of the other nations in Asia staying free would be remote indeed. Democrats everywhere need to appreciate how vital for them it is that India, by her radical planning for social justice, should succeed in a socialistic experiment. That implies no recognition of socialism as a valid commodity for export. It simply recognizes it as an alter-

[2]One Indian state, Kerala, elected itself a communist government in 1957. The communist victory there may be ascribed to local confusion, and above all to the inability of the local factions (particularly of the rival Christian sects) to sponsor a joint program for social and economic reform. In 1960, communists lost control; but the risk here and elsewhere is never far away, unless a carefully planned economy and social and educational reform build up a workable alternative.

native preferable to totalitarian communism. India is committed to democracy. Her statesmen, though many of them have proved their patriotism by being imprisoned as rebels, are also steeped in the liberal traditions of the west.

Starting out on plans of reform, however, is not the same thing as having everything ready for change. The size of India and the difficulty of communication have already been referred to; there are other handicaps of a geographic nature. Some regions are desert, and greatly in need of extensive irrigation. Most parts, however, are seasonally subjected to the swamping downpour of the monsoons. But if the monsoon fails or is substandard (as happened in several recent consecutive years) the rice and other cereal harvests are disastrous. If the monsoon is too heavy there are equally destructive floods. It has been reckoned that 82 percent of the monsoon's water is wasted anyway. The same lands will later bake in parching heat. Climate cannot be controlled, but its effects can sometimes be turned to human advantage by such things as reservoirs, hydroelectric power, and solar-heat engines. All these things are costly. Even when they are built, there are some geographic difficulties that seem insuperable. For example, Kashmir has snow for four or five months of the year; is mountainous; and has extensive forests that, because of transportation difficulties, are not yet available for silviculture as we understand it. Yet the valleys and plains are rich in crops and fruit during the summer, and even Kashmir's ruggedness is potentially a tourist attraction to wealthy people from many countries. For full exploitation, though, capital development is essential. It is far beyond the resources of the indigenous population, who in any case need educational and financial help before they can effectively help themselves on a small, local scale. At the other extreme, India has swampy, malarial plains, jungles, and the enervating heats and diseases of a tropical summer. To make the best use of her more temperate regions and seasons she is sorely in need of railways, roads, and other communications. Under British administration these arteries of the western way of life were extensively built, but an independent and self-sufficient India will need many more to support a higher standard of living.

People of widely different racial origins inhabit the various regions of India, as can be clearly seen by looking at them. It is not only that the Mogul invasion brought in conquerors of Persian and related affinity down from the northwest into northern and central India; the nations and tribes long settled in this huge country make up as many recognizable ethnic variations as we find in Europe—perhaps more. It is only to be expected that, despite certain common sympathies engendered by the great religions (Buddhism formerly, and now Hinduism), local ways of living and looking at life should be full of individuality. Diversity of idioms in practical matters is sometimes a barrier to national cooperation; yet an even greater obstacle to common effort and understanding is the great variation in language found in India. If we include the distinct dialects that have enough idiosyncracies to make them difficult to understand by those who are not native to an area, we can count well over 200 different languages in India. Some are spoken by tens of millions, and some only by thousands. (To correct a false impression given by some writers on Comparative Education, it is necessary to point out that the number of speakers has nothing to do with the distinctness of a language. Romany (the gypsy tongue) and Basque are not widely spoken in Europe; but they are nearly unique. Nothing more easily divides people from each other culturally than language).

Fourteen of the Indian languages are major regional tongues. Several of these have fine literatures reaching back into remote antiquity; others have a much humbler literary status, though they are governmental languages and widely used for commerce. Of the other 200 or so minor languages, some have not yet developed an alphabet. In mixed linguistic groups it is often an important principle that children should be given primary instruction in their mother tongue, and proceed to instruction in a major regional language later. However, in India's formative stages this raises the question whether these marked local variations should be crystallized by being accorded literary form in books. Let us take a comparison from Europe. If during the sixteenth century the Scandinavian languages (which are mutually intelligible to practiced listeners), had not been written down in distinct literatures, a common "Scandinavian" for literary use might have evolved. In Switzerland, vernacular Swiss German is very different from the literary High German of the Bible, the pulpit, and the radio stations (even as it is spoken by Swiss); but it has not been stylized in written form until very recently, for use in elementary classes. Indian reformers, who are likely to set a precedent for many generations to come, are faced with a difficult choice between sympathy for the vernacular (which coincides with the general practice of professional educators) and a realistic outlook for the future.

The Dravidian languages of the south are notoriously different from the Sanskrit derivatives in the north, and there are other linguistic families too. But in one form or another, about 47 percent of Indians could understand the languages of the northern (Sanskrit) group. Hindi and Urdu are closely related, so much so that during the British administration a kind of lingua franca, blended from them and called Hindustani, was current. Though this is (we should perhaps say "was") really a colloquial language, it could become a unifying force in India and develop literary force. Gandhi recommended this. But since emancipation and partition, Hindi (with a more Sanskritized vocabulary and in the Devanagari script) and Urdu (with a Persianized vocabulary and in Perso-Arabic script) are growing farther apart. The purely linguistic patriotism maintained by speakers of these tongues is accentuated by the fact that Hindi is more closely associated with the Hindu faith, and Urdu with Islam, though this is not exclusively so. Hindi has been chosen as the official language of India, and Urdu that of Pakistan. Because English is widely used in India (having been formerly the language of government, being still the medium of instruction in many of the universities, and having international importance in every way), there did seem to be a chance at one time that it might be chosen. But only about one percent of Indians (the educated ones) speak it, and it is understandable that an indigenous language should have been preferred.

On the other hand, the social value of the English language continues very high. In the larger towns and cities, affluent Indian parents who are eager to set their children off on the right foot, are prepared to pay what locally seem exorbitant tuition fees to Anglo-Indians or Christians who have a fairly high standard of English. Schools have sprung up to cater to this trade—sometimes in the teachers' modest apartments. Ambitious parents will often make a habit of speaking only English in the family. Others make great sacrifices to send their children away to English-language boarding schools, and, in fact, the number of such schools vaguely or directly imitating the English Public Schools has rapidly increased since independence, though the number is still small.

The reports of postwar Indian commissions on language usually agree on the following recommendations. Ideally, primary instruction should be given in the mother tongue. Sometimes, especially for linguistic minorities of small size, it may be necessary to supplement this with instruction in a very simple form of the regional language, such as Urdu in Kashmir. At the secondary stage, however, the regional tongue should increase in importance. In some cases it might be the medium of instruction, though where a language minority exists in sufficient numbers it might be possible to continue to use the mother tongue at this stage; nevertheless, the regional language should be learned compulsorily. At least a modicum of Hindi should be taught, at least in secondary schools. As time goes on it is anticipated that Hindi will be more widely and thoroughly used. Three stages of proficiency in Hindi have been recognized and recommended for schools, depending on the pupils' own linguistic proximity to that tongue.

At the college or university level, English is still very widely used as the medium of instruction, partly because that has been usual, and partly because of the supply of English and American textbooks and publications. Prospective university students, and others who are ambitious, therefore need to learn English in the secondary stage. Despite its prestige, proficiency has fallen since emancipation. It has been seriously suggested that the university is one place where English should be retained; but popular opinion is in favor of using Hindi as the university language everywhere as soon as possible instead of English. For various reasons, however, this does not yet seem feasible. A third alternative, already enforced by law in some states, is the use of the regional language in universities. This could be dangerous if it limits intercourse among scholars. There is also the problem of the exchange of students, teachers, and textbooks. India, which is after all a vast and highly diverse country, might conceivably be split linguistically and culturally if too strong a regional patriotism developed. Some educators have recommended the adoption of Hindi as the university language in the North (where it is either spoken or easily understood by the majority), in the hope that its use may spread southward in due course. Southern Indians, however, continue to campaign in favor of English for government, business, and universities. They declare that English to them is no more foreign than Hindi, and no more difficult to learn. English, too, is established already in business and educational circles. The strength of their position is shown in the declared all-India policy whereby Hindi became the "official" language in 1965, but English continues as the "subsidiary official" medium.

From what has been said already it is obvious that many an Indian child even at the ordinary school level may well learn four or five languages: his mother tongue, a regional language, Hindi, and English, together with either an additional modern language widely spoken in the vicinity or else one of the ancient languages associated with particular religious scriptures (Sanskrit, Arabic, or Persian). Among Indian students at the University of London, such linguistic expertise is common; it is, nevertheless, a skill increasingly demanded of less highly-educated Indians as mobility increases, together with all-India communications through radio, television, films, and commerce. The strain may be even greater if, for example, teachers, or public officials, or even tradesmen find it necessary to deal professionally with linguistic minorities of various affinities living close together.

Whatever happens, it is obvious that the curriculum of any child is bound to be congested on the linguistic side before anything else is learned—both for the child's own "life adjustment" and for reasons of Indian unity. It would be much easier for everybody if Hindi (or

English) were universally understood. For this reason it is required that Hindi be offered in all schools; but so far it is an optional subject for the children. If everybody learned it, communication would be easier in any one region as well as nationally; in no region or province do all the communities speak the regional language(s). In Bombay, for example, there are three of these, even though the old Bombay state was linguistically divided into two new states. A courageous attempt has been made to redraft state and administrative boundaries throughout India on linguistic grounds. Any relief of this sort will ease a grievous burden now lying heavy on school curriculums and community relationships. Those who attempt to belittle linguistic problems in India either are ignorant of the facts or ignore the powerful emotions aroused by linguistic dissatisfaction.

Distinct from language problems, though sometimes accentuated by them, are those of race and cultural pattern. Marked cleavages also exist between communities and groups, not only according to caste divisions but in respect of their varied degree of social advance. For example, some communities still live a tribal rather than a village or urban life. Others, because of their economy, consist of seasonal migrants. Linguistic factors here again can accentuate human differences. Welcome though these are in some ways because they enrich the total Indian view of life, they are nevertheless potential causes of serious discord if not handled with great sensitivity. Moreover, if books and instruction are at all unfamiliar, they are likely to be forgotten at the earliest opportunity. The problem of wastage has always been serious in India, and is certainly aggravated by linguistic and community idiosyncracies.

It is not surprising that most responsible Indians are convinced that it is impracticable to deal with Indian education wholesale on a uniform plan. That is the reason for devolving the organization of it upon the several states, subject to central supervision and advice. The Constitution of India directed that universal, free, and compulsory education for all children from 6 to 14 should be established within 10 years of its promulgation; it may be many years before that aim is nearly achieved. Plans were all ready, before the outbreak of war in 1939, for a radical reform of Indian education under British auspices. The scheme drafted by Sir John Sargent envisaged that universal free education would be provided in 40 years. After independence in 1947 Indians ridiculed the length of time estimated; they now realize that 40 years may have to elapse before all children do receive the 8 or 10 years of education hoped for, even though schooling increased threefold between 1951 and 1960.

It is almost impossible to paint a representative picture of the Indian school. In a progressive and populous city like Calcutta it is easy to find wide variation even at the primary level. Municipal schools, aided schools, and private institutions are bound to differ greatly from one another according to their clientele, teaching staff, fees charged, and amount of equipment. From area to area in any town, from district to district throughout any state, circumstances completely alter what has to happen. After all, the main concern is to get the children to come to school, and to keep them there and profitably occupied. In many country towns of reasonable size (to say nothing of the villages characteristic of Indian tradition) parents may find it necessary, or preferable, to keep the child at home or in the fields. Many adults are lucky to earn one rupee a day (if they earn money at all), and if a child's labor brings in one rupee a week, or even one a month, there is a temptation to make use of it. This is the background we start with, and we must never forget it when considering absenteeism and failure to "make the grade." Moreover, it has not yet been possible to provide free tuition everywhere at the elementary level; therefore, many parents who would wish their children to be educated just cannot pay for it.

On the other hand, those parents who can get their children to school and who know that school is the most potent means to a more comfortable life are pathetically eager to do so. In practice, the teacher does not ask too many questions about the ages of the children she has to instruct. Though the expected age of entry is 6, the majority will be 7 years old, whereas a few from more ambitious homes may be only 5. Girls may not give their age at all. So any "first class" may have boys and girls of the most heterogeneous mixture in every way. In theory, the elementary classes contain no more than 30 children, though there may be many more. In cities the children will probably be closely crowded together on straight wooden benches; in country towns they may sit huddled on mattresses; in poor villages they just sit or stand, the little boys naked from the waist up.

Great numbers of schools are operated on the principle that there are three teachers for every four classes. Much use is made of monitors to help the teacher; these are usually children of the same age as their classmates who can do the work better. The school premises range, of course, from modern buildings to the village structure consisting of a roof on four poles or even the proverbial Mark Hopkins log. It is the same with the equipment. Town teachers have a blackboard and books, while the children have slates or a painted tin or wooden rectangle for their writing. "Basic" schools in remote villages may have to practice their writing in sand. The same wide range can be found among the teachers; we may encounter a very cultivated young lady in a beautiful sari, a cadaverous elderly man imperfectly shaven, or anything in between. It is not unknown for a teacher to be a part-time farmer, or earning enough to live on outside his school in another way. So manifold and so intractable are the problems facing Indian educators!

The children may come to school at nine or nine-thirty in winter in the cities, but sometimes as early as six-thirty or seven o'clock in the stifling heat of the summer. The teacher, like teachers everywhere, has a repetitious task in teaching reading; yet with her material equipment she can seldom hope to do better than use the "chalk and talk" tradition in front of the blackboard—writing the letters, saying the sounds, and getting a chorus from the class. At the end of the first grade, the children are able to read the phonetic Devanagari script, which is, however, made more complicated because in using it the words have to be run together phonetically to show the actual practice of daily speech rather than the mere theory of how the separate words should sound. No mean achievement! There may not be too much practice in writing. Yet the children include several whose eager example in passing the grades with a view to "double promotions" is a spur to the others. Parents and teachers understandably push these children on. The full range of ten classes in the primary and secondary schools should clearly take a child to the age of 16 or 17, but it is not at all unknown for bright youngsters to be ready for the final examinations at 14, 13, or even 12. They are not officially allowed to reach the leaving-certificate before the age of 14 (a regulation which is itself significant); yet, as we have seen, a child's age is not always accurately given.

When we bear in mind the fact that two classes, and even two teachers, may be in the same room together, we realize that problems of management, no less than tradition, weigh heavily in favor of formalism. In the "middle" school, after the primary years end at 11, classes of 40 and more are authorized in districts where primary classes are kept smaller. In the top "matriculation" class 50 children may be found. This very tendency to let the top grades become larger shows to what extent bookishness and formal discipline prevail in the traditional training ground for the white-collar occupations. Rote learning and an unrealistic curriculum are only to be expected in such circumstances —the whole business being epitomized for one observer in the fact that the senior girls in an exclusive academy occupied themselves on a hideously hot afternoon by learning (in English) Shakespeare's sonnet beginning:

> *Shall I compare thee to a summer's day?*
> *Thou art more lovely and more temperate.*

It is not, therefore, surprising that a large number of children who succeed in making their way through the primary school do not pursue their studies after the age (or standard) of eleven years.

In 1964 there were approximately 370,000 primary schools with rather more than 40 million children. Secondary schools numbered 79,000 (mainly private), with over 22 million children. Some schools teach courses within the university level. Of 62 universities (1965 figure) some, but not all, are of good quality. Since 1947 there has been such a proliferation of universities that statistics have little meaning. All that can surely be said is that quality has not kept pace with the expansion. Many students, even preparing for a degree, are not in a university at all, but in some college loosely affiliated to an examining university. Some "degree colleges" are therefore really upper-secondary schools which retain some of their students for long enough to let them take the university graduating examination. In any case, discussion or independent study would be a foreign plant in India, and certainly not one likely to thrive amidst all that competition for modest posts, amidst which the goodwill of a teacher could be very influential.

In all these circumstances the importance of a good private school (frequently charging fees in excess of a teacher's average salary for tuition and board-residence) is likely to be enhanced. In 1964, in a famous city, elementary school teachers earned 80–90 rupees a month; secondary school teachers with degrees earned 125 rupees; and a fairly expensive boarding school in the same city cost its pupils 150 rupees a month, or about $32.00. Village teachers are paid much less, and are accordingly difficult to hire, even if townspeople were willing to isolate themselves in villages, as they mostly are not. Many village teachers are still recruited from among boys and girls with secondary education, or a little better; although some are of good quality and enterprising, that could not be said of most. Their morale and social status leave much to be desired. Thus, in all the discouraging circumstances, it has been an achievement to recruit some 30,000 to 50,000 new teachers a year.

The extent to which it has been possible to apply compulsion for schooling, even elementary, is of course varied. In Bombay province it was universal by 1953, except for villages with under 50 population—a fine record. It is important not to delay the provision of education in villages and small communities, in order to check the drift to the towns.

When independence was gained in 1947, barely 30 percent of the children between 6 and 11 years of age were in schools of one kind or another. Five years later the number had risen to 40 percent. The proportion has continued to rise, and school attendance trebled in the decade ending in 1960. In 1941 the literates in the age range 5 years upward numbered 14.6 percent; in 1951, after years of war and difficulty, they had risen to 18.3 percent. If we confine our attention to persons over nine years of age, which is more sensible, the figure in 1947 was approximately 20 percent. In Bombay, about 30 percent were literate; in Delhi

about 40 percent. There are great variations between regions and cities.
Universally, many more men than women can read; yet accurate figures
for literacy that is really retained and effective are hard to obtain. The
total literacy percentage in 1961 was 23 percent (a substantial increase
in view of the juvenile population explosion); for women it was 12.8
percent, compared with 7.9 percent in 1951. Village census-takers or
teachers have sometimes accepted a "yes" without verification. Some
authorities have, therefore, taken a stricter view of literacy problems
at the time of emancipation, stating that on the eve of independence
only 25 percent went to school, only 15 percent were able to read, and
only 10 percent were really able to read and write.

Many of India's misfortunes are blamed on the British, an attribu-
tion not surprising in a newly emancipated country, though opinion
now recognizes that many advantages arose during the British India
period—not least the impact of technology and science, of a world language, and of liberal and critical ideas. It is indeed surprising and
edifying to see how appreciative educated Indians have become since
1947 of some British contributions, a development that does them quite
as much credit as the British. But education as it grew in India under
the empire is rightly criticized for being defective in its aims and
methods, and for having done too little for the Indians. It has usually
been characteristic of British imperial rule to let indigenous populations develop their own culture. Religion and other life systems were
left with a minimum of interference provided that these seemed consonant with peaceful rule. Such tolerance has its drawbacks. In 1835
(before India belonged to the British Crown, be it noted), Lord
Macaulay introduced English as the medium of instruction into schools
intended to provide the administration with Indian clerks and sub-
ordinate administrators. Ever since that time Indian education has
been predominantly a white-collar, bookish, and data-packed schooling
intended to give social and professional status rather than to foster
understanding or develop character. It has been a schooling for civil
servants. In blaming the British for these shortcomings, however, most
Indians forget that secondary schooling was available to them in their
own country with tax aid under British jurisdiction some 67 years
before it was similarly available in Britain. British education, and
British technological development and mobility, might have benefited
if the United Kingdom had followed the example of her expatriate administrators in India—no matter if the instruction was bookish in the
contemporary idiom.

Bookishness and uncritical self-preparation for place-seeking, however, are not confined to any one system of schooling. They have indeed
been characteristic of Indian and most other Eastern schools almost

from time immemorial, as Indians themselves are quick to recognize in their attacks on classical pedantry, Sanskritists, and the like. However, it is unprofitable to look about for scapegoats. We must frankly recognize that until the time of emancipation there had been little escaping from the white-collar and conformist submissiveness of the complaisant pupil. There was a great need for a revitalized and Indianized schooling, especially at the elementary level.

Since 1947, an enormous impetus has been given to Gandhi's schemes for a "basic national education" of "heart and hand." Humayun Kabir well describes the main aim as being integration with daily life, and the development of educational experience around a socially useful activity like a craft. Correlation and unity are striven for by seeing the items of the curriculum as constituent parts or complementary aspects of each other. The children are taught to cooperate as members of a community. In the strict interpretation of the "basic" plan they are expected to make the school pay for itself by selling artifacts. This last proposal has been criticized both as an old-world fancy and as an exploitation of an otherwise free learning situation. In 1937 Gandhi published a manifesto recommending basic schools which was then a bombshell but which has now become part of national policy. By 1953 there were 45,000 basic schools, mostly in the state of Bihar. It is proving increasingly difficult to get sufficiently well-trained teachers for them. "Basic" schools are still almost confined to children between the ages of 6 and 11, and many think their influence is declining.

What children learn at school between the ages of 6 and 11 (the usual age of compulsion in India so far, where compulsion is applied) is of particular importance in India. Quite apart from the natural responsiveness of young children that makes this period so critical in any school system, the Indian teacher has to take account of many factors on which the future of these boys and girls will depend. For example, he may decide (often against parental pressure) not to push the bright ones on for examination purposes. It is still the usual practice in many areas to allow successful children "double promotions" so that they pass on to a higher class if they have mastered the work allotted to the one they are in. Thus a bright boy or girl might be ready to leave primary school at the age of 10 or even 9½ years instead of 11. The lucky ones may proceed to a "middle" school (that is, American junior high school, or the lower classes of a British grammar school). On the other hand, many children will leave school at this time, because parents cannot afford "middle" school fees, or because they just do not think it appropriate and need to have the child working, or even simply because the child is a girl, and soon to be married and "off their hands." Even educators in India often talk in this way about their own daughters at an age when Western girls would just be beginning their secondary school careers. When we talk of Indian mothers, we are still often speaking of girls we would class as children.

So the outlook and teaching perpetuated by teachers in Indian primary schools is vital in determining or hindering social change. It is indeed greatly to be welcomed that so much progress has been made toward all-round and life-oriented education for both boys and girls under the age of 11. It is a wonderful thing to have boys and girls at school together. Mixed schools are often regarded (as in the Catholic parts of Europe) as less desirable than single-sex schools, and are, therefore, found more frequently in villages that cannot afford two establishments. But that is precisely where their effect will be greatest. Our admiration for a more realistic and less bookish education must not make us forget certain undesirable results that may follow from it, especially in India. It may mean that children who have benefited by it will stand less chance in the competitive life of the secondary phase. Indian villagers might in fact think that their children are given only the education that will perpetuate their status as laborers or poor craftsmen, while those who have had a traditional schooling are well on their way to the job-winning and data-packed studies of the old-type secondary schools.

Many of the secondary schools of India have been missionary schools established by Europeans, and attended by Indians of all faiths (few of whom ever become converts to Christianity). The missionaries have done wonderful work for Indian education, even if their schools are frequently as scholastically formal as the worst in Europe. The personal example of missionaries is a better testimony to western ideals than the items taught. With rising costs and other difficulties it is hard for missionaries to meet the demand for secondary education. Government schools (now operated by the state governments) and government-aided schools, financed partly by local taxes and by students' fees are increasing in number, but not fast enough. The aided schools in any one state are not likely to have a uniform salary scale for teachers with any given diploma or amount of experience. Obviously, therefore, there is much discrepancy in standards, though all of them try to give the same instruction because they are all looking toward the same public examinations and certificates. The tendency in Indian education, in this respect, is toward more rather than less centralization. But there is still a long way to go. For example, in Assam as recently as 1956 there were 64 possible gradations of salary and status. And of course the 16 states and other territories differ from each other.

After passing through the "middle" and "upper" parts of the secondary school (seven years in all), the successful prepare for university entrance. The traditional arrangement has been to keep the children in secondary schools until an average age of 17, and then send them to an "intermediate college" for two years in preparation for university entrance. Thus the universities take them at the age of 18 to 19, or earlier if they have been pushed ahead by "double promotions." Recent reforms anticipate the abolition of the intermediate college stage. One of the years would be added to the secondary school and one to the university, meaning a school-leaving age of 18 and a university course of three years. The old pattern and the new are found together at present. Calcutta, Madras, and Bombay universities were established in 1857; others of remarkably varied character and status have grown up to meet the ever-increasing demand. Some are residential; some teach on a day-basis only; some do not teach but only examine. It is quite impossible to make any reliable comment on Indian universities as a whole, except that Indians themselves are dissatisfied with many of them. They are all overcrowded. The teaching is impersonal and distant. Professors and lecturers often think it beneath their dignity to talk to students. Examinations and "the subject matter of the examination" are typically what universities are for. Studies likely to lead to administrative and nonoperational occupations are the ones most eagerly pursued. Students may be very needy; most live very meagerly if not in hardship. It is common to be supported during the three or four undergraduate years by relatives (often fairly distant kinfolk) to whom they will be beholden for a long time. Students often feel thwarted, therefore, and uneasy; this helps to account for the frequently complained-of "indiscipline" which some mob-politicians turn to good account.

It may be remarked in passing that even science is often regarded as a range of studies that will not make it necessary to undertake work with the hands. Unlike most American students, Indians think of it in terms of clean laboratories and white-coated leadership. However, despite their faults, Indian universities are in the forefront of their country's advance toward industrialization and modernity. The relaxed university atmosphere of the prosperous parts of the west must not be expected in a country where success is at the top of a precipice down which it is all too easy to fall to destitution.

Indians need only their eyes and noses to remind them of what academic failure might mean to them. They live in a country where the cruelest burdens are borne on human backs. The alternative to the dreary classroom may seem to them to be the village swarming with near-naked children under the hot sun; the green village pond in which the buffalo wallow; the stinking paddy across which the rows of laborers plant the rice, nearly knee-deep in the filth; or the rough hills whose streams turn prayer wheels incessantly praising "Brahma, the jewel and the lotus." It is not surprising that parents and teachers find it hard to reorient themselves, or that if they do, they still fear to hinder their children's success.

Moreover, as we saw in the case of France (and could easily see else-where), any reform in the direction of "life adjustment" is certain to encounter bitter opposition from those who have worked out the tech-niques of social success for themselves through the use of the old-fashioned schooling. The British have gone; but all too many Indians go on aspiring to the administrative positions ever more abundantly open to them, and still think in terms of old scholasticism and competi-tions. They want an elementary education that will lead to the old-type secondary schooling, which will lead in turn to the university or pro-fessional school—and so on. If it is not a job that some of them are after, it is a good dowry or a good introduction. Recently, there has been much frustration mostly among those for whom formal education has seemed a "dead end" after all. Such men are politically dangerous.

Sincere Indian educators, however, are truly concerned that junior schooling should be a really personal experience for the child, and at the same time a social leaven or germ of new evolution. Secondary schooling they see as a self-contained and worthwhile thing. They call for a much stronger development of public secondary schools. During the years 11–18 they wish to sponsor clear thinking, with books as only a key; they wish also to pass on knowledge of practical value. These notions are commonplace in the west; but in India they are revolution-ary. It is still an unfamiliar idea that the secondary school can be an experience of fundamental value in itself as distinct from a stepping-stone to a much better place. A serious difficulty is that secondary education is still nearly all in private hands.

Community projects and extension centers are now found in over 50,000 towns and villages. These have received federal aid on an equal basis to match state aid. "Basic" schemes also have received a 30 per-cent subsidy from federal funds. Under both these plans the school is seen as a focus of community life. Increasing use has been made of radio and motion pictures. India is producing an astonishing number of mo-tion pictures, which are very popular. Some of them are also very good. Without committing India to religiosity, statesmen and educators have encouraged a revival and elaboration of song, ritual, and art in connec-tion with the village round of life. Some reactionaries fear the critical impact of science on this; but others mistrust only this mistrust, and feel that inner spiritual progress can accompany material advance. All that they are afraid of is "the hollow man." Of late there has been a widening interest in western philosophy too, as distinct from exclusively Indian or eastern mystic philosophy.

India is in some ways in a favored position. She could acquire many of the techniques of the west without suffering their "growing pains." Our mistakes have been social and philosophical as much as industrial. Indians usually believe that they can retain their traditional virtues of self-restraint, peace, and service, and still have the abundance and mass emancipation that western technology has made possible. That remains to be seen. The adoption of even one item from an alien technology is usually the beginning of altered human relationships. Some of these alterations would doubtless be welcomed by progressive Indians; but in the long run they might make the country and its system unrecognizable. But though the world seems to be growing more uniform in most respects under the impact of industrialization, that may be an illusion. It remains to be seen if Indian perceptions can add a further dimension. It will undoubtedly be a revolution in Indian education when scholars cease to be either the "withdrawn ones" of Europe or the "obedient servants" of the Indian civil service.

An All-India Commission, reporting in 1953, made the following recommendations: that one additional year should round off the secondary period (at 18); that a wider range of courses should be offered with a view to more diverse professions, but with retention of central or "core" interests; that multipurpose, rather than distinct, schools should be provided for persons following different interests. The need to develop faculties of science, technology, and agriculture was also stressed. Thousands of Indian students are now abroad studying or doing research in these fields. In time they will raise the quality of what India is able to offer, and will also direct attention more practically to the needs of a predominantly agricultural country. Scholarships are being generously granted, especially when we consider the national poverty; and a chain of national laboratories has been developed. In the arts, national academies are promoting excellent work.

The Indian Education Commission's 1966 report reinforced these points, giving top priority to improving teachers' quality and status. It is also vitally important to make sure that those most conspicuously able to profit from the few opportunities should have preferential access to them. Therefore, it seems a matter of the utmost priority, to train leaders for the next round of the educational struggle. Federal funds are being specifically assigned to teacher improvement. The several states have responsibility for promoting also the interests of depressed sections of the community—particularly the untouchables, and girls and women. The latter must obviously be about half of all the Indians, and the untouchables, according to a recent count, are estimated at 54 million—more than the whole population of the United Kingdom. Since 1947, the scheme of postmatriculation scholarships for former untouchables and other backward groups has expanded some thirty- or forty-fold. At a precollegiate level, an even greater effort has been made both to get the depressed people into school and to provide them with free opportunities of all kinds. Many civil service posts and even some high ministerial positions are reserved for them. Thus India's dilemma is being coped with at the highest level and the lowest. The nimblest brains and the most skilled workers are being trained to make their success India's success, and a sincere attempt is also being made to democratize opportunity.

The total public expenditure on education has increased more than fourfold since 1947; but costs have also risen, and in 1955 Professor Kabir estimated that India must further multiply her expenditure by three, even at existing prices, in order to provide a worthwhile and complete range of educational opportunities. Some other sources formerly available (for example, private and missionary enterprises) have not been able to keep pace with increasing governmental expenditure. An even more serious problem is that governmental enterprise itself is often outstripped by demographic growth, or by uncontrollable demands imposed by outside events. In the decade 1950–1960, the national income went up by 40 percent; but the population growth exceeded everyone's worst fears, amounting to an increase of 82 million (more than 21 percent growth). Thus the real income increase was only 17 percent. In the same period, agricultural production improved by 30 percent; but the population growth just referred to made that improvement marginal. Furthermore, persistent political-religious campaigns build up resistance to further agricultural improvement which might impinge on taboos or simply on traditional ways of life.

As we have repeatedly observed, "education" is by no means to be restricted to schooling. In India's straitened budgeting it becomes doubly important to realize this truth. It is seized upon by the followers of Gandhi's doctrines; they recommend that rural productivity should be increased through the adoption of intensive cultivation on the pattern of Japan. Thus, it is said, a maximum number of people would be responsibly employed. They could be taught to become more self-sufficient, and at the same time their marketing and other arrangements would be made educative for personal and political responsibility. Such cooperative self-help is essentially decentralized, and that would suit India. Cooperative farming and trade are themselves educative—as in Denmark. They also cause participants to learn school-type subjects, such as reading, arithmetic, and elementary economics.

Linked with this notion is the suggestion that without the disruption of the artisan system, power looms and other mechanical devices should be used more extensively. Though in some ways it looks as though any such tendency must inevitably lead toward greater urbanization and heavy industrialization, it might conceivably facilitate the retention of wholesome village independence and prevent the "uprootedness" so common in other rapidly industrialized areas. Actually, democratic co-partnership could more conceivably permeate new industries if it were once to become habitual in preindustrial life. That is what many Indians hope. It would be a welcome alternative to communist-style centralization with direction from the top. A successful experiment of this sort, even on a small scale, would be full of lessons for many of our enterprises in western countries.

An important ingredient in the whole process of leavening is the five-point program of "social education" for adults, partly through the community centers already mentioned. This has already produced notable results in the states of Delhi, Madhya Pradesh, and Mysore. Its aims are (a) to secure literacy; (b) to promote a life of health and hygiene; (c) to develop skills that will raise the standard of living; (d) to give opportunities for the learning and use of the duties and rights of citizenship; (e) to promote opportunities for, and the enjoyment of, healthy recreation. It is also assisting the social education of women along the lines already referred to, and is thus probably affecting the structure and educational relationships of the Indian family.

India has been well served by the monumental prestige of her statesmen in the postwar period. It would not have been altogether surprising if natural hero-worship had degenerated into something very dangerous to democracy in India itself and elsewhere; but fortunately there are few signs of leadership-disease. Both Gandhi and Nehru had to be actively sensitive to their people's anxieties about the niceties of democratic relationships. This is a very good thing for Asia as a whole. It is, perhaps, mainly attributable to the impressive self-restraint of postwar statesmen that India has become so jealous of the proprieties —a state of virtue which is admirable indeed. It has enhanced India's international prestige enormously. Yet it has been blemished by a blind spot or two, a sort of purblindness made harder to cure because the general moral outlook has been so high. That is perhaps why there has been so much difficulty over Kashmir, and a tragic war with Pakistan. India not unnaturally still feels insecure. She perhaps does not realize her potential example to free Asia, and the consequent need for her to be not only strategically strong but morally irreproachable.

During the past two hundred years or so the vast complex of the Hindu way of life has become entangled with the ways of the west. The

Indians have come during that period to recognize the weaknesses of both, and to aspire to the advantages of both. As dark-skinned people, and as subjects of an empire, they have struggled to equality of status with the former masters of the greatest empire on earth, and have finally been welcomed to that status by their white partners in the Commonwealth. They have generously accepted, as free men, a partnership which (though long overdue) it took unexpectedly generous statesmanship in Britain to make available to them. Indians have shown abundantly their full title to their freedom. It remains for us to observe with the greatest of humble sympathy the uphill struggle of India to cope with such a tangle of difficulties. She has to establish the life of her own people (and by implication perhaps the lives of many underdeveloped peoples) on a basis without precedent. It is not just a case of restoring a former status, for there never was one. Nor, we hope, will it be a matter of dangerous, readymade solutions from totalitarian neighbors. The experiments India will have to make will almost certainly seem to us rather hazardous from time to time; but desperate situations call for desperate remedies. We must not be so foolish as to prejudge, if only because we have no sense of India's distracting perplexities.

The ancient social problems are grievous; but and on top of them come the new ones, such as the unanswered (perhaps never finally answerable) questions about the relationship of the individual to his family. There is also to be considered the relationship of the small nuclear family (like ours) to the extended clanlike family on which Indian norms and economics have been founded for thousands of years. The critical question whether western civilization has much to offer to eastern nations (other than mechanical techniques) is bound up with uncertainties of this kind; for the whole notion of personality, with obligations and rights, depends to a large extent upon the limitations and opportunities of our social connections. The role of woman is in turn contingent upon the answers given to these questions. So are all the questions of schooling, travel, trade, careers, and personal ambition.

Indian schools themselves have difficulties of many kinds: material, pedagogical (that is, concerning orientation, content, and personnel), administrative, and social. They are weighed down with the legacies of history, politics, and ancient cultures. The child population is by western standards a phenomenally high percentage of the whole. Nearly forty percent of the Indians are under 14 years of age. The whole impact of technological change demands higher standards, and difficult readjustments; yet it diminishes or diverts the potential supply of teachers. Moreover, educational opportunity has been, so far, very unequally distributed geographically and socially.

The whole question of the nation's world role in a time of international flux is a further crisis confronting the schools of India. In her case we see the immemorial problems of food, home, family, and future reduced to their starkest form. Observing Indian progress should jerk us out of complacency and pettiness. It may perhaps in time make us re-examine our own cultural or economic hierarchy, together with notions of the relationships between home, work, and the process of learning. For what we have assumed about social life and personal education may not easily be applied to the amelioration of opportunities for most of mankind. The dreadful problems seen in India are to some degree or other the lot of more than half the human race.

8

JAPAN | ANCIENT AND MODERN

Japan is a land of surprises. The visitor, no matter how he arrives, is struck at once by a series of paradoxes. The well-publicized pictures of Japan with temple gates, cherry blossoms and Fujiyama in the background will in time become real experiences for him. They are certainly very much in the minds of all the Japanese friends he will make. Nevertheless, a first encounter with the real Japan will show either the immaculate symmetry of "Lord Fuji" towering amazingly over the industrial haze of the metropolitan region as that is seen from an airplane, or else the busy port of Yokohama, noisy with shipping construction and surrounded by the brown flotsam of the suburban sprawl. For in visiting Japan's capital we are making our way into the most densely populated city on earth—one which can outblaze Broadway with its neon signs, but one where many of the streets still have no names and the houses no numbers.

Japan has perhaps the fastest railway on earth, and certainly the most spectacular. It is a country of electronics and the industries of the future; it is also still short of an effective sanitation system in parts of the capital itself. Sandals and sunshades shuffle alongside ultra-modernity in the daily life of the Japanese, and are still inseparable from thoughts for the future. The coexistence of the ancient and the modern is stronger and more persistent in its effects than most observers seriously take account of, partly because of an oversimplification by Westerners in their histories of Japan or their present observations.

We are very often reminded that Japan was closed to Western adventurers for two and a half centuries until shortly before 1868, when the Meiji restoration finally took place. With typical Western misunderstanding, we equate that knowledge with a belief that Japan was lost to civilization. (In parentheses we should remind ourselves that the Dutch maintained some commercial and scientific contact during that interval.) In any case, we should not attribute the nineteenth-century revival solely to the sudden aggression of American "black ships" bristling with guns and threats near Shimoda in 1853, or to the great inpouring of Western technology by Americans and Europeans for the eager learning of the Japanese. Recent scholarship has shown that the events of 1868 were preceded not only by the scholarly enquiries about "the state of things abroad" by Fukuzawa Yukichi and others, but by a reasonably high literacy rate, an urbane interest in the arts and commerce, and a wide provision of schools long before 1868.

Some of the latter were established by fiefs as early as 1620. By 1755, all male children of more than foot-soldier rank were receiving formal education in one of the 200-odd fief schools, or in a temple school, or in one of the many private establishments. The fantastic red tape of the Tokugawa administration from the sixteenth century to the nineteenth century depended on widespread ability to read and write—in the extremely difficult *kanji* or Chinese script with upward of 23,000 characters. Not even the more simplified form of Japanese syllabic writing, which came to flourish alongside the classical Chinese script, minimizes this achievement.

The religious and literary conservatism of the pre-Meiji period strongly reinforced unquestioning loyalty and acceptance of the old order. The long sucession of Tokugawa regents, or *shogun,* who were generalissimos usurping the power of the emperor by relegating him to divinity, did not prevent the rise of an officially despised bourgeois population. Prosperous, urbane burgesses enjoyed the theatre, novels, and delights not too different from those in most unindustrialized countries at the beginning of the nineteenth century. Furthermore, this stable rule reinforced social cohesion, an elaborate family structure with its "circles of obligation," and a coherent picture of the world in a remarkably self-sufficient culture. Many of those skills of personal ingenuity and social organization were developed which eventually launched Japanese enterprise so powerfully forward in the last third of the nineteenth century. As has been so often pointed out in this book the real stuff of education turns on this structuring of human interrelationships and perceptions much more than on formal school structures or theoretical plans; yet even so, the basic school foundations were already well laid.

Although penned up within the tight over-all control which persisted until the Restoration of 1867–1868 gave imperial power back to the Emperior Meiji ("The Enlightened"), the already marked esthetic enjoyment, bookish curiosity, and elaborate examination system of pre-Meiji times were at least potentially modernizing. When released, their power drove Japan forward—not by rejecting the old nor by slavishly copying from the West (although this happened in the early stages), but by simply changing the management so as to redirect energies forward along a technological path. Japan's present passion for education has deep foundations, reaching down at least 300 years. Its strength lay not solely in the *samurai* schools for the warrior classes, or in the private education of burgesses, but in the *terakoya,* or village schools, dotted throughout the countryside, and still more in the meticulous craftsmanship learnt in family enterprises. All those elements underpin Japan's towering achievements in education and science in recent years.

The coexistence of tradition and progress in Japan derives partly from one astonishing power of the Japanese—their intellectual and moral strength enabling them to humble themselves so as to learn and thus in time to be exalted. In the sixth century of our era, the Japanese learnt the Chinese system of writing and also Buddhism from the Heavenly Court of the Chinese, allowing Buddhism to prevail over the animism and awe of beautiful things which is still such an important element of Japanese religious sensibility. Elements of Confucianism came in too, and were reinforced by assiduous reading of the Chinese classics for centuries. In the sixteenth century Japanese interest in trade, and respect for the Portuguese and Dutch, laid the way open to Christianity; there was also a great stir of interest in what was then modern science. After the long closure, with its attempted effacement of Christianity and other subversive importations of the "red barbarians," Japan became, in the nineteenth century, the country most conspicuous among all mankind for the total transformation of its whole social order by means of a Western device—by education as that had been systematized by the processes of the Industrial Revolution. This

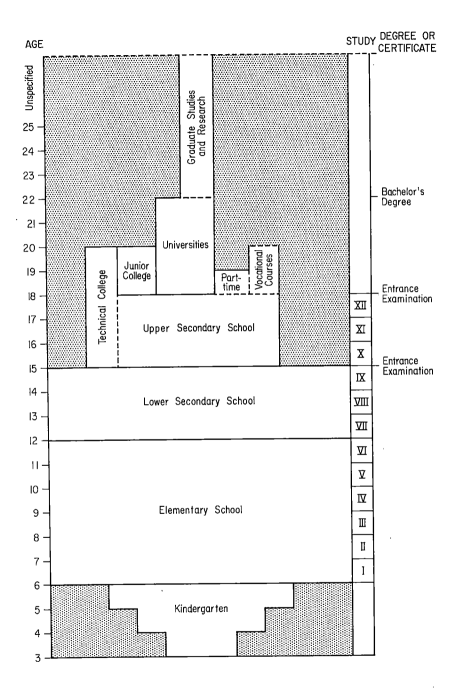

School System in Japan

transformation steadily developed from 1868 onward; but the most astonishing aspects of it were revealed before 1890—in less than a generation. For by that time the original passion for reform and democracy, which had seized the small band of oligarchs who were the real managers of Japan under the rule of the Emperor Meiji, had perforce given way to the nationalism of a conservative clique. Yet even in that partial return to the old Japanese idiom, its rulers sought to reinforce their conservatism with a technological, agricultural, and governmental modernization along Western lines, which was eventually to enable Japan to challenge the might of Russia successfully in the war of 1894.

There is no space here to detail the thoroughness with which the reformers set about their work. The pattern of government and its taxation and other controls were refurbished. Railways, telegraphs, a postal system, banks, and other public utilities were imported and controlled, bringing in great profits to the government. Papermills and textile factories, shipbuilding and a merchant marine were also owned or controlled by the government. Financial aid was given to private enterprise too, so that small firms grew rapidly into huge financial empires. Most of these came to be linked with mammoth cartels. But from the start it was recognized that none of these things could be developed without education. So the whole educational mainspring was constructed and wound. Primary schools leading to secondary schools, postsecondary institutions of several kinds, teacher-training colleges, and universities were all planned for and coordinated in precisely the right numbers at the right time and place.

Remarkable though this businesslike provision of formal education was, it was clearly not enough. The new masters of Japan recognized the need to develop their state by cultivating society *at all levels*—that is, at all levels of the social order (including the peasantry, downtrodden for centuries) and at all levels of behavior and interest. Democracy of a sort was, therefore, promised and perhaps genuinely intended. Certainly, education must be for all—and not just formal education. In the pursuit of European or American education, Western clothing, Western interests and pursuits (such as music and dancing—even Western haircuts) were all encouraged or enforced. Western food, including meat, began to enter Japan, where animals were not previously eaten. Western forms of address and relationship were (within strict limits) encouraged, so as to serve the needs of industry and a new kind of service. For the service element was strong, reinforced by a deliberate revival of the old country religion of Shinto with its deep reverence for things Japanese, and above all a reverence of Japan as personified in the Emperor's divinity. Nothing was left to chance by the rulers; but it would be folly to imagine that all this turning upside-down was

harshly enforced from above. A universal enthusiasm for Western technology, agriculture, science, and learning seems to have swept throughout the country. Diaries sent home to the United States during the
very earliest days of technical aid leave no doubt of the intelligent
diligence of the Japanese of those days—at many social levels.

In a sense, the heritage of those times lives on now in a continuum of
development—despite the nationalism of the later nineteenth century
and the first half of this. For even that nationalism was reinforced by
German philosophy. The forms of government were drawn in part from
England and later, more strongly, from authoritarian European states.
The flow of learning never ceased—in European literature, art, music
as well as in the useful sciences of the Americans. In consequence of
all this, it is now possible to see Japanese self-expression either in Eastern style or in Western style. Food and furniture, clothing and housing,
inns and entertainment—everything you might think of is to be had in
either Japanese *or* "Western style" form, though hardly ever in an amal-
gam of both, except in industry and formal education. Thus one can enjoy an unlimited flow of Western classical music on the radio in Tokyo,
perhaps a richer supply than anywhere in the world; yet Japanese
music is in constant coexistence. The same is true of drama, film, literature, sanitation—whatever you can think of. The lives of older people
who grew up before 1940 exemplify the unamalgamated separate elements of culture. So do the lives of young people today, though in a
different idiom.

Indeed, one should note the immense differences of consciousness and
conscience which must still coexist in the necessary daily contacts
made between the separated lives of the generations. Inner tensions and
inconsistencies played havoc with the peace of mind of liberals now
in their sixties and seventies when they had to live under an illiberal
regime before World War II. So they have some of the dichotomies of
Japan in their very souls. But that whole generation seems somehow
foreign to those in their forties and fifties, whose earliest consciousness
was of wars and disasters. The very young live in a yet different world.
But all of it is Japan. Despite all the sudden switching from fried
chicken to *osushi,* from the normal *tatami* matting to the little
Western-style parlor which middle-class houses proudly maintain, the
Japanese diligently maintain the progress and reorientation of Japan.
The educative or re-educative process is continuous; and nearly all
Japanese are fully committed to it.

Of course, the disasters of 1940–1945 resulted in a temporarily unquestioned repudiation of the past at least superficially, and a wholesale acceptance of the Occupation's message as a new gospel, with
Americanization and decentralization and so forth as truths which were

self-evident. But within twenty years after Hiroshima, the Japanese felt spiritually strong enough for a reappraisal of the cultural plan. Did the "West" (that is, the European tradition) only mean the American way of life, especially as packaged and exported to Japan? A huge reappraisal is continuing. To some extent it reached a climax in 1964, the year of the Olympic Games. Japan could do it all herself, with a new Tokaido railway and new superhighways cutting through the tangle of the past. These material manifestations reflected something in the collective soul. Recent years have reinvoked Japan's consciousness of herself as an Asian country with a civilization in her own right, and one which mainly by her own efforts has leapt forward into modernity— with education as the motive force.

The nineteenth-century example of Japan cannot have escaped the attention of those who, before 1917, were plotting the Russian Revolution. Education as a powerhouse, as a means of total modernization— these are concepts which recur time and again in Lenin's writing, just as they had been exemplified in Japan 50 years before. We may also be sure that the present modernizers of China can never forget that nineteenth-century Japanese renaissance, any more than they can forget twentieth-century Japanese invasions and victories. The rest of Asia is bound even more to focus attention on Japanese achievements in education and living standards, especially now that the Japanese people are so manifestly converted to peacefulness. Only one nation has been subjected to atomic destruction; the Japanese are determined to be the last. On any one of these grounds the example of Japan seems potent for Asia, the home of more than half of mankind.

Everything seems to point to Japan as an object lesson for the whole world. It must never be forgotten that in its turn the world is still one vast school for the eager Japanese, though they have now proceeded so far that they have had Nobel Prize winners in the sciences, and have long passed the stage at which they merely copied. Indeed the countries which invented and later exploited industrialization are now obliged to observe this nation which seems not simply to have progressed through their pioneering stages, but to have leapt over them into a different view of education's possibilities. This dedication to the effective *use* of education is specially potent at the present time, when the total amount of scientific knowledge in the world is doubling every 15 years, when three quarters of all the scientists who have ever lived are still alive and experimenting, and when half of all the knowledge acquired in many university courses will be more or less useless after another ten years.

Let us begin a portrait of contemporary Japan with some information about her size and resources. Japan consists of four large and many small islands, lying off the coast of Asia. The northernmost island is roughly 500 miles from the Russian port of Vladivostock, while the southernmost tip is about 500 miles from the coast of China. The total land area is about 147,000 square miles, slightly smaller than California. The population has risen in this century from approximately 50 million to little short of 100 million, a point near which many Japanese hope to stabilize by regularized abortion and systematic contraception.[1] That already places Japan in the five or six most populous nations in the world. When we recollect that roughly 84 percent of the land is incapable of cultivation, being mountain or rugged forest or built over, the concentration of population and the intensive cultivation which prevails in agriculture can be better appreciated. So intensive is rice production in recent years that, despite the enormous domestic consumption of this staple food, Japan has been able to export some. Though the Japanese are intensely thrifty, wasting no food or other shred of usable resources, the necessity for continuously expanding overseas trade is obvious; for it is not as though all of Japanese agriculture were easy, even on the cultivated land. The terracing of rice fields up the inhospitable mountain gulleys shows this fact plainly enough. Nor should we forget that Hokkaido, the northernmost island, has two meters of snow every winter, and the whole coast towards Asia is subject at regular intervals to Continental cold. In the south, at roughly North African latitudes, some sandy shores are strewn with cacti.

Though there are remarkable regularities in the succession of the seasons, Japan has earthquakes every day, some of them from time to time proving disastrous; while every autumn brings its succession of typhoons. Japan's natural circumstances have from time to time had a profound effect on her way of life. For example, in 1923 the great earthquake, which destroyed half the houses in the Tokyo area, at a cost of at least 100,000 lives within three days, and which also destroyed the greater part of its port Yokohama, cleared the way for the great reorganization of the life of the capital; but in a subtler way, the natural pattern of Japan's climate also in some ways suggests great regularity. Thus a Japanese will tell you that cherry blossom time in Osaka is on April 2nd, in Tokyo on April 10th, at Sendai about April 23rd, and in Hokkaido the first of June. By this he means one can regularly count on the best flowering time as an occasion of public outings and ceremonial viewing. Likewise, he will tell you that on or about the 21st of September the biggest typhoon will occur. The strange

---

[1] Though an official publication, *A Vision of the Affluent Japan 20 Years Hence,* envisaged a population of 130 million by about 1985.

thing is that these events follow the approximate dates given year in, year out. When we consider, too, that Japan from the sixth century onward inherited from the Chinese a profound respect for law and order with a sense of stability if not rigidity, it is not surprising to read the Imperial Rescript on Education of 1890. It insisted on filial respect and perpetual obedience to an Imperial Way which is "in truth the teaching handed down by our Imperial Ancestors to be observed alike by their Descendants and by their Descendants' Subjects, infallible throughout the ages, true in all places."

As if this were not enough, the Japanese is surrounded by reminders of the past. The ancient temples are all the more revered because their venerable unpainted timbers show the wonderful graining of the cypress enhanced by the slow wear of centuries. He reveres the patina of age shown on those ancient structures, on the even more ancient stones which are still objects of worship, and on all the slowly built up human ingredients in a beautiful landscape which still makes up the greater part of the countryside. Amidst all this reverence for the past one might wonder where any zest for the future could develop.

Yet that zest is undoubtedly there. The advertisements in newspapers, magazines and railway carriages are as modern as anything to be seen in the United States. Indeed the symbolic figures portrayed there seem often to be more American than Japanese. The visitor is gazed on by boys and girls with a kind of affectionate admiration simply because he is a foreigner (*gaijin*), a sign of Japan's expanding contacts, and a possible source of new thoughts, fashions, or contacts.

Japan has always been short of resources. In the postwar period she was also short of foreign capital and deprived of many previous overseas markets. Nevertheless in little more than 15 years Japan came to excel in such industrial fields as shipbuilding, electronics, photographic equipment, and the supply of such luxury articles as washing machines and color television sets even to the United States. Indeed, she led the world in some of these industries, increasing their productivity about twentyfold in ten or fifteen years. That is remarkable testimony to the adaptability of the Japanese, and their ability to make the educational adjustments necessary for such exacting kinds of industrial development. There are probably more graduates in the Japanese shipping industry than there are in comparable enterprises in any other country. The field of electronics and other modern industries more clearly still requires a high degree of technical proficiency superimposed on a sound basic education. These are lessons for the world. They are remarkable indications of modernity.

Living standards are now incomparably higher than they were at the end of World War II. Japan sees education as the key to further im-

provements. It is hoped to double living standards in the decade between 1965 and 1975. In a country precariously balanced in the matter
of trade it is obvious that much careful planning and the maximum development of human resources will be called for. Already Japan claims
to have more engineers than any other country in the world except the
United States and the Soviet Union. Though words like "graduate"
and "engineer" vary greatly in meaning from country to country, there
is no doubt of Japan's educational commitment or zest for the future.
Her acceleration continues; yet at the same time Japan remains deeply
conscious of ancient strengths, and is more aware of their future significance.

Of course for a very long time after the war the whole economy of
Japan was underpinned by lavish American aid. To this day there are
huge American investments. Besides one need only point to the im-
ponderable effect on Japanese economy of American armed forces'
presence and the saving made possible by the fact that Japan has
limited her military expenditure to about one percent of the gross national product. Nor can we leave out of the count the huge trade that
goes on between Japan and the United States, bringing in more than 3
billion dollars a year altogether. On the other hand, if trade relations
with the United States were to deteriorate, commerce with China
might expand, and the whole of Southeast Asia is now being assiduously
cultivated for trade purposes. The Japanese inevitably consider themselves the patrons of the East not only in economic development but in
terms of educational example. Japanese agricultural research, for
example, has already helped to save a number of Asian countries from
the periodic threat of famine.

Despite all the clockwork precision of the Olympic Games in 1964,
and the transistorized enterprises which now are winning the trade
of the world, it is strangely possible for the outsider to overestimate
some ancient aspects of life in modern Japan. Tourism is an important
industry. Glossy advertisements and magazines, therefore, publicize
prominently all those thousands of exquisite shrines, the tea ceremony,
the beautiful floral kimonos that hardly anybody wears except on rare
ceremonial occasions (if we exclude office girls on holiday in the Tokyo
parks). These are undoubtedly to be found in Japan, but far more
representative is the ordinary Western garb which predominates in
the streets of Tokyo and throughout the country towns. It is worn
with a scrupulous cleanliness reminiscent of middle-class urban Italians
and the younger salesmen of major American companies. It is true
that throughout the countryside one invariably sees farmers and their
wives hard at work in blue pantaloons or other traditional Japanese
garb appropriate to their occupation, especially when growing rice.

Here and there at holiday time, however, one may see the son of the house working alongside his parents while still wearing the dark uniform of school or university.

One of the abiding strengths of the Japanese social system, as that has been inherited from pre-Meiji times, is most clearly to be seen in the major industrial and commercial companies. The influence of these on the Japanese way of life, culturally as well as economically speaking, deserves a few moments of careful study here. In the last third of the twentieth century, the ordinary Japanese is still to a large extent dependent upon some relationships inherited from pre-Meiji times a century before. The greater part of Japanese industry and commerce is directly or indirectly in the hands of some 12 or 15 major trading corporations (*zaibatsu*). These were disbanded or decentralized for a time after the war, on American insistence; but they are now restored to full vigor. These major cartels, some initially established by the gratuities of *samurai* soon after the Meiji restoration, have grown to include not simply manufacturing and distribution, but retailing, banking, and the supply of raw materials. Such matters concern an economist directly; but some of their consequences concern any student of society, and above all an analyst of education.

The old paternal role of feudal times carries its patronage forward into the present day; so much so, that although many Japanese feared a recession after the Olympic Games (unnecessarily as it turned out) hardly anyone in Japan was afraid of it—if in employment with a major company or one of its subsidiaries in a large city, or if engaged on some of the subcontracting which such huge firms control. The reason is that when once a pupil or a student finishes his education at whatever level, and enters a firm, that is in some ways like a marriage in being a lifelong relationship. Very few people move around to other firms even in the more skilled professions. Employees and employers, therefore, tend to behave as though they were parts of an extended family. The employers are reluctant to dismiss men or women even when they are not fully employed, or when they are too old to work effectively. Likewise, the employees may tend to make free with their employer's time and resources. They certainly rely to an incredible extent upon the benefits which accrue to them directly in consequence of their employment. More than half the housing made available in recent years has been provided by big firms for their employees. Most of the commuters crowding into Tokyo and other large cities have their fares paid, with meals and clothing too. Likewise they draw on family allowances, educational costs and benefits, aid with children's other expenses, and a health service. They are helped even with being married, and having a honeymoon, with maternity benefits—and abortions when necessary

—all at the company's expense. Despite the growth in population, there is a marked manpower shortage. Nevertheless, there is little inclination among employees to try to move, and little prospect of their doing so because of the retentiveness of firms.

So while the family system is in some ways literally breaking down into the nuclear-sized family of the West, some family-type attachments are reinforced in their vigor in the patronage world of the major companies. Some firms have regular morning ceremonies at which as many as 50,000 employees have been known to gather to sing a hymn or pledge to the firm's prosperity. Sometimes they start the day together with physical exercises. Many thousands of young girl employees between about the ages of 15 and 20 are housed as the wards of a company under careful scrutiny and with many material benefits, until such time as they are returned to their village homes with a dowry and the prospect of a decent marriage. Limitations on human individuality these certainly seem to us; but they are an improvement on any feudal system elsewhere. The lot of the Japanese seems more enviable than that of many others during a period of rapid industrial growth and urbanization. Partly for this reason it is impossible to compare earning power as between a Japanese and people in other countries. At the time of writing, Japanese steel workers averaged about £500 a year, less than in England by a good margin, but no starvation wage. The exceptional benefits provided in Japan may well increase the value of this employment by 50 percent or so. Teachers and other employees of government or local authorities similarly benefit by additional allowances. In one recent official publication the teacher's side benefits in some cases amounted to 25 percent of his basic salary; and many other kinds of official or private employment pay rather better in this respect. Small firms pay considerably less than the salaries indicated above; but even workers in the small handicraft firms average about £15 a month plus exceptional benefits, and the salary structure in general seems fairly comparable with that of Italy.

Universities, too, can act like major firms in the matter of patronage. Once students are admitted into their family, professors feel a certain obligation to them, actually being reluctant to fail them. At the level of university teachers, it is noticeable that young men tend to treat their senior professors with great respect, sharing their political views and other philosophies, and often marrying into their families in a literal sense. Of course, there are exceptions to this generalized observation; but the fact that the Japanese themselves point out the exceptions shows how far the general rule may be expected to apply. A certain amount of academic inbreeding can therefore be discovered. It is usual for a university to draw its faculty members from among its

own students; and any transfer from an unfamiliar school to an important university, or from one important university to another, is duly
pointed out by the Japanese with interest. All this adds to the grave
importance of examinations, particularly those which select children
for the competitive senior secondary schools which we shall describe
later, and above all those which operate in the "examination inferno"
between the end of upper high school and any one of the more than
270 universities. (All institutions of higher education in Japan are
called universities (*daigaku*). The institutions of higher education vary
enormously in quality, in admissions requirements, and so forth. Each
has its own admission tests. These aspects will be discussed later. The
immediate point of importance for the reader is that, because of their
differences, each one of them has quite a different prognosis for employment. Thus the long arm of the *zaibatsu* reaches down through the
university structure into the secondary schools, and below that into
the primary school, and sometimes even further down into the kindergarten. So important is the element of patronage in Japanese life.

Japan must be the only country in the world with prekindergarten
tests. This fantastic concern for "brightness" in children is caused by
the wish of ambitious parents and prosperous families to make sure that
their young hopefuls will enter the right kindergarten (private) which
will lead to the right elementary school (either private or public), which
will lead in turn to the right lower-secondary and the right upper-
secondary schools with a high predictive rate for admission to the right
universities. The greatest compliment you can pay to a Japanese
parent is to call his children "bright." Eagerly and endearingly bright
so many of them are in personal encounter; but what matters is the
scholastic encounter, and for that it is important to enter the right
school. There is, of course, no certainty that one good school will follow
another in the path of the child; but there is high degree of probability
if the child is born (or taken betimes by his farsighted parents) into
one of those suburbs famous for its high success rate, or into one of the
wards of Tokyo with a famous old school (like Hibya High School).
Now we are speaking of public schools in the American sense, which
are all supposed to be equally the people's schools; but social ingenuity
will find a way, even if it means stretching the law and registering a
child for school purposes in a district where he does not actually live.

Clearly, we are talking here of somewhat exceptional cases, and
of a tendency less likely to be found in rather distant provincial cities
like Fukuoka. But that tendency is well recognized by the Japanese
themselves, though they are disinclined to say much about it to a
foreigner. Though the numbers involved are small, the numbers involved in the private "Public Schools" of England are also small, like
those in the best "preparatory schools" of the United States. Small

numbers do not say anything about the size of their influence. The
directorate and boardroom of a major corporation are small anyway.

In this connection it is worth calling attention in general terms to
the existence of a fairly large private school sector and a very large
private university sector. Some of the private universities are academically powerful and socially prophetic. If we take Keio as an example (founded by that same Fukuzawa who did so much to modernize
and liberalize Japan) we find that it has an "attached school." So do
other distinguished universities. Like the parental university, such
an attached school has high quality academically and socially. It is no
disgrace for a young university professor to take up a post teaching in
such a school. Keio's attached school shows, like the others, a "through
plan" or *ikkan*. That is to say, the relative assurance (though not the
certainty) that a child will proceed "end on" from kindergarten through
to the university enables rather different educational considerations to be developed than the competitiveness to be expected in other
places, as lower-secondary school pupils approach the diagnostic barrier line separating them from upper-secondary school. In an attached
school's "through plan," it is said, more attention can be paid to general
qualities such as character-training, esthetic sensibility, and morality.

In fact, it all sounds like the sometimes true apologia of privileged
schools in other countries, to which the Japanese frequently point.
They mistakenly believe that, for example, a particular preparatory
school in England will almost guarantee admission to a particular
Public School, and that in turn lead on nearly automatically to
a preferred university. Ways used to be cleared, no doubt, for such a
fortunate sequence of events, and the odds are still in favor of a better
chance; but the small group of highly predictive schools in Japan are
not only educationally and socially privileged—they are also more
assuredly confident of promising a rosy future in the right firm, with
all the blessings of Japanese patronage. In every country in the world
the reformers of the people's schools must measure meticulously the
likely contextual response to their theoretically admirable campaigns.
If they enhance privilege and preference for other schools, either in
the private or in the public sector, they may defeat their own ends.
(In these days of commuting and expensive residential districts it is
not difficult to develop even a publicly provided school to a position
of some privilege. This phenomenon is more likely to happen in a
decentralized system, such as was almost forced upon the Japanese
during the Occupation.) In Japan the subtleties which make so much
difference are not only those of greater wealth and physical amenities
for the school; they may also include hardheaded considerations for
a particular child's future. Educational evaluation must survey the

generalized social-emotional-moral relationship of man with society, which is inherited from the past and in some ways reinforced by the pattern of patronage.

Of course patronage is not only a matter of benefits, but of obligations too. The old importance attached to *giri,* or obligation to one's family and superiors, still forms an important part of any Japanese conscience. There must be an exact requital of work done for benefits received. Though the dependent's relationship may seem feudal to an external observer more familiar with a precisely defined contractual relationship, the emotional involvement of a Japanese because of *giri* is an important element in the cohesion of Japanese society. At all levels of the educational system, and penetrating all thoughts of its reform, these subtler aspects of communication and sharing in Japanese society are intimately persuasive.

In considering such forces as these, which the Japanese take for granted and seldom spell out to any foreigner, we see that the mere parallel tabulation of school structures or subject attainment is almost as useless as the imaginary framework of some textbook theories. Of course, we must know the facts. We must know and properly identify the institutions and what they do. It is far more important to discern the context of the past and recognize its present interaction with so many activities and considerations. But (most important) it is in the concurrent climax of all these influences on the educational decisions now being made for the future that we must look for clues as to the real significance of change in Japan's educational system.

The basic structural facts of Japan's school system are simple and widely known. The familiar 6-3-3-system of the American school pattern was adopted during the American Occupation, and still holds force. It is followed by a four–year plateau of higher education—a plateau of levels and great heights. That is to say, four years of university may be followed by postgraduate institutions, yet there is no equivalence between the various universities even at the first four–year level. A number of junior colleges have also been provided, appealing particularly to those girls who want the equivalent of finishing school or a short commercial education, or simply a chance to be in higher education and to meet a suitable young man. The former pattern of arranged marriages is breaking down, and most progressive Japanese like to feel that they choose each other as partners in the Western way. In the postwar period even nominally arranged marriages usually included a fair amount of cooperation between the young couple and their parents.

During the period since about 1963, a number of technical colleges have been set up to overlap the last few years of the school period and include the lower parts of the university structure, but with more precise reference to career prospects and technical content than had been usual in the postwar period in the normal four-year university course. Under American influence, this has attempted to be "liberal." Such minor specialization as occurs in the ordinary four-year university course is confined to the later half. The technical college, intended to provide ultimately for some scores of thousands of students, may well be a powerful institution in the future; but without a restructuring of the system of employers' patronage, it is doubtful whether it will commend itself to the ordinary Japanese parent or pupil, as it seems to restrict the prospect of employment in no uncertain way. The man in the street and a pupil in the upper-secondary school seem more inclined to take their chance in the long agony of preparation for examinations and attempts to enter a university of happy augury.

Nine years of schooling are now compulsory and free. The provision of free textbooks is gradually being extended from the elementary level up through the secondary grades. The intention is to have a free supply of books for all the compulsory years before 1970. Though school is free and books are free, other charges may be embarrassing to parents of limited means, although in this matter firms are usually prepared to help out. Of the children who leave the lower secondary schools, somewhere between 25 and 30 percent obtain employment immediately. They are likely to stay at an unskilled level for their lives. It is true that there is provision for secondary school courses on a part-time basis; but this is not easy for the pupil. Nevertheless, social stratification is mitigated by this opportunity. The other 70 or 75 percent of pupils go on full time to an upper secondary school. These are not free. Fees vary considerably, according to the locality and sometimes, of course, according to the prestige of the school. Costs are never very high in the publicly provided schools; but for any Japanese parent this budgeting must be carefully done. Tuition fees in the public schools range from about $12.00 to $25.00 a year, but the additional costs mount up. Japanese children are a shining example to others in the matter of cleanliness and smart turnout. In the higher ranges of school, and at the university, they wear a uniform if they are boys, or a standardized pattern of clothing if they are girls. Average costs are likely to come to about $100 a year for each child. The higher up the educational ladder one reaches, the higher these expenses become.

Japanese pupils and students look eager, cooperative, and also happy. As a rule they are extremely polite, not least to a visitor. Yet the seriousness of their work must never be forgotten. To the Japanese themselves, however, modern school conditions seem extremely relaxed. Those who visited Japanese homes or schools before World

War II are familiar with the insistent father, complete with chalk and blackboard, or else going through the day's work with his children in some other way. Today's schools and their curricula seem by contrast to be slack—at least to older Japanese.

In view of what has been said, it is not very surprising that after the age of 18 as many as 15 percent of all the boys and girls have been entering some form of higher education. If we leave on one side the junior colleges (numbering a little more than 300), the 270-odd universities accommodate about 750,000 students, and that number is growing fast. Of these more than 60 percent attend private institutions. There are private primary and secondary schools, but not to this great extent. About 15 percent of the regular university enrollments are girls; but more than 70 percent of the total in junior colleges are girls. Naturally, universities all have a quota; but that number has been massively exceeded in recent years. The highly selective University of Tokyo has an annual admission quota of 2614 students (a figure which we must quadruple to get the total figure). Keio University has an admissions quota of 3760; Waseda of 6480; but the actual enrollment may be indicated by the fact that in 1963 Waseda University had a total of 33,100 students.

The University of Tokyo—the former Imperial University—is a public institution, but it is the most highly selective of all. According to M. Shimbori:

> Tokyo University was taken as the very model of *daigaku* . . . the new *daigaku* all try to be a miniature of Tokyo University—a goal which can never be attained. . . . A very conspicuous and rigid hierarchy of prestige exists among institutions of higher education in Japan. As a rule the older ones enjoy a higher status than the younger; the national ones than the private; the big and many faculty ones than the small and one faculty ones. . . . Tokyo University has enjoyed the very top status, a fact which Japanese people, whether academic or not, regard as unalterable. Then comes Kyoto University, and so on down.[2]

Before World War II, Imperial universities had been established in widely separated parts of the country. As early as 1872 there had been a plan to establish a kind of Napoleonic pattern of *académies* or school regions based upon eight university centers; but the plan was never fulfilled. Reliance was placed instead upon the prefectural system tightly controlled by the central government. As far as universities go, the distinguished Imperial universities were soon followed by important private universities, of which Keio (in Tokyo) and Waseda and Meiji universities are among the most significant. Each one of the major

---

[2] M. Shimbori, *Sociology of Education,* vol. 37, no. 3, p. 230–235 (1964).

private universities seems to be associated with particular industrial or commercial corporations, on the managerial boards of which its alumni will be prominent. It also often happens that a particular university will be preeminent through one of its departments in a major profession, such as law or medicine.

In the postwar upheaval many institutions which had previously been upper-secondary schools, or had existed in the no-man's-land between school and university, all became universities. This led to an unrestrained competition for status. Those which suffered most were such humble institutions as the former normal schools or teachers' colleges. It is an open secret that in a survey conducted at the end of the war several of these were discovered to have lower academic standards than some of the best secondary schools. Nevertheless, in the postwar period they are all in the higher education arena competing together. Indeed, so important has the contest become that a few of the former normal schools, which had a secondary school or an elementary school attached, achieved importance in the public eye because those same schools (which were efficiently taught) had a high degree of prognosis for their pupils when it came to university admissions.

The emphasis must be on the word "admissions." What matters is getting into the university. It is so difficult to satisfy the requirements for the University of Tokyo and comparable institutions that a very large number of candidates for them will spend two or three years at private preparatory schools in the capital amassing knowledge which will enable them to achieve success in the appalling competition. It was not until about 1963 that some of the major universities began to take more than half of their students straight from high school, a trend which of course puts a premium on strongly academic high schools. Hitherto, they had almost invariably been recruited from among candidates who had spent an arduous period in the preparatory schools just mentioned. It has been estimated that there are between 200,000 and 250,000 young men and women in the lost world between school and university. They have been called *ronin,* like the masterless *samurai* who became such a menace in feudal times. As it is, the highest universities in the pyramid take between one quarter and one third of their freshmen from these preparatory schools. A number of university professors undertake part-time work in them as an increased source of income. They are greatly valued by such schools because of their knowledge of what is required in the examinations.[3]

---

[3] Some of these facts and problems are discussed in detail in my article in *Comparative Education,* March 1965. The conclusions reached there, and restated in the present chapter, are fully agreed with in a feature issue of the *Mainichi Daily News,* International Edition, of March 1, 1966.

After all this preparation it is not surprising, therefore, to know that in the universities with the greatest prestige the best students have already completed what might be normally considered the first one or two years of university work, and this often leaves them idle. Thus they are open to all kinds of political interference. A crisis about fees is endemic in a Japanese university. Strikes are not uncommon. Agitation is even more frequent. Many of the students join political associations, or militant unions such as *Zengakuren*. In the past few years a militant sect of Buddhism called *Soka-gakkei* has powerfully recruited disaffected students as well as many others in Japan. Liberals in general are afraid of the mass assemblies, the demagogic techniques so reminiscent of Hitler, and the other indications of hysteria which particularly affect the youth of Japan. It is said that nothing quite comparable to *Soka-gakkei* has ever happened in Japan before. Over 5 million "households" are said to have belonged to it by 1965. Since that time the movement has gone on to achieve very great political power. For us the main point to observe is its close link with the disaffection of Japanese students and their sense of social malaise. A large number of the working class are also said to belong to *Soka-gakkei;* they too could be similarly described as feeling "shut out."

Juvenile delinquency, which is growing in all countries, is particularly grievous to the Japanese, with their strict sense of social decorum and respect for elders. Loud complaints have been issued in recent years, with much prominence in the newspapers. Youngsters in the fourteen to fifteen age bracket are particularly affected. As a matter of fact, in all countries the most troublesome young people are those in the last year of compulsory schooling, although in certain instances disorders can be expected from those who are approaching some important diagnostic examination at a later age. In the case of Japan, there has been a surprising rise in organized gangsterism, as distinct from individual crime, among young people of school age. The number of gangs has increased by about 25 percent since 1958 and the membership has nearly doubled during the same period from 90,000 to 170,000. Theft accounts for most of the crimes committed by minors. In 1957, crimes committed by junior and senior high school students made up only 26 percent of the total of juvenile crimes; but by 1962 it had jumped to 42.3 percent and the figure has mounted steadily.

In a country as orderly as Japan has normally been in recent years, any figures of violence are bound to cause special concern. It is more important still to measure this increase of difficult youth against the general background of great respect for elders which can perhaps be illustrated well with reference to a Japanese film called *Tokyo Twilight*. When it was shown at an international conference in 1959 it was stated to be a film about delinquency. In fact it showed the breakdown of the family structure in Japan, or the decay of a home's ties, resulting in a broken marriage and in a juvenile pregnancy which ended in an abortion (not in itself as grievous in Japan as it would be elsewhere). When the film was shown to an international audience, several members demanded where the delinquency was. That was plain enough to a Japanese. Delinquency could be grievous in its breaches of morality without the violence associated with delinquency in some other countries. Nevertheless, the recently published Japanese figures relate to violence such as assault, armed robbery, and extortion as well as some rape and murder. It is against this background that we shall later have to consider the great concern of the Ministry of Education and other leading educators in Japan with the problems of moral education. No doubt a similar kind of unease prompts the spontaneous interest of young people themselves in mass movements such as *Soka-gakkei* which we have just described.

The liberation of youth from old time rigidities, like the emancipation of women, has often resulted in large-scale immorality on the sexual plane—if we are to apply the norms of one's parents and grandparents. In the postwar period Japanese womanhood has been legally emancipated in such matters as ability to vote, own property, and divorce their husbands. To see the young Japanese girls at present in school, robustly made and with longer legs than their mothers and grandmothers, is to recognize a state of brimming health. The kind of emancipation which allows young people to go skiing, or bathing together in the summer, or to go out on camping holidays (especially if they are students) naturally brings into question many old norms. Needless to say, the impatience of youth rejects many rules which the young people themselves would be prepared to abide by a slightly older age. All this social transformation, however, builds up an increasing alienation of sympathy between the young people and the parental generation, although in some remarkable ways old aspects of social decorum persist. For example, the ancient Japanese tea ceremony is just as important as a social accomplishment to a young suburban girl in Japan as the possession of old silver or knotted pine furniture and colonial-style equipment of the home in the United States. Such external signs, however, should not be regarded as proof of internal allegiance to the norms which the older ceremonial was supposed to develop and enhance.

Programs of democratization, and of moral or social incorporation of the young, have caused the Ministry of Education and its research teams to pay close attention to the reform of the curriculum in recent years. Some of those have been concerned to develop a new program of social studies or—above all—straightforward teaching in "morality." But before going on to the significance of this latterly-restored element of the Japanese curriculum, let us cast a brief glance at something which does not at first sight seem to be associated with it, namely the pattern of administrative responsibility.

Before World War II the pattern of control and obligation was clear. The emperor was paramount both in government and in terms of duty and moral guidance, as he was the divine representative on earth. Under him came the government, then came a strict educational hierarchy. There were 46 prefectures (as there are now); below that there was a ramification of control as in France. The postwar pattern, however, was quite different. The emperor formally disclaimed any divinity. The government was democratically elected, and represented the people. Its powers were shorn in various ways. Voters elect not only the central organs of government but two other forms of representation which run in parallel in some ways, and especially in education. In other words, they elect the prefectural assembly and indirectly, therefore, the prefectural board of education. At the same time they elect municipal assemblies, and, therefore, indirectly the municipal boards of education. Education is consequently controlled and financed at three levels. There are national, prefectural, and municipal education boards, systems of finance, and patterns of control. These are largely independent of each other. The Ministry of Education may offer guidance and, of course, assistance of other kinds to local boards of education. Prefectural boards of education can also do the same, and municipal boards do likewise in their areas. Furthermore, there has been a simultaneous development of parent-teacher associations, which were hitherto unknown. In some ways the PTAs can offer financial and other peripheral assistance to the schools. Though they are not supposed to do so, they can actually improve the teachers' salaries or offer inducements to them to fulfill parental wishes.

From this description, it follows that some of the risks inherent in the American scene have repeated themselves in Japan. Some local authorities are very progressive and generous, while others represent the opposite tendency. Furthermore, decentralization, which was introduced in the name of democracy, has often resulted in power falling into the hands of locally important people. These could be landowners or businessmen. In any case, there is no guarantee of their educational competence. In these circumstances, the Japan Teachers' Union has been able to mount locally powerful offensives against particular tendencies, especially those of a conservative kind, or those which might seem to lead to a greater amount of academic differentiation in the curriculum. In many ways the activities of the Japan Teachers' Union are extremely praiseworthy. They have helped local parents to know that they have a share in the control of the schools, and in the wider education of their children outside school. They have encouraged sports days and other elements unfamiliar in the former pattern of schooling in Japan. There is no doubt that, on the whole, this kind of enterprise is both good and in keeping with the honest wishes of the Ministry of Education itself.

However, the kind of thing that the rather socialist Japan Teachers' Union fears is most clearly exemplified in its resistance to the courses in *morality* which have been reintroduced during the past few years. In 1958 a new compulsory subject, "moral education," was introduced. Critics of this complain that it is a restoration of the old prewar code of loyal obligations called *shushin*. That code of obligations was positively feudal. Its spirit can be imagined by referring back to the insistence on obedience contained in the Imperial Prescript of 1890, from which a quotation was given earlier. Liberals of any sort were bound to object to the ethos exemplified in *shushin;* yet it is clear that the removal of a really objectionable code does not necessarily mean that young people will follow a better one. Indeed, the absence of attention in schools to the problems of moral responsibility, which receive careful attention without religion in the USSR for example, can leave boys and girls in a destructive vacuum. The area of moral indecision, in fact, is not a vacuum. It is invaded by the commercialization of advertisements, radio programs, and glossy examples from the magazines or the television screen, to say nothing of the inventiveness of young people themselves. On the other hand, the new official curriculum of moral education seems to have been invented at the Ministry, or in its research departments, without too much consultation of anybody, whether teaching or involved in moral considerations of any kind. This would be a reasonable ground for some objection. One might also say that any attempt to teach morality, instead of making young people aware of the moral considerations that may be involved, and the moral support that may be derived from various quarters (no matter whether religious or not), would be bound to result in failure. In any case, one or two of the ingredients of the moral education program could be criticized individually. In Japan's present state of tension over the question of moral obligation, with its collateral tension concerning decisions of central control on the one hand or socialism on the other, sober discussion is hard to arrive at.

In parenthesis, it might be pointed out that, whereas in some other countries it is the socialists who are accused of centralizing tendencies while the conservatives stress decentralization, in Japan political divisions are of the opposite tendency. In the interests of democracy, as

observed let us say in the United States, socialists in Japan have tended
to stress decentralization as a kind of maneuver against the overreach-
ing power of central organizations. Not only in the matter of morality,
therefore, but in questions of curriculum reform or other perfectly
neutral administrative matters, the socialists in Japan have tended to
mount embattled resistance to anything that came from the central
government. In speaking of socialists, we must certainly include the
very powerful Japan Teachers' Union, though that does not necessarily
mean that Japanese teachers or Japanese socialism always resemble
their counterparts in other countries. For example, although in the
Soviet Union and in socialist quarters in Western Europe there is often
a sympathetic consideration for such elements as the polytechnical
principle in education, in Japan there has been marked resistance by
socialists to such matters as the institution of the new technical colleges since about 1962, overlapping the last three years of the secondary phase and the first two years of higher education. Doubtless there
are questions to be asked. But in Japan they tend to be asked along
party lines. In some ways, therefore, Japan shows the Cartesian cleavages that one can also discern in France. In other countries perhaps,
this particular decision might turn upon the obvious need to provide
young people with competitive technical skills which might enable
them to bypass not only the wasteful and cruel steeplechase for university admission, but also some aspects of patronage. For the one area
in which patronage can be sidestepped in Japan is in the newer professions so greatly in demand that they can set up their own requirements
and guarantee their own mobility, as actuaries can.

Certain ministerial innovations during the past decade have been
(by external criteria) highly desirable, such as curriculum reform in
a number of subjects. Another one has been the establishment in 1961
of a national achievement test, and participation in international
evaluations of attainment like that conducted by the IEA survey associated with UNESCO. Such upgrading endeavors can only enhance
the prospects of Japanese education centrally and locally. The names,
partisanship, and statistics matter far less than the actuality of what
is going on. Japan can no longer afford pockets of underdevelopment
or incompetence. The general refurbishing now going on seems likely
to bring advantages to all the people.

There is no doubt that in Japan there are underdeveloped pockets.
The northernmost island Hokkaido is a case in point. The general vege-
tation pattern of the island seems to resemble that of Germany. Yet the
Japanese have been so committed to rice-growing that they take to
other forms of cereal cultivation only with great reluctance. Though
the northern climate is harshly indifferent to dietary habits, and causes

grievous losses to rice cultivators, farmers are reluctant to change their habits or to learn new skills. Though rice is still the staple food, and is consumed in quantities that would give any foreigner grievous indigestion, the Japanese pattern is changing with a growing demand for meat and dairy products, which (it is estimated officially) will within 20 years have increased sixfold. Localized decisions about agricultural science, however, and the technical learning that goes with it, could hardly take account of these long-term changes. Moreover, in local discussions, local lobbies like that of the farmers weigh heavily. It might be more to the point to take national account of some population and occupation changes. Not long ago farmers were the majority of the population; now they are 31 percent. There has been a great migration to the towns. Only 6 percent of school-leavers now stay on the farm, as distinct from 25 percent little more than ten years ago. These are just a few of the long-term considerations incompletely considered by local decisions or by school patterns and curriculum requirements.

In Japan there are some underprivileged people of another kind. Countries with a Buddhist tradition regard those who take life with horror. Those who are charged with the disposition of offal, or animal products such as shoe leather, are also despised. A faint echo of this attitude is found in Japan in the case of the *eta* or formerly unclean people, now more kindly called *burakumin* or "village people." Some of these are likely to be localized in depressed areas of large cities like Osaka, or in the fishing areas of the island of Shikoku. Centrally-based campaigns (like those of the American President's Appalachian and other improvement programs) may well be necessary in Japan if these and other localized unfortunates are to have equality of educational opportunity. Moreover, it seems unrealistic to insist so much on decentralization and "grass roots" when these same desiderata are vitiated from the start by the increasing centralization of industries and communications in all countries. Besides, education itself is increasing so fast in Japan both in terms of quantity and in its multiple ramifications (especially at the higher education level) that national decisions seem inevitable. In this case they will surely be imposed upon the localities and smaller interests, unless the latter can be persuaded to cooperate more fully with centralizing forces than has been the case hitherto.

To take but one other example, let us look at television. Japan excels in educational television, and perhaps also in some other aspects of its public programs. Of the six networks existing at the present time, NHK has modeled itself recognizably on the British Broadcasting Corporation. Seventy-seven percent of one of its two programs is devoted to social and educational items. One of the other television networks is devoted entirely to education. Yet another must devote at least 60 percent of its time to education. The programs in question are not mildly educational, but sometimes straightforwardly didactic. They include such things as simple instruction in quadratic equations and other regular school items. In a world which is growing increasingly short of teachers, at the same time as it is trying to catch up with all the expansion of knowledge and world events, it seems more than likely that centralized agencies of this kind will be increasingly important. In Japan's highly electronic world that probability seems more marked than ever.

To make such an observation must not be construed as evidence of a predisposition toward centralization generally. We live in a world in which three major corporations control American car production, with similar tendencies as well in Germany, Britain, and elsewhere. Industrialization's consequences are bound to overtake the schools in the long run. The very proper concern of the would-be democrat and the liberal in Japan for local endeavors, local interests, and personalized commitment to the school which can be shared by teachers, pupils, and parents alike are all very meritorious; but they must somehow come to terms with the supply of the basic necessities and the communication of the basic sources of information. What makes reconciliation so difficult in Japan is precisely the Japanese character of the institutions at work—not only in the schools themselves but in all those educative elements around the schools. Preeminent among these are the *zaibatsu* and the dependence of such a large proportion of the Japanese upon some system of patronage and obligation. Inseparable from any evaluation is the memory of the prewar period with its system of *shushin* of morality, the divine authority of the emperor, and the tight administrative control which made the life of a liberal so very difficult. Certainly all these things must be borne in mind when we try to evaluate the reform proposed in 1966.[4]

In June 1963, the Minister of Education asked the Central Advisory Council of Education to give advice on the reorganization of upper secondary education. Critics say that the advice given reflects the views of the Ministry rather than that of any independent council, and that such a state of affairs is prevalent in Japan. The main aim of the reorganization is stated to be the provision of educational opportunities for all young people aged from 15–18 "according to their aptitude and ability." The latter phrase is strangely reminiscent of the tripartite

---

[4] The leading newspaper *Mainichi* "scooped" the contents of the official report in its issue of February 4, 1966, in an account which seems reliable. A further comment on March 1, 1966, in the same newspaper (under the title "Japan's Educational Rat Race— Real Learning Suffers.") bears out the comments made throughout this chapter.

division included in the British Education Act of 1944. In consequence of this desire, it is said to be the intention to differentiate courses in general high schools. Distinctive interests or attributes such as arts, science, and general courses will be established. Girls, too, will be given separate treatment or consideration to match their feminine prospects.

Another remarkable change proposed is that of a short-course senior high school with two years as a part-time course, and a year and a half to follow as a full-time course. Such a part-time high school would have the advantage of taking care of working youth and perhaps the young people in rural districts. The level of attainment expected would be that of the ordinary full-time high school. It is clear that this last proposal is intended eventually to supply high-school education to the age of 18 for all. Moreover, alongside the regular senior high school it is proposed to establish young workers' schools which will have part-time courses of 300 hours a year providing for both general culture and vocational training. This proposal again sounds rather like the provision made of Soviet schools at the least academic levels, which nevertheless manage to provide elements of general education as well as directly useful preparation for life after the age of 15. The units or elements of education learned in such a school should qualify the young people in exactly the same way as courses provided in ordinary high schools. A further innovation proposed is the establishment of youth centers for young people aged 15–25 in large cities at central government expense. (This again resembles President Johnson's proposals in 1966.) It is impossible to say how much this "leaked information" is reliable at the present stage as an official guarantee of what will happen. On the other hand, the tendencies expressed in the interim report of 1965 already officially released, and in official circles elsewhere, indicate that what the *Mainichi* newspaper published is very much in line with trends long discernible in Japanese discussions.

It seems that the gradual development of new careers, no doubt aided by tendencies at work in the high schools and universities, and also in the firms themselves which are branching out on news lines, will before long help to challenge the powerful monopolies and "placing" advantages of the older firms. But it will be a long time before the ancient and entrenched dignities of Japan will be overthrown, if ever they are. In any case, for the student of Comparative Education it is obvious that the simple six–three–three years of the American school pattern, followed by four years of college on the American model, by no means guarantee that Japan has followed, is following or will follow American precedent. That would be impossible. In the circumstances of Japan, American-type schools have been used to turn out even more Japanese products and problems than the prewar pattern, perhaps.

One thing is quite clear: that Japan is reappraising her own position internationally: and in relation to the field of education in particular. It does not seem too farfetched to recognize some resemblance between Japanese preoccupations in education and those of another ex-imperial island power, namely Britain. Both have large populations, and must earn their prosperity and a large amount of their food by ingenuity. Both are endeavoring to democratize in different ways. Both are shifting from heavy technology toward the lighter kinds of scientific occupation which require a stronger base of schooling. Both are vigorously in search of new moral and cultural values which may or may not be based upon the existing school pattern.

What have we learned from our excursion into the world of education in Japan? We have seen beyond any doubt that education, as a whole, depends far more on the background cultural influences than on the formal school system. This takes much of its significance and certainly its dynamic from the living context and the inheritance with which people shape their lives. This basic truth is all the more important in Japan because the school system itself has been given so many tasks to do in such a coordinated way in order to reconstruct the way of life, a whole deeply rooted civilization. Even so, despite the central role of the schools and their extremely formative influence in the making of the future, the old Japan, the old aspirations, and the old value system both persist and are in some ways enhanced.

At the same time it is impossible to do full justice to the already achieved modernization of Japan or the Japanese zest for the future—based as both these are on extremely diligent work in the schools. The Japanese claim, for example, that they have the highest literacy rate in the world, and year in year out scrutinize international criteria to see how they are faring in other respects.[5] Some of these comparisons are overoptimistic, of course, as they are in all countries. And, in this case, they are hampered by the uncritical use of blanket terms—like "higher education"—as the comparisons range from one incomparable context to another. Nevertheless, if we focus on Japan itself, the scholastic achievement and the technological transformation are fantastic—especially when we relate these to the patterns of learning and social intercourse that preceded the dawn of the twentieth century, not to go back earlier.

Let us take as an example the single problem of the Japanese language and its scripts. In the millennia of almost self-sufficient isolation, despite fruitful contacts and borrowings, the Japanese developed their

---

[5] For example, many English-language publications, notably *Educational Standards in Japan, 1964.* (Ministry of Education, Tokyo 1965.)

language to reveal in infinite subtlety the decorous forms of hierarchy and social interdependence which prevailed. For example, linguists tell us that there are 36 ways of saying "I," depending on the speaker's social relationship to the person he is addressing. Yet at the same time directly causal relationships between an action and its consequences, or between a subject and its object, are not so easily designated; while there is hardly any precise way of expressing determination to do a thing or certainty that an event will follow in the future. This is not a matter of grammatical interest only. The television announcer will sometimes repeat an item of information in another form of words. A secretary will have more than one go at spelling out a telephone message, and be still more hesitant when it comes to putting that into writing in any of the three variants of indigenous writing to be found in Japan. Indeed, when transliterating any beautiful piece of calligraphy into current Japanese (or still more when translating into English), she will have particular difficulty with any names, or find it a puzzle to write in Japanese script some Japanese names correctly pronounced.

Leaving behind the purest form of ancient Chinese calligraphy with its more than 23,000 characters, Japan evolved a simplified *Kanji* (Chinese script) of her own, and supplemented that with two syllabaries, each of 48 signs representing a syllable. This facilitated the incorporation of foreign words and ideas into Japanese culture. It was in a mixture of *Kanji* and the two scripts *katakana* and *hiragana* that poems and novels were written, and such literary masterpieces as *The Tale of Genji* composed centuries ago. More recently, the total number of symbols which Japanese children must learn to be literate has been reduced—to 1850. (Compare that with our 26 letters!) In these 1850 symbols, books and newspapers are written. Stations show the place-name in both *Kanji* and *katakana*—and sometimes in Roman letters, which all Japanese children are taught too. Thus the high degree of literacy which the country can rightly boast of is not lightly achieved.

Furthermore, in relation to the modernization of the country and of social intercourse, there are other linguistic difficulties which have now largely been surmounted by the Japanese, but which may occasionally bring into prominence social divisions as irksome as those marked by color or class accent in the United States or Britain. These divisions are not in Japan primarily matters of accent (which may, however, be the subject of pleasantry). They can turn on the style of expression. Older people are much more formal in periphrasis or paraphrase; young people are more direct, if not blunt. They may use familiar forms, and address each other directly by name, extending that familiarity to older people in a way that scandalizes elders who have never called even their husbands by his personal name. Then again, men and women used different ways of talking. A male friend of mine learned Japanese well from a nurse, but caused much amusement by talking perfectly good Japanese with a color reflecting femininity at that social level. These are but a few of the complications caused by technological and social transformation. The advertisements' familiar tones remind people that they are much the same, especially in consuming the commodities offered (for they use familiar forms as they do in Italy or Germany, but not in France!); yet domestic conversation may be full of reminders of differences—if not of conflict. Then all the more credit to the Japanese for their modern society!

The use of education for deliberate planning is another aspect of Japanese experience which the student of societies in transformation must take account of. The limitations of planning and its pitfalls; the dangers of planning, especially when put to questionable use; the relation between central government planning and local or decentralized administration; the questions of freedom and independence on the one hand, as against voluntary cooperation, commitment, and morality on the other; questions of merit or of talent as distinct from family privilege; questions of a "purely liberal education" as against a form of schooling which is in some ways linked with life—all these many considerations affecting educational decision in many parts of the world are seen in the microcosm of Japan. The very isolation and special idiom of Japanese civilization make the example almost like an isolated experiment. At the same time, despite the distance from Europe and the United States and the somewhat alien features so often discoverable in the ideals and practices of the Japanese, the common human concern which the Japanese share with us are in the very forefront of our interest.

The use of a Western device, namely the schools as developed in Europe and the United States, is being widely invoked in the latter half of our present century to fulfill not only the industrial and commercial purposes of the industrial revolution but the fulfillment of its social logic. These are interests of deeply important significance for the whole of mankind. The impressive commitment of Japanese educators and administrators, and of the Japanese people as a whole, to the continuing process of education is praiseworthy in the extreme. No other country can excel the zest of this ancient civilization's inheritors for the full evolution of human talent and enterprise, with all the latest devices which our own experience and theirs can reveal to them. Last of all, at the risk of overemphasizing the case, it is important for us who are not Asians to realize the immense significance of Japan's example for the underdeveloped majority of mankind.

9

THE DYNAMICS
OF CONTEXT
AND PURPOSE

In thinking about other people's schools and children, we found ourselves involved with personal interest and sympathy. At the same time we have had serious, systematic questions to ask. Some of them have queried methods of organization; some have been concerned with the best subjects or interests to develop at school; some have asked if the schools are doing as complete a job as they might, for as many people as they are now easily able to serve; some have directly associated the schools with social or economic change; and some have raised fundamental questions about what man is intended to be.

The big point to notice is that we really have been asking questions like this—inevitably, because of our "fellow-feeling." We have not been looking out of our window at foreigners. This is no case of educational tourism, either. If we have for a few hours been able to get inside the skin of our colleagues or counterparts abroad, this is not simply a humanizing opportunity for us—though it certainly ought to be that.

The awakening of our interest has not been a passive experience; it has been all the more analytical because we have seen that our questions are living inquiries about matters of contemporary decision, worked over in actual life-involvement by real people who are increasingly businesslike in the apparatus they bring to bear on educational decision. This apparatus includes the time-honored establishments such as homes, and culture, and daily contacts; but it increasingly turns on the much more deliberately contrived machinery of government with its laws, tax support, planned priorities, and supply of teachers or other aids to education. At every point of acquaintance with other schools throughout this book we have been made aware not simply of a descriptive experience but of an increasingly penetrating analysis. We have indeed come to analyze ourselves.

Put in conventional textbook form, the items already covered in our survey include the following:

1. Education as a function of the home, or of society as a whole, or of religious or similar bodies.
2. Education as a social service somehow coordinated by public support and publicly guaranteed, or as state controlled.
3. Education on a centralized or decentralized pattern.
4. Education of an elite, or the education of a whole community.
5. Education by past prescription, or with an eye to the future.
6. Education by instruction and authority, or education by involvement and experience.
7. Education by a "pure, liberalizing essence," or vocational and civic linkage.
8. Coeducation.
9. Separated schools, or the "common school."
10. Self-differentiation in education, or imposed selection.
11. The structure and organization of the secondary school phase.
12. After-school education of many kinds.
13. Higher education, with its expansion and diversification.
14. The supply, training, and orientation of teachers.
15. The impact of self-teaching and relearning on the educative process, especially by television and other communications.
16. The planning of the "supply of education."
17. The economics of education.
18. Education for one time or place, or education with a world perspective.

If anyone needs to be reassured that we have not been idly watching the neighbors, or idly describing, the recollection of these points which have been brought to prominence throughout these pages will be a sufficient reminder. This remark introduces yet another point of the greatest importance for future comparative studies. There is no need whatever for a book to be formally didactic or "textbooky" in order to be informative—especially to that increasing band of adults or lively teachers who can stand having their academic interests brought into real contact with life. For centuries schools were thought to be the haven of the cleric, or the disagreeable exercise ground of an arduous youth, or perhaps even the refuge of those teachers who could never quite grow up enough to involve themselves in life outside. The day for all that kind of isolation has long since passed. Education is increasingly "outside." Schools themselves have their isolation broken down even during school time; as live institutions they are inseparable parts of the continuum of public involvement. They are mainly public institutions, performing a public service, with public employees officially approved and paid to assist in it, according to the decisions of parents and electors, and with the whole purpose of helping young people (or older ones) to live a full public life.

Let us be honest about it; the whole reason why schools are publicly provided or supported on such a scale is that any single part of formal education is now so intricately bound up with public considerations of funds, manpower, purpose—and indeed private possibilities for the still underprivileged (like children)—that only a public overview of what is involved could be fair all round. The most private areas need public guarantees for the supply of personal opportunity—in education especially. Our water supply is guaranteed; so (in varying degrees) is our opportunity to be healthy. Education is in the same category, only more so. We are no longer content to "let it happen." Therefore, although our whole upbringing and educative experience continues to invest our lives quasi-automatically (like language), it is no longer left as a merely casual process but is deliberately contrived. In our own private area of suburban comfort we may feel that our family is self-sufficient; yet a major economic crisis in the nation, or the outbreak of war in some distant delta, reminds us otherwise. So it is with education. We in the better educated groups are (so to speak) "suburban" to most of our fellow-countrymen; all of us in the favored nations are "suburban" to the rest of mankind. Neither our economy nor our social structure is isolatable from the rest.

Thus we come back to our reason for comparative surveys—first to inform ourselves, then to enlighten our current domestic decisions, and finally to analyze more deeply those specifically professional problems which exercise teachers, students, administrators, and now the highest level of national policy-makers. There was a time when comparative studies were "something for teachers"—or indeed just "something for students"; and there are regrettably a few professors left who behave as though that were still the case. Comparative studies must certainly be scholarly, and based minutely upon accurate information accurately correlated; but nowadays they must inevitably be comparative studies alerted to the dynamic of change and the necessity for conscious direction-taking. In other words, comparative studies nowadays must be *studies with a purpose*. Otherwise they will be both irrelevant and inaccurate—because they miss the whole point of the comparison. The comparison is undertaken in order to reveal what it is that really adds up to education in any particular context complementary to our own area of decision. What is peculiar to a context or time? What kind of "factor" or tendency seems to transcend local or topical peculiarities? What significant *pointer to the future* can be discerned to guide our present decisions which are bound to influence our children and the neighbors for at least a generation ahead?

Some guidance for future comparative study in depth will be given in the concluding chapter of this book. In greater detail the technical and academic problems involved are pursued in my *Comparative Studies and Educational Decisions* (1967). Similar reflections were contained in my article on "The purpose of Comparative Education" in *Comparative Education* (June 1965). Just now we shall do better to leave technicalities on one side, and review the purposes and conclusions of the present book. We have seen that the various questions and anxieties affecting any one case study add up to something unique in that situation—a living complex as dynamic, yet as personal, as the relationships within any one family. The constituent persons and factors cannot be pulled apart without completely altering the context. Therefore educational decisions are mainly relative, because the institutions, practices and priorities relate to particular circumstances. This recognition should hearten us when we decide to change or modify our own institutions or priorities; but it will also warn us against piecemeal copying. We must always study the whole—in our domestic setting, as elsewhere. No one item, even if it looks the same, can be presumed to have the same essence or the same effect everywhere. After all, a gift of flowers may cause a reconciliation in one family, but a grave suspicion in the family next door.

Having said all this, and having by implication warned parents and educators against assuming that what works (or does not work) somewhere else will behave in exactly the same way for us, I feel bold enough to urge a careful, comparative study both of the whole educational complex of any family or community and of the various ingredients in that complex. It does help us to understand one woman a little if we have read, heard, or discovered something about the others. Our comparative study does not deny to that one woman her uniqueness and ultimate unpredictability. It may enable us to encourage, appreciate, or even correct her; at the worst it should enable us to see our problems in the true perspective of human affairs.

That is just what parents and teachers are increasingly doing. For centuries, and especially during the past hundred years or so, educators of all kinds have been trying to pick up hints and methods from their neighbors. But as time goes on they all become a little wiser. They stop copying; instead, they think out their local problems in the light of others' experiments, and they learn to see their own involvement in a somewhat more detached way. In fact, it does us nothing but good to see just how involved we are. Those who set up and administer school systems tend to suppose that by fiddling about with them (and leaving everything else alone) they can alter the world. They can indeed, but not always in a constructive and rounded way. Education and civilization are no more matters only for the school than health is a matter only for the clinic. The school is simply the instrument that society (that is, people) selects and perfects for a particular job in particular circumstances. The mistake of leaving it to the "experts" lies in the fact that no one view can include everything that is relevant; other people's complementary views may give a perspective. So it is when we think that *we* are experts, and that we know best; we usually are all the better for letting ourselves be judged (by implication) from outside. A school or family system is most successful precisely when it is exactly matched with its context. Comparisons help us to discern that context. In no case does the school exist as an absolute.

Each one of the experiments we see going on around us highlights some particular emergency. It may be that our own problems will stand out suddenly as in relief, or that our own methods will there seem cumbersome tools. Or perhaps the things that seem "natural" to us will be shown to need re-examination. Whatever else happens, we should be able to understand the basic human problems with the sympathy that comes of having worked them over with those most immediately involved, instead of knowing only about "issues" as though they were lifeless statistics from some dreary book.

The answer to "How much or how little can the schools undertake as their job?" is conditioned entirely by the background in each case. We have seen that it can depend critically upon questions of housekeeping, that is, of national finances in relation to the many needs to be satisfied. Sometimes our answer may be determined by political objectives, like the education of an electorate or the emancipation of women or Negroes. In this last connection we are reminded that the background of social psychology is an important factor in determining

educational readiness. Fictions and obsessions can, through their practical results, become facts to reckon with. Technological changes, too,
are full of vital influence on social relationships and on school objectives. In depressed countries they tell policy makers what to seek
out first, and whom to educate; in the United States they entail the
problem of how to use up material abundance to the best advantage.
Finally, in addition to considerations of budgeting, politics, social cli-
mates, and technology, we now find we must give careful thought to
our neighbors—international as well as domestic.

This all sounds very solemn, and it is desperately important. Conscious schooling must be brought up to date for our children's happiness; but we also need to take account of very many influences that
school us quite as much as our lessons. Suggestions reaching us around
school and after it must be reckoned with and seriously studied; they
may fulfill school influences or contradict them. It will pay us to be on
the lookout for educational pressures in unsuspected places. Let us
compare police notices in Germany and Austria with those in Britain
and in the United States. In the German-speaking countries we are
simply told that something is *polizeilich verboten*—that sounds much
more abrupt than saying it is forbidden by the police, and it is all the
information you get. It is like saying, "Don't do it, or else!" In Britain
the form will probably be like this: "Passengers are requested to . . ."
(perhaps even "not to . . ."), followed by an explanation. The notice
will end: "By Order of the Police." In the United States the typical
notice runs: "$200 fine for dumping trash on the highway." It threatens
people; it assumes that people will defy the threat; and it indicates the
citizen's most sensitive point. It is easy to visualize the whole hit-and-
run drama, with states' rights and all that. These little notices are important chapters in any child's political education.

Such pleasant fancies could lead on to the sober reflections of scholarship if we permitted them. We need to do no more than notice that the
motives of authority and fear in Germany gave rise to Hitler and his
pogroms. In Britain the emphasis on responsible self-regulation, on
the whole, has in one way or another contributed to the tradition of
orderly dissent, of evolutionary statesmanship, and of personal freedom. When visitors say that the British police are "just wonderful,"
they might stop to wonder how that has come about. (Incidentally,
British visitors often report that the police in many American cities
are also exceedingly helpful.) Gracious officials both recognize that
their public is cooperative and teach them to be more so.

All kinds of daydreams could be indulged in; but there is no time for
more than a few selected at random. If boys and girls play happily
together and go to school together, this simple fact is the best of all

lessons in equality of personal worth without identity. If husbands do household chores and are willing not only to bathe the baby but to change its diapers when necessary, this again is a potential lesson in mutual regard between the marriage partners. If there is real personal appreciation, that in turn contributes subtly to more intimate felicity. So we pass on to realize why Robert Burns described the domesticity of raising a family as "the true pathos and sublime" of human life. The great passions and the rare perceptions of the most inspired poets are shared through actions around the kitchen sink—not only through black-and-white pages in the ivory tower. On the other hand, modern woman would not be what she is without the philosophic deliberations of the "highbrows." In education and culture no influence exists alone.

Sometimes educative situations like the one described above may be considered to have universal force. Others are more local and temporary, even to the extent that they are questionable in the very places where they occur. In England the importance attached to accent is exaggerated beyond all reason, as is the value of a certain poise and mannerisms. However, the fact that these tricks can be learned, and learned by increasing numbers, is in some respects an emancipating factor although it is repressive in other ways. It also indicates, no matter how ridiculously, a very real regard for education and urbanity. William of Wykeham was not altogether wide of the mark in declaring that "Manners makyth man." Behind all the frippery and folly there lies a regard for quality and values. Britain will gain if new vehicles for this appreciation can be devised, especially if any new teaching system embodies a real recognition of other men's essential worth.

In case anyone supposes that Britain has a monopoly of amusing folly among the English-speaking communities, we may note that in the United States a professor visiting a strange university needs to be very smartly dressed if he is to get a proper intellectual and material reception. Just as Americans usually ask "How big?", "How many?", and "How long?" when they visit European universities (and these are the last questions that the natives expect to hear), so they tend to think that a professor who looks like a rag bag must be a man of no significance. He evidently cannot be a "big" man, and is, therefore, hard to recognize as "important" (a dangerously favorite word in a democracy). By way of contrast, such a human scarecrow might be regarded with awe in Europe, and people would feel that he must be very distinguished. Quality counts, not dollars or productivity.

It is subtleties of this sort, so hard to pin down, that teach values and determine what the schools should or may not do. Though these influences are part of the structure of national character, they are neither unalterable nor fundamentally associated with any lasting ethical criteria. They can, therefore, be modified with the times. We have remarked that the Danes, once considered by their own spokesmen to be very boorish, and feared in centuries past as the fiends of the North Sea, are now a most highly civilized and gentle people. The once crude English have been criticized for being elegant "stuffed shirts." "Merrie England" later became a land where pleasures were taken sadly, and was the home of that aloof arrogance called *la morgue anglaise.* In postwar decades Americans have criticized British youth for being wildly licentious, however, perhaps in reaction to previous humbugs. Britons themselves are aghast at such unfairness, and believe that if there is any truth in these allegations, all must be blamed on the Puritan republic of which Cromwell was the Lord Protector. (There is strong justification for this view.) The main point to notice is that national character and normative institutions can be changed by conscious or unconscious reconstruction.

The most conspicuous changes in recent educational history are those which occurred in Japan during the past hundred years. The Japan of *Madame Butterfly* and the samurai was transformed in about 70 years into a powerful, industrialized nation that could challenge the most highly developed country on earth, and come within sight of defeating it. Japan is now faced with a critical choice for her future, and rational planning no less than the socioeconomic criteria already referred to will largely affect her decision.

Not all changes are planned, however, and many of those that are turn out unexpectedly. After World War II the United States was in a position of imperial responsibility quite unfamiliar to American political thinking, but conspicuous enough for some nations to accuse America of "economic colonialism." No one in Western Europe or North America soberly believes that the United States government is imperialistic in this or any sense, no matter what some individual Americans or corporations may dream of. For our purpose it is important to see, however, that a position of world hegemony has been achieved because of America's technological success combined with external accidents, and that this combination of circumstances has very considerably reshaped the educative context of American life. It is certainly in a very different environment from that of the "little red schoolhouse" and the congregational meetings of old New England. In such circumstances there is usually a great time lag before the formal school system catches up with the true facts of life. Quite apart from human frailty and the legendary other-worldliness of many teachers, everyone's romantic attachment to old traditions hampers a realistic readjustment. People feel they should be loyal to something, or they feel guilty about abandoning their position. Yet abandoning the position may be the very thing that a latter-day "life adjustment" and an imaginatively "child-centered" education now require of parents and teachers.

When people really do readjust themselves in order to make the most of some new opportunity, they may find themselves transformed out of all true likeness. Sometimes the results may differ strangely from the original intention. Let us take an example very familiar to Americans. It is now recognized that the majority of the settlers who pushed out into the fertile black crescent of Southern cotton country were no gentlemen in any sense. Like any other frontiersmen, they worked and fought furiously to win land for their crops; and when the cotton was ready they worked themselves (and their few slaves, if they had any) to the bone in order to build up a plantation economy. Like the homespun and ruthless Lancashire manufacturers, these were hard men, and the struggle made them harder. Yet when they accumulated capital, they set themselves up like colonial grandees and were determined to outdo the older rich in external elegance. This did not make them cultivated, any more than the same process turned the Manchester laissez-faire mill owners into the old landed aristocracy. But it did make it possible for their wives, children, and grandchildren to claim gentility with some justice. They had been to school; they surrounded themselves with fine things; they copied all the outward signs of refinement and some of the inner ones. Their comfortable paternalism did not, however, extend to a full understanding of the term noblesse oblige, limited though that concept always was in Europe, especially in regard to human rights. Southern gentility was unaffected by the intellectual inquiry which humanized so many "gentlemen" in Europe. It certainly did not lead to a local Enlightenment on the French pattern, or to a regermination of the humanitarian republicanism that enthused the Virginian gentlemen half a century before.

To that extent, therefore, it was a fantasy. It has had pernicious results in so far as human rights are still extensively disregarded, not so much by the descendants of these Southern gentry as by that vast majority of Southerners whose ancestors never owned a slave and never rose above the social position of a rural "redneck." On the other hand, we must be very careful to give full credit to the positive and constructive aspects of the Southern legend. Now most Southern children in the United States strike the observer as being even better poised than the average American child, though their ancestors not too long ago were of the humblest order. There is a graciousness in their relationship with other white people that is truly praiseworthy; and if intellectual standards are still markedly lower than in the North, that is perhaps attributable to the economic backwardness of the

South and to the many grave difficulties following the Civil War.
Urbanity and a wish for refinement are very real in the South—not
everywhere, of course, but on a wide enough scale to be a potential influence for immeasurable good in schools and homes when once Southerners see more clearly that their "peculiar institution" is still their own
worst enemy. The elegance of Natchez need not be a hollow façade; it
could transfigure American education in these latter days when all can
aspire to be ladies and gentlemen. A myth passionately believed in can
be a mainspring for reality. Even a backward-looking legend can be
made to contribute some elements of progress to the future.

The very fact that the great majority of Americans everywhere claim
to be of the middle class brings us to another illustration of formative
influences that might not be given full recognition by professional educators. The United States is without equal in the development of technology for mass production. As we have already seen, the standard of
consumption is higher there than in any other country, though the
American situation is matched in parts of Canada and a few other
countries where the same system is fast developing. Material abundance does not of itself refine humane perceptions; indeed it may do the
opposite. Yet Yankee productivity has made slavery and the drudgery
of human muscle-power unnecessary. This is potentially a releasing influence of great importance. It can free people for other things that are
traditionally supposed to be liberalizing, not just for eating, drinking
and making merry (though we ought not to forget that these have often
been the concomitants of the arts throughout the ages). Above all, the
cheap and easy flow of goods makes it possible for nearly everyone
earning a reasonable wage to look like a lady or a gentleman. This is
perhaps the beginning of thinking of one's dignity, and of cherishing
aspirations. The mere accumulation of material objects will, given luck
and proper education, eventually introduce questions of quality. Therefore the conveyor belt and the department store are potential instruments of education in so far as they provide the worker with material
adjuncts to fuller living and may help his wife to widen her horizon with
their products.

They do not do this on their own, however. Mere mechanization,
even mere consumption, may produce wage slaves and dupes for the
advertiser or expert. There is plenty of evidence that they do, and
there is no need to go to communist countries to see the tendency at
work. What transforms a negative situation into a positive movement
toward good is the precious ingredient of *value and preference*. It
may be that the first preference is for what is "bigger and better," or
for what is "important," or what is "modern"; but any society that
has retained some sense of values will reveal at least some citizens

thinking about what matters *in the long run*. People are free to do this just because they are emancipated from an urgent preoccupation with safety and livelihood for today. Being relaxed, they may actually be open to ideas as well as values; but as ideas are always likely to be disturbing, men must feel reasonably secure before they will freely entertain them. Banishing real want and fundamental anxieties has always been a prime condition of civilized life. In the past it has always been thought that "culture" depended on the existence of a leisured class, and in primitive technologies it usually has. Nowadays the *nouveaux riches* of a highly mechanized society like that in the United States include the majority of the population. With some ingenuity on the part of those concerned with public education (not just school people), the population of such a country can become increasingly sensitive to the fine and lasting products of human ingenuity.

There is some evidence that this is happening, particularly as a result of adult experience rather than of formal schooling. More and more people demand high fidelity recordings, for example, with perfect reproduction of the recorded sound. This is just a fad, of course; yet in order to play with these toys their owners listen to the masterpieces of chamber music and the great symphonies. They actually listen to prose and verse readings too. It seems likely that a moderate connoisseur of good music today has a vaster range of great compositions and first-class performances at his command than many a composer in times past. The possession of a "hi-fi" apparatus is a long way from being a participant in a string ensemble; but it is a modest step on the way there, and it is a gesture of identification with the humanizing tradition of sensibility. American orchestras are now increasingly made up of American musicians; and American composers and artists and poets increasingly claim world respect. None of these achievements are themselves factory made; nor do they come from believing that any kind of activity is equally worthy; but they have been made possible because those who enjoy them are materially emancipated from farm drudgery and the preindustrialization type of manual labor.

With the spread of modern industrialization over a great part of the world, many more people will claim for themselves those things that were once the exclusive privileges for "ladies" and "gentlemen." The way to the cultivation of civic and personal excellence is often devious and bizarre, however. The descendants of the rough and anti-intellectual frontiersman are now entitled to be genuine students in universities; but it is ironical that common parlance so often refers to them even during their university experience as "school kids." They have reached out for Olympus; they are relegated to the nursery. This is one consequence of standardization and of overlooking differences in

quality. The typical American, whose grandparents can perhaps re-
call very hard days and still harder traditions, is very tolerant and
gentle. By an odd quirk of history it was reported, in 1957, that the
sales of toilet articles for males slightly exceeded those for females in
the United States. This news item does not prove a regard for the
higher values; but it does indicate a progression in some kinds of sensibility, and it does suggest that that progression is on a nationwide
front. Once it is admitted that some things matter more than others, a
most significant step has been made in esthetics or elementary philosophy. It should not dishearten the culture-conscious unduly if their
neighbors' advance seems too little or clumsy. Nor should the established intellectual aristocrat feel too smug if the new beneficiaries of
social advance seem materialistic and vulgar; they think of good living
instead of "the good life" simply because they have so long been neglected and starved of humanizing opportunity. All too often it has been
the insensibility of the aristocrat that has caused that state of affairs;
and if it has not been heartlessness, it has been the technological system
that benefited the former elite at great human expense. There is no
need for that now. It has become technologically possible for the first
time for the mass of mankind to claim the Aristotelian "equal consideration in equal circumstances."

Therefore it is only likely that the schooling and aspirations of the
"new men" (and women) will seem grievously proletarian and vulgar
to the guardians of many countries' culture. That does not matter; it
has always been the case. Most of our present ruling classes were vulgar
a century ago. Some of the most aristocratic families in Britain were
vulgar parvenus when Elizabeth I was queen. Christianity first took
root in Rome as a vulgar faith flourishing among the soldiers and trade
organizations (*sodalitates*). History decides what is vulgar; it also decides what is merely absurd. Culture is not lace at the cuffs, peri-
wigs, and so on; it is an alert and sensitive adjustment to the problems
of working and playing with other people—or simply of tolerating
them.

Consequently, those who feel most concerned about educational
advance should exercise themselves in tolerance and patience. We
cannot expect all to have the same methods of growing up and
being refined in humanity. Neither can we expect that all nations
will choose the same industrial and social methods as Victorian England or present-day New York. One thing seems certain: factual learning, value-learning, and the development of responsible human dignity
will become ever more closely associated with jobs and vocational
training. This is a truth that very few educators have so far admitted;
still fewer have attempted to put it into practice. If they have, they

have related it only to what happens in juvenile schooling; whereas job experience and family experience, and the experience that comes from social and political participation, are the most potent influences in the long run. The totalitarian states have here seized their advantage; the liberal democracies have done little even in the way of realistically studying the context of education—a living mesh that extends through society and endures throughout life.

Moreover, we go on thinking that the schools we now know are "schools" in some absolute sense, and we make rules and philosophies for them as unchanging as the laws of the Medes and Persians. Most popular thought about schools and scholars ignores the fact that the technological and social context has radically changed, and will change further. Children now come to their teachers from a wider range of homes, and they go out again to a wider range of jobs. Home backgrounds do not reinforce schools' influences in quite the way they did a generation or two ago; nor do society and industry. Therefore the schools will have to do other things for the children. It may well be necessary to look more closely at influences working on adults. Advertisers do. So do mob politicians and all kinds of quacks. If we affect to ignore adults' learning situations we do not just "leave it to them"; we miseducate them by a void, or we turn them over to the tender mercies of "subliminal" exploiters and the like. These considerations add up to one illustration of the universal problem of adjusting homes and schools to fit social change. Never in human history has this been so rapid or so radical as in our day. Tomorrow the scope and speed of change will be greater. We have no need to fear change or fluidity, provided we face up to our opportunities. There is no sense in trying to halt change. The advantages of the Industrial Revolution are now being *socially* applied—thus transforming every relationship. We must, however, take a positive hand in shaping the future, not simply let it happen to us.[1]

There is plenty of evidence that many nations have already seen that technological change cannot be left to chance. As long ago as the French Revolution, French educators established polytechnics, advanced institutes, and the "central schools" to bring their country up to date. Germany's school development in the nineteenth century was intended to promote technical advance. Switzerland is a country whose educational administration is highly decentralized; but there is a famous federal university of technology, and the technical side of education is carefully encouraged by the central government. Both in pre-

---

[1] For some indications of what may be involved, and an account of other people's experiments, see my *Education and Social Change* (1966).

Soviet Russia and under Stalin the central government promoted technical education extensively, being content to leave other aspects to local arrangements. Wherever we look, even in the preeminently decentralized United States, we see central encouragement of practical and technical instruction. A century ago this was as true as it is today—though on a smaller scale. Yet everyone seems to pretend that technical instruction is something apart from personal "education," which in many cases the central government of democratic countries is well-nigh forbidden to touch. Far be it from me to recommend more centralization or uniformity; yet it does seem necessary to point out (a) that industrial or commercial training and activity *are* profoundly educative for better or worse and, therefore, cannot be divorced from "education"; (b) that modern industrialized life has its own tremendous drive toward centralization and uniformity in any private enterprise or consumer relationship; (c) that technical advance in any country depends on an efficient preparation not just of the top men and women but of all the citizens; and (d) that no system of schooling, or of rearing children at home, can be considered any longer as a little local game. The world is its criterion. The next generation will be its justification.

What is this next generation we so calmly talk about? And what will its living conditions be like? Will words like "school," "education," and "public opinion" have either the same dimensions or the same perspectives even in our own countries? We cannot accurately answer these questions separately; it is harder still to reckon them together. Yet that is precisely what we must do if we are to make any sense at all of our plans for our own families. Let us try and envisage some of the material changes affecting our decisions.

Since about 1925, more than 1,300,000,000 people have been added to the human race. That is roughly 60 percent increase in the whole human family. About three quarters of these were born in Asian, African, and Latin American countries—the very places least able to cope with rapid population growth in any way, least of all in terms of conventional schooling. When we consider that this population *increase* in less developed countries is more than double the entire population of the USA and the USSR put together, it becomes strikingly obvious that ancient answers to educational problems, based upon manageable numbers of children and an adequate supply of teachers fulfilling time-honored roles, are just as socially outmoded (if not pathetic) as Bostonian Brahminism or Victorian caste punctilio. For all the newcomers mentioned in this paragraph, education is an emergency need, just as if they were victims of some natural cataclysm or wartime refugees. For them, therefore, education cannot wait. It is a bread-and-butter business; it *is* the means to food and drink in the most basic terms. Teachers' textbook concepts and pious priorities are impatiently swept aside by those who see education as food, living standards, emancipation, and the factory for the future.

The state, and only the state, can provide education on such a vast scale in the developing countries. How sharp a contrast this is to our own assumptions is obvious from two historical facts: Britain did not even have anything as "official" as local school boards until 1870, and did not devise an all-inclusive public system of school organization until 1902. Respect for existing institutions and prerogatives (both educational and governmental) has everywhere hindered recognition of the patent fact that in well developed countries, too, education is already the main business of local government. In very many cases it now accounts for more than half of the local expenditure. Plain arithmetic is making it increasingly clear that reliance on local resources, though sometimes beneficial and efficient, can never guarantee over-all efficiency—much less quality. Apart from the increasing concern of all major states to improve their technological efficiency for strategic and market purposes, the very mechanics and mobility of modern living make any local educational deficiencies as great a risk to *national* well-being as is malnutrition or dietetic imperfection to one's health. Education is, therefore, a national defense, to be nationally safeguarded. Not enough is done if the nation is lucky enough to have top-level scientists, research departments, and cultural pinnacles, for the simple reason that the ordinary business of the community can not now be done unless school-induced proficiency is characteristic of all activities.

The totalitarian countries seem, at first sight, to be exempt from some of the special difficulties inherent in a more freely organized system. It looks as though orders can be sent down from above, in accordance with their governing philosophy or party handbook rules. Of course, there is always the temptation for those basically reorganizing a country's way of life to try to act in this way. But sooner or later the most tightly organized of countries comes to recognize the impossibility of ensuring automatic compliance—even in the daily fulfillment of production quotas and the like. Therefore the USSR, having long set its face against training in business administration (for fear of a "technocracy" not easily contained within official planning or ideology), has acknowledged long-standing embarrassments by deciding to found a central academy of business administration in 1962 and extended this training downward to all appropriate levels. That is to say, party prescription and the drive of the enthusiastic activist will no longer be a substitute for the expert; expertise must evidently be

devolved downwards. The present is the era of the *trained* person in
all countries.

It was once supposed that an "educated" person was equipped for
all contingencies; and by the word "educated" people meant traditionally schooled in certain forms of juvenile exercise. Severe doubts have
been cast on this notion in the most conservative countries. College
courses in the United States (not so conservative) are traditionally
"liberal"; yet the great majority of first degrees are now vocational,
and the tendency toward greater purposefulness in many studies is accelerating. Those countries which still have a somewhat protracted
"general" education are expanding, and at the same time intensifying,
their applied "further" education in one way or another. There is a
worldwide search for talent. Moreover, the sheer amount of knowledge
to be acquired and the extremely rapid change overtaking all industries
necessitate not just a system of preparatory training at one period in
life, but one which brings back *mature* learners again and again to re-
consider jobs and human relationships in a never ending reappraisal.
This is all done in the name of on-the-job efficiency, of course; but, for
the reasons already given, it is more widely re-educative for better or
worse. And, in all of it, it is impossible to think any longer of an isolated
operative down below or an Olympian pinnacle of "really educated"
demigods. The whole enterprise is either skilled or ineffective together.

Not only at the national level, therefore, or at the top directive level
of the great corporations, but in ordinary and uncountable daily situations, it is increasingly true that education is a *business* to be efficiently
organized. Life's ordinary daily business is not merely bristling with
occasions for adding this item of knowledge or acquiring that skill; it
also provides a whole vista of perspectives on life, a whole range of
occasions for assuming or declining responsibility, and (because modern
production and consumption are so "rationalized") a network of common concerns, common techniques, common language, common im-
ages, and common tastes. This kind of corporate habituation can be
evocative or it can lead to automatism. It can be commercially exploited for consumer entertainment, advertising, and similar purposes
not primarily intended to be educative. But there can be no escaping
from the truth that increasingly centralized organization is taking
place. Our only uncertainty is about its purpose, or about who does
the organizing.

Living as they do in the society that is technologically most advanced (and, therefore, most elaborately organized), Americans have
long been extremely anxious about their own acculturation by forces
and requirements that are ostensibly not "cultural" or humane at all.
Some of the serious scholarship published in recent decades on this

and related problems by David Riesman, William H. Whyte, Vance
Packard, and Martin Mayer deserves the most earnest attention of
anyone alive to the phenomena of industrialization and urbanization.
These writers' penetrating analyses are none the less profound being
sometimes presented with that flair and zest that characterize the best
of North American writing. Unfortunately, some professional "educators" are still so ignorant that they dismiss this kind of scholarship,
or completely miss its implications for their profession. It is very often
quite outside formal education that the most significantly formative
(that is, educative) influences are to be found.[2]

In the communist countries, too, the centralizing and other implications of industrialization for education have long been recognized,
theorized about, and given an ideological justification. The entire
school system and the still more formative paracurricular activities are
designed to contain all perceptions and endeavors within the purpose
of the "collective." Within this frame of reference, they are capable
of imparting conviction, securing devotion and contentment, and stimulating enterprise. Therefore the huge underdeveloped part of mankind is fascinated, both by the manifest achievements of the communist world and still more by its persistent and glossy publicity. Communist countries, whatever their drawbacks, do not represent themselves externally in contradictory terms. They do not export trashy
television programs or hideous film portraits of themselves to be endlessly relayed over the world's networks.

Outside the major countries of the western world, as well as in them,
the efficient organization of our "entertainment" business ensures that
a very colossus of communication emphasizes, through exported film
and TV, just those aspects of our life that have least in common with
civilization, religion, or humane aspirations. There is not a corner of
the world into which this portrayal is not thrust, and into which the
alternative interpretation of the nature of man fostered in the communist world does not equally push to underline our message. The
receptive audience is already half of mankind, and will soon be more
than that. The children being born in those countries are our children's
contemporaries. They are the "next generation" we asked about a few
pages ago. Their parents or national leaders are comparing systems,
making critical decisions, and, above all, are building up educational
programs without any hindrances or inhibitions. What can the little
red schoolhouse or the little old school board do about that?

It is questions like this that sharpen our realization that, within a

---

[2] Dr. S. de Grazia's *Of Time, Work and Leisure.* New York: Twentieth Century Fund,
1962, gives remarkable documentation on these.

lifetime, education has passed from being a domestic or parochial matter to a worldwide public concern that must have international perspectives if it is to be valid at all. The role, scope, and effect of the school are changing like a chameleon under our eyes, taking on new color to suit the background. Let us consider but two factors which must affect our reappraisal: television and the "youth problem."

In 1961, public television programs were just twenty-five years old. It is already impossible to think of amusements, advertising, or even teaching without them. In many countries a great number of children (not to speak of adults) daily spend the equivalent of half a school day looking at the television programs or at the comic papers associated with them. I am not suggesting that the effects are necessarily deleterious, but merely comparing the relative evocation of showy television and of a rather dull school. Moreover, where television is not of itself harmful in any way, it undoubtedly portrays life from another angle than the school. Its popularity is undoubted. In Britain, in 1951, only five percent of households had television sets; in 1961, well over 90 percent of schoolchildren had sets at home. In Italy, illiteracy is rapidly being reduced by nightly TV lessons—during which time no alternative program is shown! All over the less developed part of the world, television's effect is like a bombshell. And, when we also consider that in those very countries industry and commerce make unquenchable demands on the well-schooled minority from whom potential teachers might otherwise be recruited, it is obvious that the functions of teaching must be largely transferred to other agencies, and that the whole relationship of the person taught to these new educative agencies must be different from anything we know.

In these unfamiliar circumstances (which, in a contracting world, are already certain to be part of our children's circumstances) what rules can we lay down? The answer clearly is that we cannot lay down *any* rules with finality, if only because of our own ignorance. Vast new nations have come into being since the first edition of this book, but there is flux at home too. Time and again, for example, high-powered government surveys in a number of countries have tried to assess the number of scientists required in a given period of time. Time and again they have underestimated because they have ignored: (a) increasing government demands; (b) unrecognized but already emergent needs; (c) the growth of new enterprises to cope with those needs; and (d) structural changes both in existing enterprises themselves and in the personnel of their managements. Sitting at home, or (what is much the same thing) holding a conference with obsolescent terms of reference, we cannot see the world changing about us. The older and the more respectable we become—that is to say, the more like parents and teachers we become— the less easy it is for us to envisage the pressures and priorities of our children's world-to-be. Some comparative study of other contexts, if undertaken as objectively as possible, may help. But, by the same token, these studies dispel any idea that educational prescriptions cherished by us have some cannonical permanence.

This consideration of our foreignness in our children's world brings us directly to the "youth problem"—too big a problem by far for us to do more than acknowledge here. From time immemorial, every family has had something of a "youth problem" when the children became old enough to question parental authority. Yet that very challenge so familiar to us is mitigated in more static societies—in societies with "extended" families, in social systems with graduated initiation rituals and in places where early marriage and economic self-sufficiency are usual. The "youth problem" we face is more acute because of the absence from our midst of these bypasses to conflict with parental authority. Technological and social changes, too, have widened the gap between the generations, if only because of different worlds of awareness and different planes of expectation.

Furthermore, the extended period of dependence necessitated by our children's protracted schooling and the postponement of "fully proficient" status has brought about a completely unprecedented patchwork of maturity here, contrasting with juvenility there, all together in the same person's different social relationships. (This is very often accentuated by the mechanisms of educational selection.) But, at bottom, our "youth problem" is the same as that the world over— youth's possession of powers and perceptions that cannot be fully acknowledged and utilized.

To an unprecedented extent, today's "social migrants," or indeed whole emergent populations, also find themselves in a comparable position, introducing many educational problems. But at this point it is more convenient for us to consider the relatively clear-cut problem of our own youth. We have still to devise an effective and over-all provision for our young people, genuinely taxing their undoubted powers, improving their competence, and strengthening constructive responsibility, while keeping them at the long business of training for work, parenthood, and life. It therefore seems quite clear that the whole concept of "once and for all" schooling as a juvenile, preparatory, and sheltered experience under neatly recognizable agencies needs radical rethinking. The world is at present a workshop for the elaboration and testing of suitable expedients, involving many things much bigger than a dwindling supply of teachers and relatively diminishing scholastic influences.

These world experiments belong to us, if we are wise. Like everyone else, we have more to do than blandly observe our neighbors. Setting our own house in order entails at least the following new kinds of provision: arrangements to supplement continuously the cultural background of pupils and students; supplementation and correction of the shortcomings of specialists; preparation for new types of jobs (with new human relationships in all jobs, and a new international orientation); and some substitute for the largely broken-down continuity of family occupation or of "sense of context." These and many other needs can be studied at length, but our basic need immediately is to recognize that every problem or experiment surveyed is indirectly an examination of ourselves.

We began by looking over the garden fence. Nothing ever really happens entirely in our own back yard any more. The smoke from our barbecue is grievously tantalizing to the hungry; alternatively, the fumes of our garbage fire make our neighbor's life a misery. In these times when a day's flying takes us halfway around the world, and when radio, films, and press foreshorten time and distance, it is obvious that anyone's answers to the old questions must be different. The aims are essentially the same—the offering of a full and happy life to our children. Other people's children want that too. Unless they get it, in a way that suits their readiness and idioms, our own children's prospects will be impaired. Educational opportunity, like public health, is something we cannot afford to stint. Thinking very seriously about other people's children may be ultimately the best service we can offer our own.

required the provision of a new kind of book. "Area studies" are now respectable on the campuses of universities and in governmental departments throughout the world. So are many other kinds of "developmental studies." In each of these educational study is a necessary ingredient. No consideration of social change, economic orientation, or the deployment of manpower can be separated from an awareness of the educational background, the educational complications of the present, and the educational devices which can be employed for the future.

When considering educational development for the future, we naturally think first of the formal institutions. However, Ruth Benedict and other anthropologists long ago made it clear that it is the totality of environmental influences which are at work to make up "education." The introduction of an alarm clock or any other piece of apparatus disturbs that environment to some degree. In present reckoning for the future the whole enterprise must be envisaged together, especially as in many countries technological and social transformation is completely recasting the whole structure of human relationships. That is to say, the educational matrix is transformed by whatever we do in the economic or social sphere. Any conscious reshaping of the future will, therefore, have to take account of all the continuing re-education which will develop in consequence of our action—even if that is only the incorporation of more arithmetic or a little bit of technology in some part of the formal educational system.

In order to understand more clearly the direction in which our further studies may take us, let us see what has happened. It is perfectly true that there has been a great flowering of interest in Comparative Education proper, especially in teachers' colleges. In several of these, approximately half of all the students will choose courses in Comparative Education if they are given the opportunity. The departments of Comparative Education already established are sometimes hard pressed to provide for other colleges' lecturers the opportunity for initiation which they require to develop the subject. In consequence of this, the already existing departments of Comparative Education have tended to blinker themselves a little and concentrate only on teachers' requirements. When they think of teachers, in fact, they often envisage only students who will one day be teachers, instead of those teachers who are now actually involved on the job. These are more and more concerned with the recasting of their school systems or answering some particular enquiry about a reform of method or orientation. Moreover, mainly because of the tendency for teachers to hide themselves away (even university teachers), such instructors do not effectively heed the great growth of comparative interest elsewhere. Clearly this is to be found in governments, and even in some major corporations. But if we confine our attention to the academic world itself we can see that there are Institutes of African Studies, or South East Asian Studies, or developmental studies generally in relation to hitherto underdeveloped countries on a great many campuses. Economists and sociologists, too, branch out into comparative interests. It is a matter of the utmost regret that so many of these sincere and well-informed scholars do not seriously consider calling in the services or comments of colleagues who profess an interest in Comparative Education properly so-called. Humility should make us ask ourselves why not. Can it be that the kind of studies cultivated under that name seem irrelevant to other students of society in change?

Even within colleges of education, or university departments devoted to educational study, there are research units hived off from Comparative Education departments—but conducting what we can only call well-established and well-informed comparative studies. Some of these relate to educational policy in general. Others are concerned with decision-making processes in which education is involved. Some are more specific, being related to the development of higher education or some branch of it, such as technological education. Gratifying though this evidence of a deepening and more systematized interest is, its separation from Comparative Education sometimes reflects on the trivial nature of many of the interests pursued by teachers of Comparative Education or their postgraduate students. Perhaps, too, we must throw some of the blame on to the kind of books which have been written to further the study of Comparative Education in the past. These often reflect only pedagogical interests, or theories, or the school structures themselves which professors have seen fit to "juxtapose," classify, or pigeonhole generally.

The general feeling about academic studies nowadays is that they should not be pigeonholed at all, but should be, so to speak, in the market place or closely linked with practical decisions of some form or another. There is no question of preaching to anybody or telling them what to do. Nor is there any question of commercializing academic activity. It is simply a matter of giving to any academic study, especially in a social science, its contextual trueness and a sense of ecological dynamics. It is, therefore, arguable that a good book on the dynamics of any educational context should also be intelligible and useful to students of social, political, or technological development in any area under review.

All this means that no study whatsoever can properly lose sight of the living context in relation to which that study is made. If, for the sake of specialization, it is decided to pick on some topic or "problem," then that problem in itself must be related to the ecological circumstances in which the problem is recognized. As we have seen elsewhere, words like "home," "teacher," "child," "mother," take on a different meaning from context to context or time to time.

The time has long passed when anyone could imagine educational "laws" as though they were the laws of the Medes and Persians, unchanged and relevant for all time. We know what has happened to the laws of the Medes and Persians. The speed, scope, and complexity of present changes makes the idea of any perennial law extremely questionable. The search for "predictive laws" is a piece of early nineteenth-century romanticism, revealing ignorance of recent thought and research in the social sciences.

It will help us to sort out our aims, and methods to be used, if we spell out for ourselves exactly what we are trying to do. Are we talking about students making a first acquaintance with Comparative Education? Are we talking to people who have had some initial training in this field of interest, or perhaps to practicing teachers whose actual experience has given them the same kind of insight? Are we mainly thinking about research students doing a thesis on Comparative Education? Or are we more concerned with a student in one of the social sciences (for example, sociology or economics), already well grounded in his own field, and ready to impinge on ours, for an area study or a developmental study of some kind? Or—as is increasingly the case—are we sitting down in conference with some expert body of colleagues drawn from a variety of disciplines, helping to plan either the whole of an educational system or some detail of it, such as "equivalence of qualifications?" If we do not specify exactly what level we are aiming at, we cannot be clear whether we are providing the basic information and conspectus of aims and methods for beginners, or some enrichment for people who have had the necessary initiation, or the more penetrating kind of analysis which can be broached immediately when dealing with cooperating specialists. Here the most striking example is the International Evaluation of Educational Attainment.

The present book is intended to serve the first two levels, mainly. However, it can also offer insights important to economists, sociologists, and planners who are very well versed in their own disciplines but lack *educational* insights into the country under consideration, and therefore miss some of its dynamics. That kind of analytical insight is introduced in a somewhat descriptive way in this book. Outside experts will thus use the same kind of information as the beginner, but they will use it in a different way. Therefore this book has been written not only to be an absolute beginning for the beginner, but also to provide a beginning of Comparative Education for people already well versed either in some different academic field or in the intensive study of one particular country.

At a stage beyond that introduction, readers are well advised to pass on to a closer, more detailed, contextual study of one whole country in the present crisis of change. In order to serve the growing body of comparative interests (including that outside departments of education), a wide range of books have dealt with education and social change in whole countries or whole cultural areas. In the bibliography which follows this chapter, reference is made to the books on *Society, Schools and Progress in Scandinavia* by Willis Dixon, *Society, Schools and Progress in France* by W. D. Halls, *Society, Schools and Progress in England* by George Baron, *Society, Schools and Progress in the USA,* and other books in the same series. In a fairly homogenous series like this, the comparative study which we are pursuing is facilitated by the similar arrangement of related books dealing with various topics in an orderly sequence. But any one country so studied by itself rewards the inquirer by showing, in intimate interconnection, the whole formal and informal apparatus of public life being used for educational development and decision. The inhabitants and rulers of those countries are establishing *their* priorities. They have an eye on ours. They are aware of their neighbors' developments. They are very often pursuing comparative studies continuously. Thus a concentration and deepening of interest beyond the scope of the present book's relatively short chapters makes a rewarding case study which is at the same time, by implication, comparative in its every line. In such a living context there is more continuous comparison than could ever take place in the anatomized examinations or lifeless bits and pieces which have occasionally been used for comparative studies in the past.

Let us think what we mean when we talk about "factors" or "problems." What kind of factors or problems? Are we shutting ourselves up in our study, or closeted with a few docile students who lap up every word for examination purposes? Or are we concerned to give them something that will be a leaven in their lives, and perhaps pass on in their daily contacts and, especially through their teaching, the kind of perspective which will help educational decisions in the future, thus keeping teachers closely in touch with those they are expected to serve? Let us suppose we are thinking mainly of a straightforward instructional relationship. The "factors" often referred to in textbooks of Comparative Education turn out on further examination to be mainly elements in the historical background, such as the churches and their influence, customs and habits of various kinds, languages and philosophical assumptions (which are also largely habitual) and so forth. In other words they are historical factors and *retrospective*.

A further group could be called "perpetual" factors or problems which continue to affect us today. Among these are problems of race, of rural and similar disadvantages, of women's education, and things of that sort. But if we stop to look at these a little more critically, we shall see that although there are constant problems, the expression of the problems, and the devices used to remedy them, turn upon their present involvement in a particular social context in our time, all complicated by the impact of ideas and social possibilities or devices from outside. In other words, whatever the continuity that is present within these problems or factors, the expression and solution of the problem is highly idiomatic to our time and to one particular context. That is to say, you cannot solve or even analyze any one of these problems in a purely theoretical or static way.

No human problem of this kind simply stays put. Nor is it isolated. Language problems may be bound up with ethnic differences, possibly recognizable by color also. They may be closely associated with a particular cultural pattern or religion. Very often they also have to do with economic circumstances, or questions of social access to human rights. That is to say, even the allegedly perpetual problems are so little constant that we deceive ourselves if we think we can run across the world pursuing one problem like color, language, or the status of women. International evidence must certainly be adduced in support of whatever we have to say, but in a sense the problem is not really one of language or of color; yet more often of human relationships in which an emblem such as color or language is used as the diagnostic instrument. The *real* question at issue in such circumstances is one of equality and access to all that makes human life enjoyable.

A great deal of rubbish is talked about "problems." Possibly because they fear of a properly dynamic or contextual study, some people think they can invent algebraic formulae or abstract rules which will be perpetually valid for the handling of any problems. But because so many words, ideas, and even institutions take on different values from context to context, the very "constants" to which these theoretical formulae are applied are not the same at all. As I have said elsewhere, the Roman Catholic church throughout the world has a uniform body of dogma and a nearly uniform body of ceremony; but the day-to-day activity and the educational significance of that Church vary very greatly from country to country; and so do the characteristics of Roman Catholics in such diverse cultures as the United States, Ireland, Italy, or Poland. Quakers and Catholics resemble each other far more in the United States than do the Catholics of the United States and the Catholics of Ireland. At any rate, that is true about their social and political ideas; and therefore their decisions about educational needs and objectives. That kind of "problem" is an imaginary one. In so far as there is any constant problem, its examination may be vitiated by imperfect knowledge of social and educational facts on the part of either the teacher or the student. The example quoted is but one of dozens which immediately spring to the mind.

The really urgent questions which exercise any student of Comparative Education at the present moment, are those which arise from our present over-all context and its transcendent problems. The greatest of these is the technological transformation of our way of life, and the sociological changes which ensue. These penetrate every detail of our thinking and planning or administration. Consequently questions are raised about school organization. Who provides the schools? For whom? For how long? For what purpose? With what kind of follow-on structure? Is there to be selection? If so, how? How is "secondary schooling" to be organized? Is there to be selection according to the criteria of the educational leaders and the curricula, or according to the children's self-differentiation, or according to the envisaged structure of society in which the children will live their lives and earn their daily bread? What is the nature and function of teaching? How far is straightforward teaching largely superseded by learning, or relearning? What is the relationship of the pupil in school to the young person he or she will soon be on the threshold of marriage and lifetime's career? How is higher education to be organized? Though each one of the above questions takes on a different complexion when it is asked in quite different contexts, because the answers given must always arise from the idiom of that time and place, nevertheless there are transcendent forces at work which make some comparison really worthwhile. What makes for comparability in these cases is not so much the past as the future. Clearly the implications for social and educational reorganization of the immense change of life overtaking us all throughout the world make comparison not merely profitable but necessary.

The sort of thing that makes it desirable to have as many children as possible sharing a common secondary school experience until, let us say, the age of 14 or 15 (or perhaps longer) is the changing nature of occupations and livelihoods. We know from social surveys throughout the world that, as industrialization develops, so more and more people take up careers in what we may call the "service" bracket of occupations. In other words, they are more and more "middle class," not only socially and economically speaking, but also in the nature of the work they do. The further countries advance, the less they rely on crude labor, or even skilled handicrafts; and the more they rely on the kind of preparation previously given in secondary schools. By this I mean a firm grounding in the mother tongue, mathematics, general science, foreign languages, and fuller social studies. In other words, the more likely it seems they will remain relatively unspecialized until at least early adolescence.

Of course, the spread of middle-class ideas and expectations in ordinary life well outside the schools, and with no apparent connection with the children's own livelihood, makes parents and the children themselves expect to enjoy the comfort and opportunities previously available only to the well-to-do. It is therefore very likely that they will expect middle-class opportunity in secondary school irrespective of what they know of the world around them. Insofar as this social aspiration is politically voiced, and brings pressure to bear on legislators, it is an influence affecting the nature of the common school and its likely adoption in one country after another. The whole point is that the decisions being made on behalf of the "middle school" or the comprehensive school in the instances given have little to do with questions posed and solved in purely pedagogical terms. They are inseparable from a close study of the immediate context. They also echo all the worldwide arguments put into people's mouths because of a similar kind of technological and social advance across the world. It is the transcendent nature of some of these questions which makes comparison possible. What makes comparative study necessary is the very fact that decisions must be urgently reached in a variety of significant contexts, rather than in one easily managed context.

My whole purpose in writing *World Perspectives in Education* was to pose just this kind of question: Who was to be educated; how it was to be done and in what kind of institutions; how the program was to be divided, and how followed by further and higher education. No attempt was made to give the answers, for that would be impossible. It is wrong to speak of "the" answers, because in each particular case a different complexion of answers will be advanced by the people most intimately involved, who have to make do with the schools, economic resources, teachers, and general state of readiness in which they find themselves.

Of course, the example of other countries shows what expedients they have adopted. It also shows what institutions, ideas, or working clues may possibly be transferable from one context to another, but also what is purely relevant to one set of circumstances. Thus comparative study does two things at the same time. It heavily underlines the relative nature of nearly all educational practices and decisions; at the same time it shows that some "factors" and "problems" bear a family likeness, even if they are not identical. In any case, it obviates the necessity for working over every experiment from the beginning, and in isolation. The present-day world is one in which isolation is totally impossible.

For guidance we do not look to some holy canon of educational scripture, nor to the expedients previously used in our own country for circumstances largely historic. We look at our neighbors, whose enquiries are proceeding in a fashion complementary to our own, and relate in a complementary way to our own endeavors. In any case, in future we shall have to act in concert. Whether we like it or not, we can hardly ignore the great experiments of other people. Western technology has transformed the world. The same technology as socially applied in an early twentieth-century way by the United States has transformed the thinking habits and aspirations of Europe. The aspiration of the Europeans and the Americans affect the whole world. But we have also to think about not only the USSR but the way things may go in China. These remarks must not be construed only as a strategic comment. It is a matter of social and educational organization.

In order to serve the kind of conspectus of problems just outlined, one might also consult the excellent work *Contemporary Education* by Cramer and Browne, which analyzes a parade of problems in a different way from my own book. Others of a more sociological kind undertake an environmental study of the influences at work on school organization and decisions. Some books deal with particular educational problems like *Access to Higher Education,* edited by Dr. Frank Bowles. Of a similar nature, in relation to a particular country, one may mention the Robbins Report on *Higher Education* in Britain, in 1963. Some deal with particular lines of interest such as, for example, *Tomorrow's Education* by Jean Capelle, which is mainly about reforming education in France, but is widely relevant to European problems of education. In this connection, one should also mention the several publications of the Council of Europe dealing with common trends and problems of European countries, or with teacher education in European countries, and so on. Of a similar nature is the series at present in preparation under the editorship of Professor A. Kazamias of the University of Wisconsin, which refers strongly to educational development. A quite new empirical approach, using social science techniques, marks the *International Study of Achievement in Mathematics* (1967).

Of somewhat different character is a book like *Communist Education,* edited by myself in 1963, which is intended to portray a particular genre from several points of view—philosophical, sociological, historical, and institutional. Dr. Nicholas Hans has two reflective books related to the study of communist education. More specialized are the works of Dr. Nicholas de Witt, and the American publishers of the

Journal of Soviet Education. This kind of comparative text is analytical and philosophical. It raises fundamental questions of principle. Even in books like these, however, one discerns very easily that the aims and purposes of communist education vary in their expression and implementation in the different countries which are governed by a communist regime.

Not too dissimilar are those books which deal with the problems of certain developing countries. The latter vary in their degree of advance and resources; but there is something that can be said generically with profit to many countries. Even in what look like single-area studies either regionally or qualitatively surveyed, there are again elements of comparison which can be profitably used to the benefit of each single country. UNESCO, DECD, and ITEP studies are examples. These are "problem surveys" of a somewhat different kind from the cultural studies mentioned in the preceding paragraph. They are on a larger scale; they are less transcendent in their coverage; but at the same time they deal with education and public planning. Again we see in this connection that a comparative study suited to modern times can hardly ever escape the close collaboration of several scholars working in different disciplines, contributing ideas and insights from rather different backgrounds. Each development study is, in a sense, a comparative-analytical study within its own area.

The further we proceed along this road, the more clearly we see that the walls once circumscribing a teacher's interest, or those of a student preparing to be a teacher, are being broken down. Items of interest can be disengaged for detailed study; but they can be no more genuinely isolated as theoretical abstractions than any doctor could pretend to study an organ outside an organism, or even that organism outside its ecological context. In other words, we more clearly recognize that any educational study is also a social study. As such, it offers a leaven of personal insight to the student who feels a bond with what is observed. For he knows that a community of insight and interest is as informative as it is prerequisite. Manifold complementary insights from many disciplines, and revealed by many methods, are essential parts of any modern survey.

Simply because the facts of human behavior and their causation are never simple—especially when we study cultures—no ancient prescription and no modern gimcrack formula will really help. To look for one is like seeking a latter-day philosopher's stone. It is all very well to talk about looking for major organizing ideas; what we have to beware of is premature pigeonholing and formalization. We must also beware of applying to the living sciences criteria of attainment and measurement which apply perhaps only to physical sciences. We can never forget that in dealing with human behavior we have already passed far beyond a merely biological order. Even in biology the methods appropriate to physics and chemistry are seldom really applicable, overlooking as they do the whole concept of ecology. In mankind we have also to consider the most significant feature of any ecology—namely man's impact on the environment, his attempts to control it, the symbolism with which he organizes it and *organizes his own perception of it.*

In other words we can never overlook the vital influence of education and cultural patterns even on the human being's perception of his environment, let alone his coming to grips with it in any reformative way. In terms of Comparative Education, this means that no professor or student can decide in advance what are the relevant data. Still less can he attempt to prescribe methods; for in this he is the receiver from the social sciences and from the evidence. As a contributor, he conversely communicates his awareness of the force of the social and educational matrix shaping human endeavors. This is the kind of dynamic which he is more aware of, in terms of contexts, cultural patterns, and the recurring climaxes of educational decisions.

Insofar as the scholar working in Comparative Education is a partner in educational guidance or decision, he is simply a partner with others. The areas of crucial decision are public, not academic. Insofar as academic guidance and scholarly data are supplied, the researcher in Comparative Education is a very responsible participant; but he is no more than that, for at this level of interest and commitment he is in a very different category from the didactic writer of a textbook or the teacher with his students.

Let us look back on the suggestions contained in this chapter and back to the Introduction. We saw that there are at least three levels of making an acquaintance with comparative studies. The first is that of *factual study* through books or in the field. This is never purely observational nor descriptive. It always introduces into the view, consciously or otherwise, some working hypothesis on the part of the observer. The more informed or enlightened the observer already is, the more likely he is to derive benefit from what is done or seen. The more sympathetic he is, and more deeply able to penetrate the emotional and cultural complex of the area under review, the more *accurate* as well as more meaningful is any objective observation he can achieve. Without this kind of a beginning no later form of analysis is likely to be of much value.

The second level is that of *problem study*—an area full of pitfalls if we prematurely pick out problems, or fuss over purely academic-style problems which have little to do with the real issues at work in education today. For this reason we must be in tune with the world in change, also with the practical educators who can tell us plainly what the real questions are. We can collaborate too with colleagues in "area studies" or in contextual analyses of the kinds undertaken in institutes of developmental studies or research institutes. Both at this level and the preceding one we do well to rely on the expert biblio-graphical guidance which good librarians can give us, and on abstracts relevant to the other social sciences. Thirdly, there is the level of deeper *research,* quite a different matter from anything considered during the earlier stages, and far more practically oriented.

It will be recognized that the ascending order given in the preceding paragraphs suggests an increasing degree of academic involvement. That is the case. Moreover, we are far more likely to be involved with persons than with mere books or studies. In these days of international contacts it is of great importance to enter into this human relationship of learning in a reciprocal way. Therein inheres the essence of real communications, and therefore real comparison. Effective comparison is by its very nature a work of synthesizing conclusions from comple-mentary evidence or indications. What better way of doing this than by visiting a country or an area with well-informed insights, and pref-erably with a good guide and a good friend to receive us? Not all so-called educational travel is profitable. Much of it is little better than tourism. Some of it results in poor digestion of unrelated gobbets; but at its best this kind of human interchange is the supreme way of learning.

The use of visiting professorships and fellowships for organizing teaching or study is also an increasing feature of work in Comparative Education. So is the arranging of really well-contrived conferences dealing in a business-like way with particular themes of general current interest, to which scholars from widely different backgrounds can offer stimulating contributions. However, not all such conferences are either well contrived or profitable in result. There is no point in trying to set up just one more exclusive club, which would eventually turn Comparative Education into a pedagogical oddity rejected by the serious students and reformers of the modern world. Nor is there any point in having touristic conferences which are little better than con-ventions or jamborees. What really is needed is a sort of business meeting, which can focus attention for the expert on practical problems which are capable of solution or near-solution with the guidance of experts, and which also can give an introduction to Comparative Edu-cation's methods and possibilities to those still hovering on the fringe. Here as in other matters we should make it quite clear what we are about. No one way is right, no one level is right. All are constituent parts of promoting the great interest, and sharpening the *use* of, comparative studies in education as in other branches of social study.

The progression of Comparative Education from interest and information to real-life problem solving and scientific cooperation in building the future is traced step by step in *Comparative Studies and Educational Decision*. It would be inappropriate to take from that book (intended for more advanced students and researchers) more than the perspective of increasing purpose and usefulness ahead. Yet that concern with usefulness and helping in decision can not be overemphasized. The decision to bring about change in (and by) education has been taken all over the world on a multiplicity of fronts. If Comparative Education does not help, it will be bypassed—and the decisions will be less well informed. In fact, Comparative Education is itself in full process of change—exemplified in the remarkable teamwork of the International Evaluation of Educational Attainment (IEA), whose mathematical study of 1967 already referred to is a major landmark for our discipline.

One last remark seems justified. It has been assumed throughout this book that we really are concerned with getting to grips factually, accurately, and sympathetically with the day-to-day business of educating children and organizing the future. In other words, the aim of our comparative study is *practical and reformative* though it is also a reliable and accurate study presented as scientifically as possible. Yet inseparable from that endeavor has been the intention to link human beings together with the kind of awareness that is humane and liberal as well as scientific. Nothing could be more appropriate than to show through this method of comparative study that any old-time cleavages between the scientific and the liberal, or between the professional and the "humanizing," are so much arbitrary nonsense irrelevant in the making of the future. The really civilizing ingredient in any program of study is that which allows us to see the other man as relevant to ourselves, and equal to ourselves, even though different. It is also the best possible furtherance of education if a teacher can show that he and his colleagues are learning as they teach, not claiming certainty but exploring the unknown with others who feel their way forward at the same time as he. This is essentially the message of comparative study, and the best possible augury for human development in the future.

THE SOVIET UNION

BEREDAY, BRICKMAN, and READ, eds., *The Changing Soviet School.* Cambridge, Mass.: Houghton Mifflin Company, 1960.

COUNTS, G. S., *The Challenge of Soviet Education.* New York: McGraw-Hill, Inc., 1957.

DE WITT, N., *Education and Professional Employment in the U.S.S.R.* Washington, D.C.: National Science Foundation, 1961.

GRANT, N., *Soviet Education.* Harmondsworth and Baltimore: Penguin Books, 1964.

HANS, N., *The Russian Tradition in Education.* London: Routledge & Kegan Paul, 1963.

KING, E. J. ed., *Communist Education.* London: Methuen, & Co., and Indianapolis: The Bobbs-Merrill Company, Inc., 1963.

NOAH, H. J., *Financing Soviet Schools.* New York: Teachers College, Columbia University, 1967.

ROSEN, S. M., *Higher Education in the U.S.S.R.* Washington, D.C.: U.S. Office of Education, 1963.

INDIA

KABIR, H., *Education in the New India.* London: George Allen & Unwin Ltd., 1956.

MINISTRY OF INFORMATION AND BROADCASTING, *The Future of Education in India.* New Delhi, 1953.

NEHRU, J., *The Discovery of India.* London: Meridian Books, Inc., 1951.

NURULLAH, S., and NAIK, J. P., *A History of Education in India.* London and Bombay: The Macmillan Company, 1951.

PANIKKAR, K.M., *Hindu Society at the Crossroads.* Bombay: Probsthain, 1955.

SARGENT, J., *Society, Schools and Progress in India.* Oxford: Pergamon Press, 1967.

ZINKIN, T., *India.* London: Oxford University Press, 1964.

JAPAN

BENEDICT, R., *The Chrysanthemum and the Sword.* Boston: Houghton Mifflin Company, 1946.

DORE, R. P., *Education in Tokugawa Japan.* London: Routledge & Kegan Paul, 1965.

FUKUTAKE, T., *Man and Society in Japan.* Tokyo: University of Tokyo Press, 1962.

PASSIN, H., *Society and Education in Japan.* New York: Teachers College, Columbia University, 1965.

REISCHAUER, E. O., *Japan Past and Present,* Tokyo and Rutland, Vt.: Charles E. Tuttle Company, Inc., 3d edition, 1964.

STOETZEL, J., *Without the Chrysanthemum and the Sword.* Paris: UNESCO, 1955.

MINISTRY OF EDUCATION, Tokyo, *Education in Japan, 1964.*
———— *Educational Standards in Japan, 1964.*
———— *Educational Developments in 1964–65.*

YEARBOOKS AND OTHER SOURCES

INTERNATIONAL BUREAU OF EDUCATION, *The International Yearbook of Education.* Geneva.
    Gives an annual catalogue of educational events and changes as reported by official organizations.

UNESCO, The *Compulsory Education* series.
    Provides good accounts of the statutory minimum of education in various countries. This compulsory minimum, however, is not usually related to the highly significant sectors of education that are not compulsory.

UNESCO, The *Problems in Education* series.
    Reviews separate topics of international importance such as *The Education of Teachers in England, France and the U.S.A.; The Education of Women for Citizenship;* and *Adult Education: Current Trends and Practices.* These books are authoritative and very well written.

U.S. DEPARTMENT OF HEALTH, EDUCATION, AND WELFARE, The *Comparative Education* pamphlets. Washington, D.C.: Government Printing Office.
    These are monographs on individual countries or regions.

UNIVERSITY OF LONDON INSTITUTE OF EDUCATION and TEACHERS COLLEGE, COLUMBIA UNIVERSITY, New York, *The World Year Book of Education.* London: Evans Brothers, Ltd., and New York: Harcourt, Brace & World, Inc.
    For particular problems or factors affecting educational development. It is published annually. Despite its title, each year's issue deals with a single theme reviewed from the standpoint of particular countries or institutions which especially illustrate the theme. It is, therefore, a cumulative encyclopedia of essays written by specialists, usually contributing firsthand knowledge about their own countries. The issues in the revised series from 1953 on are the most valuable. For example, the 1957 publication surveyed philosophies and theories of education in practice throughout the world; the 1958 volume dealt with the secondary school curriculum; the 1959 volume dealt with higher education; the 1961 volume treated the concept of excellence; the theme of the 1963 volume was the education of teachers; that of 1965 was the education explosion; in 1966 it concerned the roles of church and state in education.

PERIODICALS

Comparative Education. Oxford: Pergamon Press.

COMPARATIVE EDUCATION SOCIETY, *Comparative Education Review.* New York.

UNESCO INSTITUTE FOR EDUCATION, *International Review of Education.* Hamburg.
    The above periodicals provide topical information and comment on world events or problems in education. They also review problems of method in research and teaching, as they concern the study of Comparative Education.

INDEX

DATE DUE

GAYLORD			PRINTED IN U.S.A.